A MASS CONSPIRACY TO FEED PEOPLE

FOOD NOT BOMBS AND THE WORLD-CLASS WASTE OF GLOBAL CITIES.

David Boarder Giles

A Mass Conspiracy to Feed People

Duke University Press
Durham & London 2021

Designed by Aimee C. Harrison
Typeset in Minion Pro, Univers LT Std, and Glypha

by Copperline Book Services

Library of Congress Cataloging-in-Publication Data
Names: Giles, David Boarder, [date] author.
Title: A mass conspiracy to feed people: food not bombs and the world-class waste of global cities / David Boarder Giles.
Description: Durham: Duke University Press, 2021. | Includes bibliographical references and index.
Identifiers: LCCN 2020057026 (print)
LCCN 2020057027 (ebook)
ISBN 9781478013495 (hardcover)
ISBN 9781478014416 (paperback)
ISBN 9781478021711 (ebook)
Subjects: LCSH: Food Not Bombs (Organization) | Food waste. | Dumpster diving. | Food security. | Food supply—Social aspects. | Food consumption—Social aspects. | Waste (Economics)—Social aspects.
Classification: LCC GN407. G55 2021 (print) | LCC GN407 (ebook) | DDC 306.4—dc23
LC record available at https: //lccn.loc.gov/2020057026
LC ebook record available at https: //lccn.loc.gov/2020057027

Cover photograph by Raeanne Wiseman.

contents

preface/ ACKNOWLEDGMENTS

This book will see daylight nearly in time to celebrate the fortieth anniversary of Food Not Bombs' very first meal. On March 26, 1981, its organizers dressed as self-styled hobos and held a Depression-era soup kitchen with donated castoffs outside the Bank of Boston's stockholders meeting. It was pure political theatre. (In 1981, the sight of homeless people crowding American streets remained an anachronistic novelty. If you can imagine that.) The spectacle was meant to illustrate the epic financial crash augured by the bank's investment in nuclear energy and militarism. Nobody quite guessed the soup line would grow into an international gastronomic conspiracy.

Much has changed over the past forty years—and Food Not Bombs with it. In retrospect, they weren't wholly wrong about the depression: the twin tides of globalization and neoliberalism have borne cascading, interwoven crises that have seen wealth pool among the super-rich while inequality, hunger, and homelessness grow starker by the year in many cities. That great transformation has also been the crucible from which emerged a global movement of anarchist soup kitchens.

This book tells a tale of its forging, and of the landscapes from which its raw materials precipitate. It is a work of slow scholarship, in some ways dating back to my earliest days with FNB, when both the movement and I were a spry twenty-five years old. Since then, I have watched both Food Not Bombs and the urban crises that stoke it deepen and evolve. This book aims to capture something of that long arc. I hope it contains a useful—albeit partial—map for advocates, radicals, and scholars to navigate some of the next forty years.

That future is singularly hazy right now, amid recession, pandemic, and political unrest unprecedented in recent memory. We cannot know how they will transform our world. Some of the world-class business districts described in this book, for example, have been evacuated for now—by those who can afford it. Who can say when or how they will return? Yet these crises exacerbate the underlying conditions of our era in ways that seem familiar to anyone who's spent time with FNB: supply chains are disrupted and food languishes in the fields while unemployed Americans queue for blocks at understocked food banks, yet the contradiction between squandered food and hunger has always been at FNB's heart; the COVID-19 pandemic devastates some neighborhoods and largely spares others, revealing older urban divisions that are the impetus for FNB's mutual aid; and urban uprisings proliferate globally at never-before-seen speed, emerging from the kinds of everyday structural violence, and the dynamo of police repression and grassroots resistance, that give rise to nonviolent insurrections like Food Not Bombs. (As I type this, some of my FNB collaborators in Seattle have lent their bodies to a motley, mutinous coalition, led by the Black Lives Matter movement, to peacefully occupy a six-block "autonomous zone" against police brutality and urban disenfranchisement. Within the zone—as elsewhere around the world—FNB and other activists continue to ply the skills of mutual aid and civil disobedience to share food freely, despite the pandemic.) The story of Food Not Bombs might, I hope, teach us much about the world that emerges from this moment.

Countless people have made that story, and this book, possible. Above all, I owe the book to the caring labor of the Food Not Bombs collaborators alongside whom I have volunteered. They have been friends, critics, and peers. And among the wider political landscapes that FNB inhabits, I am grateful to Victoria Law, Natalie Novak, Tim Harris, Rachael Myers, Anitra Freeman, Wes Browning, Keith McHenry, Simon Stephens, Graham Pruss, Kelly Whitmore, Spike Chiappalone, and particularly Jeff Juris, whose advice resonates through this book and whose passing is a loss to us all. For institutional support I thank Deakin University, the Alfred Deakin Institute for Citizenship and Globalisation, the University of Washington's Department of Comparative History of Ideas, the Harry Bridges Center for Labor Studies, the Simpson Center for the Humanities, and the Nancy Bell Evans Center on Nonprofits and Philanthropy. For helping me incubate these thoughts, I thank Ann Anagnost, Miriam Kahn, Celia Lowe, Phillip Thurtle, Maggie Dickinson, Patricia Lopez, Katie Gillespie, Victoria Lawson, Sarah Elwood, Teresa Mares, Trang Ta, David Spataro, Alex Vitale, Jill Friedberg, Trevor Griffey, Robertson Allen, Matt Hale, Amir Sheikh, Mariana Markova, Tim Neale, Tanya King, Victoria Stead, Roland Kapferer, Louise Johnson, Melinda Hinkson, Emma Kowal, Eben Kirksey, Bree Carlton, Jen Moore, Tamara Myers, Ryan Burt, Emily Clark, Erin Clowes, Jed Murr, Alice Pedersen, Kyle Croft, Beth Scholler, Heather Rastovac, Jessica D'Amour, Shealeigh Heindel, Ryder Richardson, Melissa Espinoza, Monica Chahary, and particularly Danny Hoffman. And my deepest gratitude is for the journey of personal becoming behind any kind of research. Thanks Laurie Penny, Jessie Kindig, Meg Murphy, Amy Peloff, Olivia Little, Noora El Shaari, Violeta Hernandez, Jill Schaffner, Taryn Dorsey, Sabrina Chap, Courtney Cecale, Risa Cromer, Lilly Frank, Lauren Lichty, Kathryn Tafra, Lily So Too, Francisco Iturbide, Peter Donahue, Joe Thompson, Jake Warga, Raven Healing, Kris Edin, Kevin "Doc" Dockery, Ash Martin-Bumpus, Amalia Davalos, Cale Wilcox, David O'Bright, Paul Ohnemus, Erin Ohnemus, Elizabeth Rard, David Wallace, Nathan Shields, Shauna "Cutter" Greene, Laura Palachuk, Kawan Baxter, Mary Holly, Ani Borua, Kevin "Irish" Kelly, Koa Kaelepulu, Corri Chase, Oats Habercorn, Wilson Shook, Eric Wirkman, Ryan Bartek, Garlicana Farms, and Annabelle Crosbie, among others. And for teaching me, in their ways, to read, care, play, endure, and help, I can thank Marilyn Boarder, Neil Blacker, and Michael Giles. These people and many more have helped make this book what it is. The errors are mine alone. But whatever it may achieve belongs to all of us.

FOOD NOT BOMBS

Free Food! Comida Gratis!

Every Sunday @ 2:30PM,

A typical Food Not Bombs flyer sums up its philosophy.

PROLOGUE

ANY GIVEN SUNDAY IN SEATTLE

On any given Sunday, the Pike Place Market in Seattle is a busy place. Just try driving a van between the throngs of tourists who seem not to distinguish between sidewalk and road. Like Hindu cows, they wander where they like without fear of reprisal. They spill out onto the street with nary a glance at oncoming traffic like me.

You can't fault them. The red bricks in the road are their domain, really. Integral to the market's image and identity, the terra-cotta-colored paving echoes the old storefronts that line it and that have done business for the better part of a century. The bricks in the road only date to the 1970s, but they're here (in lieu of asphalt) to

Throngs of tourists. The red bricks in the road are their domain. (Pike Place Market, October 2018)

lend an ambiance of seamless, world-class historicity to the place. With a panoply of restaurants, cafés, and stalls, Pike Place is one of Seattle's most iconic tourist destinations. Its produce stands have connected local farmers to the city since 1907. And it still does a brisk business in the twenty-first century. At the peak of summer, that can mean almost sixty thousand visitors in a day. Sixty thousand sacred cows (by revenue). Ten million a year. Over the course of six years, I've spent hours—maybe days—of my life behind the wheel of various vehicles waiting for them to move out of the way.

In a way, I've come here for the same reason as them: the food is world-class. The market's postcard-perfect rows of fruits and vegetables inspire high-ticket tourism. Glossy shots of its apples and avocados peek out from postcard racks across the city. The food is a symbol not only for the market but also for Seattle's global aspirations.

Postcard-perfect produce. (Pike Place Market, October 2018)

Postcards of perfect produce. (Pike Place Market, October 2018)

Like many cities whose futures seemed uncertain in the late twentieth century, as manufacturing industries ebbed south, Seattle turned its fortunes around by attracting global capital via business investment and tourism. It became the fastest-growing city in the United States at one point—and one of the richest (Balk 2014), home now to some of the wealthiest people who have ever lived. To this end, the city has capitalized on its urbane image: cosmopolitan but down to earth; diverse but not outside the middle-class traveler's comfort zone; bohemian enough to be interesting but pro-business, and with high-class shopping to boot. Qualities that appeal to a globe-trotting set with cash to spend or liquid capital to invest. Like so many cities, Seattle appeals to their bellies. And in this, Pike Place has been a perennial success.

Unlike the tourists, however, I haven't exactly been grocery shopping here. I gather the leftovers. From the rows of picturesque produce, many market-goers are looking for just the right apple. Or pear. Or tomato, or avocado, and so on. And with stalls vying to attract the attention of 10 million passersby, a lot of apples inevitably won't make the cut.

It takes a lot of waste to keep up Seattle's image.

On any given Sunday, that's where I would come in. For six years, I collected surplus food from stalls and shops around Seattle that were willing to donate it to a free meal project like ours, rather than throw it away. Many, quite upmarket: farmers' markets, high-end grocery stores, organic-friendly cooperatives, boutique bakeries, among others. They cater to the discerning tastes and disposable incomes of the upper echelons of Seattle's postindustrial economy—software developers, biotech researchers, aerospace engineers, and lawyers, for example. Seattle's median income has exploded over the past two decades, and many residents can afford to be choosy.

By contrast, the food I recovered ended up in the hands of people disadvantaged by the same economy—unemployed, underemployed, disabled, shelterless, and so on. The city's homeless population has now ballooned to over twelve thousand, the third largest in the country. Like other "world-class" cities, Seattle's postindustrial fortunes have amounted to the best of times or the worst of times, depending on whom you ask.

In this respect, the abandoned avocado, the bruised apple, and the other unwanted produce has often become part of a broad safety net of food banks, emergency meal programs, shelters, and other nonprofit organizations. A kind of aftermarket shadow economy built on world-class waste. This safety net would be unthinkable without the donated excesses of the city's consumers and markets. Then again, it wouldn't be necessary in a less starkly polarized kind of economy.

Once the surplus is taken off the shelves—and off the market—it's usually the last the tourists and shoppers ever see of it. If it doesn't end up in a market dumpster, it finds its way into charitable hands that redistribute it—normally indoors and out of sight of the shoppers. The shadow economy of wasted food moves in different spaces than they. It must. The aesthetics of abjection and poverty aren't compatible with Seattle's urbane image. My friend Carmen—alongside whom I've served free meals for a few years and who has relied on emergency assistance herself at times—puts it simply: "People . . . don't want to see the ugliness of their own city. And they certainly don't want to be faced with the challenge of finding a way to address it." It takes a lot of waste to keep up appearances.

In this respect, though, the group we both work with is unlike most other meal providers. It's a sort of anarchist soup kitchen called Food Not Bombs (popularly "FNB" for short), a motley crew of punks, students, hippies, Quakers, vagrants, itinerants, and other radicals. Whereas most meal programs are hidden in church basements and other marginal spaces, we share food in public view. In fact, there's a good chance that our forbidden gifts will reunite the tourists and their overlooked produce, passing each other unawares within a stone's throw, like ships in the night. Each Sunday, while the tourists have been off visiting the Seattle Art Museum or the Space Needle, our group takes the food back to someone's kitchen and improvises a vegetarian meal out of the waste. As those same tourists read restaurant reviews and ponder where to dine, our ragtag soup kitchen takes the meal not to a church or shelter, but to Pioneer Square, which—in addition to being home to a constellation of low-income housing, shelters, homeless services, and rough sleepers—is another popular tourist destination and a would-be hub for information technology businesses. The neighborhood is another focal point for Seattle's world-class aspirations.

And although it disrupts these aspirations, and unsettles certain tourists and businesses, we serve dinner every Sunday in Occidental Park, smack dab in the middle of the neighborhood, with the day laborers, the homeless, the down-and-out, and anyone else who happens along.

In this, we follow a forty-year-old tradition of Food Not Bombs chapters. Throughout the US and dotted across the globe, small collectives gather unwanted food from local stores (either through donation or dumpster-diving), prepare it safely, and distribute it in public spaces. Often, in the process, they challenge antihomeless measures that restrict the public sharing of food precisely because its upsets the environs of urbane, cosmopolitan consumption. In effect, these measures ban eating in public for anyone who can't afford to buy their own dinner.

On any given Sunday afternoon, we might eat dinner in the park with forty or fifty people. Sometimes more. We might also share Occidental Park's red brick paving stones (a relatively recent installation) with sports fans cutting through from CenturyLink Field. Or tourists who've come here for the popular Grand Central Bakery, adjoining the park in another one of Seattle's historic brick façades, or for the information booth on the other side of the park. When it's closed, they occasionally ask us for directions to local attractions.

In contrast, yet other sorts of visitors come to us for yet other sorts of directions. In my time with FNB, I've met train-hopping kids looking for a place to squat. A fisherman looking for space in the overcrowded shelters—he had paid his last dollar for passage to Seattle only to find that the job he was promised didn't exist and the fishing industry here had been restructured. (Seattle's homeless fishermen deserve a book of their own.) A disabled former dockworker with a third of his skull caved in by an on-the-job accident —as if a bowling ball had landed in soft mud—looking for more help than any of us could give. Other disoriented newcomers who bet on jobs or relationships that didn't materialize. Some, for whom there wasn't room in the shelters, looking for a blanket, or at least clean socks. Others looking for God. Alcoholics looking for a drink, or bus fare, or both. In six years, I saw a lot of lost faces.

The contrasts are uneasy. Between high-class consumption and abjection. Fine dining and this shadow economy of free leftovers. Ad hoc guacamole (an FNB standby) and the pristine avocados on nearby postcards racks. Sometimes businesses or tourists complain about us to the city, which in turn sends a squad car to eject us from the park. The ensuing controversies, as I'll describe in the pages that follow, throw these Dickensian contradictions into stark relief.

Nonetheless, these different spheres are integral, entangled parts of Seattle's economy. The forbidden gifts of anarchist soup kitchens like FNB, and the larger shadow economies of which they are a part, teach us a great deal about the ways in which waste and want, wealth and abjection, are manufactured in the pursuit of world-class dreams and urban renewal—in Seattle and many of the other global cities it so resembles. What follows is my own account of these urban transformations, of these shadow economies, and of my time with Food Not Bombs. It suggests something of the stakes of FNB's work worldwide and the upheavals of everyday life in the global city.

Introduction

Of Waste, Cities, and Conspiracies

If it is the misfortune of the workers' rebellions of old that no theory of revolution directs their course, it is also this absence of theory that, from another perspective, makes possible their spontaneous energy and the enthusiasm with which they set about establishing a new society.

. . . we begin to recognize the monuments of the bourgeoisie as ruins even before they have crumbled.

—Walter Benjamin

A Very Straightforward Blueprint

"Food Not Bombs is like a mass conspiracy," says Francisco, pausing for effect. He grins mischievously under a mop of curly, jet-black hair. ". . . To feed people." I laugh. And then it sinks in. In an era haunted by esoteric, far-right manifestos about the threat of outsiders and elites to take what's "ours," there's something sanguine about a global plot to give things away. Against the mythos of scarcity, FNB's propaganda of the deed is indiscriminate generosity. A conspiracy of abundance.

We're in Occidental Park. Probably half a dozen of us are lined up behind a convenient low stone wall and a row of Food Not Bombs' battered pots and pans. On the other side, ambling through the line, are a few dozen people waiting for stir-fry, a bowl of soup, or a doughnut. (Picking up leftover doughnuts from the bakery has been my job lately.) Often—and these are my favorite moments—they are here not only for the food but for the conversation. On days like today, an unlikely recipe of homeless itinerants, undocumented migrants, addicts, broke artists, musicians, students, activists, train-hopping punks, and visitors from overseas (categories that blur and overlap) all come here to hang out. Even, on occasion, a local homeless *curandera* who practices Mexican witchcraft and sometimes brings a live chicken to the park. It's late in the year and it's getting cold this time of day, but here we are eating, chatting, debating politics, and enjoying each other's society. (The curandera is largely taciturn, except in defense of her chicken.)

I have found such motley, convivial scenes reprised in parks and kitchens across Seattle, San Francisco, New York, Boston, Melbourne, Brisbane, and some of the smaller cities where I've collaborated with the movement over a decade or so. In these moments, the meal is not only a source of calories but an end in itself. Travelers look us up by name. Local activists and artists meet one another here. In Seattle, rough sleepers and hungry locals refer to us simply as "the vegetarians" and come back week after week. A handful, even year after year. Together, we form an "accidental community of memory" (Malkki 1997). But however ephemeral, it leaves tangible traces. "It kept striking me that this did make such a difference," reflected one longtime Seattle activist and teacher, Patricia, of her decade with FNB, "that notion of working collaboratively . . . to make these lives sustainable." She asked rhetorically, "How does this feed us in these other ways?"

The ingredients of this community, both human and culinary, transform from week to week and from place to place. As my friend Koa (himself a sometime-itinerant, train-hopping punk) puts it, "Food Not Bombs is a revolving door." In my time, Seattle FNB volunteers were mainly young white radicals and students, along with recent immigrants, refugees, first-generation Americans, working-class and formerly homeless collaborators, among others. (All displaced somehow, but displaced differently, as I will describe.) In contrast, twenty-five years ago, Seattle FNB was a tight-knit group of punks and squatters, much like chapters I've met in Melbourne and New York. Different again, when I visited Berkeley, where FNB were mainly aging white hippies, Quakers, and retirees. Worldwide, FNB is an eclectic phenomenon. Every chapter is a different recipe.

As transient and diverse as they are, however, in this book I argue that these accidental communities scale up. Across time and space, they amount to a transnational form of organization whose effects belie its minor footprint in recorded political history. Francisco is mainly joking, but in some sense, this patchwork is just what one might expect a "mass conspiracy" to look like. From Borneo to Buenos Aires, in hundreds of cities, in dozens of languages, on every continent except Antarctica,[1] autonomous FNB chapters gather for reasons much like those of my collaborators in Occidental Park. "I see real strengths in groups just being able to pop up, and oftentimes with no interaction at all," Patricia told me. "And they're all legitimate Food Not Bombs, you know?" In warehouses, squats, community centers, communal kitchens, parks, and sidewalks, around cutting boards, buckets, and battered old pots and pans, this unlikely constellation of co-conspirators repurpose food that would otherwise have been wasted (whether "dumpster-dived" or donated) and gift it publicly to people who might otherwise have gone hungry—often in spite of laws that forbid such largesse. Their menu is typically vegan, their organization egalitarian and flat. By convention, anybody can organize a chapter—without "needing to get approval from any central office," as Patricia puts it—as long as they agree to practice nonviolence, make decisions based on consensus, and cook vegetarian food. As one Melbourne FNB collaborator put it, "It's a very straightforward blueprint."

Simple enough. And yet such a modest proposal might open new windows onto our economic and political lives. Food Not Bombs becomes a lens all the better with which to interrogate hunger, homelessness, our increasingly divided urban landscapes, and perhaps the shape of protest to come. This is not, therefore, just a book about FNB (of which several already exist; see McHenry 2012; Parson 2010; Shannon 2011). Rather, this is a tale of waste, cities, and conspiracies. It aims to capture something of the inexorable churn of mighty metropolises, and to make visible some of the communities and the political possibilities cultivated amid their detritus, where people and things that have been abandoned or overlooked gather. In this sense, FNB is the tip of an iceberg of postcapitalist surpluses.

> What does Food Not Bombs achieve? It redistributes food that would probably get fucking trashed. It feeds people good nourishing organic food that they probably wouldn't come across. It teaches people skills. It can be really fun, 'cause you're working with friends.
>
> —Frank, Melbourne FNB, ca. 1999–2005

> Well, that's the beauty of the potential of the design, right? . . . It creates this very practical entry point. We're fulfilling a very obvious need. No entry requirements. All you have to do is be willing to chop vegetables. And in the process of doing that obviously good thing, you'll often be subjected to state repression and you'll see even more dramatically the nature of the problems we're confronting and become radicalized in the process.
>
> —Allan, San Francisco FNB, ca. 1990

Although "mass conspiracies" belong mainly to lurid fiction, as a metaphor they are nonetheless good to think with in a few ways. First, they are politically inscrutable: they hide in plain sight like the city's discarded people and things, as we will see. Second, they are paradoxically esoteric and all-inclusive, organized and decentralized, much like Food Not Bombs. How both of these things might come to be, and what they have to do with each other, is at the heart of this book's argument. Taking a cue from Francisco, the figure of the mass conspiracy is intended to capture those emergent forms of generosity, solidarity, and resistance that spring from the city's overlooked remainders. Wherever capitalism's leftovers have been scavenged and shared, its rule queered or held in abeyance, there might we find our conspiracy at work. In these decades of political uncertainty, it may be valuable to bring such illiberal, egalitarian political possibilities into better focus (lest authoritarian visions dominate the void left by the increasingly tattered liberal social contract).

The book's "conspirators" work both with and against the contradictions of capitalism. Follow the trail of abandoned food, hungry mouths, forbidden gifts, and urban developments from FNB chapter to FNB chapter, continent to continent, and it leads to larger intuitions about transnational capital, about its handmaiden the "global" city, and about the forms that political resistance may take in the years to come. To connect these dots, in this book I ask questions that seem initially unconnected. Why should our market economies (touted as bastions of efficiency) abandon so much unspoiled food? Why should it be illegal to feed the homeless? What makes a city "world class"? How does one organize a mass conspiracy?

Consider two facts. Since the 1980s, major metropolises around the world have increasingly been remade in the image of the so-named "global" city. From São Paulo to Dubai, their metastasizing glass-and-steel skylines glint from the pages of in-flight magazines in honor of their accession to a privileged niche at the apex of financial, managerial, and informational food chains. They perform the "command functions" of global capitalism (Sassen 2001, 6). Meanwhile, during precisely the same period, chapters of FNB have steadily multiplied, scavenging for leftovers the world over and feeding those at the bottom of the same economic food chains. These trends are related. Although FNB crops up in diverse places for diverse reasons (like crabgrass or any other rhizome), the oldest, most storied chapters—the ones that touch the most diverse lives and anchor an oft-ephemeral, swarm-like movement—have tended to assemble in globalized cities such as Seattle. Not only because these places are crossroads for teeming flows of people and ideas. But also because such mighty conurbations unremittingly manufacture the very surpluses, scarcities, and dispossessions that make FNB's labors both possible and politically meaningful. Food Not Bombs has been formed in the crucible of these cities' divided landscapes and it has, in turn, shaped those landscapes after its own fashion. In short, global capitalism and the global city create the conditions for a worldwide conspiracy to feed people.

This book develops a toolkit to sound out these entanglements between capitalism's wastes, urban transformation, and political resistance. Based on six years of collaboration and participant-observation with Seattle FNB (from 2005 to 2011), shorter, recurring research expeditions to FNB in San Francisco, New York, and Melbourne, and more than a decade of volunteering and personal affinity with FNB in the other cities in the book, it follows three lines of thought across time and space, each suggested by FNB's global scope and its location at the margins of economic value and urban space. First, FNB's redistribution of discarded food throws into relief the rhythms by which waste is produced and circulated under contemporary capitalism. Second, its struggles with food-sharing prohibitions highlight the relationship between waste-making, (bio)political power, and the production of urban life. And third, FNB serves as one possible map of the political potential of that waste, or what Anna Tsing calls "the possibility of life in capitalist ruins" (2015). Briefly, the book argues that capitalism manufactures scarcity through waste-making, world-class cities create both world-class waste and massive displacement, and from those discarded surpluses and displaced people may emerge novel forms of political organization and nonmarket economy, emblematized by FNB.

Accordingly, three themes wind their way through this argument. First, the book excavates what I term *abject capital*, those once-commodities that are still useful but that are more profitable to throw away than to sell. If capitalism is "patchy," as Tsing (2015, 5) puts it, these goods are banished to some of its most obscure patches. Out of sight, out of mind for many businesses and theorists alike, they are paradoxically discarded and yet still captured within the process of capital accumulation; their abandonment actively manufactures scarcity itself. So cast aside, however, abject capital is a kind of "latent commons," a hidden commonwealth that may be "catalyzed by infraction, infection, inattention—and poaching" (255). In this vein, I'll trace some of its social afterlives and the abject economies made possible by its banishment. They belie the myth of scarcity that is a cornerstone of market economics and capital accumulation.

Second, I explore strategies of municipal governance, particularly antihomeless measures that punish public food sharing and privilege a world-class, commerce-friendly kind of public life. Among other things, this keeps waste matter in its place, out of public view. In the same move, certain modes of living are excluded and rendered "surplus life," "life that is considered unnecessary, and that is nonetheless productive of surplus value in neoliberal capitalism" (Willse 2015, 49). I'll call the urban polity by which these lives are excluded a "market-public."

Third, I chart some of the emergent forms of resistance and "counterpublics" (Warner 2002) cultivated in their exclusion from this version of public life. They share abject or marginal embodied political-economic practices that I call "illiberal embodiments." Here, I mean by *illiberal* not authoritarian or conservative, but rather queered with respect to the liberal social contract (following the term's older meanings of "vulgar" or "ill-bred"). In their alienation from the mainstream public and its liberal economies, the city's residua are freer to find unexpected affinities and allegiances, as Anna Tsing (2015) teaches us. They nurture the kinds of nonmarket shadow economies described in the prologue. Crucially, their fluid, heterogeneous forms of material solidarity are not neatly captured by the ascendant terms of political analysis that reduce affinity to identity. (Whether one's preferred critique centers "workers," "whiteness," or what have you—although these are surely part of a larger, messier recipe.) Yet over temporal, spatial, and social distances, they emerge as an unstable yet effective political object. Both oppressed and released by their exclusion from the public sphere, and by the desuetude of its unwanted excesses, they form the kernel of political resistances like Food Not Bombs—something I will describe as a kind of slow insurrection.

In the coming decades, as growing ranks of people concentrate in increasingly polarized megalopolises around the world, these three dynamics may increasingly shape the fates of those cities that call themselves "global" and those people and things that are marginalized under their mighty economies. The nonmarket economies and forbidden gifts described in this book highlight relationships between food (in)security, municipal governance, and the global economy that hold broad implications for urban governance and political mobilization in these places. (The slow insurrection of FNB, for example, partially prepared the terrain for faster insurrectionary movements such as Occupy Wall Street, which likewise reassembled abandoned people and things in a global fashion.) And more broadly, the relationship between waste-making and political exclusion plays an often overlooked role in capitalism's constant transmutations. In all of these ways, therefore, FNB's example may hold valuable lessons for the twenty-first-century city.

The Global City

"This city is so fucked, I don't know where to begin," says my friend Rose, a tattooed artist who knows FNB from her time in the punk scene. "It makes me want to throw up. They are doing absolutely everything they can to push low-income folks out. Which, by the way, is now anyone who makes under $72,000 for a family of three."[2]

This is Seattle in 2018. Only two decades ago, its sleepy reputation was such that "Weird Al" Yankovic could rhyme "garage band from Seattle" with "sure beats raising cattle." But now, all anyone can talk about is the rent. Seattle has become a boomtown. Cranes dot a skyline that I barely recognize from a mere three years before, and the cost of housing chases these brand-new towers skyward with reckless abandon. Rose is a single mother and dance instructor whose teaching studio rent has just increased by 40 percent all at once. (Her name is a pseudonym, like that of anyone else in this book who isn't already a public figure or hasn't requested otherwise.) Her sentiments are shared by countless friends and collaborators who have seen the city transform over the past decade—and their rent hike literally overnight. At one point, Seattle's housing prices were increasing by an astounding five dollars every hour (Adolph 2018). As Seattle-area multinationals such as Microsoft and Amazon expand voraciously, and as transnational capital flocks into local markets, the city's "growth machines" (Logan and Molotch 1987) fete its success. They're not alone in the celebration, as various knock-on benefits—from world-class shopping to appreciating home values—trickle down to the middle class.

But others can't fail to feel squeezed. As well-paid information technology workers with expensive tastes flood the labor force, beloved local haunts are shuttered or slated for redevelopment. Communities of color and blue-collar residents are priced out of their neighborhoods while offshore corporations park the anonymous wealth of global elites in luxury real estate and empty condominiums—which have, in the years following the global financial crisis of 2008, become a sort of global "currency" with increasing significance (Madden and Marcuse 2016; see also Sassen 2015; Florida and Schneider 2018). Meanwhile, FNB has seen growing lines of unhoused and food-insecure people join it for dinner in the park each week. Seattle follows the example of cities like Los Angeles and New York, where the ranks of people sleeping on the streets swell in proportion to housing costs (Glynn and Fox 2017). More than twelve thousand people now experience homelessness in the city—a threefold increase over the past fifteen years (All Home 2018). (Although a persistent myth envisions the homeless as drawn to the city's bounteous social services—in reality an overstretched, ad hoc patchwork—the majority of Seattle's shelterless were here before they lost their homes [City of Seattle and Applied Survey Research 2017].) The mayor declared Seattle's runaway homelessness a state of emergency in 2015, but it grows apace, nonetheless.

"Now leasing": reflections of downtown Seattle (2017).

On any given night, more than twelve thousand Seattleites experience homelessness. (First Hill, Seattle, 2017)

Yet the problem is more complex than gentrification or rent gouging; it's also a question of political power. Consider, for example, the 2018 "head tax"—a per-employee levy to be paid by high-earning corporations that was championed by Seattle's City Council to fund solutions to the housing crisis (the burden of which falls increasingly on city coffers in an era of dismantled state and federal welfare supports). Political resistance from business leaders such as Jeff Bezos, Amazon's CEO and now the richest man in the world, blocked the tax (Semuels 2018). In the subsequent City Council elections, Amazon devoted more than $1 million—the largest individual donation in recent memory—to challenging progressive candidates (Beekman and Brunner 2019). Meanwhile, spurred on by the head tax controversy, a constellation of city elites and "Not-in-My-Backyard" homeowners' coalitions have spun a partisan narrative about homelessness to stir up popular resentment against the same progressive politicians, perceived as being permissive or enabling, and to divert money from prevention to prosecution.

The city's successes have not, therefore, trickled down to unhoused Seattleites. One longtime homeless advocate recently summed up the net gain of Seattle's boom: "There's sixty-five cranes on our skyline, and all we got were nineteen units of affordable housing. Beyond pathetic."[3] As Seattle ascends to the rank of global city, it is easy to read its trajectory in Manichean hues. ("This city is so fucked.")

Rose could easily have been talking about most of the other cities I will describe in this book. Particularly Melbourne, New York City, and San Francisco—to which I have returned often in writing and in person, along with Seattle. Each city's experience is distinct, of course. Their waves of transformation reflect local histories and geographies as much as global trends. But their parallel evolution over time is striking. Far-flung cities converge in form; they "move toward" one another (Simone 2010, 15) in such a way that three decades ago and eight hundred miles away, San Francisco FNB found itself pitted against much the same dynamic Rose decried in Seattle, expressed in much the same terms by Peter—who himself lived in a tent in Golden Gate Park when he began serving food with FNB in the late 1980s, in that very park. "What was happening was a transformation," he explained. "The city was . . . moving out poor people wholesale."

In part, these cities express the age-old story of haves and have-nots. But the restructured landscape of post-Fordist capitalism calls for more specific comparisons. Geographically distant, they are nonetheless bound by common ties to the world market. Following Saskia Sassen (1990, 2001), I use the word *global* to describe their shared patterns of development. All cosmopolitan, postindustrial cities that have gradually been abandoned by manufacturers (and many stable middle-income jobs along with them), they have reinvented themselves as powerhouses—either emerging or established—within the informational industries that organize the world economy.[4] In pursuit of that goal, coalitions of businesses, developers, and public officials work to give their landscapes a "world-class" makeover, but at the cost of great polarization and displacement.

There have long been "world cities" of great renown and influence (Geddes 1915; Hall 1966). But the "global city" is something newer: a metropolis transformed by the "new spatial division of labor" that emerged from the globalization and deregulation of production and finance in the late twentieth century (Friedmann 1986, 70). Coined by Sassen in the 1990s, the term *global city* captures the emerging command functions of cities like New York, London, and Tokyo—those industries central to regulating and directing the global economy (Sassen 2001). Although the global playing field has evolved since then, as different "global" cities adopt diverse strategies to compete with one another within the same niches (see Ren and Keil 2018), Sassen's remains the canonical model. One of the ironies of the new world order, she argues, is that capital is both more mobile (in its investment) and more centralized (in its ownership and management) now than ever. As industrial production is increasingly atomized, far-flung, and flexible ("made in Mumbai-Detroit-Tokyo-Juarez-Shenzhen . . ."), and the international movement of finance has asymptotically approached a kind of tractionless instantaneity, global cities have concentrated the management of this production and movement, accumulating the relevant "producer services" (finance, information technology, research and development, corporate management, accountancy, and so on) and infrastructure (stock exchanges, office towers, high-speed broadband, etc.).

Sassen describes a hierarchical network of such cities fanned out across the world, facilitating flows of wealth and information—a postmodern, multimodal expression of Wallerstein's "world systems theory" (1984), splintered and flung about the globe according to the needs of global capital. Seattle, Melbourne, San Francisco, and New York City have all become regional and/or international nodes within this network over recent decades.[5] Although they vary in power and connectivity, they each have a stake invested in their command functions and the distinctive forms of urban transformation Sassen associated therewith.

Moreover, though most cities are not global cities strictly speaking, according to Sassen's model, many aspire to become so. They are "globalizing cities," as John Rennie Short (2004) puts it; a common sense of global "becoming and longing" animates them (Short 2004; see also Marcuse and van Kempen 2000; Ren and Keil 2018). And the contest is always changing. World leaders like New York City seek to maintain their status just as important regional centers such as Melbourne aspire to become global cities. Throughout this book, therefore, I describe my objects of study as both "global" and "globalizing" to capture the tension between extant and virtual, being and becoming.

As many have suggested, calling them "global cities" implies a certain ethnocentrism—even racism—as if the toxic fields of Delhi's electronics recycling industries or the Taylorist barracks of Shenzhen's factories were any less products of globalization. Surely, a city can be global in myriad ways (see N. Smith 2002; Mayaram 2009; Ong and Roy 2011; Simone 2010). But precisely the point here is that elite, ethnocentric visions of New York, London, Tokyo, and so on become hegemonic. The "global city" (and its cognate adjective, *world-class*) therefore becomes both a framework of analysis and an emic, ethnographic term embraced by cities that aspire to defend or usurp the command functions of such economic powerhouses (Sparke 2011). Representations of the global hold a weighty cultural cachet invoked in these places, a cipher to international economic and political success within what is not quite the smooth playing field the word often seems to claim.

Such global imaginaries enable an enormous project of place-making that remakes many of the everyday surfaces of metropolitan life. The global city itself is therefore a product, a sort of metacommodity, that emerges from such economic and cultural restructuring, and enables distinctive regimes of urban accumulation and agglomeration. That urban life, remade, turns out a wealth of world-class waste (food wasted in the interests of commodity aesthetics, buildings left empty for property speculation, and so on) and yet puts food and shelter financially out of reach for many. These conditions are ideal for scavenging, redistributive movements like FNB. As Marx and Engels might have it, therefore, what the global city produces, above all, are its own gleaners and garbage collectors.

Food Not Bombs

Meanwhile, back in Seattle, I'm at a meeting. A semiregular Food Not Bombs convocation to hash out the perennial quandaries of an anarchist soup kitchen. Whose house to cook at next month? Who'll pick up the food? Will we cater for the upcoming demonstration? Could more people please stick around to wash the dishes? (Long-term FNB collaborators may feel pangs of burnout just reading this.) Not a very romantic place for the reader to join the fray, but an inescapable one. These are the messy, quotidian details that sustain a "mass conspiracy." We'll visit more rhapsodized episodes later in the book. (The clashes with police. The gleeful trespasses in back alleys and overflowing dumpsters.) But the mundane moments—that never rise to the level of an "event" in Badiou's ([1988] 2013) sense yet constitute its necessary conditions—are just as crucial. With apologies to Gil Scott-Heron, the revolution will be full of meetings.

It's 2017 now. I haven't been actively involved for five years (after chasing various teaching posts), so I recognize only a few friends. There's Jules, for instance. She's a core organizer, or "bottom-liner," as we call them. A single mother who has juggled raising two kids with casual employment and public assistance, she still routinely makes space for FNB in the small kitchen of her low-income apartment, embodying the can-do-make-do ethic that makes FNB possible. She's hosting this meeting in her living room. One or two friendly faces aside, however, these folks are all new to me. Yet the group feels instantly familiar. Its similitude underscores a par-

Food Not Bombs, New York City (2016).

adox: like many radical political projects, FNB is simultaneously ephemeral and perennial. In each city I have visited, FNB crews turn over as a matter of course, as volunteers move on and are replenished. "There were people all the time, every week, that were new . . . just coming through the same outlets that I did," explained Kris, who as a teenage punk found FNB via flyers at Seattle's Left Bank Books in the mid-nineties. "And you know that's what Food Not Bombs thrives off of," he beamed. "Long as you got bodies, that's all you need. In a thing like Food Not Bombs, you don't need, you know, a structured group of people. Like it's kind of beside the point." Yet though people come and go, the common conditions of the city reproduce shared dynamics and struggles that resonate from chapter to chapter across the movement. Forty years old now, Food Not Bombs represents a sort of global, recombinant commons (no longer latent) assembled largely of capitalism's excesses. Although it fluctuates from week to week and cohort to cohort, it has expanded across decades and cities steadily, like the mounting food waste, hunger, and neoliberal globalization that have been its backdrop during the same time frame.

The familiarities are manifold. Like so many FNB conclaves before, a dozen or so of us are crowded around an ad hoc meeting space. If it's not a living room, it's a church. Or a park. Or a community center. Whatever can be begged, borrowed, or occasionally rented at a cut rate. By necessity FNB becomes expert at rendering the common at the margins of other economies, bearing out Bataille's dictum that "life occupies all the available space" ([1949] 1991, 30). Similarly, logistical considerations like those rehearsed above echo from meeting to meeting and chapter to chapter. In fact, during my six years of previous involvement I learned many of the answers to the questions raised by relative newcomers at this meeting: Should FNB seek a permit to share food in the park? (Probably not, as we'll see in chapter 4.) Who updates the web page? (That's my old friend Vijay, a refugee who donates his IT expertise to grassroots groups rather than make a cent from it. He makes a cameo in chapter 5.) Veterans hand down some of this information. Other knowledge is acquired by each new generation under the selection pressures of food recovery in the global city.

From these conditions emerge a shared constellation of dispositions and skills—the know-how to open a locked dumpster or facilitate a meeting, for example. "There was just so many places where I've used the model of Food Not Bombs, that notion of just being able to grab whatever is accessible, and create this meal out of it," reflected Patricia. "I was very compelled by the consensus model that was being used," she said. "The fact that there was basically no budget, and that there didn't really need

Passersby, Food Not Bombs, Seattle (2017).

to be. That it ended up being people just kind of diving in and taking responsibility and working cooperatively." Such shared, embodied knowledge often knits together the disparate global constituents of radical political movements (Juris 2008).

The mood in the room is familiar, too, a predictable spectrum of responses to the sometimes exhausting, sometimes exhilarating endeavor of feeding the city's most vulnerable members and improvising with the surpluses at hand, week in, week out. Some people here are earnest and idealistic. Some are restless and bored. Some, quietly pragmatic, and perhaps suffering burnout born of years of unpaid caring labor, working against the grain of a market society. (As one old hand from Melbourne FNB told me pithily, "There's always somebody doing too much.") And yet meetings like these are often warm, affirming affairs. Jules has made dinner for everyone. My new acquaintance Matt's irrepressible sense of humor means he can't hold himself to his promise of making only one pun per agenda item. This buoyancy and solidarity, too, is familiar from my years with FNB in Seattle and elsewhere. As I argue in chapter 5, such a mass conspiracy is animated and organized precisely by such bonds of feeling and affect.

> It was a crew of friends, and a big group of friends, you know? There was a hundred people in the punk scene, even more, that all supported in one way or another Food Not Bombs . . . Because we were cooking in our own houses . . . you know you'd always get your little things of households complaining, "Oh, bloody Food Not Bombs has been here again and they left a huge mess!" And then other people were like, "That's what I did—I cleaned up Food Not Bombs and that was my little bit that I did!" . . . It's a really positive, amazing, empowering thing to achieve—and the excitement and the little smile you see on people's faces when they hear that, wow, Food Not Bombs is still kicking off, and that it is worldwide . . . . You just want it to spread. And that was always the philosophy of everyone I knew in Food Not Bombs: "This is not owned by us. This is something to be owned by every individual. And to be taken as far as you can take it." And, what we used to say to a lot of people when they say "Oh, you know, I want to help, I wanna help." And we'd go, "Start one up in your own area."
>
> —Kay, founding member, Melbourne FNB, ca. 1992

If the things that make this meeting feel familiar spring from FNB's common urban context, so do the things that make it feel different and new. The new faces here, and the movement's constant turnover, are reflections of the diverse forms of mobility fostered by cities like Seattle. Social and economic "drift" are both a reflection of the precarity and flexibility of post-Fordist economies (Ferrell 2017) and also distinctive to globalizing metropolises, which tend to be nodes for larger patterns of domestic and international labor migration (Sassen 1996, 2001). Indeed, during my time, most of my FNB collaborators were touched by drift and displacement—from broke, train-hopping punk rockers and other unhoused volunteers who met us while lining up for dinner, to transplanted university students; from migratory service workers (international and domestic) working in the bottom rungs of the postindustrial economy, to underemployed youth following the suburban-to-urban exodus in search of a supportive counterculture and a better job. This not only afflicts FNB with a high turnover. It also lends FNB a distinctly networked, heterogeneous character that weaves together the largely white radicals and students who are the mainstay of much far-left protest with a spectrum of other differently displaced outsiders in ways that remain illegible to frameworks that center class, race, or nation. (As such, FNB complicates some of the stereotypes associated with young, privileged, radical activists, as I argue in chapter 6.) And as diverse FNB collaborators move from city to city for diverse reasons, they often seek out new chapters, molding Food Not Bombs into a "network of networks" (Castells 1996; see also Juris 2008). As Vikki, a squatter and radical journalist from New York, put it, "I think it's one of those things that's on a circuit, so while I was doing Food Not Bombs if I went to another city, I went and I tried to find Food Not Bombs." Corrina, an ecologist from Oregon, agreed: "I definitely started traveling differently than I would have maybe in college before I was, I don't know, more open to the radical community if you want to call it that. Like Food Not Bombs, and that kind of circle. Now, when I go to a city, I expect to be able to find a community there."

Nothing illustrates this networked structure better than the Five Degrees of Food Not Bombs, a game I developed almost accidentally through chance run-ins in FNB kitchens early during my research. So mobile and well networked were my new friends, I realized that I could trace networks of personal acquaintance between literally any two of the FNB collaborators I met in any of the six cities on two continents I had visited at that point, within only five degrees of separation—without including myself. (It's a variation, of course, on the popular Six Degrees of Kevin Bacon, played by connecting actors to Kevin Bacon via shared film billings. Aptly, a friend taught me that Five Degrees of Food Not Bombs could readily become Six Degrees of Kevin Bacon, because a close relative of the actor apparently once played in an East Coast punk band and was loosely associated with the local FNB chapter.)

> When I was in Toronto, I went and I visited my cousins—who are very sort of straight-laced, Hong Kong Chinese, living in Canada, working straight jobs. They study business or something like that. And they were really puzzled because I was walking around that part of Toronto where crusties hang out, and I would stop every single crusty on the street and ask them if they knew if there was a Food Not Bombs. Like every single one of them, and my cousins were really sort of puzzled by this. They were like, "She has stopped every homeless person under the age of thirty and asked them about something called 'Food Not Bombs'" . . . so I think if I hadn't been involved in Food Not Bombs, I wouldn't have that sort of like, "I want to plug into this and see how it's done someplace else. Gee, I don't know where there's a Food Not Bombs. Let me just ask homeless people." Or "Let me decide to go an hour before my cousin is supposed to get married, wash cabbage with a really nice dress on."
>
> —Vikki, New York City FNB, mid-1990s

After I had interviewed dozens of collaborators, some of whose stories date back to FNB's salad days in the late 1980s, it became clear that the shared urban landscapes and cultural logics described in the last section have been a crucial medium for the movement's growth. Although the name "Food Not Bombs" was first coined in Boston in 1980, it began as a different kind of project, under different historical conditions: the group was an outgrowth of the antinuclear Clamshell Alliance, and founder Keith McHenry described the original dinners to me as a sort of political theatre. Ironically, they had hoped to evoke the shocking spectacle of Depression-era soup kitchens and breadlines—happily unaware that within a decade such spectacles would become an unremarkable part of the American landscape. FNB's most explosive growth only came later, with the metamorphosis of American cities, particularly San Francisco. In 1988, after a relatively controversy-free eight years in the Boston-Cambridge FNB chapter, McHenry moved to San Francisco and organized a new Food Not Bombs chapter there. By that time its urban conditions of possibility were transformed. The deregulation of the global economy, the Reagan-era rollback of the welfare state, and the corresponding restructuring of US cities rendered the intersection of homelessness and public space a site of intense political struggle—acutely so in globalizing cities like San Francisco, Seattle, and New York. Those struggles are the primary content of FNB's particular conspiracy. As I describe in chapter 5, the new San Francisco chapter faced intense opposition by police and public officials, and this newly globalized urban landscape became ground zero for the movement's growth. By 1992, new chapters had formed numbering perhaps in the dozens, enough to hold the first national FNB gathering; and within another decade the movement spanned the globe. Food Not Bombs chapters therefore each represent an expression of a kind of many-headed hydra growing out of the surpluses, excesses, inequities, and deterritorializations of urban globalization.[6]

> I have this really great visual memory of people marching down Haight Street and having fun and, you know, like banging on soup pots, you know what I mean? It was really colorful. I mean Haight Street was really colorful anyway . . . So I was very taken by that. It was a total California experience. And very friendly people . . . I just felt like I quickly found a very welcoming community of people, friendly people, and people who were interested in a lot of the same issues that I was. I have a good visual memory—people were having fun, chanting "food not bombs" and all that. You know, it's a very concise expression of a lot.
>
> —Erin, San Francisco FNB, ca. 1990

Methods

In investigating this, I have followed anthropology's signature approach, ethnographic participant observation. Ethnography's firsthand, quotidian optics are well suited to exploring a patchy sort of global capitalism. Its local footing puts the ethnographer on the trail of concrete, lived traces of global phenomena—or as George Marcus (1995) famously described it, "ethnography in/of the world system" (see also Ong 1999; Tsing 2004, 2015). I have therefore framed my field sites at multiple scales. On one hand, I have worked at the local scale of FNB chapters and the genres of space they inhabit (the park, the kitchen, the dumpster, and so on). On the other, I have imagined "the field" at the scale of two emergent, transnational phenomena: Food Not Bombs and the global city. Both figures describe rhizomatic networks simultaneously global and place-based, moving assemblages of goods, people, information, and value—albeit of very different kinds. As Nik Heynen writes in his own work on Atlanta FNB, "Ethnographers have shown that the combination of local participant-observation complemented by engagement with these kinds of global networks can facilitate more meaningful understandings of the 'global as local practice'" (2010, 1228).

Mapping these formations has demanded that I, too, be in motion. To that end, I have juxtaposed the kind of long, intimate participation for which ethnography is famous with shorter forays into the network of networks that is Food Not Bombs. In the former, I spent nearly every Sunday for the better part of six years with Seattle FNB, collecting, cooking, and sharing food, and then washing up afterward. In the latter, over a decade or more I made recurring visits to chapters in San Francisco, New York City, and Melbourne (Australia, not Florida), along with more limited visits to other chapters in the United States (Boston, Worcester, Berkeley, Davis), New Zealand (Wellington, Christchurch, and Dunedin), and Australia (Brisbane)—many of them facilitated by acquaintances within the Five Degrees of Food Not Bombs. Like so many other new FNB initiates, I chopped vegetables, cooked dinner, and shared it with new friends at each chapter. Not all of these places are "global" cities, of course. Like any good rhizome, FNB has many faces; each is the sum of its local, historically particular contexts. Nonetheless, even chapters in smaller cities offered a valuable vantage point from which to trace the movement of people and ideas, and their embeddedness in a trans-local political economy.

Additionally, none of these chapters represents a single "site." As nodes in various larger networks and flows, every FNB chapter enables what Celia Lowe has called a "multi-sited ethnography in a single locality," insofar as each can "reveal the travels of cultural meanings, objects, and identities across wider fields of engagement" (2006, 6). As has been well established by now, the locations we might describe as "field sites" in a narrowly geographic sense in fact contain multiple forms and structures—and don't even contain them very well (Gupta and Ferguson 1997; Malkki 1997). In the same way, a single chapter of Food Not Bombs becomes multi-sited over time as its personnel and clientele turn over and the city churns with redevelopment.

And not only that. As we saw earlier, Food Not Bombs collaborators themselves are often on the move, and are avid networkers. Everywhere

I went, I met a Babel of itinerant co-conspirators from other chapters in countless cities and perhaps a dozen countries. I could have perhaps even stayed in one place and let the world come to me—and all the more so in the global city. Following the example of Jeffrey Juris's (2008) work on protest networks and global informational flows, however, I found it invaluable to follow the global distribution of embodied practices that make those flows possible. The best way to learn about FNB was to visit numerous kitchens and get my hands dirty.

It is helpful that Food Not Bombs is a cosmopolitan affair that welcomes sundry newcomers (and, indeed, anyone willing to chop vegetables). It comprises countless strangers who—not unlike anthropologists—often turn up enthusiastic and green, get to know their way around the kitchen and lesser-known corners of the city (dumpsters, shelters, and so on), and often drift from chapter to chapter, mapping out the larger social worlds of FNB as they go. It becomes an open book to collaborators, yet remains anarchic and illegible from without (as Francisco suggested with the word *conspiracy*).

It is also helpful that I identify as an enthusiastic co-conspirator. For more than a decade, I have been connected to FNB and the political and countercultural communities in which it is embedded—dumpster-divers, squatters, homeless advocates, punks, anarchists, and so on. My own experiences with FNB date back to age twenty-three, when I worked in the back of a thrift store in Davis, California, sorting through a cornucopia of unwanted, donated ephemera. I saved backpacks and personal hygiene supplies from the pile and handed them out alongside FNB. I had heard the group's recruitment messages on community radio: they always ended with, "And remember . . . Food is good, bombs are not." When I later moved to Seattle for graduate school—before I ever thought about writing this book—I sought out FNB and became quickly committed. In the process, I also cultivated relationships with a range of advocacy groups in Seattle, often cooking with FNB for fundraising benefits, demonstrations, marches, and anarchist book fairs, cultivating individual relationships with communities of homeless advocates and service organizations.

This is all the stuff of ethnography. Jeffrey Juris (2007), who found a productive synthesis between ethnography and activism during the counterglobalization protests of the early 2000s, writes: "One has to build long-term relationships of mutual commitment and trust, become entangled with complex relations of power, and live the emotions associated with direct action organizing and activist networking. Such politically engaged ethnographic practice . . . generates better interpretations and analyses"

(165–66). In the same fashion, I and other FNB collaborators have put our bodies on the line in visceral, practical ways, from doing outreach in some of Pioneer Square's darkest alleys to throwing my back out carrying too many boxes of produce. I, along with my co-conspirators, have lived the feelings associated with FNB's brand of direct political action, from the anger stoked by police pressure to the despair shared with homeless friends at their desperate circumstances, the joy of finding the perfect peach in a dumpster, the frustration of washing dishes until midnight with too little help, or the gratitude at finding a couch upon which to stay the night. I lost many an hour of sleep looking for new kitchen spaces. I literally wore out my car's shock absorbers driving nigh on a half-ton of food and volunteers around Seattle each week. Juris (2007) defines this embodied political engagement as "militant ethnography."

This political action becomes differently legible in a global perspective, against the backdrop of the global city. In that sense, the global city is my primary "field site." Its transnationally networked character and the flows of people, things, ideas, and money to which it gives rise lend it a multilocal ethnographic reality. I therefore follow urbanists such as Joanne Passaro (1997) who suggest that the cultural politics of homelessness are embedded in a globalized political economy in a way that constitutes a coherent heuristic for fieldwork (see also Bourgois 2010; O'Neill 2017). Passaro argues that the chaotic experiences of urban life in a major city like New York are no more complex than those at any other point in the (post)modern, globalized world. Or, as she puts it, you can, in fact, "take the subway to the field" (Passaro 1997). In these ways, this book aims to present a multiscalar account of both Food Not Bombs and the global city, informed by local ethnographic realities and transnational trends.

Plan of the Book

The book is divided into three parts dealing with waste, cities, and political organization, respectively. Ideally, the argument will unfold like a three-course meal, inspired by the models and methods of discard studies, global urbanists, and radical social movements. Following the venerable example of *Das Kapital*, it begins with a symptom, the humble commodity (and here, its route to the dumpster); connects the dots that trace its origins; and highlights its political implications.

Part I, "Abject Capital," traces the origins of our mass conspiracy's raw materials, both people and things. It asks why capitalism should abandon edible food and other useful surpluses to the dumpster and how the act of their abandonment circumscribes political membership and exclusion. The first chapter explores the cultural economy of commercial waste and the reasons it might be profitable for businesses to throw away goods that are still useful. This waste, I argue, represents an ongoing contradiction for capital that inflates the value (and price) of newer stock. Paradoxically abandoned and yet still part of the process of capital accumulation, I define such waste as "abject capital."

The second chapter explores the social spaces that are implicated in the creation of abject capital. Under liberal capitalism, the creation of value defines a particular kind of public sphere, an imagined community of people who are understood to share the basic language and conventions of commerce and exchange. If abject, wasted capital has a role to play in establishing the value of those things left on the shelves, it must remain absent from this particular public sphere. If it circulates at all (and it must, for it cannot be willed into nonexistence), it must do so apart from those people who participate in the market, both spatially and socially. This sphere is what I call a "market-public." The chapter explores the disenfranchisements that result from the weld between its economic and political imaginaries, as public needs and priorities are defined in ways that privilege commerce. At the same time, I suggest that other nonmarket "counterpublics" (Warner 2002) might be constituted in the recirculation of capitalism's excesses. It is exactly this counterpublic dimension that is expressed by Francisco's metaphor of the mass conspiracy.

Part II, "World-Class Cities, World-Class Waste," explores the relationship between waste, political inclusion, and the transformation of cities by neoliberal globalization. Chapter 3, the first in this section, describes the concrete processes by which abject capital and market-publics are produced in globalizing cities, particularly in the speculative and spectacular projects that lend global cities currency and prestige within the world market, and in their reimagining of the urban landscape, from luxury consumption and gentrification to inequality and displacement. The process intensifies turnover of capital of all kinds, much of which is rendered abject and removed from circulation.

Chapter 4 teases out the implications of this waste for urban space and policy. It describes the forbidden gift—the efforts of Seattle and dozens of other cities to restrict the free outdoor distribution of food and other necessities. These prohibitions against sharing represent an instrument with which to remake public life in the image and interests of the global city, and they constitute the chief site of struggle for our book's conspiracy. Meanwhile, the circulation of abject capital—wasted food in particular—

is consigned to marginal spaces within the city. The chapter looks more closely, too, at the assumptions and attitudes of policymakers, public employees, and philanthropic organizations in Seattle, many of whom accept the basic priorities and claims of a market-public and are distrustful or antagonistic toward counterpublic efforts like Food Not Bombs that circulate these free gifts.

Having described the provisions and proponents of the conspiracy and the counterpublic shadows in which they operate, in Part III, "Slow Insurrection," I describe their forms of organization and mobilization. Chapter 5 explores the uneasy relationship between city governments and Food Not Bombs—from the hundreds of arrests of Food Not Bombs volunteers in San Francisco during the 1980s and 1990s to the episodic police pressure enforced in Seattle and my other research sites. Drawing on Zibechi's (2010) model of insurrectionary political movements, I sketch out a symbiotic relationship between a peaceful, "slow insurrection" like Food Not Bombs—one that unfolds opaquely over decades—and the municipal state apparatuses with which it is entangled and which have an interest in keeping out of public circulation precisely the abject capital and surplus life that are FNB's raw materials. In policing the ways and spaces in which people can survive in the globalizing city—particularly by limiting the nonmarket circulation of food—they provoke FNB's mobilization and expansion.

In chapter 6, I explore Food Not Bombs' global proliferation not only through conflict with municipal authorities but also through mutual aid among nonmarket counterpublics of dumpster-divers, squatters, gleaners, and other scavengers. This chapter asks what new forms of global, embodied relationships are made possible by the availability of global capitalism's wasted surpluses, particularly food and shelter. These counterpublics hold open the possibility of assembling a diverse spectrum of bodies and practices excluded from mainstream, liberal public spheres. Illegible from without, this assembly nonetheless makes new lives and embodiments possible.

Finally, in the conclusion, I recap the book's arguments by way of teasing out four political conclusions pitched at a broad readership, from activists and policy makers to everyday readers. These conclusions aim to complicate received political and economic wisdoms, contextualize or critique urban policies (such as the feeding restrictions described throughout the book), and suggest strategies for political organizing. In these ways, perhaps the experiences and intuitions of FNB may be put to further work.

The thesis was that if there's technology and machinery on the planet that can make a television set for every man, woman, and child on the planet, and you don't have a television because you don't have the money, the money is a way of inventing scarcity.

—Peter Coyote
(December 2008)

Locked bin, locked restaurant dumpster. (Melbourne, 2018)

PART I

ABJECT CAPITAL

SCENE I

IT'S THANKSGIVING IN SEATTLE

It's Thanksgiving in Seattle, and I'm up to my elbows in garbage—giving thanks, as it were, for the harvest I'm about to reap.

I'm in a dumpster at Pike Place Market. Halfway in, actually, headfirst, balanced awkwardly on the edge. I'm sorting through produce discarded by the market's stalls, which closed early today. A crate full of green beans. Asparagus, only a little wilted (by retail standards). Potatoes—we'll mash these tonight. Pineapples with a few brown spots—we might save those for pie, along with the strawberries and apples from the last dumpster. Or bake them with dumpstered yams and a little brown sugar. My friend Meg keeps watch.

Among the soggy cardboard, only slightly sullied by coffee grounds, are untold postcommodities: some beyond hope, some ready to eat, all purged to make room on the shelves for newer stock. With a few precautions and a good rinse, they're no more dangerous than the recalcitrant leftovers in the back of your refrigerator. Better yet, the market compost dumpster never sees the kinds of detritus that accumulate in the average rubbish bin. It even smells nice. Like a salad or a garden. And in these piercing, grizzled Seattle Novembers, the chipped green dumpster walls are cold to the touch and keep the contents fresh—relatively speaking. (As we'll see in this book, value is always relative.) The experience is not completely unlike going shopping.

I only have to dig a few handbreadths down to excavate the ingredients for our Thanksgiving meal. The red brick road, worn smooth by decades of teeming wheels and feet, is deserted as Meg packs the food in waxed cardboard boxes, also from the dumpster. We'll take our haul to a friend's house to make dinner: stuffing,

On a characteristically grizzled winter Seattle evening in 2011, I balanced on the chipped green walls of Seattle's "burrito dumpster." (Photo by Raeanne Wiseman)

mashed potatoes, sweet potato pie, apple pie, and stir-fry. In all honesty, it will be the best Thanksgiving meal I've had in a long time (with apologies to my family). Then we will drive to Pioneer Square, the original "Skid Road," to give it away.

It's two in the afternoon, but the usual tourists and patrons are elsewhere for the holiday. The stall-keepers have gone home. Their dumpsters sit at the curb, padlocked. (Taking a cue from Ziploc, "the freshness is locked in.") We can open their lids just enough to peer inside, but that suffices to let us know which one to plunder. Then it's a matter of prying out the pin that holds the lid's hinge in place, removing the hinge—a long, simple iron bar—and opening the dumpster from the wrong side. One doesn't normally do this in broad daylight, but we're running late: this was something of a last-minute "plan B." In fact, for the Seattle chapter of Food Not Bombs (which does Thanksgiving sometimes, qualms about colonial dispossession notwithstanding), dumpster-diving is usually supplemental. Most Food

Not Bombs groups find enough vendors to donate their "seconds" that we don't need to spend the hours it takes to prospect in the rubbish. We had originally secured donations for this week from a local supermarket. Amid the tumult of Thanksgiving crowds that morning, however, they'd forgotten to set anything aside for us except a small bag of flour. (They'd thrown away the rest of the day's surpluses, so naturally we checked their dumpster too.)

In a pinch, we knew Pike Place would bear fruit. On an average day, the market's detritus reflects its vast turnover. The goods passed over in the course of its postcard-perfect commerce are world class. Its dumpsters overflow with slightly bruised peaches, perfectly tender mangos, and barely overripe avocados—some of the hundred billion pounds or so of edible food thrown away in the United States every year. Food that has reached the end, not of its usefulness, but of its social life.

Fortunately for the abandoned peach, mango, or avocado, many people like Meg and myself are there to intercept it. While millions of hands around the country, and around the world, labor first to make it valuable—cultivating, harvesting, packing, and shipping it—and then to devalue it (pulling it from the shelves, trucking it to a landfill, where commodities go to die), thousands of hands also work to resuscitate it. Countercultures of gleaners, dumpster-divers, squatters, punks, hippies, Food Not Bombers, and so on, for whom the value of a thing doesn't follow the economic or cultural logics that banish it to a dumpster. They'll tell epic tales of their favorite discoveries and found new movements, networks, and kin on the reliable availability of resources beyond the capitalist market. Even the dumpsters themselves take on a new kind of currency, as bespoke monikers circulate along with their contents—the "Bread Dumpster," the "Chocolate Dumpster," the "Burrito Dumpster." They become, quite literally, household names among a certain scavenging coterie. People drive to Seattle sometimes just to hit the Juice Dumpster. Rumor has it there's a Cookie Dumpster in Boston somewhere.

This anecdote is also an allegory of everyday life in what Karl Polanyi ([1944] 1957) called the "market society," into whose political and cultural institutions are woven the assumptions of capitalism, from its tax code to its tastes and values. The story suggests daunting questions about the way markets, small and large, (de)value goods. We might ask: Why do people throw such useful things away? What can we learn about them, and their society, from their trash? What becomes of that trash once it is thrown away? What sort of afterlife does it find? What new economies—or mass conspiracies—might be built on the detritus of the old? These theoretical questions are at the heart of this part of the book.

After all, when we made it down to Pioneer Square with our offerings that night, although different charities had been serving turkey all day (unlike most of the other days during the year), and despite the quickly dropping temperature, we still found people waiting for us. And we still ran out of food. One older shelterless man I met under the viaduct that night summed it up for me: "There's always more hungry people around here."

A typical night at the chocolate dumpster. (Seattle, Washington, 2015)

1

The Anatomy of a Dumpster

Abject Capital and the Looking Glass of Value

Beginnings and Endings

This chapter begins where many things end: the dumpster. Or, for that matter, the garbage can, the landfill, or the sewer—all seemingly points of no return in the "social life" of a thing (Appadurai 1986). And yet, in this chapter I argue that these ends are only apparent. They veil the ways in which the thing persists and, in strange, subterranean ways, continues to *produce*. In the trash heap, things secrete a kind of abject value, central to but invisible within the social and financial calculus of market societies. Waste of all sorts, in this way, haunts our cultural economy.

> The works of the roots of the vines, of the trees, must be destroyed to keep up the price, and this is the saddest, bitterest thing of all. Carloads of oranges dumped on the ground. The people came for miles to take the fruit, but this could not be. How would they buy oranges at twenty cents a dozen if they could drive out and pick them up?
>
> —John Steinbeck

Waste also haunts this book—in particular the squandered surpluses of capitalism. Just as every bread riot begins not with a broken window but an empty stomach (while others feast), our mass conspiracy begins in the dumpster. Waste is its condition of possibility. Without the food industry's excesses, Food Not Bombs and projects like it would not be possible. Without the disparities of a market-driven food system—simultaneous waste and want—they would not be necessary. To make sense of the cities and social movements in this book, therefore, we need to know how waste is made under capitalism. To that end, this chapter raises some very theoretical questions: What is value? What is waste? How are they related? It also raises very concrete questions: How does a commodity meet its end? Where does it go afterward?

Of all these terminuses, the dumpster has been most accessible to my soggy research expeditions. Scavenging practices, and especially dumpster-diving, are the economic foundation of Food Not Bombs and many of the political communities into which it is woven. As my Seattle FNB co-conspirator and dumpster-diver Koa told me, describing the mysteries of the waste stream and the joys of scavenging, "Stuff always appears, out of nowhere, you know? It's like 'Ah, cool. *It's ours now*.'" More than that, however, these practices are a form of everyday research into the circulatory systems of modern capitalism. As any good dumpster-diver must to be successful, in this chapter I develop a theory to account for why so much is thrown away before ever reaching the consumer. Especially what I call "abject capital," material wealth that could be used but instead is sequestered in the bin because it is profitable to do so. Like so many of the scavengers I have met, I ask why the production of cultural and economic value should generate such waste, and how that waste in turn might produce cultural and economic value. In an era colored by the memory of multiple global financial crises—marked equally by bread lines, million-dollar bonuses, and rotting food in the fields—waste is a cipher to the cultural logics that create and distribute wealth.

> KAREN: I mean things that you find in dumpsters, you know? A whole bag of plastic chopsticks that haven't been opened. And dolls. And clothes. And—what else—mango chutney. Ha. Yeah.
> TERRY: Anything you want.
> KAREN: Toilet paper.
> TERRY: *Scented* toilet paper.
> KAREN: Yeah scented toilet paper. Anything and everything, if you keep it up. I mean just the other day, an entire dumpster full of oranges. *An entire dumpster.*
>
> —Karen and Terry, Melbourne FNB, ca. 2006

I ask: What can we learn from those commodities that migrate from the shelves to the dumpster but still have use values? Or, if you like, *why do people throw perfectly good things away, and what can we learn about them and their values from their trash?*

What I describe below is a looking-glass economy of trash in which Marx is turned on his head, labor *devalues* commodities, and things somehow become trash merely by being thrown away. I take a cultural-economic approach to make sense of the ambiguities of this valuable garbage, which confound the mathematical rationale of economics but are nonetheless part of an economic system. To that end, this chapter borrows poststructuralist philosophy's knack for the uncanny, ambiguous, and occluded. I decode the back-to-front logic of waste in terms of Giorgio Agamben's notion of the "relation of exception" (1998) and Julia Kristeva's "abjection" (1982). Both concepts capture the ejection of people, places, or things from our social worlds in ways that leave a stain. As both thinkers argue, those stains—here, the prejudices and hidden meanings attached to the trash—form the very foundation of our systems of meaning and value. Whereas Marx taught that things gain value through productive labor, Agamben's exception represents a conceptual boundary across which all things must pass when they finally abdicate that value. And Kristeva's abjection—the unsettling, intimate, gagging estrangement of the strangely familiar—highlights the bilious affect with which those boundaries are often policed. At political and personal scales, Agamben's and Kristeva's work highlights the stakes of these boundaries, which in very real ways define life and death, value and valuelessness.

Briefly put, I suggest that the dumpster, the garbage can, the landfill, and so on are exceptional, abject spaces where the lapsed value of their contents is paradoxically relinquished and retained in ways that lend value, comparatively, to goods still in circulation. They are part of the material and social infrastructure of capital. In short, *sometimes the value of things is determined not by what we keep, but what we throw away.*

This research, for better and for worse, demands a look at the trash itself and the point of its inception (read: demise)—that moment in which a thing migrates from valuable to worthless and is discarded. This transmutation is riddled with indeterminacy, aesthetics, prejudice, and moment-to-moment reckonings that demand firsthand participation and observation. To trace the contingent processes through which value is determined, I borrowed Food Not Bombs' tactics, making our food recovery strategies—via both the dumpster and grocers' donations—into a research methodology and inspecting the still-useful stuff junked at each point in the commodity chain. In this way, for several years I became a weekly visitor to Seattle markets and grocers, soliciting for FNB donations of fruits and vegetables, bread and doughnuts, pastries, coffee, you name it, before they hit the dumpster. I developed relationships with the employees and learned from them why they were throwing it all away. With friends and informants from Food Not Bombs, I've explored Seattle's back alleys and parking lots, from the wholesalers and producers of the industrial districts to the supermarkets, produce stands, and retailers of the suburbs. And I have inspected, excavated—and, yes, eaten from—dozens and dozens of dumpsters.

In this way, I have tried to describe how and why things might come to end up here in the trash, and what they portend for the social life of things.

The Quiet Crisis of Waste

The first time I climbed into a commercial dumpster, on a winter's night in 2004, in the alley beside a Trader Joe's supermarket on Seattle's upmarket Queen Anne Hill, my antibacterial scruples evaporated at first sight: immaculate, individually wrapped slices of pie; imported cheeses, still sealed, on the very date of expiry; prepackaged salad mix; fresh fruits and vegetables; bread; and a small mountain of fresh-cut flowers. The contents represented an almost random sample of what was on the shelves.

That night, several friends gave me my first lesson in "dumpstering." I knew them from Seattle's loose network of communal houses, which served as a sort of grassroots infrastructure for radical activism. FNB often borrows their kitchens, for instance. I set off from Sherwood Co-op (a long-standing, communally owned student house) with my housemate Scott, a wiry white vegan with an asymmetrical haircut, and we picked up his partner, Tanya, a longtime anarchist and antiracist educator, from

Dumpster still life: fruit, vegetables, and fresh-cut flowers in a grocery dumpster. (Seattle, Washington, 2017)

Sunset House, another share-house full of like-minded hippies, punks, and radicals, mainly in their twenties and thirties. I was surprised that there was no "trick" to deciding which food was safe. Scott and Tanya had simply learned to trust their noses and eyes, and to follow the kinds of basic food-safety principles that guided our grandparents' choices in the days before refrigeration and the rise of abstract industrial rationalizations like the expiry date. (Note that, of all the dumpster-divers I've met, only one has ever reported getting sick. If only I could say the same about my track record with certain commercial restaurants.)

They knew which dumpsters to check, and on what days, to find more or less exactly what we needed. A friend from another share-house had also done in-store reconnaissance earlier to let us know which dairy products were due to "expire" and be pulled from the shelves. The abundance was reliable, predictable even. We discreetly visited four or five alleys and parking lots in the wee hours of the morning and left with a carload of what had been, just hours earlier, hundreds of dollars' worth of food. We stopped by another share-house to rinse the food and stock the refrigerator. On the way home we dropped off a box of groceries at yet a fourth share-house—decorating their windowsill with a lovely dumpstered flower arrangement to boot.

Corrina, a dumpster-diver and FNB collaborator from Seattle, once told me, "the biggest reason that you throw stuff out is that you take too much. And you can't fit it all in your refrigerator and then you can't give it away fast enough. Even if you're throwing bags of bread at everyone you see on the street—*literally*." Ever productive, however, even the twice-abandoned food becomes the basis of yet other ecologies and economies: "That's what chickens are for," she said, winking. "We had fantasies about taking our chickens dumpster-diving, but we decided not to."

Such was the dumpsters' bounty that a year later, one Seattle collective known simply as "the Pantry" bought an industrial refrigerator (secondhand, of course) to store it all. It was located in my old share-house's basement. Perhaps two dozen scavengers from across the city all deposited their regular haul in it, taking whatever they needed and leaving the rest. They thus divided their anticapitalist labors and multiplied their efficiency and range (in ways that, ironically, might have made Adam Smith proud). The Pantry partly supported a citywide network of communal houses and at least two distinct Food Not Bombs chapters before dissolving after several years. Seattle's dumpsters had become the basis of a friendly little gift economy—less in the sense of obligatory gift exchange (see Mauss [1954] 2002) and more the "generalized reciprocity" (Sahlins

1972) of anarchist "mutual aid" networks (Kropotkin 1902). A modest sort of grassroots safety net for local activists, many of whom are precariously employed and (contrary to popular stereotypes) don't have middle-class families to fall back on (more on this in chapter 5).

The material wealth we found cloistered in Seattle's factory, wholesale, and retail dumpsters isn't out of the ordinary. Rather, it's *business* as usual. The market has not been the efficient arbiter of resources some free-market ideologues still imagine. As my friends taught me that first day, it makes waste in astounding, predictable quantities.

For scale: in the United States, although most still-useful food is wasted by consumers—91 billion pounds per annum, by the most comprehensive estimate[1]—the US Department of Agriculture estimated that retailers throw away 5.4 billion pounds of unspoiled food without it ever reaching the point of sale (Kantor et al. 1997, 1). Although the US produces enough food to feed its populace almost twice over each day, a third of it is thrown away before its time; retailers alone throw away enough of it to feed more than 4 million people daily (Kantor et al. 1997, 2–3). Contrast that with the 15.8 million American households (more than 40 million individuals) that were "food insecure" at some point in 2017, meaning that they were unable to, or unsure of whether they could, adequately feed all their members (Coleman-Jensen et al. 2018, 7). The two trends, toward surplus and scarcity, are inextricable.

Waste is a quiet, ongoing crisis at the heart of capital that, no less than want, stalks the noisier, episodic economic calamities we are more accustomed to hearing about. The American foreclosure crisis of the past decade, for instance, was characterized as much by empty houses as by evicted families. But any crusty squatter punk can tell you there is nothing new about empty houses in the United States.

Researchers have mapped numerous dimensions of this crisis. This book builds on their work. Archaeologists, for example, have documented the growth of postconsumer garbage in recent decades (e.g., Rathje and Murphy 1992; Jones et al. 2002a, 2002b). Economists and sociologists have studied the steady increase of abandoned housing in the US.[2] And a growing literature that goes by the name of "discard studies" explores the implications of all this excess, often approaching the question of value from *behind*, asking what detritus and desuetude can tell us about the way people, places, and things are valorized, ordered, and abandoned. As the economic anthropologist David Graeber (2001) points out, we can think of value in at least three related ways: in terms of semiotics (the value of symbols and signifiers), economy (exchangeability and price), and ideals (cultural notions of the good). In each sense, waste is revealing: *semiotically*, the rejection of dirt or "matter out of place" lends coherence to our systems of symbolic and spatial classification (Douglas [1966] 1984; see also Thompson 1979; Hetherington 2004; Hawkins 2005; DeSilvey 2006; Munro 2013); *economically*, many scholars suggest that capitalist value is *defined* by the production of material excesses, particularly surplus commodities (e.g., Baran and Sweezy 1966; Henderson 2011; Vaughn 2011; O'Brien 2013; Barnard 2016) and "relative surplus population" (Marx [1865] 2000); and *politically*, ideologies of progress and development are often constructed in opposition to notions of "ruination" (e.g., Navaro-Yashin 2003; Scandura 2008; Stoler 2013; Gordillo 2014; Tsing 2015; Gupta 2016).

This book aims to connect some of these dots and asks how they might outline the conditions for a mass conspiracy. In particular, it takes its cues from Gidwani and Reddy, who synthesize all three lines of inquiry, describing waste as "the constitutive outside" to capitalist value and political modernity (2011, 1628). As such, waste is a translation matrix that links the nested scales at which the market is reproduced through signification, economic exchange, and the designs of state apparatuses. In this book I follow suit, describing the workings of the "market" on both experiential and abstract scales, from discrete marketplaces ("Pike Place Market," "the supermarket," and so on) to the metanarrative of the Market-with-a-capital-*M*. The double meaning folds in a dialectic between particular cultural-economic practices of exchange and their larger discursive formations. And by "waste" I mean both "detritus" and also "unnecessarily thrown away." As the market carves out the *profitable* from the *merely useful*, the dual meaning of the word is appropriate. In this sense, the production of waste is the production of wealth. And the distribution of wealth is also a distribution of waste.

On the face of it, such waste seems illogical according to the rationality of the market, which, it is often claimed, connects supply to demand with sweeping efficiency. But the deregulated markets and globalized commodity flows of recent decades have done little to stem excesses. On the contrary, waste is inherent in the corporate agribusiness model that dominates the global food system (Cloke 2013). Indeed, the United Nations Food and Agriculture Organization found that up to a third of the globe's annual food yield is wasted, particularly in developed nations by retailers and consumers who can count upon its relative abundance and low cost (Gustavsson ct al. 2011, 14). At the same time, average food prices around the world climbed prohibitively higher throughout the past decade, elbowing millions of people beyond the poverty threshold.[3] These two facts are entangled. In the same way, the global food crises of 2008 and 2010 were not a matter of scarcity per se, but rather of distribution.[4] Nor were they fundamental changes in the pricing mechanisms of the global food system, but rather quantitative spikes—de rigueur, in fact, for the workings of the market. In other words, the "crisis" is incipient in markets themselves.

Wasted surpluses are not confined to food. Consider the following tip from an anonymous, experienced dumpster-diver: "Do what any savvy shopper does—look in the yellow pages! Chances are, if they sell it in front, they throw it away out back . . . There's bound to be a dumpster out there to serve you: food, bike equipment, construction materials, kitchenware, books, electronics, clothes, flowers, shoes, bread, bread, bread" (CrimethInc. 2004, 220). In my own research, I have recovered virtually everything on this list. (I didn't need the kitchenware.)

Yet the grocery dumpster is singularly symptomatic. Writing about the United States, Janet Poppendieck observed: "Poor people routinely suffer for want of things that are produced in abundance . . . but the bicycles and personal computers that people desire and could use are not perishable and hence not rotting in front of their eyes in defiance of their bellies" (1998b, 127). This conspicuous decadence, and the instrumental relationship between food, life, and culture, makes food waste an especially transparent variable in the social calculus of economic value (and therefore the focus of the remainder of chapter 1).

> The best peach that I have ever eaten in my entire life was in the Larry's dumpster. It was the size of a cantaloupe—and I'm not exaggerating. And it was perfectly ripe. It was absolutely perfectly ripe. And, of course, you don't want to eat stuff without washing it but the skin just *slipped off.* And, so I ate it. It was *so good.* It melted in my mouth like butter.
>
> —Corrina, Seattle FNB, ca. 2005

The Bulimia of Late Capitalism

At the outset of the global financial crisis in 2008, Seattle's gunmetal-gray autumn days portended a winter of discontent. The recession decimated job markets. Food stamps surged in popularity.[5] Meal programs and food pantries were swamped, according to my acquaintances working in, or relying on, Seattle's emergency food system. Queues of people waiting for Food Not Bombs in the biting cold evenings grew from dozens to sometimes hundreds, stretching across the damp red bricks of Occidental Park. We usually ran out of the soups and stir-fry first. (The hot stuff.) After that, we'd run out of dessert. (Fat and carbohydrates to sustain people through the night.) Sometimes even the nearly bottomless flats of doughnuts donated by a local vegan bakery would run dry. Next, the fruit dwindled. (Late arrivals could at least carry it with them, saving it for later.) The last thing to go was the salad. (Nobody ever really wanted salad.)

But while demand grew, *our supply kept up*. Donations remained steady and the dumpster-divers I knew saw little change in the waste stream. In fact, that year food waste amounted to the greatest recorded proportion of Seattle's commercial waste stream to date (Cascadia Consulting Group with Seattle Public Utilities Staff 2008). The proportion had increased steadily since 1996 irrespective of economic boom or bust, and it has remained stable since.[6] While I was collecting produce donations from Pike Place Market, a vendor told me he had noticed more customers shopping at the discount tables—the last stop for produce before the trash—but when I told this story in the park later that day and speculated that the markets might cut back on donations, other volunteers were doubtful. One reminded me that even during the Great Depression, food had been left to rot rather than be used to feed the hungry or be sold at a discount.[7] They turned out to be right. The crisis certainly unsettled our home economics in other respects: the unluckiest among us lost jobs and moved onto friends' couches in Seattle's network of share-houses, or into local squats; the luckiest lent out money and couch space. (One twenty-something friend, Food Not Bombs collaborator, and former cook at a local diner moved into my basement for six months. Meanwhile, I used my student loans to pay my roommate's rent and my parents' mortgage.) But among FNB collaborators and other dumpster-divers, larders remained well stocked with scavenged groceries. The dumpsters and their contents seemed to have quietly escaped the recession, despite the incipient panic inflecting other spheres of city life.

In other words, the waste cannot be explained simply as a symptom of American opulence, as many do. Nor is it merely an unfortunate side effect of a booming free market. Rather, the imperative to expend and abandon surpluses is often primary, even in the face of collapsing markets. Waste represents a cultural logic unto itself, with the potential to drive the expansion and evolution of capital—particularly in the last four decades of neoliberal transformation. Indeed, in Marx's seminal description of capital, wasted excesses cast a definitive shadow: overproduction was, he wrote in the *Grundrisse*, the "fundamental contradiction of developed capitalism" ([1941] 2000, 399). This contradiction seemed to Marx so inescapable as to be capitalism's downfall. Instead, however, capitalist industries have often made lemons into lemonade by making this overproduction fundamental to their reorganization in the wake of periods of crisis (see Baran and Sweezy 1966). During the postwar boom, for example, both built-in and perceived obsolescence became the norm, and the contradiction of excess became the basis of rapidly growing consumer economies that prized constant, disposable novelty (Packard [1960] 2011). The neoliberal capitalism of recent decades has only accelerated this waste-making, assuming an unprecedented capacity to mediate life itself and translating the barest of human necessities (food, shelter, water, health) into commodities. The imperative to produce and squander excesses is a key dimension of this transformation (see O'Brien 2013; Giles 2015, 2016; Barnard 2016).

Even the consumer's appetite—literally—has been subject to inflation in capital's renewed search for new markets during the neoliberal era: between 1970 and 2003, the average American's caloric intake grew by 523 calories per day (Wells and Buzby 2005). The greatest increases by far were of fat, oils, and grains, reflecting not just a net increase but a qualitative change in the American diet. Correspondingly, the quantity and diversity of foods available per person in supermarkets have grown significantly in the United States and Britain over the past two decades (Stuart 2009). Indeed, Guthman and DuPuis (2006) suggest that in the neoliberal market society, the consuming body itself is being remade in the image of capital, whose contradictions are temporarily resolved therein as it absorbs more calories more cheaply—becoming, in effect, an expanding market for new products.

But a body can take only so much. When the upper limit of a body's caloric intake presents a problem of "inelastic demand" (Guthman and DuPuis 2006, 439), waste becomes a way for markets to overcome the barrier: Guthman and DuPuis describe a "bulimic economy" of paradoxically excessive portions and empty calories, overeating and expensive dieting—of economic binging and purging—which has the effect of encouraging us to spend more, and more disposably, on our bodies. As they put it, "neoliberalism's commodification of everything ensures that getting rid of food—whether in bodies, municipal dumps, or food aid, for that matter, which has been shown to open up new markets—is as central to capitalist accumulation as is producing and eating it . . . . In other words, bulimia is not simply a way to read bodies; it is a way to read the neoliberal economy itself" (442).

Correspondingly, Americans' per-capita food waste grew steadily by about 50 percent between 1974 and 2003 (Hall, Guo, Dore, and Chow

Dirty dozens: out of its material and semiotic packaging, the lone egg is not a legible commodity, so good eggs and bad eggs alike are abandoned together when a carton contains both. (Seattle, Washington, 2017)

2009, 1–2). Their diets have thus been reorganized in myriad ways according to the food industry's particular mode of production—in the image not just of the market, but of the *supermarket*. Dumpster-divers often find eleven perfectly good eggs in the bin alongside one cracked one, for instance, because they fall short of the humble egg's standard commodity form, the dozen. Similarly, expiry dates represent factory-stamped estimates, projections of the conditions of production, transportation, and sale that are largely unregulated in the United States and vary from producer to producer ("enjoy by," "use by," etc.). In this way, industrial algorithms are incorporated into consumers' foodways and waste-ways.

Therefore the slow-motion crisis of waste, like its faster cousins the global financial crisis and the global food crises, can be quite profitable. The more life itself is carved up and parsed out into capital—even, and especially, food—the more waste is left in the dumpster.

The Social Afterlife of the Commodity

My argument here sets out not from within any particular dumpster (the technological limits of word-processing hardware being what they are), but rather the notional space of the dumpster and places like it. They are integral to the waste-making mode of production I have just described. Indeed, waste-making and waste management represent forms of infrastructure that are simultaneously technical and affective, material and immaterial (see Fredericks 2018). They organize and bound the entire economic system. This section gives an account of the cultural work that happens in these places, where waste is symbolically secluded and its value neutralized.

This description is necessarily theoretical—in contrast to actual dumpsters, which come in all shapes, sizes, colors, and textures. They are filled and emptied by diverse actors, reflecting distinct technologies, infrastructures, and "waste regimes" (Gille 2010; see also Nagle 2013; Reno 2016). And that's to say nothing of their contents: no two dumpsters are the same. (In fact, no single dumpster is ever the same for very long—trash is always becoming trash.) Nor of the myriad reasons things might end up there. (Bad memories. Broken glass.) They span such a range of human endeavor as to have absolutely no common denominator except that somebody saw fit to throw them away.

So, from the outset, we could define the dumpster as simply "away." That place where things are thrown. The dumpster, trash can, landfill, sewer, and other such spaces serve as a kind of conceptual *elsewhere*. An outside to their former sociality. An end to the "cultural biography" of a thing (Appadurai 1986, 34). Although it may go on to lead myriad social and ecological afterlives, the everyday lexicon of waste tells us little about them. Instead, *rubbish, trash, garbage, detritus, refuse*, and so on, with their various etymological roots and associations,[8] all rattle their chains from a kind of "cultural no-man's land" (Navaro-Yashin 2003). The nature of this exilic realm depends on two questions. First, what kind of a social life did it lead? And second, what constitutes its outside?

The social life that leads to the commercial dumpster is, of course, the life of a commodity. A "shelf-life," if you will. A commodity is, after all, not simply a category of thing but rather "one phase in the life of some things" (Appadurai 1986, 17). For many goods, that phase comes to an end in alleys, loading docks, and parking lots at every point in the commodity chain before the point of sale. If the contents of those dumpsters are still useful, then their former lives cannot have been defined by utility alone—what Marx called a "use value" ([1865] 2000). Rather, the definitive feature of the commodity's social life is its *exchange value*. Its going rate. For our purposes, although this waste is still useful, its exchange value is essentially zero. (Sometimes even negative: once in the dumpster, businesses usually pay by volume to have it removed). It is de-commoditized, or, in Igor Kopytoff's words, "priceless in the full possible sense of the term, ranging from uniquely valuable to uniquely worthless" (1986, 75).

Of course, this status is unstable. What is thrown away might yet be re-commoditized: sold, traded, or given away under other circumstances or in different spheres of value. Waste materials such as scrap metal may be big business, for instance.[9] Likewise, some supermarkets now generate electricity from their organic wastes through anaerobic digestion. Even so, these wastes usually have been diverted to different "commodity contexts" (Appadurai 1986), arenas of value outside those that initially determined their sticker price. The dumpster therefore marks both a conceptual and a spatial boundary between those arenas.

What, then, constitutes an "outside" to that former commodity life? Poststructuralist political theory comes in handy here: with respect to its former life, the trash stands in what the philosopher Giorgio Agamben calls a "relation of exception" (1998, 18). For Agamben, the exception highlights a structural boundary between socially and politically meaningful forms of life and their "outside." This boundary defines the exception by what it is not and repels it on those grounds. In Agamben's words, it is "included solely through its exclusion" (18). For example, the refugee is defined by their lack of citizenship. The prisoner by their lack of freedom. The homeless individual by their lack of shelter. And the trash by its having been thrown away. Indeed, something of "waste" resides in all of the exceptional categories listed above. The exception, Agamben writes, is "not, in fact, simply set outside the law and made indifferent to it but rather *abandoned* by it" (28; emphasis in original).

At first glance, his definition seems somewhat circular. But it tells us something about the power to sustain a given order and to establish its limits. Agamben cites Carl Schmitt's proclamation, "Sovereign is he who decides on the exception" ([1985] 2005, 5). In other words, the exception not only proves the rule, it justifies rule itself (Agamben 1998, 18). Unlike thinkers who envisioned sovereignty as the freedom *from* rule,[10] for Agamben, sovereignty is a structural characteristic of systems of rule. It is manifest in any sociopolitical order that is "biopolitical," which is to say that it regulates life itself, reproducing and legitimating certain forms of social life while rendering other lives unprotected, unrecognized, and "bare." In Michel Foucault's famous formulation, such "bio-power" makes live or lets die ([1978] 1986, 138).[11] Such sovereignty is not exclusively the provenance of the state,[12] but may also be expressed structurally in the ways in which capitalist norms come to remake and capacitate certain lives and bodies (as we saw in the previous section) while abandoning others. When so many go hungry, it could be none other than the sovereignty of capital that banishes the edible ex-commodity to the bottom of the dumpster. Like the lost freedom of the prisoner, or the noncitizenship of the stateless refugee, the former value of the once-commodity in the commercial dumpster is a kind of absent presence that authorizes the calculus of for-profit exchange and private property (rather than bare human necessity) to define the value of everything left on the shelves. Such waste is "included as an exclusion" in the commodity chain (see also Thompson 1979; Henderson 2011). Thus does the dumpster's very existence authorize the entire system of market exchange, in ways inadequately acknowledged by political economy (Marxist and classical alike). One needs only to observe the suspicion—and sometimes anger—of some retail employees toward dumpster-divers who violate those principles to see this sovereignty at work.

This means that *what we throw away serves a function through its own absence.* Abandoning a commodity that still has use value paradoxically inscribes it within a sort of shadow commodification under a regime of market value even as it becomes an ex-commodity (Barnard 2016). It remains a kind of commodity fetish—and therefore an organ of capital accumulation—long after it hits the dumpster (see Giles 2015; Barnard 2016). Otherwise, if it could be "simply set outside the law and made indifferent," in Agamben's words (1998, 28), it could be given away, eaten, worn as a hat, or forgotten completely, with no meaningful consequence for the market. The fact that it is not (and is sometimes even sequestered behind a padlock) reinforces its relation of exception to the social world of commodities.

Consider the following thought experiment: If the supermarkets' edible surpluses were given away indiscriminately, instead of thrown away, we can predict that it would be hard to ask "full price" for what was left in the stores. (Philanthropic donations represent another exceptional case, as I describe in the following chapter, and are only viable insofar as they do not disrupt the market.) Even if the surplus were sold at a significant discount, the exchange value of the newer stock would suffer, according to the logic of supply and demand. They cannot be "made indifferent" to each other. To paraphrase Steinbeck: Why buy it new, when it can be had for less, albeit not quite as fresh, in the alley?

In other words, *waste manufactures scarcity*. Indeed, governments and farmers have relied on this principle whenever they have purchased and dumped agricultural surpluses to inflate prices, from Steinbeck's "grapes of wrath," rotting in the fields, to the European Union's "milk lakes" and "butter mountains."[13] In the same way that "negative externalities," expenses deferred or passed on by the market (e.g., agricultural subsidies, environmental damage), are echoed in a price structure, keeping costs down, so is waste. Waste, though, is an externalization of product. It keeps prices up. In some sense, it passes its value on to the stock left in circulation.

Milk lakes and butter mountains are destroyed almost instantaneously, however. In

> No moment illustrates the morally and practically contentious status of edible garbage more ironically than the curmudgeonly market worker I met who insisted on throwing away the same melons twice. I was on my usual Sunday routine at Pike Place, picking up FNB donations, but had been noticing over the preceding weeks that there were plenty of treasures that had been thrown away before I arrived. I was indiscreet, upon this occasion, and took to dumpstering during store hours. I had pulled out a box full of melons and set them aside to look for more produce. I'd put them down maybe two meters away while I went back to forage in the bin. But when I returned they were gone. I went searching for them along the market sheds. I met him instead. I asked naively if he had moved a box of melons, and he told me crankily (and confusingly) that he had thrown them away (again) because I hadn't "taken care of them." He seemed to have been watching me. I asked what he meant and he repeated with some ire that I wasn't "taking care of them," so he had. I explained that I wasn't taking them for myself, but would be taking them to share with people who couldn't afford to buy melons for themselves. I told him about Food Not Bombs. "Maybe I didn't realize that," he said, and then begrudgingly, "and maybe I'm sorry." But he rebuked me angrily for persisting in search of them. If I take him at his word, he was acknowledging the inequity of waste in the face of hunger. He was regretful, and yet still cranky with me, it seemed, for taking them. And in any case, he wouldn't give back the melons.
>
> —Author's notes, Pike Place Market, autumn 2007

the same way, the trash compactors increasingly encountered by dumpster-divers destroy use value. As do the employees who sprinkle their trash with bleach. (Although those stories circulate mainly as rumors. I have only once met a dumpster-diver who found bleached garbage.) By contrast, many former commodities retain their use values. The difference is critical. It sets the useful ex-commodity in an ambiguous, exceptional position—both part of the calculus of supply and demand, yet excluded from the market. Like the zombie or the revenant, neither dead nor living, the useful ex-commodity is undead to the world of capital accumulation. (It threatens to rise again from the dumpster.) It is an *uncommodity*. Such uncommodities are an ontological precondition of scarcity, an ineluctable substrate of market exchange and capitalist value. The dumpster materializes that space of exception that makes this paradox possible, a frontier beyond which the normal rules of exchange value no longer apply.

Where Meaning Collapses

Of course, most shoppers do not object strenuously to this state of affairs. They have little business with the dumpster, which has been kindly removed from their social worlds. Beyond the pale of market sociality, it is poorly legible and best avoided. This mistrust is echoed by coverage of dumpster-diving in the popular press, which often conflates it with criminality, homelessness, or illness, or presents it as a kind of entertaining sideshow.[14] Like other spaces of exception (the prison, the asylum, the camp), the dumpster is segregated by a spectrum of exclusions, formal and informal, abstract and embodied, reasoned and felt. All these exclusions lend momentum to the circulation of things, both in the sleek consumer playgrounds of global cities and the aftermarket shadow economies that are the subject of this book.

> "Sometimes I start to think 'hey maybe dumpster-diving wouldn't be so bad' . . . then I remember the things I throw away in dumpsters."
> "Obama has reduced us to the level of rats: eating out of dumpsters."
> "Sorry dumpster diving dudes and dudettes, but dumpster-diving will always be gross."
> "I've got a great way for this 31[-] year-old who is still in college to help solve hunger. Get a job and donate part of your salary to the food bank."
>
> —Selection of readers' online comments regarding *Seattle Times* coverage of my research (Long 2011)

Indeed, most shoppers are not merely estranged from the dumpster and spaces like it. They are *repelled*. This point is crucial to understanding why waste stays wasted. "Disgust," as William Ian Miller puts it, "helps create conditions of scarcity which build up demand and increase value" (1997, 114). To explain this phenomenon, we must think carefully about affect. As the embodied substrate of culturally coded sentiments and feelings, affect represents the realm of contact between the structural, the signified, and the embodied. It is precisely at the intersection of these forces that value is made and unmade.

If waste is a constitutive outside of economic value, then to understand it we must remember that value is no mere formal quantity. Instead, value reflects both quantitative and qualitative aspects of capitalist social relations. It is a "social hieroglyphic," in Marx's terms ([1865] 2000, 475; see also Harvey [1982] 2006, 36). Its qualitative aspect therefore embraces the demand, desire, and "libidinal investment" of its constituents (Gibson-Graham 2006, xxxv). In this way, affect does the work of valorizing and devalorizing things. (Indeed, as Sarah Ahmed [2004] has pointed out, affects themselves circulate in value-laden ways that might be called "economies.") Further, it enforces capitalist social reproduction and marginalizes noncapitalist forms of economic practice, such as dumpster-diving.

After all, the trash's "elsewhere" is, ironically, not usually very far away at all. It hides in plain sight, in the backyard, the alley, the parking lot. But despite its closeness, it often escapes notice. Its conceptual space is quarantined, worlds apart, by that strange, fascinated repulsion that is "abjection." For Julia Kristeva (1982), the abject is intangible but real. It can inhabit any experience, from an act of social deviance, to the touch of a corpse, to the off-putting skin on a glass of oversimmered milk. It is the threatening, the disturbing, the contaminating. Like Agamben's relation of exception, abjection is included in the psyche through its exclusion: "There looms, within abjection, one of those violent, dark revolts of being, directed against a threat that seems to emanate from an *exorbitant outside or inside*, ejected beyond the scope of the possible, the tolerable, the thinkable. It lies there, *quite close, but it cannot be assimilated*. It beseeches, worries, and fascinates desire, which, nevertheless, does not let itself be seduced. Apprehensive, desire turns aside; sickened, it rejects" (Kristeva 1982, 1; my emphasis).

For Kristeva, the abject refers not to a semiotic or phenomenological object. Rather, it is purely affective, a sense of disruption within the self. While this may manifest as an uncanny, gagging aversion to a particular person, place, or thing, its ultimate source resides in a threat to the coherence of self-identity. Like Mary Douglas's ([1966] 1984) "matter out of place" (one of Kristeva's inspirations), what is abject is reckoned largely through (dys)classification: "It is thus not lack of cleanliness or health that causes abjection," she writes, "but what disturbs identity, system, order" (4).

The threat of abjection, therefore, haunts any given "cultural no-man's-land" and guards its boundaries. Whereas Douglas and Agamben both emphasized symbolic threats and structural limits, Kristeva explains why they might be experienced so viscerally. What Agamben describes as "exceptional" at a formal, structural scale therefore often corresponds, at an embodied scale, to "abjection." Where the exception has been spatialized, its structure mapped in the dimensions of affect, of tactility, of the viscera, the possibility also exists for a disruption to that structure—and the experience of that disruption is abjection. Like the exception, therefore, the abject reinforces a social structure, cordoning off potential sources of disruption. "There," writes Kristeva, "abject and abjection are my safeguards. The primers of my culture" (1982, 2).

In other words, if a space of exception, like the dumpster, manifests the laws and exclusions of a given regime—in this case, capital accumulation—abjection polices them at the gut level. What is most important about the dumpster's contents is that—except for once a week when the garbage truck comes to remove it—they remain *in there*, rather than *out here*. (In other words, ". . . and stay out!")

Like the exception, the abject cannot quite be named directly. Importantly, it is a space of contradiction and paradox. Kristeva writes: "If the object, however, through its opposition, settles me within the fragile texture of a desire for meaning, which, as a matter of fact, makes me ceaselessly and infinitely homologous to it, what is *abject*, on the contrary, the jettisoned object, is radically excluded and draws me toward *the place where meaning collapses*" (1982, 1–2; my emphasis).

In like fashion, trash cannot be named directly. It must simply be understood as that which has been thrown away. Or, more precisely, it refers to the "collapse" of meaning that occurs at the point where something has been thrown away. For that reason, ironically, here in the trash, where the sheer tactile reality (color, texture, smell) of a thing has never been more apparent, its continued materiality is overlooked or misapprehended.

These twin dimensions of waste, the exception and the abject, therefore define the dumpster's role in the production of value. Although not all contact with waste threatens to disrupt identity or order (making and handling trash may be embedded in everyday systems of signification in innumerable ways, from peeling a banana to taking out the recycling [Hawkins 2005]), the commodity form embodies a logic of estrangement that culminates in waste, and abjection is fundamental to the integrity of this order.

By exactly the same token, a discarded avocado, saved from the space of dumpster, is still unmistakably an avocado (albeit with a bruise or two). On its merits, it is edible once more. Its former stigma becomes negotiable. As such it represents a rebuke to familiar modes of consumption and commerce. Indeed, the very existence of such valuable garbage poses an existential challenge to the taken-for-granted-ness of market norms. If, therefore, the uncommodity qua uncommodity is a crucial component of capital accumulation, then it simultaneously embodies the possibility of capital's dissolution. (Indulge me, if you will, in a daydream: Shoppers everywhere wake up one morning with a strange amnesia and no memory of the stigma of the dumpster. Rather than shop, they wrench open bins by the thousands, plundering their contents. Supermarket managers look on, helpless. It's an absurd caprice, but then so is capitalism in its way.)

Here, then, is the secret of abjection: *It is revolting, in both senses of the word.* The paradox of abjection's "dark revolt of being" is that while it secures a system, it also undermines it. Kristeva points out that the threat of disruption contained in abjection's fundamental ambiguity is also the fundamental *weakness* of abjection: it is always on the verge of becoming sublimated. Of being renamed, recategorized, and diffused. "Through sublimation," Kristeva writes, "I keep it under control. The abject is edged with the sublime" (1982, 11). In other words, the abject, indeterminate frontiers between meaning and its collapse are also manufactories of new meaning. The abject can be *recouped*, its taboos reimagined or revalued. Like Kafka's open door,[15] what initially seems to be a prohibition is also a threshold to be crossed.

Dumpster-divers sometimes contrast, for instance, their initial gut hesitations at dumpster-diving with expressions of subsequent liberation, accomplishment, and joyful transgression at successfully living on the leftovers. In this vein, Dylan Clark (2004) describes the import of these symbolic transgressions for dumpster-diving punks in Seattle, whose initial revulsion is sublimated, relocated from waste to the economic system responsible for it.[16] "Eating food from dumpsters is, for a generalizable American whole, repulsive," he writes. "Food in a trashcan becomes spiritually and materially *polluted*," he says. "In this sense, *the downward descent into a dumpster is literally an act of downward mobility*" (11; emphasis in the original). Rather than rejecting this sense of pollution, the punks in Clark's work often embrace it, celebrating new, anticapitalist identities in the process (see Edwards and Mercer 2007). As we will see, that very sublimation is the organizing principle of this book's titular mass conspiracy.

If the price-less uncommodity in the commercial dumpster represents a kind of lapsed *almost-capital*—the capital that *very nearly was*—the ambiguity and weakness of abjection, and the infinite possibilities for its sublimation, also frame it as capital that very nearly *could be*, finding new utility in sublimation, revolt, or recovery. It could indeed be reintroduced into the market. But more interesting are the ways in which these goods may undergo parallel kinds of nonmarket economic circulation that obviate in some small way the logic of the market. The ubiquitous possibility of such practices is the precondition for our mass conspiracy. The threat of such alternate forms of circulation is that they demystify the commodity form itself, as the deliberate labor of its disposal is immediately apparent in a way that its production is often not. In this capacity, as incipient disruption to capital, we might think of this waste not only as an uncommodity but also as a counter-commodity. What is most significant about waste is its ambiguous *itinerancy* between these two poles. The

A rough sleeper in Melbourne's Central Business District underlines—literally—the manufactured scarcity of the Victorian housing market while awaiting eviction from the sidewalk later that day by local police. (Melbourne, 2017)

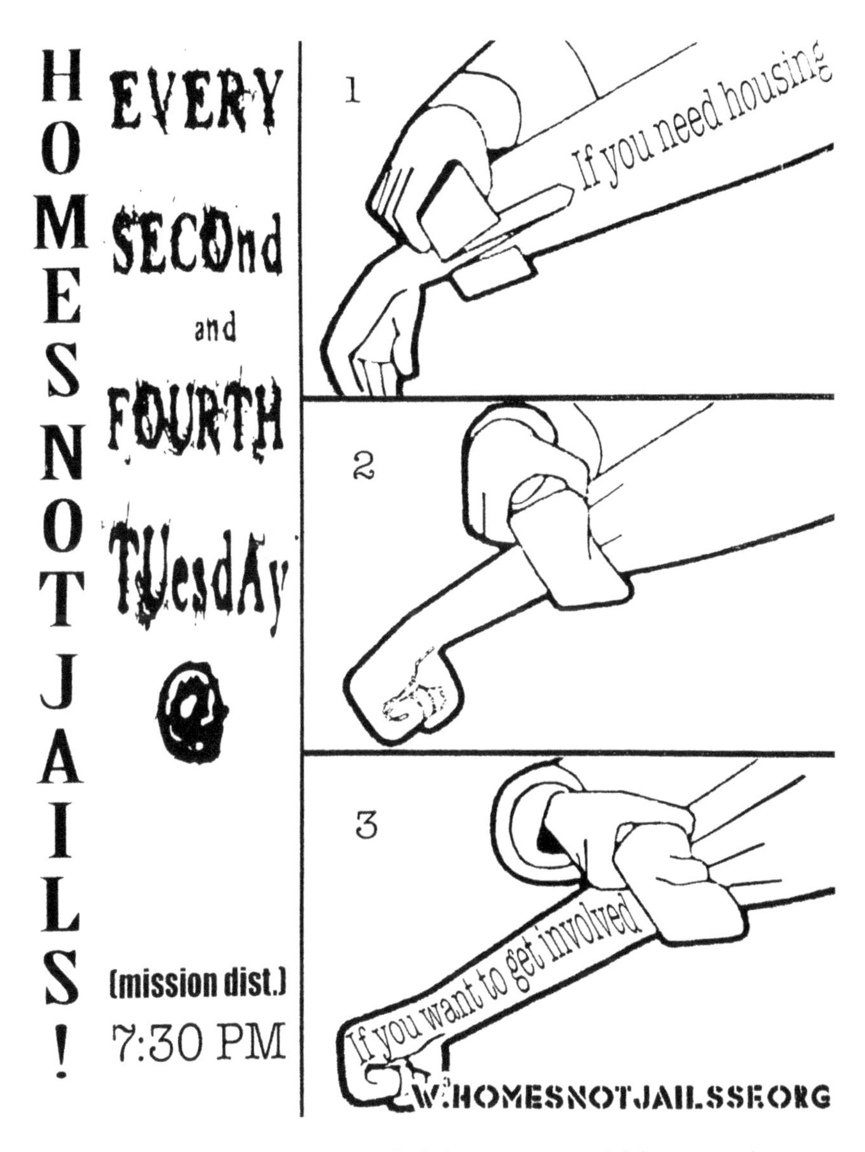

Homes Not Jails handbill. (San Francisco, California, 2017)

boarded-up houses of the 2008 foreclosure crisis, for example, were simultaneously cold harbingers of the crash (note that while housing prices plummeted, rental costs in some places piqued at the sharp spike in demand)[17] and a few discreet squatters away from becoming residences. (Homes Not Jails, an offshoot of Food Not Bombs in San Francisco, in which several friends and collaborators have been involved, takes advantage of just this ambiguity, temporarily squatting abject housing when the property title is being disputed by multiple financial institutions.)

In the nineties in Lower East Side Manhattan was an amazing phenomenon many of us punk kids called "Crack Treat Swap Meet." It was a flea market of sorts that seemed to be quite unofficial but was quite large and would happen every week at the same time. I'd say it was half folks, including myself, who dumpster dove throughout the week and then would sell what they would find, and then literally leave much of what they wouldn't sell to be re-dumpster dove. It was amazing, and of course was one of the many awesome things that was driven out of the area with gentrification.

—Helen, former itinerant dumpster-diver, Seattle and New York City

Taking direct action and engaging in civil disobedience, Homes Not Jails publicly occupies vacant buildings to demonstrate the availability of vacant housing, to promote proposals to utilize the housing, and to put people in the housing. Furthermore, we provide information on squatting and network with other squatting groups. . . . Homes Not Jails opens up vacant buildings and helps homeless people move into them—because people need housing NOW! Over the years hundreds of vacant buildings have been opened, providing housing for people and reducing the overall demand for housing—making housing more affordable for all of us. Many have lasted for years, many are still happening, and more will be opened as long as people are forced to live on the streets.

—Homes Not Jails, "About Us" (ca. 2011)

In its paradoxical capacities as both uncommodity and counter-commodity, then, useful waste constitutes a kind of *abject capital.* As we have seen, although it is ejected from circulation, its absent presence in the market contributes to the constant accumulation of surplus value that Marx called "capital." It emits a kind of abject value in comparison to that of the stock that remains on the shelves. In its ambivalence, the relationship between abject capital and active capital is that of both a functional boundary and the possibility of its negation—not completely unlike the relationship between antimatter and matter.

Remember, here, that value is a social hieroglyphic. A complex cultural calculus. And one that must be constantly realized and reified through social relationships. Right up until the point of sale, a commodity's value is therefore only *virtual.* (Like Schrödinger's cat, its fate hangs ambiguously upon a moment of inscription.) The abject capital quarantined in the dumpster is both the product of this calculus and one of its many variables. In this way, its function is analogous to fixed capital—productive goods and infrastructure, from factories to farm equipment, that are not deployed as commodities to be exchanged but rather expended as a means to create more value. Although abject capital is not itself sold, it is put to work in order to establish the conditions for other goods to realize their value. It thereby marks a possible future for every commodity that defines its social life. As we have seen, however, that possible future is twofold, simultaneously death and undeath. *This is where meaning collapses for capital*, at the temporal, spatial, and semiotic extremities of the market, which are also the necessary complements of its everyday workings. After all, if capital remains capital only when in motion, it's no good to the market gathering dust on the shelf. Such is the mantra of the market: if it cannot be profitably converted into cash, it must be converted promptly into abject capital.

Conclusion: A Certain Usury

This chapter ends at the beginning. Like T. S. Eliot (1942), "the end of all our exploring will be to arrive where we started, and know the place for the first time."[18] Novel kinds of meaning, labor, and value, I have argued, are all submerged in the cultural economy of trash. And like Bakunin and Schumpeter alike,[19] our interest in destruction is also an interest in creation, and the end of a thing's social life from one point of view is the beginning of a new existence from another. Abject capital, in its ambivalence—outside the law but not indifferent to it—is both new and old, alpha and omega.

From the perspective of capital, it is made obsolete in comparison to what remains on the market. As an uncommodity, its exchange value is (for most intents and purposes) null, *and yet it is still not free.* Sometimes they padlock the dumpsters to prove the point.

From the perspective of the dumpster-divers, gleaners, and scavengers I hang out with, however, its ambiguity—abandoned but useful—is exactly the source of its freedom, if you know where to look (or how to break into the dumpster). A counter-commodity, it costs nothing and yet is the foundation of friendly little gift economies everywhere.

The frontier between these two kinds of economy, then, is a space of possibility, where the same labor may both devalue and revalue at the same time. The mass conspiracy that is the subject of this book depends on this very possibility: *what is revolting may also revolt.*

Because the market trends toward overproduction, toward abundance and waste, the work of capitalist production is constantly reproducing this frontier, multiplying both active capital and abject capital. We may see the dumpster as part of the holistic process of capitalist production rather than its end—as a safety valve that allows capital to keep moving, to recoup its value in the market even as its abject personae (non grata) are locked away. If capitalist crises result from capital's inability to move or turn over, then *waste of all kinds is constantly rescuing capitalism from itself.* Waste is a deferred crisis.

Of course, this deferral imposes a certain usury. The more capital accumulates, the more it must be spent. Many have suggested that in market societies, the turnaround time for capital, along with the pace of everyday life, is accelerating (Agger 2004). Money changes hands more quickly. Novelty endures less and less. Trends, investments, and shelf stock turn over at a rate that approaches "instantaneity" (Agger 2004). At the same time, not only the pace but the saturation of market norms increases as new realms of life are increasingly annexed under the sovereignty of capital (see Hardt and Negri 2004; Cooper 2008). As all these kinds of production are multiplied and accelerated, the abject production of waste, too, must be multiplied and accelerated.

If the horizons of capitalism are expanding, and with them the sovereignty and guiding logic of a market regime of value, we increasingly have to ask what abject forms of life and sovereignty are cultivated at its frontiers. The more capital accumulates, the more it must spend, the more it must throw away, and the more there is for those left behind to recover.

SCENE II

RECKONING VALUE AT THE MARKET

The reckoning of value at any given moment is a shifty business: part mathematical calculation, part cultural judgment, and part fortune-telling. Value is a multidimensional equation. But it is useful to remember that equations are also always comparisons. In other words, value is always relative. And a thing's route to the dumpster is reckoned in juxtapositions. It's not necessary to fathom emergent trends in the global market or embark on an analysis of global food prices to see these comparisons at work. It is enough to watch, over employees' shoulders, the moment-to-moment decisions in which products win or lose their place on the shelves.

At Seattle's Pike Place Market, for example, and any number of other farmers' markets and supermarkets across the city, I have often waited patiently as produce workers expertly culled unwanted goods to donate. Dodging and pushing to hold my ground as the standing-room-only Sunday crowds teemed through Pike Place's fruit and veggie stands (pondering just which avocado to bring home, which peach is too ripe), I'd watch produce workers' deft hands blur as they spun between giving away free samples, making sales, and filling boxes with donations from across the vegetable kingdom. They made split-second decisions about what was worth leaving on the shelf a bit longer and what they'd just have to throw away later in the afternoon if they didn't give it to me on the spot.

But the choice is often a vexed, ambiguous one. At one moment, to my dismay, an older employee thinks better of his coworker's quick decision, and grumbles at her "that'll sell." He grabs a box of peaches or apples from my arms just as I'm about to wade back to my car through the crowds. On other occasions, an experienced worker glances across the rows of what seem to me to be perfectly salable fruit, and at the throngs of tourists milling past, and culls all but the most picture-perfect items, either for the sake of creating a more attractive display or simply to make room for newer stock waiting in the back. It's an art that's remarkable to watch—each apple or peach hanging on a fraction of a second's consideration.

The variables at work are not necessarily less complex than they might be at the New York Stock Exchange. While the price of a *type* of thing at Pike Place—say, avocados—may be more stable over a day than the Dow Jones Industrial Average, the real exchange value of any *specific* avocado is constantly shifting depending on how many people will visit the market that day (and how picky they are), whether it's sunny and warm (and therefore how long produce will keep on the shelves), when the next shipment is arriving, what's popular this month, what any given customer wants it for (and how quickly they need to use it), and how it looks on the shelf next to the other produce. In this way, vendors are doing the expert work of evaluation, not unlike real estate appraisers, stock consultants, and other gatekeepers who, as Anna Tsing (2015) suggests, are crucial to turning things into commodities. Except that here they're doing what I call "the work of waste-making" (Giles 2015)—turning once-valuable commodities into waste. Of course, not every vendor is the same. Some donate their produce. Some have a discount table. At the Pike Place Market, many of the workers are punks and dumpster-divers themselves, already familiar with Food Not Bombs, and some of them graciously err on the generous side.

As the day goes on workers inspect their avocados, or apples, or dragon fruit (or, or, or . . .) and make the kind of spontaneous decisions I've described above. The ones that won't sell—or won't sell *quickly* enough—disappear from the shelves to make room for newer stock. "For," as the theorist Wolfgang Haug puts it, "the existence of old stock spells economic death for any capital trapped in commodity form . . . here the commodity has to perform its salto mortale, the death-defying leap, which carries the risk that it might break its neck" (1986, 23).

In each of these day-to-day considerations, we can read the imprint of the entire food system. The real exchange value of an avocado reflects the racism and classism that determine how much—or how little—we value the workers who picked it, packaged it, shipped it, and stocked it. Exchange value, after all, derives from labor.[1] Productive human life. "Whenever, by an exchange, we equate as values our different products," Marx wrote, "by that very act, we also equate, as human labor, the different kinds of labor expended upon them" ([1865] 2000,

475). Similarly, when we dismiss a thing's value, we dismiss the different kinds of labor expended therein. (As a sidenote: ironically, it's rare that actual dirt—soil, rocks—ends up in the dumpster. Sometimes it comes in on lettuce that wasn't washed thoroughly when picked. But for the most part, what is thrown away is the product of human work upon raw materials.) The mechanisms of immigration and labor exploitation that keep the price down and make agricultural laborers invisible also make it thinkable to throw away—unspoiled and uneaten—the foods they cultivate and harvest.

Commodity capital lives and dies in all of these comparisons, small or large, implicit or explicit. All the work invested in an avocado's cultivation, packaging, and transport may or may not pay off in one particular avocado. The producer, the wholesaler, and the retailer all gamble that on balance they'll make a profit on their investment. But capital remains capital only when it is in motion. Live or die, in a competitive market, it cannot sit still for very long.

Live or die, capital cannot sit still for very long. Many of the goods in this Seattle grocery dumpster, for example, are shelf-stable. They are weeks or months from expiry. Yet here they are, just after Christmas, making room for new stock on the shelves. (2017)

2

Market-Publics and Scavenged Counterpublics

The Proverbial Free Lunch

Waste is always productive. As Georges Bataille (1991) pointed out, the "general economy" of nature knows nothing of the social life of things. When we throw a thing away it takes little notice. Forgotten or ignored, it goes on expending energy and matter: mold transfigures bread in the depths of the fridge; rust forges complex new topographies on derelict cars; decay and photosynthesis cultivate overgrown postindustrial ecosystems in the evacuated suburbs of America's "rust belt"; and the sandwiches cleared from the Safeway deli counter, which once might have fed paying customers, will instead feed colonies of microbes and worms. Or, if they're well packed, they might feed opportunistic dumpster-diving scavengers. The destruction of value from one point of view is the production of value from another.

> The living organism, in a situation determined by the play of energy on the surface of the globe, ordinarily receives more energy than is necessary for maintaining life; the excess energy (wealth) can be used for the growth of a system (e.g., an organism); if the system can no longer grow, or if the excess cannot be completely absorbed in its growth, it must necessarily be lost without profit; it must be spent, willingly or not, gloriously or catastrophically.
> —Georges Bataille

> . . . publics don't shit.
> —Gay Hawkins

Likewise, the taboos of one cultural economy are the thresholds across which other economies may trespass. The specter of waste, never entirely forgotten, haunts the calculus of the market through prohibition and abjection. But the material waste is free to be spent in new ways. This book hinges on the relationships between that specter and the obscured afterlives of abandoned people, places, and things. Picking up where the last chapter left off, below I sketch out a theoretical framework with which to think about this book's main characters—its key "conspirators," if you like—the dumpster-divers, gleaners, and scavengers with whom I have worked and their relationship to the predominant politics of the market. Mindful, in their own way, of Bataille's general economy, these marginal figures quietly salvage the unspoiled surpluses of the commercial waste stream. They recirculate them within subcultural networks that are anathema, in myriad ways, to the dominant market calculus by which this excess is discarded. They consume the leftovers. Meanwhile, the realpolitik of urban development privileges that market calculus, forcing both the waste and the alternative economies built on it from public view. Their obscurity is precisely the condition of their conspiracy. (Every conspiracy is hatched in the shadows.)

What is at stake here, and throughout this book, is the meaning of *public*. When city officials prohibit food sharing in the name of public health and safety, for example, whose interest is the "public interest"? Who is left out? Whose bodies are deemed a threat to public order? And when store managers refuse to let the public eat from their dumpsters, where else will their waste circulate? What people and things are treated as "matter out of place" when they cross the threshold of public visibility? To answer these questions, we must understand the relations between markets, values, surpluses, and the publics that circulate or abandon them.

The market and its ambulant garbage relate to each other as a kind of "public" and "counterpublic," categories I borrow from the queer theorist Michael Warner (2002). For Warner, the public sphere represents a matrix through which values and discourses are translated into political imperatives. At the same time, the negative dialectics of the public imagination afford those who are excluded a certain radical freedom to reconstitute meaning and value. In this radical freedom lie the political possibilities that underwrite the slow insurrections of Food Not Bombs and movements like it.

This chapter therefore introduces two theoretical questions that will guide the rest of this book. First, what has waste to do with the constitution of a hegemonic public sphere? Second, how is that waste simultaneously productive of new counterpublic spheres of value, sociality, and sovereignty within the spaces abandoned by capital? In the process, I foreshadow two ethnographic dynamics that will be central to parts II and III of the book, respectively: the regulation of urban public spaces, and the proliferation of Food Not Bombs chapters and their associated spheres of dumpster-divers, squatters, and other scavengers.

In part, the answer to the first question is that commercial waste of all kinds draws the boundaries of a *market-public*. A public sphere whose lingua franca is pecuniary and whose conversations are carried on among consumers, merchants, and producers through the medium of the transaction itself and through a range of secondary literatures. Waste establishes the parameters of that public—the terrain within which supply, demand, and exchange value are reckoned. The anxieties and repulsions inspired by waste designate an abject realm anathema to public decency (which, as I suggested in the previous chapter, keeps things off the market even if they are still useful). It is often the job of city officials to manage these anxieties and defend the norms of such a public.

The answer to the second question follows from that of the first. The abjection that keeps things off the market is also the condition of possibility for the development of counterpublics with an abject relationship to these market-publics. If food, clothing, durable goods, and housing are all routinely abandoned by the market, they are also free to those who know how to obtain them. (How to unlock dumpsters, how to squat and discreetly turn the water back on, and so on.) This freedom to renegotiate a lived economy in nonmarket terms—to live for free—is the basis for distinct social spheres and identities with considerable autonomy from the larger market-publics.

Here, then, I make three related arguments: first, the circulation of—and the refusal to circulate—wasted surpluses defines and is defined by a "market-public," constituted as much by the exceptional spaces wherein its waste is enclaved as by those public spaces where commodities are exchanged and economic value circulated. Second, it is not only through acts of exchange and circulation but also through formal political exclusions that this public is maintained (such as the antihomeless statutes I discuss as the book unfolds), which simultaneously define a corresponding series of exceptional spaces wherein circulate those people and things abandoned by the market. Third, it is this very abandonment that inspires and facilitates the slow insurrection of FNB and its conspiracy of dumpster-divers, squatters, and anticapitalists.

The Difference between Dumpster-Diving and Donation

Not all scavenging is created equal. Different pathways of recovery elicit different responses from those who discard the food. Throughout my fieldwork, one difference stood out in particular: businesses are often happy to donate their surpluses to food banks and meal programs that feed the hungry; but they rarely invite people to help themselves to these surpluses directly from the dumpster. *What, then, is the difference be-*

"Do not play in, on, or around this container for any purpose."

tween dumpster-diving and donation? Why let one group collect the waste by one means but not another group by other means? A range of factors are surely at work, from class-inflected indignation to insurance costs. But I argue here that there is less difference between charity and landfill than meets the eye. In both cases, waste remains banished to exceptional spaces, out of public circulation.

This banishment is not a formal, ironclad kind, but it works. Consider the spectrum of responses with which my collaborators and I have been met while dumpster-diving: from hospitality to hostility. The latter is more common. One young bike punk told me, for example, about fretting when a worker popped out unexpectedly from the back door of a Seattle bakery and caught her in the bin; he disappeared back into the bakery almost immediately—to call the police, she expected—only to emerge a second later with an extra bag of bread for her. She told this story precisely because it was a happy surprise; I've heard *more* tales of angry and forbidding employees (see also Vaughn 2011). One twenty-something friend even described being beaten by police who discovered him beside a dumpster with several housemates from his Buffalo punk house. That degree of enforcement is extreme, however; usually it's the staff who warn dumpster-divers away, often obligated by management to do so. One night, upon finding me and several FNB collaborators behind one of Seattle's Trader Joe's markets, a terse manager even asked us to *put back* everything we found. Quietly incensed, we nonetheless obliged. Like dumpster-divers I've met across the United States and Australasia, we observed an informal "code" of respect for other scavengers: don't take more than you need, and don't risk getting the dumpster locked (see CrimethInc. 2004). When caught, some scavengers politely explain themselves, and one Melbourne anarchist would even ask for a few extra minutes to tidy up after himself before leaving. As one Seattle graffiti writer (ironically) wrote on the side of my old neighborhood Trader Joe's dumpster: "Rule #1: Always leave the dumpster cleaner than you found it."

> We knew all our favorite places we'd go. And some places it was easy—we didn't have to hide or be sneaky. Other places were in neighborhoods where we were always worried about getting the shit beat out of us. There was a QFC on Capitol Hill up on 15th that always had a good dumpster but, boy, they were always really tight about kicking us out if they caught us. So it was always a matter of sneaking in and out of that dumpster. If you were in the dumpster when they came, you just had to sit in there and wait for them to dump the garbage on you and be all quiet and then sneak back out.
>
> —Lisa, Seattle punk rocker, former squatter, and organizer of the unnamed dumpstered street feeds that later evolved into Seattle's first FNB chapter in the early 1990s

Nonetheless, despite these cautions the bins are periodically locked. Indeed, my Seattle favorites—the Bread Dumpster, the Chocolate Dumpster, the Juice Dumpster—all suffered this fate after becoming too popular. The locked dumpster therefore becomes a common trope among dumpster-divers, who often gleefully swap strategies for bypassing it. Some suggest Allen wrenches to remove the hinge. Others call for bolt cutters for the padlock. (Once it's locked, there is, after all, no longer much point in being discreet.) I have even heard uncannily similar anecdotes (or maybe urban legends) from people in cities in the United States, Australia, New Zealand, and Europe, who all claim to know someone in possession of a skeleton key that opens all the city's dumpsters. Like a punk rock "key to the city."

The lock constitutes both a symbolic and material enclosure, segregating resources from people who might reclaim them. "They want it all hermetically sealed—the whole production process, from production to final disposal," one twenty-something Melbourne anarchist and political science student explained, speculating on why he, too, had been chased away from a few dumpsters. Although he puts it a little conspiratorially, he poetically describes the hegemony of a certain post-Taylorist economic rationalism and, more importantly, a corresponding distrust of whatever, or whomever, is not legible in economic terms.

And yet. In contrast, many of the very same businesses who have turned us away from their dumpsters, or locked up their trash, also regularly donate their excess. (Though clearly not all of it.) "We can go around to local markets, like PCC, and they are more than willing to contribute to the cause," explained Kris, who volunteered with Seattle FNB in the mid-1990s, "because they recognize that this food that they have to throw out isn't bad. It's fine. And they know that we're going to get it, cook it that day, and they recognize the irony in the fact that they have to throw it out just 'cause there are new shipments coming in." Of the retailers I have described above, for example, Trader Joe's has often donated surplus produce. Similarly, two-day-old artisanal loaves from the Bread Dumpster's upscale bakery were a routine sight at Seattle food banks. And multiple employees responsible for policing the Chocolate Dumpster have likewise reassured me (in language so similar that it might have been rehearsed) that their spare chocolate was donated. Unwanted produce from Pike Place is picked up seven days a week, often multiple times a day. And so on. Indeed, at times retailers even *relied* on donations to remove their excess. Another Seattle FNB organizer and punk rocker from the 1990s who goes by "Ingrate" explained for example that "Greenlake PCC said 'Listen, we need you guys to be picking up stuff on Saturday *and* Sunday, if you're going to do this.' Because . . . it started taking up too much space, and so they said, 'We really need this stuff gone on Saturday,' so we said, 'Great, we'll come by.'" Kris drew a direct analogy between these donations and the dumpster. "There's nothing they can do with them once the new product comes in," he said, "except give it away . . . or throw it away. Which is usually what happens. Ninety-nine-point-nine percent of the time."

"Herein lies the particular genius of emergency food," writes Janet Poppendieck: "much of the food distributed by the emergency food system is food that would otherwise go to waste . . . and many corporate donations to the emergency food system would otherwise end up in the landfill" (1998a, 42). Indeed, the very concept of a "food bank" was inspired in 1967 by food waste at local grocery stores; it was founded on the willingness of those grocers to let their products be recirculated under the auspices of social service agencies rather than throwing them away (St. Mary's Food Bank Alliance, n.d.). Five decades later, extensive networks of such food-recovery organizations continue to grow, from grassroots efforts like FNB to formal, nationally affiliated nonprofit organizations like Food Lifeline in the United States and OzHarvest in Australia, connecting these commercial food surpluses with food-insecure people. Growing public concern over commercial food waste has amplified this trend, leading to legislation in places like France and California that obliges grocers to donate their waste. These networks typically leave intact the linear structure of the commodity chain, linking charities (in lieu of consumers or the dumpster) to retailers or wholesalers rather than producers. During the 2020 coronavirus pandemic, for example, when those intermediaries were interrupted by the consequent recession, farmers were forced to destroy produce, milk, and other raw goods despite soaring demand at food banks across the United States.

Commercial grocery surpluses typically constitute such an important part of the emergency food system in the United States, and increasingly other industrialized nations, that we might imagine it as a sort of aftermarket shadow economy made up of people, places, and things passed by in the course of commerce-as-usual (along with federal commodity surpluses that, in their own way, prop up capital accumulation).[1] And a bountiful shadow economy at that: although food banks and meal programs certainly occasionally experience shortfalls, they nonetheless constitute a robust layer of many urban food systems. One Seattle street youth said bluntly, "You can't starve here."

Although many large nonprofit organizations benefit from incorporated status and a steady stream of grants—referred to by some as a "homeless services industry" (Willse 2015)—many grassroots groups also recirculate food surpluses less formally, through direct relationships with employees and businesses. In approaching vendors at Pike Place, for instance, and perhaps a dozen other donors over the course of my work with FNB, I often found that invoking the phrase "soup kitchen" unlocked the goodwill of store managers (even if it doesn't capture all the nuances of a mutual aid project like FNB). Some remained mistrustful, but many were glad not to throw away good food. They were willing to set it aside for us, no questions asked, as long as the effort didn't cost them too much in terms of time or space. (Sometimes the more sympathetic employees would scan the shelves with a particularly generous eye as I waited to do the weekly pickup, winking as they handed me exotic or expensive donations that I couldn't tell apart from the goods left on the shelf.) Similarly, even with no formal status or tax ID number, most of the FNB chapters I met were able to rely primarily on donation (which is less time-consuming than scavenging). And this despite the fact that many of the Food Not Bombs volunteers are the same sort of dumpster-diving riffraff (a compliment, mind you) likely to be chased away from the dumpsters at a different hour of the day.

Wherefore the difference? By any other mode of recovery, the food still tastes as sweet, and it is still eaten. If waste, or abject capital, cannot be simply given away without upsetting the market, why, then, should donating food surpluses to a soup kitchen not be comparably disruptive? From the on-the-ground paradox of these two distinct afterlives we can infer an unspoken parallel between the dumpster and the soup kitchen or food bank. Each, in its own way, must be some sort of exception with respect to the logic of the market. In other words, they are places with which the market's agents are nominally and structurally unconcerned, except insofar as they are explicitly abandoned. This abandonment defines a series of exceptional spaces through which abject capital can move without ceasing to be abject—spaces where it neither forfeits its use value nor is reincorporated into social relations of supply and demand.

Of course, like market value itself, this relation of exception exists not simply between places and things. It defines a power-laden, biopolitical relationship between people and the means of sustaining life. This exception outlines both the "inside" and the "outside" of a collectivity of people who are imagined to constitute the market through buying, selling, and producing, and those people who are imagined not to. Another way of putting this might be to say that patrons of the soup kitchen are assumed not to have been potential customers anyway. In this way, they are excluded from a critical dimension of public life.

I mean, at first, back in the day with Food Not Bombs, I remember when we first hooked up the gig [donations] with the Vic Markets, you know, they just thought, "Oh, here we go: bunch of drunk punks getting food. Whatever. Rah rah rah." And we'd just get boxes of slop. And we'd have to search through the slop, to get to the good food, you know? And once it sort of—within a month, they realized what was happening, and we gave them report backs on little stories that we got off a lot of homeless people—whose favorite fruit was a peach, and they haven't eaten one for fifteen years, and, they only wanted *one* 'cause they wanted to make sure that everyone else around them had one too, you know?—and the little stories like that that we'd take to the vendors and stuff that, it just touched their hearts and it made them realize, "Well these kids are really really serious," you know? And, slowly they started being educated that—I mean from a monetary perspective to them too, it was actually better off to give us that food three days earlier, instead of trying to sell it off cheap, knowing that it was going to a good place, and it was actually being used instead of—and it would cost them to throw away food, as well—and so they sort of cut costs in that way too and started to give us food, really good quality.

—Kay, founding member,
Melbourne FNB

The Market-Public

"The public" is a consequential fiction. It is both everywhere and nowhere. Throughout this book, we find it functioning as a discursive resource, a tool with which to claim various entitlements (as when activists and shelterless people occupy public spaces) or to translate cultural and economic values into political projects (as when "the homeless" are identified as an implicit threat to public health or safety, or when for-profit developments are imagined to benefit the public). Yet the public is no mere collective figment. Publicness, I argue below, is produced not only discursively through the circulation of texts and discourse, but also materially and spatially through the movement and association of people, places, and things. It determines where surplus food may and may not circulate, where people may and may not eat, how they may and may not share with one another (as we will see later in this book), and other material practices of distribution. Therefore, an intimate relationship always exists between publicness and economy, broadly understood.

In this section, I build on the work of Michael Warner to describe one particular kind of public, defined by its participation in the creation and circulation of market value. It is constituted through material and spatial practices that circulate (or refuse circulation to) people and things, and through the discursive circulation of economic and social values realized in the process. This market-public amounts to a key player in this book, one embroiled in creating both world-class cities and world-class waste, as I describe in the next chapter. In this way, it is both benefactor and adversary to the book's mass conspiracy.

"The public" is also a misnomer, however. A singular being marked by a commanding article, *the*, its boundaries are both too nebulous and too exclusive to be meaningful. The more benign, neutral, and universal the term aspires to be in principle, the more terrifying its exclusions in practice. Whose lives matter enough to be protected in the name of *the* public? Whose bodies are marked—whether by race, religion, nation, class, or otherwise—for surveillance, restraint, or death in the name of that same leviathan? In lieu of *the* public, then, Warner suggests that we speak in terms of *publics*, plural (only some of which persuasively perform the confidence trick of hegemonic self-evidence connoted by the definite article). Like a nation or polity, a public is an "imagined community" (Anderson 1983) in which membership confers entitlements and value. Unlike nations, polities, classes, mobs, movements, subcultures, or most other imagined communities, however, which are defined by ideas, identities, or attributes, Warner's publics are defined by their circulation of discourse and texts. Thus, a public is both audience and actor—that imaginary that creates the conditions for texts, ideas, and affects to circulate among strangers. It is defined and limited by the extent to which it shares vocabularies, media, and spaces of discursive circulation. So we might speak of a feminist public, a Spanish-speaking public, or a punk public, for example, who consume, produce, and/or recirculate feminist discourse, Spanish-language media, or punk rock, respectively.

Warner owes a debt to Jürgen Habermas (1991), who identified a public sphere of free, rational discourse as a distinctive, integral element in the development of contemporary liberal democracies, wherein "the public" assumes a vital, oppositional role in constituting the nation-state. It was for this reason that classical liberals such as Rousseau and Thomas Jefferson touted "Public Opinion" as the ultimate source of both wisdom and authority for government (see Johansen 1982). Feminist critics like Nancy Fraser (1990), however, raised an astute hackle at Habermas's description of "the public sphere" in the singular, heedless of the ways in which it submerges or marginalizes diverse voices and rationalities. As a corrective, she identified competing "subaltern counterpublics" who vie for recognition and legitimation by state institutions. Whereas Fraser's influential formula is most concerned with the adjunct relationship of these counterpublics to government, however, Warner dwells on the ways in which publics and counterpublics become meaningful in their own right. With or without the state, he says, they are capable of their own "poetic world making" (Warner 2002, 114). It is exactly this sort of world-making that has rung throughout recent decades of neoliberal reform, for example, as citizens have been rebranded "consumers," welfare programs reimagined as "investments" (with an expected return) and entitlements as "services," and "the economy" everywhere conflated with "the people." In this way, the neoliberal project has successfully annexed vast folds of the social fabric under the discursive frame of the market. These transformations in public discourse resonate throughout this book and bare their teeth through such articulations as the municipal fixation on "civility," "order," and "quality of life" described in the next section.

But new buzzwords are the tip of the iceberg. Although Warner's public is primarily implicated in the circulation of texts and ideas, his framework may also help us describe the ways in which the "social hieroglyphic" (literally "sacred text" in Greek) of economic value, as Marx put it, is reckoned and circulated on the market. If, as we saw in the previous chapter, value is a qualitative reflection—a looking glass—of social relationships of production, distribution, and consumption, it must be made manifest through socially legible, widely recognizable transactions. Therefore, although value itself is not purely discursive, as David Graeber puts it, it "can only be made into a reality ('realized') in a relatively public context, as part of some larger social whole" (2001, 70). In short, *value must be realized in public.*

Markets therefore necessarily entail a distinctive kind of public. Without it, they cannot create or circulate market value. (Warner himself lists markets among his taxonomy of publics, though he does not elaborate further.) Although markets are mainly imagined to move concrete goods and services about, they are only markets qua markets insofar as they circulate economic values, mainly in the form of capital and currency. In the same way that liberal states have presumed the existence of a public to circulate ideas and opinions, and to which government may address itself, liberal economies have presumed the existence of a market to circulate economic value, and to which products, prices, and transactions are advertised. These markets are often radically disembodied in economic and political rhetoric, but they rest on the assumption that an embodied collectivity of economically literate, interested parties constitute them. (Adam Smith's magisterial Invisible Hand, in this way, is analogous to Jefferson's Public Opinion.) The collectivity whose public discourse consists of exchange values, transactions, and a variety of secondary literature—from price tags to stock analyses—is therefore a species of public.

In principle, of course, this kind of public is a component implied by the term *market* itself, which we might understand to refer to the practices, contents, outcomes, and agents of exchange. Its agents and their discourse, however, are often lost within impersonal, economistic abstractions—like a too-small child on the mathematical seesaw of supply and demand—or else reduced to essentialist caricatures like "homo economicus." Indeed, as economic anthropologists have argued, the disembodied, ahistorical model that is the foundation for so much of our thinking about markets today represents in some ways a willful erasure of the social contexts and relationships that make a market tick (e.g., Gregory [1982] 2016). The market, so abstracted, is also depoliticized. Its entanglements in the gyre of public discourse and policy so overlooked, its logic is rendered as mere "common sense" (Gibson-Graham 1996; Harvey 2007). Ethnographers of modern market societies, therefore, draw crucial attention to the social formations to which market exchange is addressed and by which it is constituted and legitimated. It helps to think here in terms of "market-publics."

In contrast to the rhetorically disembodied market, Warner's (2002, 87) model emphasizes the relationality of a public—a constellation of autonomous strangers, personally interpellated, hailed into being, through their "mere attention" to a discourse that addresses them as such. In this way they generate their own social worlds and subjectivities. Through their interpellation, this constellation also produces its own spatiality and temporality: a headline-reading public acts in different spaces and rhythms from an academic public, for example. Whereas Warner, however, emphasized the discursive "scenes of disclosure" (63) that a public produces—the shared semiotic space of texts, publications, and publicity—we cannot forget that, like all social practices, discourse is always *embodied*. Therefore, a public's space of circulation, that locus of attention that reproduces a public's "relationship among strangers" (76), must also entail, as Kurt Iveson points out, a "material structure," a constellation of corporeal spaces "which influence the political possibilities and opportunities it affords" (2007, 13). Those sites might comprise the armchairs and morning trains where we read our newspapers, the basements and clubs where we hear our favorite punk bands, or the public parks where we give away dinner, among others. In other words, publics depend on public spaces, discursive and material, semiotic and spatial, that make us intelligible or visible to one another as such. Further, such a shared topos is necessarily reproduced and contested through ongoing struggles for legibility and inclusion (14), in which recognition by public institutions often plays a crucial role, as we will see below.

As a framework, these principles are good for the economic ethnographer to think with. Taken together, they highlight concrete, historically specific forms of agency, spatiality, and sociality through which different markets may realize both economic value and a shared cultural imaginary, from local farmers' markets to international commodity futures.[2] By way of a limited example, think back to the Pike Place Market. Its sixty thousand daily visitors, its vendors, its suppliers, and so on are collectively strangers to one another, yet they are all interpellated within a common market. Inextricable from Pike Place as tourist destination, historical site, or urban metonym, the Market as an economic organ entails a range of shared forms of public address, from postcards to sticker prices, that bespeak the value of the stock on the shelves and produce distinct rhythms and circuits of movement. Crucially for FNB, those rhythms and circuits are corporeal and finite. They don't extend to the hungry people in Occidental Park with whom we share the leftovers—which renders the food free to us. And, of course, different markets entail different publics, with distinct temporalities and spatialities. The notion is therefore scalable, drawing our attention to the public dimensions of local and global markets alike. In contrast to Pike Place, for example, the market-public constituted by the range of competing twenty-four-hour supermarket chains has a far broader material, spatial, and temporal structure. And in my experience, they are correspondingly less likely to donate their surpluses. (As a matter of corporate policy, for example, for a long time the University District's largest corporate grocery franchise donated only its day-old bread to the University District Food Bank and disposed of the rest of its edible waste in their locked dumpster.)

Finally, what also makes the "public" in a market-public useful to highlight is its entanglement with other dominant social imaginaries and institutions. Too vague or heterogeneous to serve the purposes of punditry, the body politic called "the public" has a string of body doubles. As Warner puts it, certain dominant publics are able "to stand in for *the* public, to frame their address as the universal discussion of people" (2002, 117). Or, put another way, they "can take their discourse pragmatics and their lifeworlds for granted, misrecognizing the indefinite scope of their expansive address as universality or normalcy" (122). Thus, for example, the American public is often spoken of implicitly (and increasingly explicitly) as a white public, a Western public, an English-speaking public, a Christian public, and a market-public. It is in this way that the norms of capitalist social organization come to speak through the "general public." *Consumer* stands in for *citizen, the economy* for *the people*, and so on. The hyphen in *market-public* therefore captures this weld between the self-evidence of capitalist norms and the hegemonic credentials of *the* public.

In this way, the fiction of the public emerges from stratum upon stratum of exclusion via other dominant publics along the lines of race, class, gender, sexuality, ability, ethnicity, religion, and so on. Further, these exclusions contribute to the mutual articulation between market and public because, as Audre Lorde puts it, "institutionalized rejection of difference is an absolute necessity in a profit economy which needs outsiders as surplus people" (2007, 115). These exclusions are never total, however, as Eva Cherniavsky (2006) points out, but rather reflect "differential incorporations" within that biopolitical regime that relies on difference to produce value. (Consider the ways in which cities celebrate "multiculturalism" while simultaneously enacting policies that segregate and marginalize ethnic minorities.) Indeed, feminist scholars and theorists of racial formation have long argued that the construction of spatial, racial, and gendered differences—and the differential values thereby ascribed to different lives and labors—is fundamental to capitalist accumulation (e.g.,

Luxemburg [1913] 1951; Gibson-Graham 1996; Lipsitz 1998). Cedric Robinson (1983), for example, famously described the differential incorporations of racialized bodies into capitalist modes of production as "racial capitalism." This observation applies isomorphically to the public sphere of consumption—because, as Hannah Appel (2018) puts it, "race makes markets."

Our market-public, therefore, which ostensibly consists of the collectivity of people implicated in economic circulation, is itself conditioned by nonmarket distinctions and exclusions. In simpler terms, "the public," so called, is largely identified with those of its members who are willing and able to participate in the market economy, while many otherwise willing customers simultaneously find themselves overlooked or rebuked by the public sphere of the market as a result of racism, classism, sexism, and other prejudiced imaginaries that are not strictly economic. In both ways, people find themselves abandoned by the concerns of public policy and public discourse.

"For a Few People to Disrupt an Entire Society": Homelessness, Civility, and the Public

The market-public I have described therefore emerges not only from the circulation of economic value, strictly speaking, but also from the spectrum of public pronouncements, spaces of visibility or legibility, and moments of exclusion that underwrite that value. Some of these exclusions are indirect and partial, as when the shadow economy of emergency food described above is reckoned a world apart from the grocery-shopping public. Others are violently explicit and given the force of law, as when those who can't afford to purchase even food or shelter are framed as an alien threat to the public and ejected from its ambit.

Recent years, for example, have seen escalating numbers of government evictions (often referred to informally as "sweeps") of homeless encampments from public land in West Coast cities from Los Angeles to Seattle—driven partly by a semiconcerted backlash from media commentators, conservative political elites, and Not-In-My-Backyard (NIMBY) groups with names like "Safe Seattle" and "Seattle Looks Like Shit." Such commentators describe homelessness in the most abject, dehumanizing terms, as an existential threat to public life. (Often they back this up with distorted, cherry-picked crime statistics and offhand dismissals of the structural factors that contribute to homelessness.)[3] Consider one lu-

Before and after a "sweep" of one of Seattle's downtown parks, December 2017.

rid 2019 documentary, for example, entitled "Seattle is Dying" that was rebroadcast nationally. In it journalist Eric Johnson blames Seattle's titular demise on the "filth and degradation" of people he claims choose homelessness and addiction (Johnson 2019). The film frames their intrusion into the public eye as an unjust disruption of a public life premised on the private accumulation of property—whose most paradigmatic subjects are the homeowner and the local business (sometimes imagined as the "real" victims in all this, in an ironic twist on Lefebvre's [1968] "right to the city"). In such ways, shelterless subjects are made exceptional, ejected symbolically, procedurally, and materially from public view on the basis of their failure to consume in the usual way. And ejected to where? With surprising frequency, pundits sidestep any meaningful answer to the question (along with the perennial problem of inadequate, underfunded shelters and services). Like other abjected surpluses, they are left to circulate, simply, *elsewhere*.

Here, the fiction of *the* public becomes a translation matrix through which the interests and exclusions of other publics are afforded the weight of law. The market-public thereby assumes a discursive and legal instrumentality. In turn, this instrumentality lends it a palpable materiality as it restricts the circulation of people, things, and modes of living to indistinct, exilic spaces. Just so, friends and research collaborators in Seattle have been fined or arrested, had their tents and belongings confiscated, and been given what the city calls "exclusion orders" banishing them from parks and other public spaces (exclusions that disproportionately target poor people and people of color; see Beckett and Herbert 2010). Although, encouragingly, a Ninth Circuit Court ruled in 2018 that the criminalization of basic survival practices constitutes "cruel and unusual punishment" anywhere adequate emergency shelter is unavailable (US Court of Appeals 2018), local advocates tell me that, for now, that ruling has made no practical difference to Seattle's policies or enforcement. Advocates and city employees have told me that as long as a single shelter bed is empty, the sweeps can continue. It will remain for the courts to show that Seattle's six thousand or so shelter beds are not equal to its twelve thousand or more shelterless residents (All Home 2018). Each of the cities where I have worked has invoked similar rhetorics of public health and order to similar ends. As such, the "poetic world-making" of a market-public remakes urban space, forging distinct spheres of discursive and material circulation, with the effect of both cultivating and segregating distinct modes of living—and surviving—in the city.

Such violent language and policy inherit a legacy dating back to what geographer Neil Smith (1996) called the "revanchist" period of the 1990s (from the French *revanche*, "revenge"), during which "white flight" to the suburbs was reversed, giving way to an impulse to "take back" the city center from the working classes and minorities who occupied it. The homeless became instant scapegoats for white and middle-class anxieties; they were punished precisely for failing to uphold or enable dominant modes of consumption. During that period, municipal politicians in Seattle, San Francisco, and New York took pioneering steps to identify their public interest with the fortunes of their markets by passing a string of "civility ordinances" (in Seattle) or "quality of life" laws (in New York) (see Mitchell 1997; Vitale 2009). (San Francisco's campaign was more cryptically called the "Matrix" program, but its discourse was comparable.) Among other things, this revanchism spurred on what homeless advocates call the "criminalization of homelessness," policies that spread across US cities and beyond during the ensuing years, banning survival practices synonymous with homelessness (see National Law Center on Homelessness and Poverty and National Coalition for the Homeless 2009).The laws are often explicitly designed to defend a threatened downtown business climate. They do not address particular market practices, but rather prohibit things such as public urination; sleeping, sitting, or lying on sidewalks during business hours; and "aggressive" panhandling—perceived social obstacles to downtown commerce.

This logic is not completely unfounded. Unapologetically mercenary, perhaps, but not without a rationale: since the 1980s, postindustrial cities like Seattle have increasingly relied on tax revenue from local commercial investment and real estate, and have taken a series of pro-business measures to attract it, or at least to keep it from fleeing to more profitable locales. Haunted by the specter of the rust belt's twin abandonment by industry and retail, these cities have been increasingly obliged to accommodate the interests of businesses and of high-income consumers (see Gibson 2004).

Particularly in the early days of revanchism, city politicians were compelled to articulate new rhetorical frameworks and political subjects in order to justify these goals. Some were euphemistic about their motivations. Others were refreshingly blunt. Defending Seattle's civility ordinances, for example, former city council member Cheryl Chow in 1999 declared, "I feel it's not right for a few people to disrupt an entire society" (quoted in Bush 1999). By implication, those homeless people targeted by the ordinances were apart from and at odds with "society."

Similarly, in a 1993 polemic, Seattle city attorney Mark Sidran implored *Seattle Times* readers to embrace his early civility ordinances. He threatened them with the fate of the rust belt: "We Seattleites have this anxiety, this nagging suspicion that ... maybe we are pretty much like those other big American cities ... 'formerly great places to live'" (Sidran 1993). The city's retail core was indeed in decline. But rather than blame diminished consumer spending power, postindustrial transformation, or a shrinking welfare state, he decried a climate of "incivility" constituted by the multiplication of "usually tolerable 'minor' misbehaviors"—like lying down on the sidewalk or panhandling "aggressively" (Sidran 1993). In the decades since, a parade of public figures have taken up Sidran's mantle, drawing on the same rhetorical frames and calling for new measures to disappear various avatars of homelessness from Seattle's streets and parks.

Sidran's rhetoric was borrowed almost verbatim from the influential, if highly contested, "broken windows" theory of policing, which called for aggressive prosecution not of violent crimes but rather of minor moments of disorder (Wilson and Kelling 1982). Such misdemeanors—so the theory goes—chased off law-abiding citizens and in their absence encouraged worse crimes to go unchallenged. (The theory doesn't cite Mary Douglas's "matter out of place" but it easily might have; the symbolic danger invested in disorder is analogous.) Although the broken windows theory lacked supporting empirical evidence[4] (even the authors admitted that crime rates and public order weren't *directly* correlated; Wilson and Kelling 1982, 29), it conveniently justified a "project of reassurance" and consolidated class power for anxious middle classes and businesses (Gibson 2004). In rapid succession, cities like Seattle, New York City, and San Francisco assimilated broken windows theory into programs for "civility" or "quality of life" (Vitale 2009).

Almost needless to say, poor people and people of color have disproportionately borne the effects of these policies, which instrumentalize prejudice against a range of suspect bodies, from the implicitly racialized "superpredator" to the explicitly gendered, proletarian "working girl."[5] Chief among these imagined specters is "the homeless body," a brutish, corporeal figment that occupies the negative discursive space of citizenship and agency (Kawash 1998). The homeless—people who can't purchase shelter in the usual way—are thereby imagined as bare life, asocial bodies that are dangerous or incapacitated, rather than political subjects who are vulnerable and vested with political and economic agency (see also Hopper 1988). (Such tropes date all the way back to the sixteenth-century Tudor Vagrancy Acts, motivated by the myth of the seditious vagrant—one of the earliest "broken windows" to attend the development of agrarian capitalism and its corresponding state institutions; see Woodbridge 2001.) This obscures the ways in which people who inhabit these suspect bodies do indeed participate actively in political and economic systems, with the effect that those who would otherwise have a claim on the protection of the welfare state are instead increasingly managed by the criminal justice system.

Closely following the theory, Sidran argued that moments of disorder caused by the homeless "cumulatively become intolerable" to the public (whom he avoided defining). Not only intolerable, they are never far from the specter of violence. Sometimes a mere comma away, in fact: Sidran (1993) predicted a hypothetical future Seattle "where the simplest rules of civility are ignored without consequence, where random senseless acts of violence become pervasive." What both lurid sentence fragments have in common, as theorist Samira Kawash might put it, is that they "correspond to a rigorously normative definition of the public that views the propertylessness and displacement experienced by the homeless as a threat to the property and place possessed and controlled in the name of the public" (1998, 320). If Sidran identifies Seattle's public life as one threatened by "incivility," he is therefore also defining a "civil" society of bourgeois consumers whose comfort, personal space, and consequent ease of access to the market are public entitlements. Sidran (1993) insists that these constituents shouldn't have to put up with it "when incivility begins to threaten their sense of security." (As an ironic sidenote, the word *bourgeois* in Habermas's "bourgeois public sphere"—"burgerlich"—can also be translated as "civil" [Habermas 1991; see the translator's note].)

These civility ordinances, and the larger pattern of criminalization they betoken for shelterless people, simultaneously instantiate and segregate two social imaginaries: a market-public and a social world antagonistic to the market. The latter poses an existential threat precisely analogous to that of abjection, in Julia Kristeva's terms: "It lies there, quite close, but it cannot be assimilated" (1982, 1). Kristeva might as well have been writing of Sidran's incivility: "Many people," he wrote, "see those sitting or lying on the sidewalk and—either because they expect to be solicited or otherwise feel apprehensive—avoid the area" (Sidran 1993).

This rhetoric frames not only acts but also modes of living—from "sp'anging" (punk vernacular for panhandling or "spare changing") to pissing in the alley—as anathema to public decency. Ironically, what marks most of these modes of living as exceptional is their very publicness. They are predominantly private behaviors that a sheltered public would normally do at home (Waldron 1991). They represent the logic of privatization, extended to the public sphere. Transported into public spaces, such modes of living become abject and exceptional with respect to the conventions of this market-public.

Yet they must happen somewhere. Without them, some people cannot live. Where, then? If publics are constituted by mere attention and manifested in the space of that shared attention, then abject bodies and practices are not banned so much as banished to spaces where they do not command such attention. In Seattle, for instance, there exists a single permitted outdoor meal site for emergency meal providers. It is located under the freeway, a stiff uphill walk from downtown, and well out of sight of downtown tourists and businesses. This hidden locale, along with the variety of permitted *indoor* meal programs, represents a space of exception, carefully segregated from the commerce and concern of Seattle's market-public (a point to which we will return in chapter 4). And as we saw earlier in this chapter, these cleavages emerge not by design, at the stroke of a single pen, but through the accumulation of partial exclusions, material and symbolic, formal and informal, de facto and de jure.

The market-public is therefore a holistic phenomenon that entangles political, economic, and cultural vectors of circulation. Recall, for example, that Seattle's shadow economy of emergency food segregates not only people but things. Just as the dumpster keeps useful food surpluses out of public circulation, so does the soup kitchen or the food bank. These institutions represent an alternative to the dumpster—both for the ex-commodity and for the people who might otherwise have to eat out of it. The exclusion from the market that extends on a human axis to abject poverty extends on a different axis to abject, wasted capital. Such spaces of exception therefore segregate not only people but economies. They sequester goods, use values, and categories of people anathema to the market-public. And the modes of living they render exceptional are nonmarket subsistence practices.

In policing its boundaries, however, the market-public also outlines spaces of survival beyond the realm of commodity exchange. These spaces of exception represent some of those "exilic spaces" described by Grubačić and O'Hearn, located at the margins of capitalism, "where groups of people gather in escape or forced exile from state control and the processes of capitalist accumulation" (2016, 4). However incompletely, they create geographic or structural locations for mutual aid and other nonmarket forms of economy. It is precisely these exilic spaces to which I turn next, along with the dumpster-diving counterpublics who exploit them.

Scavenged Counterpublics

Revolutionaries are often forged in exile. What form of revolution, then, is fomented in the exilic spaces of the city? If the market's public is formed by the "mere attention" of participants, as Warner suggests, what happens when they aren't looking? (Or are failing to see, which amounts to the same thing.) The mass conspiracy that is the subject of this book avails itself of such lacuna. Like any conspiracy, it is inscrutable from without; it becomes possible in the obscure space where attention is not. It prospects for abandoned or overlooked space in the same way that it scavenges for discarded and undervalued goods, it is necessarily *counter*public, as Warner would have it. Whereas a market-public accomplishes a kind of "poetic world-making," lending an aura of common sense and self-evidence to capitalism, the shared whispers of this conspiracy poetically make other worlds of capitalist detritus.

Before anyone in Seattle had heard the phrase "Food Not Bombs," for example, its ingredients were already at hand. In the early 1990s, the small coterie of radicals who would eventually call themselves FNB were already squatting, dumpster-diving, and putting on occasional public street-feeds to redistribute the riches they were finding in the bins, sharing them sometimes among the homeless and sometimes among other radicals (although one can't always draw an easy distinction between the two, as I describe in part III). A spectrum of working-class and formerly middle-class artists, musicians, punks, and anarchists, mainly but not exclusively white, motivated by outsider sensibilities, anticapitalist outrage, cross-class solidarity, and broke self-preservation alike, found common cause in scavenging and sharing. Across the city, they had this practice in common with other groups out of which would grow projects parallel to FNB, such as the collective of volunteers who would go on to call themselves "Friday Feast" and associate with the Seattle youth shelter ROOTS, for example.

This Seattle scene was echoed by similar social worlds in cities around the globe. Already linked through spheres of radical politics and music, they have only become more so through Food Not Bombs' proliferation. By 1993, for example, the Seattle community described above had learned of Food Not Bombs from fellow dumpster-divers, squatters, and punks in the San Francisco chapter (including several people interviewed for this book). It was no great leap for their Seattle counterparts, inspired by epic tales of San Francisco FNB's countless arrests for sharing food in Golden Gate Park (see chapter 5), to adopt the slogan and begin sharing food weekly in Pioneer Square, bringing them into conflict with the same market-centric laws and spatial segregation. (A quarter-century later, the Seattle chapter still serves a block from the original spot and still faces periodic pressures to move.) Similarly, within two years of the Seattle chapter's beginning, dumpster-divers and squatters in Melbourne's punk scene learned about the project from a recording entitled "Bombs, Not Food," by the San Francisco punk band MDC,[6] and organized their own chapter. Dozens of other groups around the United States and beyond followed suit during the early 1990s, culminating in the first of an ongoing series of international Food Not Bombs gatherings in San Francisco in 1995.

> Everyone was squatters and lived communally in warehouses and would rely upon each other to bring in food. Pretty sure the crew at Brown Warehouse already had established constant gigs, a café, once a week that would come. They'd sort of done it DIY style. Like maybe not a soup kitchen out on the streets, but definitely to feed themselves and friends within the scene—that can be quite self-destructive—so it was a way of joining together to kind of look out for each other and make sure at least once a week everyone was fed really well.
>
> —Kay, on the community of squatters and punks who went on to found Melbourne FNB

Embedded in a larger constellation of radical social worlds, FNB was and remains heterogeneous. One dumpster-diver and Food-Not-Bomber from Melbourne, for example—a punk who has herself often relied on FNB and dumpster-diving for food in the past—described some of the diverse identities and motivations that draw people to Food Not Bombs: "Poor people, homeless people, and lots of punks as well . . . do it because, at times they've relied on free food. And so they're giving back. And for students I think it's a little bit different; they're doing it as more, a statement or something." Just so, in Seattle, Melbourne, or any of the other cities where I've worked: participants have included privileged teens rejecting their parents' consumerism, the working poor trying to stretch their grocery budget, or crusty punks who haven't held a job and a permanent address in years; they have been recent immigrants and tourists, queers and indigenous activists, software engineers and broke college students, and so on.

> That's how Suzie and I ran into each other. She came over to the Ballistic Chicken Co-op [a share-house] . . . because we had a posting that we had random bike parts for barter. And she had just moved to Seattle, and needed to get her bike together. So she came by and she was working on her bike in our yard. And we got to know her and said, "Just take whatever you need. We're not going to try to make you do anything for them." And so she cooked dinner with us for trade. And she had a Food Not Bombs patch. And I hadn't been *that* involved in Food Not Bombs. But when I was in Boston I was on Critical Mass. And at the beginning of the Critical Mass ride . . . Food Not Bombs was finishing up, so we'd eat with them. And that's how I learned about it. And I had a few friends in Boston that were a lot more involved. So that's how I learned about it. And then when I saw the patch on Suzie's bag, we started talking about it. And started doing research and figured out that there wasn't actually a hot meals program going on in Seattle.
>
> —Corrina, on starting a new Seattle FNB chapter with Suzie in 2004 (after its previous hiatus)

Between them, they constitute a shared social world of surpluses. Surplus food abandoned by retailers. Squatted homes and low-rent kitchens overlooked by the real estate market. A surplus population abandoned by labor markets and underserved by social welfare agencies. We could go on. These add up to a kind of "latent commons" (Tsing 2015), which becomes the raw material for a minor economy both necessitated and facilitated by their exclusion. Where those exclusions incentivize profitable commerce, this commons emerges from recovery and reclamation. Where goods once circulated in the form of capital and exchange values, its denizens revalorize and recirculate them as use values. Where public space had been reserved for bourgeois consumption, they reclaim it for symbolic and practical ends through various motley incursions. We might think of them as a counterpublic. A dumpster-diving, scavenging, squatting, gleaning counterpublic who imagine themselves picking up after the market-public and exploiting those spaces overlooked or abandoned by it. These counterpublics are patchy: less contiguous than a "network" or "assemblage," more ephemeral and heterodox than a "movement" or "subculture" (although they may give rise to both). And yet they *matter*—both in the sense that they make possible new meanings and politics, and that they reorganize matter and material practices.

Like other publics, the alternative public sphere out of which Seattle FNB grew in the late 1980s and early 1990s was already a "relationship among strangers," as Warner would have it, dotted thinly across the globe, sometimes only indirectly aware of each other, yet with dispositions and sensibilities in common. This relationship was forged not by common identity, strictly speaking, but rather by shared attention to common practices of recovering and recirculating wasted surpluses. And like other publics, FNB's proliferation was possible not simply on the basis of existing social networks or affinities, but also on the basis of a concrete possibility of address, "both personal and impersonal," to an imagined plurality of those strangers (Warner 2002, 81).

"People just found out and came," as Vikki put it when describing her time as a core organizer in New York City FNB during the mid-1990s. Much like other chapters, the group rarely bothered to seek out volunteers because they could rely on shared counterpublic spaces to funnel strangers to FNB:

> People would just show up . . . there was a more thriving squatter community and more of the anarchist activist community was centered around the Lower East Side. It wasn't as far flung as it is now. So there is like sort of like, I dunno, a triangle or square where you could go—maybe it wasn't quite a shape but it was a general area where there was like Blackout Books, on Avenue B and 4th street, so that's the anarchist infoshop. So you go there, find out what's going on. Somebody will tell you, if you're hungry, Food Not Bombs meets on these days. If you're hungry and it's Sunday, you sit here and Food Not Bombs will pass . . . And there are other different squats where sometimes things would be going on, other times things wouldn't be going on, but there's sort of like that locus of activity. So people would eventually make their way over to Food Not Bombs. So we didn't feel like we needed to go out and recruit people.

Further, the explosion of self-published punk 'zines and other kinds of do-it-yourself (DIY) publication during the 1980s and 1990s, often photocopied and distributed for virtually no cost, also provided a venue in which not only to write about dumpster-diving and related topics, but also to exemplify nonmarket exchange. DIY performance spaces and records served the same function, as do web-based publications and social networks today. Through such shared spaces of circulation, people who already shared marginal economic practices came to share a counterpublic sort of imagined community, and vice versa.

Despite their multiplicity, they share space in a class-inflected cultural economy of waste with respect to the market-public. Abject or undervalued surpluses are the raw material of their economic practices, from dumpster-diving to perusing the food bank, from squatting in warehouses to renting in dilapidated neighborhoods. They put these surpluses back into motion by way of a raft of subsistence strategies and nonmarket innovations. They live amid dense networks of communal houses, performance spaces, and arts or activist projects. They deliver extra food and durable goods to friends, compile them in DIY community pantries or "free boxes" in their houses, or publicly swap and gift them at collective giveaways known as "Really Really Free Markets."[7] Such strategies cultivate a lexicon of marginal value and postcapitalist home economics with far-reaching political possibilities.

In all these ways, Food Not Bombs is embedded in, and emerges from, a broad public. And yet it is also a kind of conspiracy, illegible in the light of an even larger public's gaze. As we will see later in the book, not only their scavenging but their practices of public gifting, and the antiauthoritarian, swarm-like structure behind them, render FNB inscrutable and suspect to many. FNB's species of publicness is therefore counterpublic in the sense that it is defined precisely by its tension with "mainstream" public spheres. Counterpublics are realms of publicity that contravene the norms of circulation obtaining in larger, dominant publics. In a word, they are *queer*: they define "not a positivity but a positionality vis-à-vis the normative" (Halperin 1995, 62). They exist through the looking glass in both their own eyes and those of the dominant public. Counterpublics are therefore inherently spaces of social change—"spaces of circulation in which it is hoped that the poesis of scene making will be transformative, not replicative merely" (Warner 2002, 122).

In a practical sense, this means that counterpublics disclose the very possibility for unthinking certain received wisdoms and discursive norms. What once seemed like common sense may be turned on its head. Food Not Bombs, for example, is often the place where new volunteers learn for the first time that it is possible to dumpster-dive without getting sick, that squatting is something people might do voluntarily, and so on. Moreover, shared spaces of counterpublic circulation—of people, things, and ideas alike—incubate and disseminate the practices, material and discursive, that make possible an alternative community. Whereas dumpster-diving in isolation can involve a frustrating, lonely learning curve, for example, conversations around the FNB cutting board are one excellent way to learn where the best dumpsters are along with other such specialized knowledge (e.g., which vegetarian restaurants give away their leftovers at the end of the day, how to turn the water on in an abandoned house).

Further, counterpublics cultivate the forms of embodiment and affect that sustain them. Rage. Affirmation. Inspiration. Etcetera. As Terry, from Melbourne FNB, told me, for example: "I was doing it [dumpster-diving] for a long time and, just wasn't any good at it, wasn't getting anything. So I'd come to Food Not Bombs and say, 'What's going on?' [i.e., 'Why aren't I finding more?'] And they'd say, 'Oh yeah, it's okay.' . . . Because maybe fifty-fifty—maybe a bit, even more—it's a dud, and there's nothing or it's locked. So you've got to hear these success stories to inspire you. . . . People only ever tell success stories. They don't say, 'I went and I got nothing for months!'"

This affective support is analogous to the ways in which, as Warner describes it, gay counterpublics overcome and transform the internalized homophobia that often haunts them: "Styles of embodiment are learned and cultivated, and the affects of shame and disgust that surround them can be tested, in some cases revalued. Visceral private meaning is not easy to alter by oneself, by a free act of will. It can only be altered through exchanges that go beyond self-expression to the making of a collective scene of disclosure. . . . Publicness itself has a visceral resonance" (2002, 62–63).

Like the prejudices a market-public may promulgate toward trash, the affect Warner describes is abjection, a collapse of meaning and self-identity (at least from the perspective of the straight world). And like Warner's visceral revaluations of sex and gender, dumpster-diving counterpublics also create spaces where the usual, embodied antipathies toward waste can be tested, altered, and sublimated. (As Kristeva reminds us, sublimation is never purely abstract; it must be embodied.)

To the extent that they can make or break new meanings, counterpublics may be said to exercise a kind of sovereignty. That term has complex structural and symbolic implications,[8] some of which we will come back to in later chapters, but what is perhaps most important about the sovereignty of scavenged counterpublics is its experiential, affective quality—

the kind of palpable, lived freedom to persuasively define and circulate new meanings. As Lauren Berlant suggests: "To have sovereignty is to *feel* sovereign" (2010, 29). FNB and the exilic spaces in which it is embedded stake out just such a feeling of distinction and independence from the market-public, however patchy, ephemeral, or bracketed. They express a kind of marginal sovereignty that takes exception to the social order from which they are excluded. For both public and counterpublic, this exception is also therefore an umbilicus, a common axis along which they reject each other. What is abjected (literally, "cast away" in Latin) by one public becomes the currency of another—from the slurs reclaimed by drag queens to the waste reheated by dumpster-divers.

This sovereignty is more than symbolic or performative. While it would be a mistake to romanticize counterpublic agency and resistance—which are, after all, predicated on exclusion—they nonetheless have material consequences for their constituents. Avery, for example, a punk and squatter who cofounded Seattle FNB in the 1990s, described the practical and political benefits of their scavenged economies: "I never felt that squatting was in itself anything radical . . . but the time that it gives you—I mean sure, it takes a lot of time to scavenge but beyond that—it gave us the time to not have to pay off a landlord, to engage in meaningful projects like Food Not Bombs or Books to Prisoners. And because we had more time than maybe others who were renting or working, the project got molded into our political proclivities, as it were."

The possibilities many itinerant punks, hippies, and anarchists realized, for example, in migrating to a new city such as Seattle and availing themselves of a countercultural economy of dumpsters, free boxes, Really Really Free Markets, FNB chapters, and so on represent limited but nonetheless real, pragmatic kinds of sovereignty. Not least of these is a form of marginal food sovereignty, a measure of choice, independent of the strictures of a paycheck or food bank, about what to eat. Similarly, the proliferation of countercultures of squatters represents the freedom to snub the housing market and still have some say over where one sleeps. Often very efficiently—as when one train-hopping friend and collaborator, Jennifer, arrived at Seattle FNB broke and hungry, and that very night found a floor to crash on with other FNB volunteers. Then, within weeks they had found a room in a local punk house and became a mainstay of the local anarchist scene.

In such ways, Food Not Bombs' weekly meals in Seattle and other such sites are spaces where dumpster-diving counterpublics may generate "communities of affect" (Fredericks 2018), where dumpster-divers, squatters, train-hoppers, punks, hippies, and other countercultural voyagers may begin to meet each other, to plug into the local scene, and to discover local resources. As the punk band Gogol Bordello put it: "There is a little punk rock mafia everywhere you go; she is good to me and I am good to her."[9]

Conclusion

The borderlands between a market-public and its exceptional counterpublics are productive, porous, and busy places. The traffic across these thresholds, discursive and physical, is both constitutive and transformative of the publics themselves. It is the productive friction between these spheres that makes possible mass conspiracies and slow insurrections like FNB.

On one hand, as I have described, some of this traffic is antagonistic and results in prohibitions and blockages—new penalties for pissing in public, new locks on old dumpsters, and others. These antagonisms, I have argued above, both cultivate and segregate distinct modes of market and nonmarket circulation. More particularly, I have argued that processes of valorization and devalorization that constitute the work of capitalist exchange—and the abject capital they discard—are underwritten by a social imaginary that I have called the market-public, an imagined community demarcated not only by its participation in the market, but also through municipal policies that enforce a social and spatial segregation between the market and those people, practices, and things excluded from it.

On the other hand, the traffic between these spheres is often generative. The circulation of abject people, practices, and things in certain spaces—or the refusal to circulate them—may in turn enable the development of scavenged nonmarket counterpublics and economies that recirculate abject capital in other spaces. I have described above some of the affective transformations made possible in the dumpster, from getting over one's aversion to garbage to cultivating a shared subcultural identity. As these transformations scale up, so too does their significance: the anonymous, expanding horizon of a counterpublic represents the practical value of the autonomy its members assert; the possibility for new forms to grow from the umbilicus of exception that ties it to the liberal state or its dominant publics, though they are often illegible to those larger publics.

Coda: Keeping an Eye on the Dumpster

Scavenging, gleaning, dumpster-diving counterpublics, and the abandoned surpluses they exploit, have been incubators for a universe of radical political projects, from the Wobblies to the Wombles of Wimbledon. The movement of civilly disobedient encampments inaugurated by Occupy Wall Street, for instance, was bolstered by a steady stream of free food, blankets, books, and other surpluses, many of them dumpstered or donated to the cause (see Gordinier 2011; see also Barnard 2016). Compare those surpluses with the abandoned rural lands fringed with the signature bamboo and black plastic outposts of the Brazilian Movimento Sem Terra, living rough at the property line in order to eventually claim squatters' rights. Or, at a more personal scale, consider the experience of my friend Vikki, a Chinese American artist, activist, independent journalist, and former FNB bottom-liner in New York City who has researched, written, and published four books and countless articles and 'zines, organized international exhibits of her own photography, and raised a daughter with a miniscule budget and a part-time job thanks to the low overhead of their squatted apartment—complete with electricity, hot water, and insulation, mind you. This was only possible, she explained to me by email, through the shared efforts of a larger constellation of scavengers

> in the 1990s/early 2000s LES [Lower East Side] squat context in which there was an organized community that was built in the 1980s that enabled (some) buildings to get to the point where there was enough stability that people would be able to put in plumbing, insulation, heat, etc., because they were anticipating a long-term stay. And that this kind of long-term squatting was only possible given that, in the 1970s and early 1980s, the real estate market had gotten to the point where landlords preferred to torch their buildings for insurance money or had stopped paying taxes on them (which meant that the City of New York seized those buildings) and so there was an abundance of abandoned buildings in the Lower East Side (and in the South Bronx).

Large and small, these projects are no picnic. They demand an intensive, anticapitalist kind of labor and endurance to accomplish. Vikki, for example, upon reading a draft of this chapter, hastened to add: "You may want to clarify that when you visited my place, I had enough electricity to power a couple of space heaters to take the frigidness out of the air and keep us from freezing, but it was far from warm during the bitterest days of winter. (I still have very un-fond memories of evenings spent bundled up sitting in front of the heater or wrapped in blankets 'cause it was too cold to do anything else.)"

These projects and movements are more concrete than Warner's counterpublic "relation among strangers." But the former are only possible because of the latter. No conspiracy is possible without an opening scene of disclosure. Novel forms of life and sociality are based on the possibility of reaching out to strangers, imagining them as a community, and on that basis setting out to find them and conspire with them. If a shared public of scavengers is what makes this possible, then to see which way the political winds will blow, we might do worse than to keep an eye on the dumpster.

. . . cityness also includes a sense that behind the present moment there is another time operating, other things taking place, unfolding, waiting, getting ready or slipping away, and that we know only a fragment of what is taking place.

—AbdouMaliq Simone,
City Life from Jakarta to Dakar: Movements at the Crossroads, 2010

Senior citizen, supplementing her pension by dumpster-diving after hours at Melbourne's iconic Queen Victoria Markets (2018).

PART II

WORLD-CLASS CITIES, WORLD-CLASS WASTE

SCENE III

IF YOU BUILD IT, THEY WILL COME

At first glance, everything else made sense except the bocce courts. Pulling out a third of the park's trees made sense to city planners, for example, who were anxious about drug dealing, public drinking, and other shady details that they claimed went on in the shadows of the park's canopy. And dismantling the pergola made sense to those who felt the enormous rain shelter underutilized the public space or encouraged the wrong people to congregate. The local business association, for instance, supported the new design of Occidental Park. They had their own reasons for imagining the park better off without the proverbial huddled masses huddling less proverbially under it during Seattle's infamous downpours. Food Not Bombs, on the other hand, shared dinner under the pergola on rainy Sunday afternoons, so its removal was counterproductive for our purposes—and for the sixty or seventy people who queued up each week to eat with us. The park's new designers had also judged its benches to be "antisocial" and recommended removing most of them, along with the (only) neighborhood public toilet, at the north end of the park (Project for Public Spaces 2004, 39). The handful of "more inviting" (39) replacement benches installed afterward differed in one key respect: iron armrests subdivided them and prevented unhoused locals from lying down.

At the public commentary session I attended, along with several FNB volunteers and dozens of other homeless advocates, then–Deputy Parks Superintendent B. J. Brooks suggested that the pergola's location might be earmarked for an outpost of Tully's Coffee or Starbucks. This, too, from a pecuniary perspective made sense for local businesses: with relatively few long-term residents or dwellings, the surrounding Pioneer Square neighborhood is an awkwardly matched quilt of

A new notional vision for Occidental Park from the Project for Public Spaces, ca. 2005.

tourist-friendly bars and restaurants, homeless shelters and drop-in centers, corporate offices, emergency meal programs, warehouse spaces, and tech startups, all stitched together with aging red brick and stone walls that seem like equal parts heritage site and safety hazard. Anything that attracted extra financial or cultural capital to the neighborhood could help tip the balance. In this context, a new Starbucks in the park could both "activate" a place and contribute to city revenues, according to the Downtown Parks and Public Spaces Task Force. Selectively channeling the spirit of urbanist Jane Jacobs, they wrote: "Retail activity can create

Existing Conditions
OCCIDENTAL PARK

Dark area under trees.

Uneven surface.

Presence of homeless people.

Retail obscured by trees and landscaping

Blank edge.

"The presence of homeless people" under the pergola and other aesthetic drawbacks in the park before its renovation, according to the Project for Public Spaces, ca. 2005.

interest and bring activity to the parks, which will, in turn, improve park safety and perceptions about the parks as attractive, welcoming destinations" (Seattle Downtown Parks & Public Spaces Task Force 2006, 8).

The million-dollar facelift of Occidental Park in 2006, described above, was part of the Task Force's scheme to make the city's parks more "people friendly and diverse" (Seattle Downtown Parks & Public Spaces Task Force 2005, 3). They wrote, "As rising numbers of individuals and families look to downtown as a livable and active residential area, it's time for Seattle to make its downtown parks the beautiful, vibrant and welcoming public spaces they were meant to be. *As downtown booms, the parks should bloom*" (Seattle Downtown Parks & Public Spaces Task Force 2006, 1; my emphasis). Borrowing the metaphors of "revitalization" and "renaissance" from so many other urban redevelopment projects, the Task Force argued that the parks should answer to the urban landscapes of prosperity attending Seattle's recent economic successes. Their vision for a people-friendly space was tailored to a market-public.

That the park was already friendly (or at least not totally hostile) to a different, largely unsheltered kind of public life did not go unmentioned. The fact that homeless people and substance abusers regularly used the park was consistently mentioned in the same breath as its need for change in newspaper reports and blueprints of the new park. One local resident was quoted as saying, "Almost anything [the city] could do would be an improvement. [The park] has been such a disgrace. On the north side is where the mentally ill people congregate, and the south side is where the drug dealers hang out. This is going to let some sun in" (Murakami 2006a). Implicitly, here the interests of the mentally ill, the addicts, and the homeless users of the park are framed as being at cross-purposes with Seattle's sunny social and economic prospects. Putting it bluntly, Katie Comer, of the local business association, defended the new design: "What we're trying to do is replace the negative activity with positive activity" (Murakami 2006b). The winter of Pioneer Square's discontent made glorious summer with a bit of landscaping.

None of which quite explains the bocce courts.

Bocce ball isn't particularly popular in Seattle. Even then-mayor Greg Nickels, a proponent of the new park, needed a bocce lesson when the game was introduced to it.[1] My Food Not Bombs comrade Meg, who grew up in New England before moving to Seattle in her twenties for casual work, contrasted Seattle's near-nonexistent love of bocce ball with her experiences in Boston's North End, where bocce ball is part of the neighborhood's rich Italian-American heritage: "Did they think if they installed bocce courts, packs of old Italian men would suddenly materialize in the park?"

She may be on to something. Although bocce is hardly Seattle's Next Big Thing, the bocce courts were suggested by a New York design firm which specializes in what it calls "placemaking." In other words, "If you build it, they will come," as Meg described the logic behind the bocce courts and the heralded Italian septuagenarians. The group, Project for Public Spaces, has consulted on redevelopments in such high-profile destinations as New York's Times Square and Boston's Haymarket District. For them, place-making is "both a process and a philosophy" (Project for Public Spaces, n.d.). On paper, their approach to planning is driven by a community's expression of its needs and desires. But in the case of Occidental Park, the firm's suggestions were openly "heretical" to local residents' sensibilities—in the director's own words—taking more after Copenhagen than the Pacific Northwest (Project for Public Spaces, n.d.). In this way, the firm and the Parks and Public Spaces Task Force enacted a virtual, speculative version of Seattle. The philosopher Michel de Certeau might have described it as a *concept city*, "a *universal* and anonymous *subject* which . . . serves as a totalizing and almost mythical landmark for socioeconomic and political strategies" (1984, 94–95; emphasis in original).

Fortunately, at planning meetings, local residents had the chance to "red-light" the worst of these suggested heresies. The AstroTurf remained a mere splotch of green pencil. And the park's existing totem poles, ivy, and firefighter statue escaped the chopping block. (Although the trees weren't so lucky, they were at least in some way commemorated by the ex post facto judgment of the courts in favor of several residents who sued to keep them in the park.)

Nonetheless, the Costneresque globalism at work here (Seattle–cum–Copenhagen–cum–North Boston by way of New York) reflects a speculative, utopian, and ethnocentric vision of the future of public life that many urban redevelopment projects share, along with their vitalistic euphemisms. For world-class cities like Seattle, a key export has been their own urbane image and lifestyle. Envisioning Seattle's park of the future, for example, the Downtown Parks and Public Spaces Task Force describes "a vibrant gathering space for a broad, urban democracy" (2005). Their meeting notes proffer evocative sketches of this urban vision, from "a visual outdoor gallery" to "the backyard for downtown residents . . . a place for a picnic, barbecue, or a glass of wine" (Downtown Parks and Public Spaces Task Force, 2005).

It's telling that they describe it as a *backyard* rather than, say, a *living room*. A place to play a civil game of bocce ball, but not to get a night's sleep. A place to drink a glass of wine, but not a forty-ounce bottle of malt liquor. The residents of the concept city conjured up in this speculative vision invariably engage in a bourgeois, market-centric kind of public life, and then they go home to their private residences at night. (Seattle's "civility codes" still include an 11:00 p.m. curfew for the parks.)

And it's even more telling that, surpassing all these sketches, the first priority listed for the park of the future is that it be "clean, clean, clean" (Downtown Parks and Public Spaces Task Force, 2005).

In other words: "Out, damned spot."

The actually existing grit and disorder of urban living are characteristic stumbling blocks for the speculative utopianisms of city planners and developers. From the ongoing influence of the "broken windows" theory of public order all the way back to the sixteenth-century French edict to lock up one's own "sullied waters" indoors rather than disposing of them in the street (described in Dominique Laporte's *History of Shit* [2000, 4]), cities have often reckoned their worth through the rejection of dirt and dereliction. But these incipient utopianisms are never very far from their erstwhile dystopias. Although the ideals of urbanists are put to work fashioning values and goods, waste is every bit as much their product: "The necessary outcome of socially profitable production, it is the inevitable by-product of cleanliness, order, and beauty" (14).

This idea underscores the irony of the following observation: On the Sunday after Occidental Park's grand reopening, when the chain-link barriers had come down and Food Not Bombs was once again able to hand out food from the middle of the park, neither the old Italian men nor the young urban professionals materialized to take advantage of the bocce courts. But undeterred by the new courts and the absent canopy, the crowd of hungry and homeless people still waited to eat with us—no smaller than on any given Sunday in the old park. And, while they waited, some of *them* were playing bocce ball.

3

Place-making and **Waste-making in the** Global City

Big-City Dreams

Big-city dreams and urban dereliction are inseparable. The markets and publics upon which world-class cities hang their collective aspirations are built equally on place-making and waste-making. On one hand, if you build it (the stadium, the art museum, the symphony hall, the bocce courts, and so on), the markets may come. The wealth and growth of the cities described in this book rely on such constant "place entrepreneurship" (Logan and Molotch 1987). On the other hand, as I have argued, the production of value in one form is inevitably the production of obsolescence, desuetude, and abjection in another. As Michel de Certeau wrote, the "concept city" that inspires great place-making projects "repeatedly produces effects contrary to those at which it aims: the profit system generates a loss which, in the multiple forms of wretchedness and poverty outside the system and of waste inside it, constantly turns production into 'expenditure'" (1984, 95). Place-making and waste-making represent an inescapable urban dialectic. In this chapter I argue that one characteristic product of the churn of the mighty metropolises of the capitalist world is abjection, particularly abject capital.

> The colonist's sector is a sector built to last, all stone and steel. It's a sector of lights and paved roads, where the trash cans constantly overflow with strange and wonderful garbage, undreamed-of leftovers.
>
> — Frantz Fanon

Cities materialize this dialectic. The "urban process under capitalism" (Harvey 1978) valorizes and devalorizes places according to the needs of the market, creating relationships that in turn set people and things into motion in three dimensions. Their rhythms of circulation keep what is valued and what is wasted out of each other's way, enclaved by the bounds of showrooms and back alleys, tourist destinations and underpasses, gentrified neighborhoods and derelict properties, and so on. The markets and publics I described in the first part of this book therefore produce a spatial order whose geographies are metropolitan in scale. As Dominique Laporte puts it:

> The town, as opposed to the country, becomes the site of the rot-proof and advances a new space of the visible. *Where shit was, so shall gold be.* And with its entrance, gold proclaims its implicit and ambivalent relation to excrement. Beautified, ordered, aggrandized, and sublimated, the town opposes itself to the mud of the countryside. But in so doing, it also exposes itself, in the notoriously virginal face of nature, as a place of corruption. . . . If the shit that glows in the fields becomes the lasting gold of city streets, the stench of shit lingers where gold sleeps. (2000, 39; emphasis in original)

The "shining city upon a hill" of popular imagination is inevitably superimposed onto erstwhile metropolises of surfeit and scarcity, waste and want, distributed according to the spatial logics of urban commerce. This chapter therefore turns to the question of place-making and locates the book's key conspirators in a specific kind of urban landscape: the global city.

Consider Seattle. Its wealth was first built on the fortunes and detritus of lumber and resource extraction in its founding neighborhood, fortunes that earned the district two distinct names: the heroic "Pioneer Square" was also the first place to earn the nickname "Skid Road." Originally referring to the logs that skidded down Profanity Hill toward the city's first sawmill, the term became synonymous with the cut-rate bars and hotels that served the mill's precarious, itinerant workforce. In the neighborhood's Janus-faced nomenclature are recorded the fortunes and misfortunes of the archetypal Western boomtown.

Plus ça change. Seattle today is a different kind of boomtown, global in scope, a hub for shipping, research, and high technology, built equally on the fortunes and misfortunes of its day. In Pioneer Square, they are still mapped onto the old geographies. The neighborhood is still a focal point for entrepreneurs who can afford to dream, a node for technology, tourism, and development. And at the same time, the rescue missions concentrated there still cater to those hard cases who have been let down by the city. "It's just a vortex," as Kris described it, recounting his time sharing food in Pioneer Square with FNB:

It was a communion of frat boys and sorority girls on Friday, Saturday nights. But it's also surrounded by shelters, and King County Jail, and the International District, and people getting on ferries to Bainbridge Island. I mean it's just this weird mix of rich and poor, and crazy, and minority, and so ... It's the perfect spot to have some sort of political forum, and to exchange ideas, but it's always been a place where people come to party, and go to the ridiculous bars. And so, I mean, it's kind of a gross American reality really. It was then and it still is now.

Pioneer Square is still where many a recent, broke arrival to the city begins to map out her chances. Passing through the Food Not Bombs line on a Sunday afternoon, I've met military veterans looking for a new start, undocumented migrants between construction jobs, and train-hopping punks, among many others. In a way, they're all chasing big-city hopes.

The Bread of Life Mission, 2017. Bread of Life is one of several shelters and homeless drop-in centers in Seattle's Pioneer Square neighborhood, the original Skid Road, a block away from Occidental Park. (The Mission took Food Not Bombs' leftovers for a time and let us rinse out our pots and pans there.)

In turn, the city has long relied on those hopes to drum up labor. Pioneer Square is an entry point for many such unlucky initiates into the social spheres of homeless shelters, meal programs, caseworkers, panhandling, squats, drug dealers, and other kinds of marginal lifeworlds.

That the social and economic worlds of a city's most successful and least fortunate are intimately interwoven is not in itself a novel observation. It resonates from Dickens's unequal cities, or Marx's industrial reserve army of restless labor, down to the slogans of contemporary slum dwellers and homeless activists. What I have added so far to this tale is that the diaphanous membranes between such worlds also set *things* into motion. They determine objects' circulation across different states of value and worthlessness. In part II of this book, I trace those pathways as they weave across the city, producing distinct urban spaces as they go.

The political tensions and traction between these spaces are at the heart of my argument. They are the conditions of possibility for this book's eponymous "mass conspiracy." And as these urban geographies are entangled in global currents of people and things, so too does that conspiracy become global (as I describe in part III). To put it bluntly, globalizing cities like Seattle, San Francisco, New York, and Melbourne produce waste and want in such proportions as to make a global movement like Food Not Bombs both possible and necessary.

The seams between these urban spaces are formed and re-formed according to the contours of capital. Global cities and their wastelands are reorganized according to the needs of global economies. This chapter therefore describes some of the social, economic, and geographic processes by which globalized, post-Fordist cities have invested in spectacular and speculative efforts at place-making and have cultivated corresponding terrains of abject capital. To the extent, therefore, that these cities converge, emulating each other in appearance and structure, they also produce the globalized wastelands of excluded people and things that form the conditions for the "conspiracy" of Food Not Bombs to flourish. With apologies to Marx, the global city creates its own (would-be) gravediggers. To account for these conditions, this chapter turns to the work of urban theorists to describe the relations between cost of living, commercial waste, and material privation; between real estate speculation, vacant properties, and unsheltered citizenries; between market-publics, utopian urban spectacles, and their erstwhile metropolises.

World-Class Waste

In these opening decades of the twenty-first century, cities of all shapes and sizes have found their fates inexorably tied to the rhythms of a singular global economy. In a sense, they are all "global cities" (see N. Smith 2002; Mayaram 2009; Ren and Keil 2018). Their waste-ways are no less global. Transnational entanglements inflect the place-making/waste-making dialectics that animate them: ethnic trash-pickers in places as far-flung as Cairo, Egypt, and Sofia, Bulgaria, for example, find their livelihoods encroached upon by the interests of transnational waste disposal corporations and the European Union, respectively (see Fahmi and Sutton 2013; Resnick 2015); informal recyclers in the slums of Bangladesh, Bangalore, or Delhi transform flows of electronic waste from the Global North into crucial sectors of the local economy (Lepawski and Billa 2011; Gidwani 2015; Reddy 2015); communities of dumpster-divers in Seattle or Melbourne rely on world-class consumers to pass over food, shelter, and other goods. The list could go on. There is not, alas, space in a single book to account for all these diverse forms of global waste-making. But the cities where I have worked have more specific landscapes and waste-ways in common.

Globalizing cities like Seattle, San Francisco, New York, and Melbourne jockey with each other for the "command functions" of global capital and concentrate wealth, elites, and intelligentsia at the top of a global pecking order (Sassen 2001). They therefore exemplify a paradigm of "neoliberal urbanism" that privileges market-centric forms of organization and governance (Theodore, Peck, and Brenner 2011; see Hackworth 2007). The terrain on which they compete is not only economic but cultural, and the public lives of these cities are tailored to a fit a particular market-centric vision of world-class success—a vision shared and cultivated by elite transnational networks of investors, managers, architects, developers, and others (see Castells 1996; Zukin 1998; Sassen 2001). In other words, the global city cultivates a market-public that is global in scale. It concerns itself with building the perfect container for market-centric forms of life like those personified by Seattle's Downtown Parks and Public Spaces Task Force, as we saw in scene iii: forms of commerce and consumption that are civil, utopic, and as they put it, "clean, clean, clean."

It is according to such lofty urban imaginaries that people and things are made matter-out-of-place. From such commanding heights there inevitably precipitates a large share of gilded waste. (In the global city, gold still smells a little like shit.) The world-class aspirations of globalizing cities therefore follow the pattern of waste-making described in part I. If cities of all shapes and sizes make haste and waste in diverse ways, globalizing cities make waste according to their globalized modes of production, distribution, and consumption. Or, if you like, *world-class cities make world-class waste*. That waste takes a variety of forms, from abject surplus populations excluded from labor markets, to edible surpluses consigned to the dumpsters, to abandoned properties that stand, padlocked, waiting for the market to develop an interest in them. Such desuetude—of labor, food, shelter—is endemic to the polarized lives of great metropolises and an invariable consequence of the rhythms of market exchange and circulation that make and break global cities.

This polarization is the most relevant feature of Sassen's model for my argument: the global city tenders the best of times and the worst of times. Echoing Friedmann (1986), Sassen (2001) argues that as global cities have been reorganized to serve command functions within the global economy, they have been both socially and spatially polarized. Distributions of wealth are bifurcated, the haves and have-nots increasingly segregated. In the absence of the relatively well-compensated, stable employment once typical of the Fordist city's key industries, the global city's booming informational economies have tended to promote expansion at the top and bottom of the labor market, now respectively consisting of largely high-income, white-collar sectors directly employed in the various managerial or informational command functions, and low-income sectors associated with blue-collar service industries and casual labor. Now twenty-five years old, Sassen's case for polarization still holds water. Although it has been complicated by subsequent research that suggests a more contingent, multiscalar relationship between the concentration of global managerial services and the growth in low-income job markets (e.g., Hamnett 1994; Elliott 1999; Sassen 2001), her thesis nonetheless remains consistent with on-the-ground polarization in many global cities (Sassen 2001; Fainstein, Gordon, and Harloe 2011; van der Waal 2015).[1] In fact, the model's salience has grown over the past quarter century: when it was first published, only a small network of core cities could be said to be truly "global" in Sassen's terms; however, as economies have continued to be reorganized and liberalized planetwide, their command functions have become distributed across a broader constellation of cities, which have therefore been reorganized according to comparable social and spatial patterns (van der Waal 2015). The polarization that Sassen originally observed in New York, London, or Tokyo, therefore, is now more and more in evidence in smaller, less strictly global cities (Hackworth 2007; van der Waal 2015; Florida 2017).

Such polarization, Sassen argues, fosters elite forms of consumption and social reproduction. For instance, she writes, "The expansion of the high-income workforce, in conjunction with the emergence of new cultural forms in everyday living, has led to a process of high-income gentrification, which rests, in the last analysis, on the availability of a vast supply of low-wage workers" (2001, 285). In this way, working-class neighborhoods near the urban core, like New York City's Lower East Side, San Francisco's Mission District, Seattle's Central District, or Melbourne's Inner North, have been steadily revalorized and redeveloped, while their former residents, particularly migrants and working-class people of color, have been displaced to the urban peripheries by white-collar workers in these cities' managerial and informational sectors. Further, in each city growing incomes among the top tiers of the labor market drive soaring housing costs,[2] intensive foreign and domestic investment in luxury commercial and residential construction, and a corresponding spatial polarization. A consequence is the explosion of homelessness in these places (Bartelt 1997; Sassen 2001; Byrne et al. 2012).

As this polarization and gentrification proceeds apace, it has cumulative, qualitative effects on the public life of these places. As Jackson Hackworth describes it: "Gentrification is much more than the physical renovation of residential and commercial spaces. It marks the replacement of the publicly regulated Keynesian inner city—replete with physical and institutional remnants of a system designed to ameliorate the inequality of capitalism—with privately regulated neoliberalized spaces of exclusion. Gentrification is also much more than the small, idiosyncratic neighborhood process that it is often framed to be. No longer limited to 'islands of renewal in seas of decay,' redevelopment pockets have melded into a larger zone of exclusion that now forms the reinvested core" (2007, 122). This zone of exclusion applies not only to people but to things, as we have seen. This polarization therefore fosters luxury consumption and bourgeois social reproduction on one hand and disinvestment and dereliction on the other. These conditions incubate the place-making/waste-making dialectic of the global city.

The Mass Consumption of Style

These new landscapes are perhaps easiest to grasp from a great height. The god's-eye elevation of postcards. Or of Seattle's Great Wheel, a fifty-three-meter white Ferris wheel that is the centerpiece of the city's redeveloped waterfront. Viewed from atop it, the city resolves majestically into a luminescent panorama of glass and steel, trailing off toward northern and southern horizons. I once took one of my best friends there for his sixty-sixth birthday. A Vietnam veteran, a black man who lived through the era of segregation, and a former resident for several years of one of Seattle's homeless-run tent cities, my friend knows something about the spaces of exclusion that make up Hackworth's "reinvested core." But from 175 feet in the air, that wasn't what he saw. Like most other visitors, he was just impressed with the view.

Which is, of course, the point. Global cities dress to impress. Thus do they perform their "world-class" credentials. As they are polarized, gentrified, and reorganized to bear the stamp of the global economy, they are also remade to reflect the world-class tastes and vision of their upper echelons. (Quoth the Seattle Downtown Parks Task Force: "As downtown booms, the parks should bloom.") In other words, they produce a shared set of cultural imaginaries and social expectations for a successful global city—expectations that privilege the arts, entertainment, spectacle, and the visual consumption of public spaces (Zukin 1998, 2010; Florida 2003; Gibson 2004). These imaginaries presume a hierarchy of global connectivity, within which cities compete for financial, cultural, and human capital (Wetzstein 2012). Sharon Zukin described the cultural terrain on which they all compete as a global "symbolic" economy "based on such abstract products as financial instruments, information and 'culture'—i.e., art, food, fashion, music and tourism" (1998, 826). It is largely this symbolic economy, and the forms of elite consumption it fosters, that produce the world-class waste of the global city.

One symptom of all this world-class competition is the global rash of giant white Ferris wheels they have built from which to see themselves. The view is just as spectacular from the Melbourne Star, for example, at 120 meters the seventh tallest Ferris wheel in the world. Both are emulations of the London Eye—which, at 135 meters, was the tallest Ferris wheel in the world when it first opened in 2000. Never to be outdone, however, New York has planned a wheel to dwarf them all at 193 meters. Countless other cities with global aspirations have followed suit. These projects are placed strategically along their waterfronts—dazzlingly lit by night, iconic white by day—all the better both to see the skyline from and to be photographed against it. (And while San Francisco has no wheel yet, at least some San Franciscans are feeling the pressure to catch up.)

> Imagining this high-flying ride on the Embarcadero is a no-brainer. All you need is a little piece of property at the end of a pier and the backing of some eager tycoon . . . Even at $13 a ticket, the Great Wheel is getting long lines in Seattle and no doubt a similar ride would get them in S.F. as well. If people are willing to wait a half hour for a pricey coffee at Blue Bottle in the Ferry Building, what's another half hour and a few more bucks to experience vistas only available to seagulls for the past several centuries?
>
> —Dave Curran, *SFGate*, July 27, 2013

This global game of keeping-up-with-the-Joneses is an example of what Hardt and Negri (2004) call "biopolitical production," the production of new needs, desires, and forms of social life to meet the demands of global capitalism (see also Lazzarato 2006). As they produce the global economy, so too do global cities engage in their own biopolitical production (Giles 2015). Like these Ferris wheels, other forms of spectacular consumption proliferate wildly in these cities, catering to their higher-income strata—the software engineers, the corporate accountants, the market researchers, and so on—whose relatively disposable income fosters distinctive patterns of urban consumption, from the gentrification and soaring housing costs described above to the niche goods and postcard-perfect produce of markets like Pike Place in Seattle or the Queen Victoria Market in Melbourne. (Both donate excesses to FNB.)

These forms of elite, world-class consumption become one of the chief products of the global city. In contrast to the twentieth-century predominance of middle-class consumption in the Fordist city, Sassen writes that in global cities

> style, high prices, and an ultraurban context characterize the new ideology and practice of consumption, rather than functionality, low prices, and suburban settings. This is not merely an extension of elite consumption, which has always existed and continues to exist in large cities. It is quite different in that it is *a sort of new mass consumption of style*, more restricted than mass consumption per se because of its cost and its emphasis on design and fashion. There are distinct areas . . . where this new commercial culture is dominant and where one finds not only high-income professionals for whom it is a full-time world, but also "transients," from students to low-income secretaries, who may participate in it for as little as one hour. (2001, 323; my emphasis)

The new mass consumption of style is about far more than fashion. It inspires cuisine, art museums, boutique breweries, world-class concert halls, shopping malls, and massive waterfront development, among other things. It is the portrait painted in architects' sketches of new shopping malls and concert halls, the face of the market-public invoked in the "broad urban democracy" of Seattle's Downtown Parks Task Force. As Sharon Zukin writes of New York's spectacular consumer lifestyle, "It has also generated new, complex retail strategies, combining advertising, sales, real estate development and entertainment" (1998, 825; see also Zukin 2010). And, of course, this is equally true in San Francisco, Seattle, Melbourne, and other cities with analogous global aspirations (Zukin 1998; see also Stevens and Dovey 2004).

This nexus of retail, real estate, and world-class style is not merely incidental to the life and death of global cities. City governments often have a lot riding on it. It is precisely the kind of cosmopolitan public life to which officials have often looked to attract investment and revitalize their retail cores, as we saw in chapter 2. "Thus urban lifestyles are not only the result, but also the raw materials, of the symbolic economy's growth," Zukin (1998, 826) wrote. (It's no accident that it was in the middle of the first properly neoliberal decade, the 1980s, that the cocktail named "Cosmopolitan" was invented and popularized throughout the US on the strength of the iconic, urbane martini glass in which it was served [Regan and Regan 2006].) The mass consumption of style, therefore, has become a definitive currency for global cities, defined equally by the spectacles of the perfect avocado at the market, sidewalks full of expensive jeans and cutting-edge tech, bocce ball courts and Starbucks stands in the park, and so on. This symbolic economy expresses and addresses a globalized, multiscalar market-public that weaves together the lives of white-collar workers with disposable incomes, restless Fortune 500 headquarters, real estate developers, tourists, urban planners, and readers of in-flight magazines, among others, implicating them all in standardized (as distinct from homogenized) vernaculars and patterns of attention and accumulation (Zukin 1998).

Such standardization, however, also creates matter-out-of-place. Beneath the overtones of style and prestige is the aversion to disorder described in the previous chapters. Abject people and things mark the discursive and spatial boundaries of this globalized, urban(e) market-public. Particularly in light of the polarizations of the global city, this aversion often takes the form of punitive exclusions that inherit the logic of "broken windows" theory. The same exclusions inspire the subsidized processes of gentrification. In *Times Square Red, Times Square Blue*, for example, Sam-

Advertisement at Melbourne's Tullamarine Airport for "Exciting New Stores Coming Soon," 2017. This ad ambiguously refers both to airport retailers under construction and Melbourne's highly aestheticized, world-class retail core. The spectacular white circle of the Melbourne Star, to the left, complements the composition. Without it, the image might be mistaken for any other city's waterfront of oblong high rises.

uel Delaney (1999) described the cultural standardization that accompanied Times Square's gentrification—one of the most paradigmatic transformations to express and effect New York's becoming-global in the 1990s. New public-private partnerships with such squeaky-clean corporate citizens as the Walt Disney Company underwrote retail and entertainment developments across the infamously sleazy neighborhood, while the city forcibly acquired local businesses, condemned buildings, and discouraged or criminalized pastimes perceived as marginal, low-rent, or deviant. Delaney's favorite gay porn theaters, for example, were tainted with associations of moral and material pollution for the neighborhood's new straight, white, bourgeois clientele and forced, one by one, to close. The sexually permissive, interracial, cross-class sanctuary these theaters once afforded to gay people living in Manhattan was nothing if not "out of place" with respect to the staid civility of Times Square's new symbolic economy.

In this fashion, the fear of pollution and disorder that animates the global city's highly aestheticized spheres of consumption result, in the final analysis, in exclusion and displacement, both of people (whether Delaney's theatergoers or the homeless denizens of Occidental Park) and of things (like the abject capital I have described in this book). Below I describe some of the more specific mechanisms by which not only people but also unwanted goods are obsolesced and made abject.

Excursus: Speculative Global Futures in Occidental Park

All of this returns us, not for the last time, to Occidental Park. We might think of its million-dollar facelift, described in scene III (bocce courts and all), and the efforts to discourage homeless people from congregating there, as a speculative investment in just such a symbolic economy. Occidental Park represents a fault line where Seattle's histories of labor exploitation and lumpen abjection intersect with its speculative, world-class visions. It is one of the places in Seattle where investment and policy trade on global urban futures, where membranes between different lived and imagined social worlds determine the value of things and people. (That interface haunts the next chapter of this book.)

Bordering the park, for example, for many years sat a large, overgrown, fenced property and a poorly attended parking lot. On Sundays, FNB would park there gratis, watching hawk-eyed for the infrequent parking inspectors. And when the park itself was closed for renovation, we used the parking lot to share food. When Occidental Park was first built in the seventies, however, the designers imagined that these lots would one day be filled with apartments and residents who would treat the park like precisely the backyard imagined by Seattle's Downtown Parks Task Force three decades later. Instead, those spaces sat largely derelict, waiting abjectly on the right moment to realize their potential value. One version of that potential value was scripted into the South Downtown Vision Project by Seattle's Major Property Owners Group (MPOG), a consortium including three of Seattle's biggest developers, in 2003—the year before the Project for Public Spaces published its recommendations for remaking Occidental Park (Holter 2004). An artist's rendering of the vision, commissioned by the MPOG, imagined these two expectant spaces (along with a swathe of territory stretching south from Pioneer Square all the way to Sodo) as home to luxury apartments with a luxury hotel on the pier a few blocks away. The neighborhood blueprints were partly modeled after Portland's revamped Pearl District, "the Rose City's most cosmopolitan urban area, with rows and rows of residential lofts, trendy art galleries and antique shops, and superb dining and retail" (58).

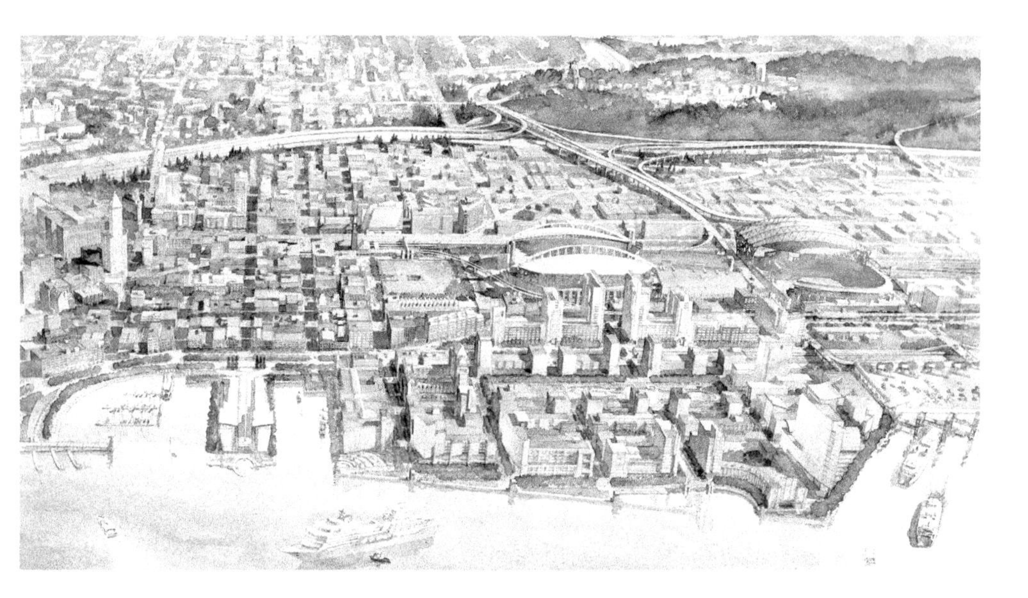

The vision of the Major Property Owners' Group for Pioneer Square seems to have replaced the blue-collar industries at the Port of Seattle with luxury housing and high-rise hotels. (Artist's rendition by Bill Shook, 2006)

Unsurprisingly, Pioneer Square's rescue missions and homeless drop-in centers weren't clearly depicted on the map. (One hopes that this was merely a stylistic choice rather than a planning one.) The vision makes only one veiled reference to the future fate of the neighborhood's entrenched social services and their clients: "Most of the new housing is gauged for middle- to upper-class incomes, [one of the developers] says, to *balance the many low-income living quarters already here*" (Holter 2004, 54; my emphasis). The MPOG's vision rested explicitly on the transformation of the region into a globalized space of stylish and stylistic consumption. (It also called for the Port of Seattle to relocate the shipping facilities and blue-collar jobs at Terminals 37 and 46, and lobbied the city to raise the height limit for construction in the area.)

Now, nearly two decades on, the MPOG's vision for the neighborhood has made some advances. The vacant lots next to Occidental Park now host a brand new, aesthetically impressive office complex for Weyerhauser, a timber company that is one of the world's largest private owners of commercial forestry land. The cheap art studios and low-income living quarters a few blocks away have been replaced by high-income rentals. The rescue missions and homeless drop-in centers persist for now. The

The newest addition to Occidental Park, 2017. As intended back in 2006, after thinning out the trees, adding Christmas lights, café tables, and red bricks, the adjacent parking lots would eventually make way for new up-market neighbors. Sure enough, upon returning in 2017, I found Food Not Bombs sharing the park with a new corporate neighbor—the purpose-built headquarters of timber giant Weyerhauser.

city's prominent street newspaper, *Real Change*, even moved its offices into the neighborhood in spite of the local business association's efforts to block it.[3] The ongoing contact between these two realms, the urbane lifestyle of historic Pioneer Square and the historic Skid Road in its midst, illustrates the fault lines of abjection and ambivalence that continue to haunt the neighborhood's property values and revenues. Big-city dreams remain inseparable here from urban dereliction.

Abject Capital in the Land of Plenty

Having tarried awhile with urban theorists, gazing down from above the city, I invite the reader back to earth, just a few blocks north of the Great

Wheel, to Seattle's Pike Place Market. We have already visited its dumpsters, but let's take another look. They begin to make a new kind of sense here in the shadows of the mass consumption of style I have described above. Each day's verdant archive of abandoned pomegranates, star fruit, heirloom tomatoes, and so on serves a crucial sacrificial function, ensuring a postcard-perfect experience for the market's annual millions of passersby. But we can now better situate those passersby, and the market itself, within a symbolic economy that is crucial to Seattle's global standing. Not only as a tourist icon but also as an engine for the mass consumption of style, Pike Place's importance is inestimable. And the dumpsters make it all possible. Thus does world-class commerce cut short the social life (or shelf-life) of things. Particularly in the world of upscale consumers who can pay a premium for the newest, the freshest, and the most stylish, premium goods. Vikki, who we met in previous chapters, summed it up succinctly: "Actually I think it [dumpstering] might be easier because there's so much waste in New York, just in terms of *everything*. People are like, 'Oh, I don't want this.'"

This world-class waste is also evidenced by the size of a city's scavenging, gleaning, and dumpster-diving counterpublics. Not only do prestigious, high-traffic locales like Pike Place or Melbourne's historic Queen Victoria Market richly supply produce to local Food Not Bombs chapters; large metropolitan hubs like New York, Seattle, San Francisco, and Melbourne attract and sustain itinerant radicals partly according to the extent and vibrancy of local scavenging. Corrina, originally from coastal Oregon, for example, gushed about Seattle's dumpsters compared to those in several other cities where she had dumpstered or collaborated with FNB:

> Seattle is the land of plenty. Both in terms of there are a lot of people there that are pretty wealthy and upwardly mobile and all that; but also, you can get pretty much anything you want for free. Usually legally. And other cities aren't like that . . . Just Craigslist[.org], is

> A lot of times when we were in between places that would give us regular donations, we would go out dumpstering. And there was sort of like the route of dumpsters you could hit up that would always have their stuff separate from the garbage. So it's like all the vegetables would be in one bag, and all the crappy stuff would be in another bag. There was one place for a while that we used to get really nice bread from . . . and they would always separate their stuff. And then they must have figured out that people were going through their garbage, because one day I opened a bag and it was all, like, chicken bones mixed in with the bread. And I was like, "Okay, forget it." So at times when we didn't have the regular thing, we would dumpster. And it was always just as good as what we would get directly, you just had to work for it more. So for a while there was a route of dumpsters where it's like on Thursday night, these five places all put out relatively good stuff.
>
> —Vikki, on dumpstering for FNB in New York's Lower East Side in the 1990s

a resource, or walking down the street and finding free piles, you find things in Seattle that are worth a lot of money and are very valuable... But that's something about Seattle that probably makes it easier to do Food Not Bombs. 'Cause we get gorgeous donations, you know? Organic fresh delicious produce. And, I think, you know, also the dumpster-diving reflects that, because people throw away anything that isn't perfect, in many of the stores and so that means that what's in the dumpster is going to be just slightly less than perfect.

Other constituents also make more targeted, short-range journeys to the city: whether at Food Not Bombs or in the dumpsters themselves I have often met scavengers from smaller outlying towns on pilgrimages to forage in well-known bins.

The city's abject capital takes at least two distinct forms: abject mobile capital (i.e., food and other movable goods whose value travels with them) and abject spatial capital (i.e., real estate, the built environment, and other place-based commodities, dependent on location), which I describe in this section and the next, respectively.

The global city's dumpsters are rich with abject goods for at least four reasons. First, urbane, world-class consumers can be choosier, and retailers' strategies correspondingly more exclusive, than in smaller towns where I have dumpster-dived and interviewed scavengers.[4] Aesthetic standards are exacting, conforming to Sassen's mass consumption of style. As we've seen at Pike Place, even small imperfections consign goods to the bin. Retailers often cultivate this rarefaction of style and supply, of course, conscious of their implications for cultural capital and brand identity. Consider the bourgeois clothing chain H&M (itself a sprawling global creature involved in high-profile place-making and retail developments), which took serious criticism after the Manhattan store was caught regularly bagging up unworn clothing and putting it out to the curb with its trash (Dwyer 2010). Many of the clothes were deliberately cut up or torn to prevent anyone recovering them, lest they be recirculated in the wrong places or by the wrong people. The end of their social life was defined in part by the exclusivity of their label.

A second factor in the production of abject mobile capital is the sheer diversity of options from which the world-class consumer may choose. These globalized spheres of consumption amount to a sensory buffet of competing products, from jeans to avocados to smartphones, all of which are subject to stylistic obsolescence.[5] Crucially, diversity itself can accelerate obsolescence. As the Arizona Garbage Project's exploration of American garbage discovered, for example, across both generations and geography, the more diversified a household's diet was, the more food they waste (Rathje and Murphy 1992). The global city's dumpsters attest to a similar pattern emerging from retail diversification and competition. Among the garbage, just as in the supermarket, there is more to choose from than in smaller cities.

A third factor comprises the global city's greater concentrations of people and commerce. More densely populated places make more waste of all kinds. In the same way that global corporations benefit from the "multiplier effects" of large cities that have a critical mass of requisite industries and workforces, dumpster-divers benefit from their own multiplier effects. The resourceful Seattle dumpster-diver, for example, has several branches of each major grocery chain to visit, as well as a wide range of independent grocers and produce stands. And Seattle consumers' taste for local, organic, expensive produce supports more than a dozen farmers' markets, some of which operate year-round and all of which have produce to discard or donate at the end of the day. The city's size also supports a range of niche businesses, with equally niche dumpsters like those I have already described. This fact has important implications for those in the city's dumpster-diving scene, who come to enjoy a certain luxury, relatively speaking. In this way, communities of scavengers and activists can more dependably rely on a critical mass of raw materials, which in turn attracts a larger pool of potential collaborators, friends, housemates, and so on.

Finally, the value or obsolescence of goods is intensified by citywide spatial and temporal patterns of circulation. Will Straw (2010), for example, describes how the prestige and cultural capital of a locale like "downtown" is transferred to individual goods, which can command higher prices in the retail core than the very same goods would in more peripheral locations proximate to abject or devalorized people, places, and things. In this way, tourists at the picturesque Pike Place Market pay more for an unspotted potato than at the utilitarian, wasp-colored Cash and Carry, decked out in spotlight-yellow and black just two miles south along First Avenue, in the industrial district. (Granted, they both throw potatoes in the dumpster at the end of the day, but the Pike Place dumpster is literally and figuratively more fruitful. It often smells like a salad. The Cash and Carry dumpster smells like soggy paper bags and stale urine. I didn't go there often.) Similarly, charity shops, Straw points out, can sell their once-discarded wares for higher prices if they're surrounded by a built environment dominated by luxury consumption, while the same kind of merchandise at the city's pawn shops is tainted by the stigma attached to their suppliers and neighborhoods. For the same reason, informal markets for secondhand goods and other surpluses are pushed to the social, spatial, and temporal peripheries of the global city, where they cannot taint more rarefied spaces of world-class consumption (see Duneier 2000; Trang 2017). Thus do the graduated zones of exclusion that constitute a city's "reinvested core" valorize and devalorize goods and determine when and how a city's wasted surpluses may circulate.

Speculation, Warehousing, and Abject Spatial Capital

In addition to these movable commodities, abject spatial capital is routinely abandoned in the global city. Unsold condominiums, foreclosed houses, empty storefronts, vacant lots, and so on all represent potential commodities, and yet they are kept off the market, sometimes sitting disused and derelict for years. Admittedly, they are not thrown away in the same way as a carton of eggs or a torn pair of jeans. Indeed, places are a very different kind of commodity from other goods.[6] But like other abject capital, they are abandoned according to the rhythms of market exchange—often in ways that inflate the price of things. In other words, they, too, represent a kind of manufactured scarcity. Although abandoned properties are a ubiquitous feature of the cycles of valorization and devalorization that characterize the urban process under capitalism (Harvey 1978), these cycles necessarily reflect the specific political economy in which they are embedded, and globalizing cities demonstrate patterns of abandonment and dereliction that correspond to their characteristic patterns of gentrification and polarization.

Chiefly, in Sassen's polarized city, high-income gentrification, real estate speculation, and soaring housing costs affect properties in a manner parallel to the pressure of commodity aesthetics and luxury consumption on food and other goods. Just as the symbolic economies of the global city attract prestige, value, and investment to theaters of au courant consumption at the expense of yesterday's avocado or last week's jeans, finance capital may pour into real estate markets (and sometimes "bubble" over) in highly valued localities or properties while others are passed over or depreciated a stone's throw away. Properties are often left to sit abjectly, off the market until their value has increased or until they can be put to profitable use. Picture the Homeless, a coalition of homeless and formerly homeless New Yorkers, calls this process "warehousing"; they pointed out that warehoused properties often exceed the number of unsheltered people in a given city at a startling rate.[7] This amounts to a kind of property speculation, be it deliberate or de facto. In aggregate, it contributes to the spatial polarization described earlier, spatially delimiting the attention of global market-publics and valorizing or devalorizing different regions of the city.

Moreover, not only have the local dynamics of real estate and housing markets been reshaped by the global city's reorganization; they have often been significant sites for global investment in their own right, both of development firms and elite investors for whom real estate markets in global cities have become a new kind of global currency and a safe place to park their capital.[8] This currency holds its value whether it is occupied or not (Madden and Marcuse 2016). The globalized economies of scale of such international investments, of course, absorb the costs of speculation and hiatuses in the circulation of abject spatial capital more easily than residents who've gotten the short end of stick in the housing market.

Just as the dumpster-diving communities described earlier are an index of the global city's world-class waste, so is abject spatial capital evidenced by the counterpublics of squatters I have met in my research. Through my work with Food Not Bombs in Seattle, New York City, Melbourne, and San Francisco, I have met small but thriving communities of squatters who take direct advantage of these vacant properties, as well as artists, punks, anarchists, hippies, and nouveau bohemians who also benefit from cheap or free access to such would-be wastes of space. I return to these communities and their housing practices at more length in chapter 6.

Conclusion

Real estate and the consumption of style are far from homogenous from globalizing city to globalizing city. Property markets from Buenos Aires's bourgeois Porteño playgrounds (Guano 2002) to Bangalore's emerging software campuses (see O'Mara and Seto 2012) to Mumbai's ephemeral, interstitial housing tenancies (Appadurai 2000) are part of each city's distinctive experiences of becoming global, and they abandon people, places, and things in their own fashion. In this chapter, however, I have argued that the specific kinds of economic restructuring entailed in Saskia Sassen's model of the "global city" implies distinctive patterns of elite consumption and investment that produce corresponding patterns of waste. In such global (and globalizing) cities, a symbolic economy of aestheticized urbanity is increasingly the currency in which capital is rendered and transacted. They compete with each other for investment, industry, and labor partly according to their ability to perform their world-class credentials. The prevailing upmarket urban lifestyles and market-publics conjured by their parks, museums, markets, shopping malls, luxury apartments, waterfronts, Ferris wheels, and so on are cornerstones of this currency.

Yet it represents a currency backed by a cultural economy of world-class waste. Food, shelter, and other goods are routinely abandoned in order to keep up the exacting aesthetic standards and high turnover that make possible what Saskia Sassen calls the global city's "mass consumption of style." It renders obsolete and abject a great many goods, and at the same time, the confluence of this stylish consumption with intensive global investment leads to the devalorization, dereliction, or desuetude of abject spatial capital.

These forces don't only shape the social lives of individual goods and properties. They constitute a citywide spatial order. Urban geographies and rhythms of circulation directly inflect the value ascribed to individual commodities and vice versa. Food, shelter, clothing, and other necessities are stalled, obsolesced, and rendered abject in their circulation partly according to their social and material location within these geographies. For the same reasons, world-class cities are often compelled to keep abject capital, abject bodies, and market-publics out of each other's way. The matter-out-of-place I have described so far in this book therefore holds broad social implications with regard to people and public life, as I will discuss in the next chapter. In any case, I have made the case here that these wasted surpluses are partly a consequence of the speculative valorizations and investments built into the market-publics of these metropolises. If the global city's streets are paved with gold, they are also secretly lined with waste.

SCENE IV

LIKE A PICNIC, ONLY BIGGER, AND WITH STRANGERS

The squad car pulled into the park, right onto the paving stones, and stopped eight paces from the planter. Not much of a planter, mind you. Two anemic elms and a scrubby young Douglas fir, not so much tended to as kept from dying by the Parks Department. They served mainly to frame two commanding Chinook totem poles, carved by a local artist, at the center of the triangular patch of woodchips and dirt. The totem poles are majestic and survived Occidental Park's million-dollar facelift two years before by the skin of their wooden teeth.[1] But the planter itself was unremarkable. A low stone wall bordered its north edge, where we clustered. Lined up on the wall: Food Not Bombs' battered pots, pans, plates, cups, and cutlery. We stood behind them as people filed past for dinner.

The officer walked purposefully up to the four or five of us serving food, forgoing any small talk whatsoever. "You are being audio- and videotaped," she said, resting her hands on her duty belt, "and I have warned you about this before." It wouldn't be too much to say she was being surly. Not to mention redundant, in a way, because we were videotaping her as well. (This is why I know how many paces away she parked. I'm a decent ethnographer, but not that good.)

There's some irony in the fact that both she and our ragtag soup kitchen felt the need to document each other's presence here in the park. In her mouth, it was a warning—which she followed up by reminding me personally that she had already copied down my name and address during her last visit, a few weeks ago. For us, it was a kind of protection—we thought the city might be less willing to prohibit public food-sharing if we could publicly circulate images of them doing so.

The officer went on: "Right now, I'm going to suffice it [*sic*] to say you are to step *out of the planter*. I already talked about this. This is a planted area; you cannot be in there. You cannot serve hot food in the park. You know that already."

On her previous visit, she had told us to pack up and vacate the park. The order was poorly received by a number of our diners, who lobbed jokes at her with impressive comic finesse given the situation. ("Calling all cars: felony feeding at Occidental Park," if memory serves.) With some effort I kept a straight face. Perhaps picking her battles, and preferring not to address a small crowd of understandably pissed off homeless people, she had ignored them and took the issue up with me, chiding us for standing in a planted area. Meanwhile, picking our own battles, we had finished feeding the people in the line and packed up the remaining food before anyone else showed up.

Upon her return, she remembered me and addressed me directly. This time, she said, she wasn't going to make us leave. Instead, she told us to get our stuff out of the planter. "I won't have you standing in there," she said, and gestured with concern toward the planter. "*That* I have a problem with." Not much of a planter, recall. Her priorities can't have been lost on the diners within earshot, most of whom were sleeping rough or paying five dollars a night to stay in the nearby rescue missions. The scrubby trees, such as they were, seemed to be framed as the hapless victims in all this.

Or, more precisely, such were the priorities of the Mayor's Office. While the officer seemed to take personal offense at our operation, she was, after all, enforcing a policy. This was the summer of 2008, before the global financial crisis stalled the city's growth machines. It was our fourth visit from the police in two months (and our second from her). One of them had told us that the mayor had asked Parks Department employees to "dial 911" whenever they saw anyone handing out food. (It wasn't clear whether the officer was speaking figuratively or not.) Mercifully, not all parks workers complied. Sometimes we offered them doughnuts and promised to be out of the park promptly. (And even when they did call, presumably the police often found more pressing things to do.) Before that, city workers had carried copies of an open letter from Parks and Recreation informing would-be do-gooders that the city allowed outdoor meal programs to operate in one place and one place only: Sixth Avenue and Columbia Street. They'd hand us a copy when they came through the park to empty the garbage cans. On the heels of the downtown parks' 2007 "renaissance," the Mayor's Office made a concerted push to channel rogue soup kitchens like ours up to the permitted meal site at Sixth and Columbia. We'd

Gregory J. Nickels, Mayor

Seattle Parks and Recreation
Timothy A. Gallagher, Superintendent

Central West Downtown District
4209 West Marginal Way SW
Westbridge Building
Seattle, WA 98106

April 23, 2008

Dear Meal Provider:

I am writing to this letter to notify you that you must move your meals program to the permanent location of the Outdoor Meal Program. The site is administered by OPERATION: Sack Lunch and is located on the corner of 6th Avenue and Columbia Street in downtown Seattle. The City of Seattle opened this site to continue to provide safe and nutritious meals to those in need and offer meal providers and hungry persons a safe and inclusive atmosphere. Currently, the eight providers using the 6th and Columbia location include: Operation: Sack Lunch; The Lord's Table; Mt. Zion; Bible Street Ministries; Neighborhood Cooking; Snoqualmie Valley Church; Mother's Kitchen and Curry Temple. Times are available for other providers.

OPERATION: Sack Lunch and the City of Seattle have been working hard to make the 6th and Columbia site meet all public health codes and City regulations. It is our expectation that **all** organizations providing outdoor meals to those in need within the City of Seattle will get on the regular schedule at the 6th and Columbia site. This is the only approved outdoor meal location within the City. Un-permitted food distribution in the area of City Hall Park has caused numerous rodent problems and other health issues and is not allowed.

By being part of the official Outdoor Meal Program it assures your compliance with City ordinances and health codes intended to protect the health of those you serve. Please contact Beverly Graham of OPERATION: Sack Lunch for an application.

> Feel free to check out the site when the programs are serving:
> Monday – Friday: 8:00 AM – 9:00 AM and 1:00 PM – 2:00 PM
> Monday – Thursday: 8:00 PM – 9:00 PM
> Saturday: 12:00 PM - 1:00 PM, 1st, 3rd, 5th Saturdays: 4:00 PM – 5:30 PM,
> Sundays: 10:00 AM – 11:00 AM, 3rd Sundays: 2:00 PM – 3:30 PM

OPERATION: Sack Lunch staff are available during all meal times if you would like to visit the site and ask additional questions. Please contact OPERATION: Sack Lunch's toll free line at 1-866-277-9252.

Sincerely,

Timothy Gallagher
Superintendent, Seattle Parks and Recreation

cc: Beverly Graham, OPERATION: Sack Lunch
Al Poole, Homelessness Intervention and Block Grant Administration
Judy Summerfield, Survival Services Unit
Fe Arreola, Survival Services Unit

Printed on 100% Post-consumer Recycled Paper

100 Dexter Avenue North, Seattle, WA 98109-5199
Tel: (206) 684-4075, TDD: (206) 233-1509 Internet: www.seattle.gov/parks
An equal employment opportunity, affirmative action employer. Accommodations for people with disabilities provided upon request.

A scanned copy of one of five such letters both hand-delivered and emailed to Food Not Bombs in 2007 and 2008 by Seattle Parks Department employees. (The image has been altered in order to anonymize the Parks Department employee whose card was paper-clipped at the upper right of the page.)

received copies of the letter no less than five times from parks employees and other meal providers; they had even been emailed to us at Seattle FNB's website.

Nevertheless, having browsed the parks code without finding any unambiguous prohibition of public sharing, we persisted. "Events" required a permit, but these were ill-defined. We resolved that it was more like a picnic than an event—only bigger, and with strangers. Even now, despite ambitious redevelopment visions and this antifeeding campaign, the park remains a place where people who are hungry or homeless pass the hours on a Sunday afternoon. The winners and losers in Pioneer Square's economy continue to lay competing claims, formal and de facto, to the area.

The territory of the official Outdoor Meal Site (OMS), in contrast, is subject to few claims. It is something of a no-man's-land: under the freeway, outside the old metro buses' ride-free zone, uphill, and relatively distant from many of the city's shelters and from downtown foot traffic. And although police crackdowns on unsanctioned meals were ostensibly intended "for safety's sake and public health's sake," according to the Mayor's Office (quoted in Spangenthal-Lee 2008), the effect of deliberately concentrating those seeking outdoor assistance under the same freeway pillars is not necessarily to create a safe, antiseptic dining experience. Although meal providers working there make unimpeachable efforts and feed thousands of people every year, the space can be crowded and force people into close quarters with others they might rather avoid—whether because of concerns about communicable disease, violence, or other reasons. One diner explained to us that the police sometimes patrol the line, looking for people with outstanding warrants. (In a city where camping or even sitting on the sidewalk is prohibited, it's easy for homeless people to acquire arrest warrants.) And, of course, the shelter of the freeway accommodates diverse bodily functions overnight. It often smells like stale piss. All of which raises questions about whose security and well-being counts as "public safety" and "public health." The site's very existence is a trace of the fractious politics of hunger and homelessness in the city, which ultimately leaves out the voices of people who are homeless, hungry, and would rather eat elsewhere.

During her first visit, our aforementioned officer of the peace had in fact asked me why we hadn't relocated to the official site; I replied with the afore-cited reasons. Her solution: We should focus on providing transport to anyone disabled or too ill to walk to the OMS. I think she knew she'd lost the argument on pragmatic grounds at that point, but she nonetheless (or maybe consequently) threatened to issue me a parks exclusion ticket. I was thankful that she didn't. (Although the

Seattle police instruct Food Not Bombs to leave Occidental Park, June 2008. (I am largely obscured; I'm in the polka-dotted shirt, standing second from the right.) This image appeared in Seattle's weekly paper, *The Stranger*, perhaps deterring the city from further police action. (Photo by Jonah Spangenthal-Lee)

next time I saw her she suggested that I had provided her with false information—another reason it's nice to have a videographer handy when you're talking to the police.)

Fortunately, that was the last we heard from the police for quite a while. Conceivably, in the shadow of the global financial meltdown later that summer, the Mayor's Office decided we weren't worth the hassle. A local journalist had also visited us and photographed one of our conversations with the police, which perhaps also deterred city authorities (Spangenthal-Lee 2008). (His piece earned a great deal of attention. People who knew nothing else about FNB or homelessness cited the article to me in appalled tones for months after it was published—not realizing I was *in* it, quoted under a pseudonym.) In any case, they left us alone after that. In the intervening decade or so, Food Not Bombs has continued to share dinner in Occidental Park on Sunday afternoons. And in more recent years we have increasingly been joined by new informal meal projects in the neighborhood throughout the week. Meanwhile, the planter survives to this day, unperturbed by our efforts.

This was not the only moment of discord between FNB and the Seattle Police Department. Participants from other phases in the group's quarter-century tenure have described similar periods during which their efforts provoked city agencies, local businesses, or both to pressure them to move. Nor is Seattle unique in this respect. Food Not Bombs co-conspirators from cities across the globe have told similar stories. In such ways, publics and policy makers have often reacted to the growing global crisis of homelessness by controlling the free public distribution of food.

Like homelessness itself, these prohibitions represent transformations in the fabric of urban living that have been both cause and effect throughout these vexed decades of political and economic transformation. If restrictions of free, public meals have spread from city to city in the United States and elsewhere, they are remaking not only the lives of people without reliable incomes or shelter, but the cultural economy of eating itself. Mighty urban economies such as Seattle's produce waste and abjection in proportion to the economic value they create, and yet to function they must keep each circulating away from the other. This is most poignantly true of eating, as the geography of food surpluses and scarcities, waste and want, are carefully managed. To remake urban life in such a way asserts a powerful form of governmental control. But this urban life, remade, neither sits still nor does what it's told. Its component elements—variously segregated, sanctioned, submerged, or subsidized—emerge from and thresh against each other's edges in myriad ways. Homelessness, hunger, and survival itself are not only in a sense *created* by these policies; they also exceed every effort to manage them, and in turn, they unravel and reform the city, the state, and the social.

4

Eating in Public

Shadow Economies and **Forbidden** Gifts

The Very Stuff of the Metropolis

"The merchants hated me, the city hated me . . . inside their public space," Genevieve exclaimed. "I was fined. I was—I'm not going to say *threatened*, but, you know, police followed me everywhere. And me, saying, 'But this is a park, right? Can't anybody go into this park?'" In the 1990s, just as downtown Seattle's homeless shelters and real estate markets both showed early signs of the three-decade boom and polarization that has earned the city world-class status, Genevieve began handing out sandwiches from her van in Pioneer Square. Like Food Not Bombs—which began sharing food in the same neighborhood during the same period—she quickly found that her free sack lunches weren't welcomed by city authorities. Cannily, she recognized that the prohibition of such public generosity reflected a transformation in the fabric of urban space and citizenship. She went on: "You know, it used to be that this part of town, it was Skid Row—this was where everybody congregated. And then all of a sudden all the people who have resources came in and started purchasing and remodeling and renovating. And now it's had this revitalization, and the people who were disenfranchised to begin with are disenfranchised again."

> We can only point to a few facts. To refuse to give, to fail to invite, just as to refuse to accept, is tantamount to declaring war; it is to reject the bond of alliance and commonality.
> —Marcel Mauss

Genevieve's experience is common. Such forbidden gifts, and the reinvention of public space they betoken, are widespread. Why should the two be so entangled? To answer that question, this chapter traces the relations between markets, publics, wasted surpluses, and the governance of eating in the global city. The central fact of this inquiry is this: over recent decades, the apparatuses of city government have often attempted to regulate who can and cannot eat in public. Or, in (slightly) less Machiavellian terms, they have imposed a range of schemes to dissuade private citizens from sharing food, particularly with homeless people, in public spaces. Fines for giving away meals. Selectively issued permits for the use of city parks. Public "education" campaigns to discourage alms. Informal agreements among police, officials, and service providers. And so on. In early 2018, for example, at least a dozen people were arrested for sharing food in El Cajon, California.[1] The previous month, activists had been ticketed for the same thing in Atlanta, Georgia.[2] Throughout my work, I have spoken with Food Not Bombs collaborators and other meal providers from half a dozen cities who have fallen afoul of these policies at various points during the past thirty years or so.[3] The courts have sometimes challenged, sometimes upheld the prohibitions, depending on their formulation. Nonetheless, variations on the theme are in effect in dozens of US cities, perhaps more.[4] They also crop up around the globe, from London to the Philippines.[5] It follows that anyone in these cities who can't afford to buy food is prevented from eating in public (at least in those spaces where the policies are actively enforced).

The salty constable of the last scene is therefore the tip of an iceberg. One face of a transnational assemblage of prohibitions that contribute to the transformation of foodways in the global city. Already in this book, I have argued that food surpluses and people experiencing food insecurity—both affected by these restrictions—represent twin exclusions, abandoned excesses whose removal from view underwrites the economic and political order of the city. Feeding restrictions are a fulcrum for those exclusions. Lisa, one of Seattle FNB's founding organizers in the 1990s, directly identified their struggles over food sharing with revanchist policies that transformed public life during that period: "When we were feeding was right before they passed these so called 'quality of life' rules where you couldn't piss on the street or sleep on the street or sleep on sidewalks . . . So the crackdowns were just kind of starting, and it was around the same time the massive gentrification was starting to kick in."

With a deceptively small footprint, feeding prohibitions have far-reaching implications. Enforced less frequently or consistently than other quality of life policies, they nonetheless play a symbolically and politically pivotal role in secluding wasted surpluses, segregating abject populations, and reproducing the biopolitical terrain of the archetypal global metropolis.

That still sounds a bit Machiavellian. I don't mean to suggest that city officials are twirling nefarious moustaches. Rather, as cities become "global" the stakes of eating in public are raised. Particularly so in the commanding metropolises of the Global North. As we have seen, investments, incomes, and inequality in these mighty towns have taken on Dickensian proportions during recent decades of economic globalization and neoliberal transformation. In these polarized burgs, characterized equally by world-class excess and manufactured scarcity, the circulation of wasted food surpluses has become a critical site of struggle for government, commerce, hungry people, and would-be do-gooders alike. That struggle is the chief object of the "mass conspiracy" that is at the heart of this book.

Sharing prohibitions are at the center of this. They recast the relationships that make a city, intervening in the social reproduction of urban economies and publics. Or, if you like, what is at stake is the content of public life itself. Most fundamentally, these policies define the means by which food and other excesses may circulate legitimately and legibly in public spaces. Which is to say, *the ways that it is allowed to change hands*. This transfer is usually in small quantities, by commercial exchange, or both. Other economic relations are thus excluded from the public sphere. Eating—and by extension, surviving—in the city is reckoned a private affair or a business venture. Except in moments of commercial transaction, food (like money) sparingly crosses the frontiers that segregate social classes in the city. And the instances in which it does become the source of quite a fuss. They provoke disgust, disdain, and anxiety among many as the abject capital and broken windows of the urban economic order threaten to crowd too close.

These are questions of how we value life in the city and what kinds of urban lives we foster. They reflect a fundamental entanglement of aesthetic, economic, and political values. In this way, health and safety regulations become a palette for bourgeois aesthetics; the management of downtown parks and sidewalks articulates a de facto austerity policy; and distinct subjectivities and economies are woven into the resulting tapestry. The economic structures, public prejudices, and personal struggles cobbled together in a word like *homelessness*, for example, are not things that simply exist a priori, apart from law, economy, or society—only to be "criminalized" after the fact. Rather, homelessness is this crumpled dollar bill, this generous stranger, this free doughnut, this scavenged piece of cardboard, this eviction notice, this busy sidewalk, this new bylaw,

Gifts among strangers. Seattle Food Not Bombs volunteer and diner, Occidental Park, 2017.

this unpaid ticket, this seat in the park, or this queue outside the shelter, among many other things. These things are the raw materials of lived economies. The very stuff of the metropolis. Like minimum-wage service jobs, raucous football games, gleaming shopping malls, and so on, they compose the social life of a city. They are made and remade in precisely such lived moments as Food Not Bombs' episodic run-ins with the law. Therein, diverse modes of living in the city are rendered visible, viable, and even grievable (see Butler 2009). (Think of the victimized planter in the last scene.) Other modes of living are left bare, hiding in plain sight. In such moments are forged the ontological and experiential boundaries of metropolises, markets, and publics.

So far, to capture these landscapes I have told a tale of the global city, cut from a cloth of market-publics and abject capital. These market-publics, with their currency of urbane spectacle and consumption, are anxious to keep their scavengers and their world-class waste out of view. In the process, those excluded surpluses—people and things alike—are left to circulate elsewhere in the shadows of the global city. They are set into motion in ways that produce new, marginal economies and scavenged counterpublics. Indeed, some of those marginal spaces foment our book's mass conspiracy.

In that, this chapter picks up right where the others left off, offering an extended example of one political technique by which these exclusions are accomplished: the *forbidden gift*. Policies restricting the sharing of food and other surpluses don't just passively reflect public anxieties about homelessness or hunger. Rather, to forbid the gift is to remake the "relationship among strangers" that is a public, curbing the circulation of surpluses among them and reproducing the norms of the market. (As nineteenth-century American frontier authorities knew all too well when they banned the Kwakiutl potlatch.) These prohibitions both enact and enable the world-class symbolic economies of the global city, which include homelessness and hunger among their ontological preconditions just as surely as they are built on world-class waste and manufactured scarcity. Sharing prohibitions articulate these symbolic economies with the techniques of urban governance and biopolitics: they discipline individual bodies and regulate populations, producing new genres of urban life and imprinting them with the stamp of the global city. Further, they marginalize alternative, nonmarket modes of survival—such as the free, shared meal—that might abridge the challenges of housing and food insecurity. They add inconvenience and indignity to the daily grind of shelterlessness. As sharing prohibitions spread from city to city, these forbidden gifts are themselves increasingly part of cities' experiences of becoming "global."

Forbidden Gifts

Early in 2017, Melbourne's sidewalks were especially crowded. Almost two thousand new Melburnians moved to the city every week.[6] And the number of rough sleepers had grown starkly over the previous two years as a result of soaring rents and shrinking safety nets.[7] By February, semipermanent encampments of tents, mattresses, and sleeping bags had become a regular feature of Melbourne's busy thoroughfares, prostrate islands in the stream of otherwise standing-room-only foot traffic. The *Herald Sun* newspaper ran lurid headlines, pitting these ragged bivouacs against the global renown of the nearby Australian Open ("Gland Slum" was my favorite).[8] The state's chief of police, Graham Ashton, called a press conference to accuse campers of "pretending" to be homeless in order to "shake down" the tennis-goers (Dow 2017a). It was a "very ugly sight," he said.

Abandoning its long-standing reputation for progressive approaches to homelessness, Melbourne's City Council responded by proposing bylaws to ban camping or leaving unattended possessions on the footpath. But even more tellingly, the city earmarked funds for an education campaign to *dissuade passersby from giving gifts* directly to homeless Melburnians. Spare blankets. Backpacks. Groceries. The inventory of Melbourne's sidewalk camps. They would be asked instead to make donations through more "appropriate" channels, charities like the Salvation Army or the Brotherhood of Saint Laurence. The bylaws were defeated, partly by voluble outrage from Melburnians with homeless sympathies.[9] But the education campaign was not so disavowed and remains a nominal possibility. It illustrates the work of urban transformation that I am concerned with in this chapter. Its explicit aim is to remold urban sociality, redirecting economic largesse and discouraging mutual aid between strangers. What does it tell us that such gifts must be actively suppressed? And that, in particular, we mustn't share the things that keep us alive, like food and blankets?

Like the other annulled generosity described in this chapter, the most immediate goals of this antisharing campaign were aesthetic and geographical. As Ashton made clear, it aimed to segregate homelessness from commerce and render public space a worthy world-class attraction. In that way, like the civility ordinances described in chapter 2, it articulates the priorities of a market-public. It and the other proposed bylaws are enrolled in a larger "politics of containment" that disciplines the poor by regulating their survival strategies, forcing them to accord with the temporal and spatial regimes of capitalist social reproduction (Heynen 2010, 1225). In effect, it curbs their mobility in space and time. In the polarized cities with which this book is concerned, which have been remade to varying degrees by decades of deindustrialization, global finance capital, and neoliberal austerity, the growing number of lumpen poor raise the stakes of these policies (see Mitchell 2011). Their containment, in turn, is a symptom of the ways in which economic globalization's "collateral casualties" the world over are made surplus to requirements and excluded from state concern (Bauman 2004, 40), simultaneously abandoned and enclaved, much like the abject capital I have already described (see J. Ferguson 1999; McGregor 2008; Reddy 2015). So we might say that sharing restrictions militate against the circulation of both abject capital and surplus populations in public space.

In so doing they enforce capitalist norms of exchange and disrupt what David Graeber playfully calls "baseline communism," the practice of economic largesse that refuses the logic of a transaction (2011, 98). Unlike other kinds of gift economies, such gifts are debt-free,[10] perfectly alienable, and come with no strings attached—except the implicit obligation to treat others with the same kindness. But whereas such humanitarian food projects (the proverbial free lunch) thus eschew any "spirit of calculation" (Appadurai 2012), feeding restrictions presume that food and other necessities should circulate among strangers—in other words, in public—chiefly in the form of commodities. Similarly, those "appropriate channels" of gifting that *are* permitted often perpetuate a discourse of "deserving poor" who reproduce the expectations of government agencies and service providers, and "undeserving poor" who haven't yet earned their charity. Sharing food via these appropriate channels amounts to a private courtesy—or even a coercion—rather than an entitlement (see Poppendieck 1998b).

"Testing for random acts of kindness," Seattle sidewalk, 2008. Panhandling is a sort of anticapitalist mutual aid among strangers, an economy of debt-free kindness.

In these ways, sharing prohibitions construct the public as necessarily a market-public and obstruct the nonmarket circulation of resources. In particular, they refuse recirculation to the abandoned, abject capital that stocks soup kitchens, food banks, and other humanitarian food-sharing projects. Although it is the market that produces and discards abject capital, it is urban policy that keeps it that way, and that delineates the counterpublic spaces within which it may circulate.

In both of these ways, therefore, feeding restrictions comprise one frontier of what Foucault ([1978] 1986) called "biopower," that quintessentially modern form of power that works simultaneously through institutions and individuals, disciplining discrete bodily practices and regulating whole populations. Crucially, for Foucault, biopower not only governs life but remakes it. Life does not simply exist, fully formed, waiting to be discovered and regulated by state agencies—although the state's technicians and critics alike sometimes tacitly accept this sequence, as when they describe the "criminalization" of homelessness or hunger, for example. (So goes the old myth: "the poor will always be with us," immutably and ahistorically.) Rather, as Craig Willse (2015) has argued, diverse biopolitical entanglements of policing, welfare agencies, housing policy, commercial enterprise, and social services constantly reproduce a genre of lives like "the homeless." Feeding restrictions play their part in producing such lives. Moreover, in the same fashion, they transform space and sociality more broadly, cultivating the economic order of highly aestheticized, world-class market-publics described in the previous chapter. Insofar as their ultimate product is an urban sociality that enables cities' successful integration into global circuits of capital accumulation, they represent an apparatus of "biopolitical production" that tends to remake social and biological life itself in the image and interests of capital (Hardt and Negri 2004; see Lazzarato 2006). Feeding prohibitions and other forbidden gifts therefore play a role in the biopolitical production of the global city and by extension of the global economy itself.

The Legacy of Broken Windows

Where biopower, matter-out-of-place, and urban policing intersect, policy makers often imagine "broken windows." Now three decades old, that phrase has fallen somewhat out of fashion, but it nonetheless captures the logic of the forbidden gift. Behind these prohibitions is the implication that free food and other forms of generosity-in-public represent a threat to urban order. As David Spataro writes, "During the era of neoliberal urbanization that forces all visible signs of poverty and 'disorder' out of public space under the guise of zero tolerance for quality-of-life violations . . . every FNB meal represents a potential subversion of neoliberal public space because *all publics are welcome*" (2016, 194; my emphasis).

The broken windows theory of policing still casts a shadow on contemporary antihomeless measures. Its discursive effects continue to inform zero-tolerance policies and public figures who, like Graham Ashton, are keen to quarantine the urban poor in order to appease anxious middle classes and create an ideal landscape for consumption and investment. But in addition to treating homeless bodies as matter-out-of-place, the theory also implicitly criminalizes the movement of actual *matter*, pathologizing the informal circulation of goods. Consider, for example, the wares of the pavement vendors in Mitchell Duneier's *Sidewalk* (2000), many of whom sold previously discarded books scavenged from New York's world-class waste stream. Duneier describes the crucial role business improvement districts, empowered by broken windows theory, play in reorganizing such economic behaviors in New York. He underlines the entanglement of symbolic and financial capital involved, quoting one district member who said, "It's not just that they're selling things in public space, but *they don't look like they've made a capital investment* in what they're doing. . . . It's not clear that they're part of the social fabric" (234; my emphasis). The admission is rare and telling: it takes a capital investment to be a full-fledged member of this public. For similar reasons, concerted opposition to public food sharing has often come from local business associations such as the Pioneer Square Community Association, whose events manager paid FNB several visits in 2005, when I had first joined the group, in an attempt to dissuade us from using the park alongside other events like the monthly Art Walk. (Relatedly, the event manager's LinkedIn profile advertises that he "Doubled PSCA's operating income via the . . . monetization of existing programs," many focused on Occidental Park, thus marketizing its public function.)[11] "He just seemed to have a power trip going and didn't have much to actually enforce it," as my FNB collaborator Corrina remembers, "but he liked

> Me and my ex-girlfriend showed up one day—well, this is when we were squatting the Washington Shoe Building [near Occidental Park]. And there was a bunch of home-bums sitting at the park bench, and they were there for about a half hour. And this tan van's sitting there. And, soon as this home-bum cracks open a beer, five or six cops hop out of this van and they come bum-rush this home-bum and his buddies. And toss him on the ground and arrest him. Throw him back in the van. Ha. It was a total snatch squad for some guy drinking a beer.
>
> —Koa, Seattle FNB, early 2000s

to inform us that the mayor didn't want us there and that we needed to leave."

In this fashion, although zero-tolerance policies (and their proponents) emphasize aesthetic order, they are profoundly economic in nature. They target informal economies, mutual aid, urban subsistence, and other non-market-friendly forms of life, comparing them to the first cracked panes in a downward slide toward urban ruin. (Here we might be reminded that Eric Garner, the unarmed African American man choked to death on camera by New York Police in 2014, had been detained for informal economic practices: he had been selling loose cigarettes on the sidewalk.) Whereas its technicians often framed broken windows strategies as chiefly *reactive*, "restoring" order, the chief function of biopower, according to Foucault, is to actively produce and inculcate new practices and subjectivities. In this way, the policing of minor disorder becomes one frontier in the production of a new kind of economic life in the global city.

Sharing prohibitions are thus frequently justified in language that echoes broken windows theory, positing food sharing as a dangerous form of public disorder, often expressed in terms of health or safety. One senior public servant I interviewed in Seattle, for example, rehearsed for me a common argument for restricting public meals: "A number of different low-income and homeless people come, food is provided, and then they leave, leaving trash and other refuse in the area," he explained. In like fashion, other Seattle public figures have often invoked the specter of consequent rodent infestations. (This is not entirely unfounded, but it reflects a telling double-standard. A certain amount of clean-up necessarily forms part of FNB's weekly work. But our meal surely does not contribute more half-eaten hotdogs and other debris than the unruly sports fans and bar crowd with whom we share Pioneer Square. And we are perfectly capable of tidying up after ourselves in the park.)

With few exceptions (as I describe below), in effect these perceived threats force economies of generosity, hungry people, and donated groceries indoors, mainly into churches, shelters, and drop-in centers. Through policies that establish distinct spaces of circulation for distinct types of food, people, and economic practices—and through the assumptions, prejudices, and political-economic calculations that inform those policies—municipal governments thereby articulate boundaries between public space, where market exchange dominates, and private or exceptional spaces, where poverty and generosity can show their faces. In all these ways, broken windows theory articulates the demands of world-class symbolic economies—with their emphasis on elite consumption and aesthetic order—with the regulatory and disciplinary techniques of biopolitics, the quintessential logic of which is the *ban* (Agamben 1998). The theory authorizes juridical exclusions that are marshaled to produce public spaces of world-class consumption, on one hand, and spaces of exception wherein abject people and abject capital may be contained, on the other.

Sharing restrictions vary in formality and severity. But all cast the shadow of a ban. Seattle's are positively warm and fuzzy compared with those in San Francisco, where a thousand or so Food Not Bombs volunteers were arrested for serving food in Golden Gate Park between 1988 and 1992,[12] or in Orlando, Florida, where for several years FNB fought explicit ordinances against sharing one's dinner with too many people in the park. Seattle's example is telling for its subtlety. In contrast to explicit prohibitions and arrests, Seattle's outdoor assistance is curtailed and channeled through a simple refusal of permission to use the parks. Although the reader will recall, it's not altogether clear what requires a park use permit. One officer admitted to us that there were a "lot of grey areas." Indeed, pursuing such a permit through official channels may be fraught with ambiguity, as Ingrate, a co-conspirator from the late 1990s, pointed out:

> There's a funny cyclical thing that we went through a couple times where we were told we needed a permit to serve. We said, "How do we get a permit?" "Well, you've got to have a Health Department permit." We went to the Health Department, said, "How do we get this permit?" They said, "Well, you've got to talk to the Parks Department." Spoke to the Parks Department, again. It was like, "No, talk to the Health Department." So, as far as we could tell, we actually did very earnestly start investigating that, thinking, "Well, if we're operating out of a kitchen that's good, and we have folks

> I remember in '96 when we were in the week between us almost getting thrown out of the park and fighting back, and the next week where we thought the cops were gonna come and get us en masse, and everybody was prepared—so, like, what are our roles gonna be? Who can get arrested? Who can't get arrested? Who needs to be on the outskirts and able to get away? Somebody actually went and looked up the NYC Parks Department rule book and there is a rule that's like, "You need a permit to serve food. You need a permit if more than twenty people are going to eat it." So if you're having the big Smith family gathering in Central Park, and you're going to have like twenty-five relatives, supposedly you would need a permit. I guess somebody called to clarify, and they were like, "Well what if I have twenty-five relatives?" And they were like, "You need a permit." And so we were debating whether or not—well how about this? We get people to get the food and then we kind of like ask them to go a little away so they're not all congregated? And somebody else was like, "Well let's just say if we had fifty cups there, would they then say you have fifty cups, you're expecting more than twenty people?" . . . Well as far as I know, that might be why none of the other established Christian groups serve in the park.
>
> —Vikki, Lower East Side FNB, mid-1990s

with food handler's permits, if it's easy enough to get a permit, why not just do that? As long as we're not changing what we do to meet their requirements." But, we discovered that, in fact, that was just a red herring that they were throwing out. They just didn't want Food Not Bombs happening.

"You know you're not allowed to do this, right?" the officer said, from the driver's seat, through her passenger-side window . . . "No, actually I didn't know that," said Sarah. I think Sarah tried to offer a short explanation, which seemed like it irritated the police officer, who said that if we wanted to argue, she could make more of an issue of it and give us all tickets. I didn't think Sarah was being particularly argumentative, but she was not agreeing with the officer's basic premise, so maybe that's enough to call arguing? I tried a different tactic, and asked the officer if I could ask a question . . . from a significant distance, of course, but as politely and nonconfrontationally as I could. She seemed a bit more amenable to that—her tone softened ever so slightly. I said that we had in fact looked into the law, and [had] not found any laws that we were breaking, and so I was curious if the officer could tell us what the relevant laws were that we should look into . . . She replied fairly bluntly that there were "a lot of grey areas" involved, which was why, she said, she wasn't going to get out of the car and make more of an issue of the whole thing. But she said she felt like she wouldn't be doing her job if she didn't tell us we weren't supposed to be doing this.

—Author's field notes, FNB, Seattle, February 9, 2010

All of this has the effect of a ban. Outdoor meal projects in Seattle have historically been consequently unpermitted in all but a single Outdoor Meal Site. In fact, that particular spot was not within the jurisdiction of the parks code or other "civility" ordinances anyway because, as we saw in scene 4, it's under the freeway.

Less subtle, more direct legal instruments such as Orlando's ordinance or the one implemented by Las Vegas in 2006 help make crystal clear the logic behind the ban. Orlando's law legally recognizes citizens' entitlement to an ill-defined "aesthetically pleasing atmosphere." Of course, this invokes the interests of style and symbolic economy described in the last chapter. Even more brazenly, Las Vegas punished citizens for sharing food in the park with "the indigent," defined as anyone "whom a reasonable ordinary person would believe to be entitled to apply for or receive" public assistance (quoted in Archibold 2006). In other words, the ordinance literally obstructs food from circulating freely across class boundaries.

It is worth noting that such prohibitions have been challenged in court on numerous occasions, with mixed results. In 2011, for example, the Eleventh Circuit Court upheld the Orlando ordinance, overturning a previous ruling that Orlando's arrest of FNB participants violated their freedom of speech (United States Court of Appeals for the Eleventh Circuit 2011; cf. American Civil Liberties Union 2008). Encouragingly, however, in August 2018 another Eleventh Circuit Court seemed to disagree, ruling that the arrest of several Fort Lauderdale FNB activists did indeed constitute a violation of protected speech (United States Court of Appeals for the Eleventh Circuit 2018). It remains to be seen whether future rulings will again reverse this. It is worth noting that neither of these rulings had any impact whatsoever on the status quo in Seattle, where food sharing is not prohibited by the same legal mechanisms.

Nonetheless, whether through direct interdiction, as in Orlando and Las Vegas, or through indirect refusal, as in Seattle, the forbidden gift constitutes a mechanism of biopolitical production that bans those people, things, and forms of exchange that represent disorder with respect to the market-public's aesthetic and economic norms. Indeed, if the right to exist, as Jeremy Waldron (1991) has argued, is tantamount to the right to occupy space, then the spatial exclusions of outdoor meal projects from public spaces like parks are tantamount to a refusal of the right of hungry people to exist as public, political entities. In this way, such mechanisms establish the order of these cities' symbolic economies as well as the "broken windows" against whose outline they are defined.

"WHEREAS, the City of Orlando encourages use of City owned or controlled parks by City residents in *a safe, sanitary, and aesthetically pleasing atmosphere*; and

"WHEREAS, unregulated large group feeding in public parks in the *Downtown Community Redevelopment Area* (CRA) has resulted in litter on park grounds and surrounding rights-of-way such as food, containers, and other food wrappings creating *hazards to the health and welfare of citizens*, and is *detrimental to the aesthetic atmosphere of parks* . . .

" . . . now therefore, be it ordained by the city council of the City of Orlando, Florida: [. . .]

"It is *unlawful to knowingly sponsor, conduct, or participate in the distribution or service of food* at a large group feeding at a park or park facility owned or controlled by the City of Orlando within the boundary of the CRA without a Large Group Feeding Permit issued by the park official . . .

" . . . *Not more than two (2) Large Group Feeding Permits shall be issued* to the same person, group, or organization for large group feedings for the same park in the CRA in a twelve (12) consecutive month period."

—Chapter 18a, Parks and Outdoor Public Assemblies, Code of the City of Orlando

"That's Not My Constituency": Locating the Outdoor Meal Site

At Sixth Avenue and Columbia Street, shrouded in the perpetual shadow of Interstate 5, beyond the sun's compass as it sets over the Puget Sound and turns the rest of downtown to gold, is the only place in Seattle where strangers were, for many years, sanctioned to share food with each other with any great scope or regularity. Behind several towering cement pillars, where the asphalt parking lot rises to meet the underside of the six-lane freeway, a chain-link fence marked the threshold between the city proper and its surplus shadow economy. Seattle's Outdoor Meal Site offers a window onto the realpolitik of keeping up a city's world-class image.

The Outdoor Meal Site, 2010. Gifts are forbidden beyond the shadow of the interstate.

In other words, the place-making politics behind the Outdoor Meal Site (capitalized on the city's web pages) offer a telling example of the mechanisms of biopolitical production at work, fashioning a market-public that reproduces the aesthetic, economic, and political norms of life in a global city—with respect to which the unchecked conglomeration of poor people appears as a broken window. The negative space implied by this public outlines exceptional spaces, subjects, and things that must be quarantined in order for it to function. Their geography, as I describe in this section, owes its existence to an outright refusal of permission in conjunction with the exercise of softer sorts of power—through ad hoc task forces, resident complaints, nonprofit partnerships, and occasional police pressure. These exceptional spaces circumscribe the geography of survival for many unlucky Seattleites.

It took at least four months in the winter of 2004 to decide on a new location for Seattle's Outdoor Meal Site. For those four months, no public food sharing was allowed anywhere, after which a provisional location was secured before the eventual long-term site could be agreed upon. An ad hoc task force spent that time searching in good faith for a safe, accessible place for the endeavor. As locations were proposed, according to two task force members I interviewed, businesses, residents, city agencies, and homeless service providers registered their respective opinions and concerns about them. By contrast, the direct input of homeless people themselves was largely absent from the task force. As one member told me, having suggested to one unsympathetic city councilor that the Outdoor Meal Site might be expanded into a larger indoor-outdoor social justice center, the councilor retorted bluntly, "Over my dead body ... that's not my constituency." (To their credit, Operation Sack Lunch, which manages the Outdoor Meal Site, continued to push for a better, purpose-built location. In its absence, however, the freeway represented the best available compromise.) Guided by such selective consultation, therefore, the committee was remapping one crucial aspect of the geography of survival in the city along the exclusionary lines of tenancy and investment. In other words, it redrew the boundaries for the nonmarket circulation of food. And it did so with an ear for the complaints of Seattle's market-public over those of marginalized and displaced diners in the city.

This constituency of tenants and investors found a willing ally in City Hall. Then-Mayor Greg Nickels framed himself as a "pro-business" mayor and was openly concerned about the impact of homelessness on the business climate. He had such an antagonistic, vexed relationship with home-

I went to City Council and said, "Why don't we turn this into a social justice center? What a win-win is this? To have a social justice center that feeds people . . . and the social justice center would also have hygiene, it would also have different parts of the building that were used for, you know, maybe domestic violence" . . . And one of the City Council members looked at me and said, "Over my dead body." And they're no longer a City Council member, but, you know, this was a few years ago, but it was: "That's not my constituency. They're not the ones who are voting me into this office, so I'm not even going to think about all the people who are disenfranchised."

—Seattle homeless advocate on participating in the ad hoc task force to locate the Outdoor Meal Site

less advocates that one tent city was eventually named after him: Nickelsville (evoking the Depression-era Hoovervilles). A few homeless advocates privately confided in me that they had heard Nickels describe outdoor meals as "undignified." So, when the OMS's predecessor, a walled plaza at the Public Health and Safety building, closed down in 2004 and the building was scheduled for demolition, Nickels refused to sanction another one. Citing the usual "health and safety" concerns,[13] he effectively banned all complimentary outdoor meals in the city. This ban went over like a ton of bricks with many advocates, meal providers, and diners. Along with sympathetic City Council members, they protested by continuing to distribute food outdoors in City Hall Park in a surprising coincidence of political clout and civil disobedience. "The interesting thing about that moment," according to one of the protesting meal providers, "was it [got] a lot of publicity—every news station in Seattle. But all the City Council came down, rolled up their sleeves, and served the meal. So, you know, the mayor was embarrassed." After a few weeks, Nickels agreed to reinstate the Outdoor Meal Site and called together the committee that, after deliberation, negotiation, and experimentation,[14] decided on the ultimate OMS.

Still, its continued existence was never secure. In 2012, Dannette Smith, the director of the Seattle Human Services Department, echoed Greg Nickels in deed and word, calling the Outdoor Meal Site "inhumane" and "undignified," and proposing to shut it down. Like Nickels, she relented (Burkhalter 2012), and the Outdoor Meal Site persisted at Sixth and Columbia until 2020. But as this book goes to press, it appears that such views have finally held sway, and the Outdoor Meal Site has in recent months been replaced by the combination of a mobile meal kitchen and the ambiguously named Open Meal Service (retaining the acronym OMS), located apparently indoors in a "safe, permanent, and sheltered meal site" (Operation Sack Lunch n.d.).

Ardent prejudices against homeless people from concerned citizens and businesses had always made determining the tenuous location of the ultimate Outdoor Meal Site especially hard, particularly in and around Pioneer Square. As another 2004 task force member told me, "We looked at a number of sites . . . But it was very contentious, and not pleasant, to work with people who said very unkind things about low-income and homeless people." The search was protracted as various proposed locations were rejected out of wariness of complaints from neighboring stakeholders. This is in keeping with a pattern: as Timothy Gibson (2004) has documented, Seattle business elites may exercise strikingly direct behind-the-scenes influence on the location of homeless services.[15] And more generally, Not-in-My-Backyard resistance often consigns new homeless services to those neighborhoods with the least political and economic clout (Brinegar 2003). In a similar fashion, the concerns of stakeholders like Pioneer Square businesses directly inform the policies that affect shelterless people in the neighborhood and represent some of the driving forces that put the issue of outdoor meals on city government's agenda in the first place. One longtime city employee gave a particularly enlightening explanation of the political process by which outdoor meals end up in the City Council's crosshairs:

> I mean, essentially, it's difficult to site things that are connected to homeless people. Pioneer Square is the historic area that's perceived as the place for homeless people. Pioneer Square has stated in the last twenty years that they have more than their share. And that any new program involving homeless people should be elsewhere. Because they have missions, they have shelters, and it isn't sort of the "go spend a day with the homeless people" place. They want to try to revitalize their neighborhood.
>
> —Participant in the Outdoor Meal Site ad hoc task force, on the group's decision-making process

> Complaints are made by residents or tourists—but residents certainly have more sway. And the complaints go to the police. And the police say they can't do anything about it. And so then the complaints may go to public health. And they'll say they can't do much about it. So then they go to a City Council member or to the mayor. And if enough of those complaints kind of pile up . . . if complaints reach a certain level, and the mayor feels that he or she or a Council member will try to do something about it, they'll convene a team of people of the city. . . . As I went through different mayors, it seemed like after about a year, a new mayor would say, "Here's this problem, what are you going to do about it?" And so then they would bring in others who are stakeholders to see what can be done.

In this case, "residents" explicitly refers to both commercial establishments and people living in the neighborhood. This is telling. In the fi-

Pioneer Square convenience store, 2017. Not far from Occidental Park, this store has served homeless locals for more than fifteen years. They sell socks, hygiene products, canned food, high-carbohydrate snacks, beer, wine, and other items in high demand by rough sleepers. In my time, Food Not Bombs spent a *lot* of money here on plastic cups, plates, and utensils.

nal analysis, city government's constituency is framed in terms of a market-mediated territoriality. (Territory, after all, is more than just space; it comprises specific vectors of power and claim-making [Sassen 2011].) Homeless and hungry people, therefore, are not afforded the same territorial constituency as businesses and residents with titles, leases, and formal lobbying groups. The anxieties and prejudices of these squeaky wheels carry more weight. Through such channels, homeowners' associations, neighborhood organizations, business communities, and so on are made legible as constituencies to city officials. They lay claim to the protections of government in a way that shelterless people cannot. (And this in spite of Seattle's long-standing history of organized activism by and for unhoused residents.) They are, in effect, afforded a kind of tenancy-cum-citizenship.

This tenant citizenship is consonant with the market-public articulated by public officials and the symbolic economies upon which they stake their cities' success. Thus do city politicians and civil servants imagine the city's well-being as synonymous with the health of its businesses, shoppers, and property owners, who become legible as job creators, as taxpayers, as residents, and so on. In this imaginary, homelessness and free public meals seem to be little more than noise or disorder.

Keeping Matter in Its Place

Yet noise can be provocative. The anxieties provoked in the process of locating Seattle's Outdoor Meal Site continue to percolate and periodically erupt at those junctures where competing modes of eating in public collide. Like the OMS itself, these conflicts variously reassert and test the place-making efforts of city officials and local businesses. Food Not Bombs has therefore continued to experience occasional, inconsistent phases of police pressure, receiving repeated visits in 2001 and 2008, for example. As Koa, who volunteered during both periods, told me, "It would go in spurts. You know, sometimes it would last for a month or two. And sometimes for five or six months nothing would happen." Like the feeding prohibitions that inform them, these conflicts often reassert the legitimacy of tenancy and investment to define the public life of the city and articulate the scope of the possible—establishing de jure and de facto geographies of eating in the city. It is also significant that sharing prohibitions in particular often focus on one of the few notionally public forms of urban territory: parks.[16] Unlike even libraries and footpaths, whose purposes are clearly delineated, parks represent urban spaces wherein the vectors of power and claim-making are by definition more heterogeneous, and the outcome of these conflicts therefore more pivotal.

One period of regular police contact with Seattle Food Not Bombs, for example, in 2001, resulted from a protracted, if somewhat one-sided antagonism between the group and one Pioneer Square resident, who for some months called the police any time he saw FNB handing out food in Occidental Park. Volunteers discovered the impetus for these visits only after swapping their faded black T-shirts and political patches for collared shirts and attending, incognito, a meeting of the Pioneer Square Community Association, where the resident admitted to making the calls. His sentiments, of course, were not isolated. According to Patricia (whom we met in the introduction):

> There was a time that some members of [Food Not Bombs] would go down and attend some of the neighborhood meetings there that the city would sponsor. And a lot of the issues that were being discussed was what to do about the park and what to do about factors that ended up being distressing to business owners or potential shoppers. So usually it was in the midst of those discussions that people would express frustration with our group. Because we definitely weren't discouraging the homeless from being in that area. And that's one thing that they were trying to do was make that area much more pro-business.

Partly in deference to the same kinds of prejudices, the phase of police pressure on Food Not Bombs to vacate the park in 2008 was motivated directly and explicitly by instructions from Mayor Nickels's office, according to the police officers, parks workers, and meal providers with whom we spoke. Whether they are motivated by concerned tenant-citizens like the cranky Pioneer Square resident or by the explicit directives of elected officials, these pressures produce an officially sanctioned geography of survival. Consequently, relatively few rogue meal projects besides Food Not Bombs have challenged it for any length of time.[17]

Feeding prohibitions and complementary projects like the Outdoor Meal Site therefore represent a fulcrum in the biopolitical production of urban lives and economies. Although they are relatively minor expressions of municipal sovereignty and resources, their reach is great. Compare, for example, the occasional periods of police pressure on Seattle Food Not Bombs—with nary an arrest in twenty-five years—with the $2.3 million or more Seattle spent over a five-year period on ordinances that more directly criminalize homelessness, such as Seattle's anti-sitting ordinance (Howard, Tran, and Rankin 2015) or the million-dollar contract with private companies the city signed in 2017 to dismantle Seattle's homeless encampments (Olsen 2017). And yet, despite their modest scale, they have capacious implications for public life. Although they are not routinely or consistently enforced, they define a public territory that is, in principle, citywide, and they mandate within it certain forms of economic life, the only exception to which is the Outdoor Meal Site.

The tacit legitimacy of this arrangement for much of the city can be perhaps best gauged by the intensive response to its suspension, described in the previous section: when Nickels attempted to suspend the OMS, activists, politicians, and news media responded viscerally and immediately, and the mayor was forced to relent. That ardent, motley coalition, however, wasn't fighting for the freedom for strangers to share food anywhere in the city. Rather, they were calling for the maintenance of a *single exception* to the otherwise hegemonic rule that food of any appreciable quantity must change hands outdoors by private acquaintance or commercial exchange. Having achieved that, they accepted this exception as a victory. As the director of the OMS told me, they were obliged to observe the political process: "You don't have to agree," she said, "but you have to respect that there are other views." Nonetheless, that process itself depoliticizes the segregated geographies of eating in the city (see Spataro 2016).

Through concrete processes like these, the anxieties and prejudices of a globalizing city's tenants-cum-constituents, and the larger symbolic economies of which they are microcosms, are inscribed in the territory of the city. They map out strategic places to assert their claims, leaving other, more marginal spaces where both people and things that are unwelcome downtown are allowed to move more freely. Pioneer Square is just such a strategic territory in Seattle's symbolic economy, where rescue missions, low-rent hotels, homeless drop-in centers, and so on compete for space with historical tourism, property development, and information technology businesses. Particularly in such contested places, the geography of eating and surviving downtown becomes a key site of political struggle, both for producing Seattle's market-public and for constructing a geography of survival for those excluded from it. It is also this struggle that represents the *content* of the mass conspiracy that is Food Not Bombs—a point to which we will return in the next chapter.

Discipline and Expertise: The Meals Partnership Coalition

Once a month, on a Thursday, in the shadow of yet another freeway, a coterie of advocates, social service providers, and nonprofit staff meet to talk about sharing food in Seattle. They sit in a large circle in a meeting room at a homeless drop-in center in Pioneer Square, adjacent to the Highway 99 viaduct where dozens of rough sleepers take shelter. Sometimes there's coffee. Aptly, sometimes there's free food.

It's a winter morning in 2010. On this occasion, maybe fifteen or twenty people are at the Meals Partnership Coalition general meeting. Officially they're here to discuss "current triumphs, difficulties, and ideas surrounding meal provisions" in the city (Meals Partnership Coalition n.d.). Most of them seem to recognize each other and know the drill. They're mainly in their forties or fifties. Almost all of them are white, unlike the rough sleepers who wander in from the cold. The meeting starts with introductions for the newcomers: the Union Gospel Mission, the Chicken Soup Brigade, Food Lifeline, the Hunger Intervention Program, St. Paul's Archdiocese of Seattle, the Phinney Neighborhood Association, the Seattle Indian Center, the Young Women's Christian Association, Angeline's Day Center, and the Millionaire Club Charity. They're all local meal programs, congregations, shelters, community centers, or nonprofit organizations committed to food security. Nominally the Coalition includes dozens of organizations, although they clearly don't all come to meetings regularly. Representatives are here from the Census Bureau and the City of Seattle too.

And then there's me. I'm representing Food Not Bombs.

This is a little uncomfortable. It's the first time in perhaps a decade that anyone from FNB has come to a Coalition meeting, and there are reasons for that. To be sure, we all care about hunger. And for my part, I have a suitable respect for the decades many of them have devoted to homeless advocacy and service. But in some critical ways, we are at cross-purposes. The Meals Partnership Coalition, and its parent organization, Operation Sack Lunch, illustrate the slightly Faustian bargain many advocacy coalitions and service providers make with city government. It's a bargain most Food Not Bombs collaborators will not countenance. The compromise makes it possible for the Coalition to serve as a crucial mouthpiece for people experiencing homelessness and food insecurity, and they've won significant concessions from the Council, not to mention funding. But having the ear of the city comes at a cost. The Coalition is entangled in the realpolitik of governance and commerce that molds the city's geographies of eating and surviving. Perhaps even more than the police, groups like the MPC play a constitutive role in transmitting the biopolitical forces that animate municipal sharing restrictions and reproducing the social and spatial order of the global city. Not only do they extend governmental optics and influence over the populations they serve; they also share a role in conditioning and legitimating some modes of eating and sharing in public while excluding others.

In concrete terms, their compromise is twofold. First, like advocacy coalitions whose members I have met in Melbourne and San Francisco, the Coalition must observe—and even enforce—the conventions, explicit and informal, of city agencies. And second, like other coalitions, they are obliged to be careful about what they endorse publicly. They mustn't speak too stridently against the wrong politicians, and they most certainly can't routinely flout the law or capitalist property relations à la FNB. These consequences correspond roughly to two definitive aspects of biopolitical production: first, its disciplinary mode, which conditions bodies and practices; and second, its discursive mode, which produces and legitimizes certain norms and expertise. In both of these ways, Craig Willse suggests that a broad "homeless services industry" plays a crucial role in producing the "housing monster" that perpetuates homelessness (2015, 1). The Meals Partnership Coalition is necessarily part of that industry.

> The institutionalized groups, the charities, they just won't touch Food Not Bombs with a ten-foot pole. The San Francisco coalition is somewhat supportive, but even they couldn't quite figure out what to do with us . . . I was on the staff eventually. So they knew what was going on [with Food Not Bombs], and they were generally supportive, and occasionally wrote stuff in the *Street Sheet* about what was going on. But, you know, the Coalition on Homelessness in San Francisco, like most of them, is mostly a coalition of nonprofit service providers. That's their primary constituency, as much as they try to involve homeless people or whatever. And those groups were scared to death of touching something so overtly political. So they weren't about to start organizing—what were they going to do? Organize homeless people to get arrested, serving food? That wasn't really their charge anyways, so at least they didn't speak badly about [Food Not Bombs], or do stuff behind our backs that was bad, which I think has happened in some other cities. So they never did that. Rhetorically, if asked, they always spoke positively about us. Of course people shouldn't be arrested for giving away free food.
>
> —Allan, San Francisco FNB, San Francisco Coalition for the Homeless, ca. 1990

Yet this proximity to power affords the Coalition the capacity to do crucial work. After all, whereas Food Not Bombs might serve dozens of people each week—up to one hundred on an especially long night—Operation Sack Lunch alone has shared more than 3 million meals in its quarter-century of existence.[18] It supplies 48 percent of the city's emergency meals (and continues to feed people even in the midst of a pandemic). In practice, the Coalition comprises a robust network for distributing resources and knowledge. (At today's meeting, for example, somebody has forty thousand recently donated tiny bars of hotel soap to share with other members.) Perhaps even more crucially, the Coalition is a powerful vector of resistance against the more severe forces of city administration. When Mayor Nickels shut down the Outdoor Meal Site—and later when the Human Services director threatened to do so again—these people were some of those who raised the alarm and kept on defiantly sharing food, as I described earlier. And not long after today's meeting, when the City Council will seem poised to cut funding for homeless services, these are the people who will intervene for a better budget. For all these reasons, FNB will send a delegate to these meetings off and on for a few more months. But the relationship will prove untenable. Our scavenging, civil disobedience, and decentralized organization don't lend themselves to the Coalition's disciplinary or discursive functions.

For my purposes here, the Coalition's most pertinent role is to advance the Outdoor Meal Site, channeling hungry Seattleites and meal providers alike to the underside of the freeway. In so doing, they necessarily reproduce the spatial and social segregation of the city. Thus, Coalition members do occasional outreach to noncompliant groups like FNB, encouraging them to relocate to Sixth and Columbia. It was one such visit, in fact, that brought me to today's meeting. I told the Coalition member we preferred to stay in Occidental Park, and he nonetheless said we'd be welcome at their general meetings. We accepted tentatively. It was unclear whether he knew this was a conversation we'd had several times before over the preceding decades. In fact, during the mid-1990s, FNB members even accepted the invitation, relocating briefly to a previous incarnation of the Outdoor Meal Site at Fourth Avenue and Cherry Street. Patricia, who volunteered with FNB at the time, explained why the site wasn't suitable: "We struggled with that decision for a while, ended up saying, 'Let's give it a try.' And a lot of people came to the meals. But one of the things that we decided was that by and large it wasn't the *same* people who were coming to the meals [as in Occidental Park]." In other words, the site did not accommodate a broad enough population. Moreover, FNB objected to their segregation. "There was this kind of big, physical barrier around it," she said, "so you could even barely see what was going on in that plaza just from the street—you'd drive right by it." Thus, FNB rejected the site's disciplinary and discursive implications, containing generosity and obscuring poverty from the public sphere. (Although in more recent years FNB members *have* reached out to Operation Sack Lunch about other vectors of collaboration, such as sharing kitchen space.)

The most immediate subjects of this disciplinary function are the diners themselves. Corrina contrasted her FNB experience with the ways in which diners are managed and marked at some more traditional nonprofits: "I volunteered for another free meal program once and they actually had the volunteers eat first in front of the waiting 'clients,'" she explained. "Along with who they recruit for helping and the attitude that giving food comes with the right to demand folks pray first, don't cuss, etcetera, this is . . . not an act of solidarity." Behind these coercions, Corrina recognized the imperatives of a market-public, "the insistence on calling folks 'clients,' as if making it capitalist helps them have a legitimate relationship and place in the world."

As Piven and Cloward argued in their seminal *Regulating the Poor* (1971), government-sanctioned relief in market societies has never been solely a matter of generosity; dating all the way back to the Tudor Vagrancy Acts, it has always contained unrest and disciplined the poor themselves. Sanctioned charity therefore usually has strings attached. It's a lopsided gift exchange: the "deserving" poor who are its beneficiaries owe a debt of compliance in order to earn their lunch. Insofar as it takes on this disciplinary function and picks up slack where neoliberal reforms have scaled back government safety nets, the Meals Partnership Coalition fits Maggie Dickinson's description of nonprofit meal providers as an outsourced "third tier" of the welfare state (2014, 118).

> So our center gets a lot of their funding from the city. And the city is getting pressure from all the Pioneer Square businesses on that particular block of the street, because there are a lot of homeless people that hang out there because of the center and because of the nearby shelter. So the Pioneer Square businesses are bitching about all the homeless people hanging out, and they get mad at the city. Well, the city wants to placate the businesses, and so then they talk to the center . . . and then the center has to act. So it's just this filter. And they ask their—the people that come in often hang out in the street—and we ask people not to hang out in the street and we try to institute a lot of various ways of getting people to not hang out on the sidewalk.
>
> —Roxanne, former Seattle homeless services employee, ca. 2004

Not only are people experiencing food insecurity therefore diverted from public spaces by Seattle's feeding restrictions; they are also funneled into spaces of surveillance and management. Aside from the police who might patrol the Outdoor Meal Site, Meals Partnership Coalition partners facilitate such surveillance and management in a range of ways. There are some humanitarian reasons for this, of course. The longest conversation on today's meeting agenda, for example, is about how advocates should tally Seattle's ever-growing shelterless population during the city's annual "One Night Count" of the unhoused population. Coalition members can even shield their clients from the state's gaze in some ways. (At the meeting we learn that if clients don't want to use their real names, they can write "Emily Person" on their Census form instead.) Surveillance is never innocent of biopower, however, and enumerating the homeless can foster a nonprofit industry that reproduces rather than challenges the principles of a capitalist housing crisis (Willse 2015). Moreover, Coalition partners are forced to participate in more Kafkaesque sorts of tallies, like the federally mandated Homeless Management Information System database that logs the lifetime use of services by specific individuals.[19]

A humanitarian argument can also be made for concentrating emergency meals, along with other resources, in a single location in order to streamline users' access. According to one ad hoc task force member quoted earlier, for example, "Mayor Nickels . . . felt [that free meals] should be more appropriately provided indoors, connected with services. And I think in an ideal world, that is absolutely true." Many shelterless people would appreciate more convenient access to a continuum of services; however, the obligatory connection between those services and *indoor* assistance reflects a coercive logic of spatial management whose effect is to contain homeless bodies. Moreover, this rationale promotes the widespread paternalist myth that the homeless lack the agency or interest to seek appropriate help and must be disciplined into doing so. From local pundits to national experts, policymakers are often quite candid about this paternalistic assumption.[20] As the Atlanta Department of Public Safety put it, in a flyer distributed after two Food Not Bombs volunteers had been ticketed for sharing food, "Many people *become dependent* on these activities, leading them to stay on the streets instead of seeking the help and support they truly need" (Jilani 2017; my emphasis). This myth not only implies that they are homeless by choice, it also ignores the considerable agency it takes to survive without stable shelter and the ways in which such coercive management can *undermine*, rather than empower, that agency.[21] In this way, meal providers are by implication enrolled in the disciplinary functions of government.

The Meals Partnership Coalition also has disciplinary effects on its own members, reproducing the norms and expertise of institutional charity. Coalition meetings thus represent a micropolitical, "capillary" vector of biopower (Foucault 1980, 96). Although, to their credit, members welcome FNB and the chair makes it clear after today's meeting that, whether or not we choose to move to the OMS, we can expect a seat at the table, in informal ways they would nonetheless prefer to bring FNB into line with the norms of state-sanctioned charity. This is understandable, and yet limiting. Take, for example, one Coalition member's offer to help Food Not Bombs find a new kitchen. Upon learning that our current cooking space is closing, he generously offers to ask around. But he insists that he will do so only if FNB agrees not to share dumpster-dived food. We won't take him up on the offer.

It's a redundant stipulation—at this moment our food is exclusively donated by stalls at Pike Place—but it illustrates the micropolitical, capillary scale of power. At heart, his is a genuine, understandable concern for food safety (although he seems to wholly misunderstand the art and science of dumpster-diving). As another Coalition member reminded me, "The fact is that when someone is driving up to a street corner and putting down a pot of chili that has been sitting on their oven, on top of their burner, for twelve hours, unheated, that somebody's going to get poisoned and might even die." But tellingly, the request isn't framed in terms of food safety. Had it been, nobody in Food Not Bombs would have objected. Indeed, many FNB collaborators, having worked in the food service industry, possess Washington State food handlers' permits. And as Ingrate points out, "Health inspectors have actually shown up to Food Not Bombs meals in the past and found nothing that they could actually cite Food Not Bombs for really." Rather than enquire about food safety, however, the Coalition member challenges the group's fundamental scavenging-sharing economy. In some small way he is reasserting the norms of market exchange and coding alternative economic practices as deviant.

> SPD . . . were fucking with us pretty good and they called the Health Department. And the Health Department came out. But the guy was actually pretty cool. He's just like, "Yeah I'm not here to bust your balls or anything but you guys got to do this and this. But we can totally appreciate and understand what you guys are doing." So, I mean, they were totally cool about it and they never came back. . . . There's a church group that came out, and the Health Department busted *them,* though. It was pretty funny. And this church group was always coming up to us and trying to offer us food. And totally trying to preach to us, and give us tracts and stuff out of their little handbills or whatever. And it got to be a point where they'd show up, and it's like "Oh, hey, have you heard of the word of Jesus Christ? Blah blah blah." It was like, "No, you guys want some tofu?" Ha.
>
> —Koa, Seattle Food Not Bombs, ca. 2001

Moreover, this positions the Coalition as a gatekeeper with the legitimacy and know-how to share food. In this way, the Coalition enacts a form of institutional authority. (This idea partly explains why the city consults advocates and service providers on decisions like the location of the Outdoor Meal Site rather than consulting homeless people themselves.) This expertise is necessarily conservative and leery of difference, leading some Coalition members to take a skeptical attitude toward what they call (not without reason) "drive-by" meal programs. As the meal provider quoted a second ago put it, "There's a lot of crazy people out there that could poison homeless people just because they don't want them in the world anymore."

This fear is the same kind of stranger danger that deters parents from sending children trick-or-treating—even though the evidence lends no credence to the poisoned candy of urban legend, and suggests that strangers are no more likely than known parties to abuse children (Best 1993). Although its merits as a risk-management strategy are unclear, this sort of caution effectively attenuates practices of economic generosity-in-public and stigmatizes efforts at grassroots mutual aid—despite strong evidence that such approaches have important benefits.[22] Such a confluence of discipline and expertise therefore places a brake on the engagement of a wider public in sharing and mutual aid, and it renders illegible or illegitimate alternative forms of organization and economic practice such as Food Not Bombs.

Conclusion

Virginia Woolf once ventured out across London on the thin pretext of needing a new pencil. Perhaps she had just read the sociologist Georg Simmel. For Simmel ([1903] 2002), relations of commerce and consumption were the pretext for most urban relations. Whether it bought pencils or built office complexes, he believed that the spirit of the financial transaction was what lent city life its impersonal, anonymous character. But where Simmel saw a mercenary, calculating sort of alienation, Woolf was a keen flâneuse. "As we step out of the house on a fine evening between four and six," she wrote, "we shed the self our friends know us by and become part of that vast republican army of anonymous trampers, whose society is so agreeable after the solitude of one's own room" ([1927] 2016, 1). For Woolf, one's home was full of stiflingly inalienable objects (an impulsively purchased china bowl on the mantelpiece, a brown stain on the carpet, and so on), every bit as anchored to memories, relationships, and obligations as a ritual *kula* exchange in the Trobriand Islands, half a world away. In contrast, she took comfort in the perfectly alienable company of the crowd.

Both writers describe the production of an urban public. In many ways, the two contemporaries describe the *same* public: that of the great occidental metropolis, full of impersonal objects (like pencils) and anonymous passersby. Yet they inflect this public differently, with communion or calculation, amity or anomie. Perfectly alienable from one another, these "anonymous trampers" may resolve into the solidarity of perfect strangers or into the transactional disinterest of a market-public. What determines the character of its anonymity?

In a way, this is the question I have been asking throughout this chapter. Surely, one answer lies in the way we eat and share food in the city. Not unlike Woolf and Simmel, Michael Warner described a public as a relationship among strangers. Above, I argued that the gift of food changes the quality of our strangeness. The anthropologist Richard Wilk underscored this very point before a Florida appeals court in defense of the Fort Lauderdale Food Not Bombs volunteers described earlier. He wrote, "gifting and sharing are important acts of communication in all human societies. Gifts of food are particularly meaningful" (Wilk 2017, 154).

The forbidden gift, then, makes a particularly meaningful statement about the quality of public life and economy. Chasing global capital and heavily investing in a vision of world-class prosperity and quality of life, city officials and constituents alike feel actively threatened by competing visions of public life. Many policymakers have therefore aggressively prosecuted those conspicuous modes of living and surviving in the city that offend a market-public's sensibilities: informal exchange; public food sharing; economies of largesse and mutual aid built from those people and things rendered superfluous by the prevailing norms of capitalism; and so on. Sharing prohibitions in Seattle and dozens of other cities therefore contribute to the formation of metropolitan market-publics and insulate them from their unwanted surplus goods and abject others. These banished people and things are contained at the peripheries of urban life, along with those nonmarket forms of economic life that represent matter-out-of-place with respect to the city's world-class image. These exceptional modes of living are either prohibited outright or geographically marginalized in the city's symbolic economy—consigned to those territories on the city's map not already claimed by influential players within the market-public. Officially, in Seattle, this has typically meant under the freeway. Elsewhere in the city, feeding prohibitions also make it harder for people to share food with one another in any but the most narrowly circumscribed way. In other words, feeding prohibitions ensure that if food in any significant quantity changes hands in public, it is not free. And by the same token, if food *is* free (meaning both wasted and given away), it is not in public. It can be donated to meal programs and served under the auspices of these meal providers—but indoors or out of view.

The production of these lived urban economies—both the market-public that dominates the urban imagination and the shadow economies of surplus people and things contained under the pall of freeways and drop-in centers—is the work of biopolitical production. Public officials, government agencies, and private charities work in conjunction to recast public life in these molds, to divorce the society of anonymous trampers from the largesse of perfect strangers. City-sanctioned networks of meal providers, like Seattle's Meals Partnership Coalition, assume the exclusive mantle of authorized charity and discourage the city-goers' inclinations to unrestrained mutual aid. Spaces of exception, like Seattle's single Outdoor Meal Site, prove the rule of market exchange across the rest of the city's public spaces. In this way, cities like Seattle produce the very "broken windows" that cause them so much alarm. Homelessness, hunger, and other abject modes of being-in-the-city are forged in a negative dialectic with the aspirational city. They are literally unimaginable in their present form without reference to the conventions of a world-class market-public—not only in an epistemological sense but also in a very practical one: feeding prohibitions and other means of effectively "criminalizing" homelessness simply make it harder for people without property or money to eat, and therefore to regain that private existence that the market-public so privileges.

Coda: Other Futures for the City

Lest it seem that I'm overstating my case, a variation of my utopian thought experiment from chapter 1 might help. Imagine the explosive growth of hunger and shelterlessness that has characterized cities like Seattle, San Francisco, New York, and to a lesser extent Melbourne, occurred instead in a city where people regularly shared food with strangers in public and where the abject capital abandoned by their high-ticket grocery and real estate markets was free to be reused by others who live on nonmarket terms—and where, therefore, the terms *squatting* and *dumpster-diving* were meaningless. Such a city is a surreal contradiction, of course, but it throws into relief the contradictions of our own.

It also raises new questions. Another kind of becoming-global is incipient in the observations I have made above. If I have outlined the work of government to produce a certain biopolitical order and its exceptional others, I have also described the conditions of possibility for the growth of the ranks of those others. As the number of people without shelter increases, as the incidence of food insecurity in the city escalates, the broken windows of the globalizing city play a more and more significant role in the political and cultural life of the city. In part III, I explore the cultural logic of these others who share a counterpublic relationship to the market-publics of the globalizing city. Therein lie other equally important sorts of life and labor, other equally compelling futures for the city. There bubbles the conspiracy at the heart of this book. The scorned surpluses of the global city are its inventory. The exceptional, overlooked spaces of the city, its cover. And the struggles over nonmarket sharing, the content of its conspiring—the forbidden gift, its call to arms.

The transformation of
waste is perhaps the oldest
preoccupation of man. Man
being the chosen alloy, he
must be reconnected,
via shit, at all cost.

—Patti Smith,
"25th Floor"

Artist's representation, Melbourne Food Not Bombs (2007).

PART III

SLOW INSUR-RECTION

FOOD NOT BOMBS

SCENE V

"RABBLE" ON THE GLOBAL STREET

"The evicted poor are at your door. Get used to it!" We're chanting. Those last four words are given a defiant, hoarse emphasis. It's about ten o'clock in the evening, and we're outside the Lord Mayor's house. We're on the footpath of one of Melbourne's well-kept inner suburbs, surrounded by stately houses with the shades drawn. It's a summer's eve and the air is still—aside from our remonstrations. There are perhaps a dozen of us, holding hand-painted banners, banging pots and pans, playing accordions, and making what could fairly be called a brouhaha. As it turns out, the mayor is inside, calling the police (although noise restrictions don't take effect until eleven). I was not expecting any of this when I woke up this morning.

It's early in 2017, and Lord Mayor Robert Doyle has just proposed to fine unhoused people for sleeping rough and leaving belongings unattended in the Central

"The evicted poor are at your door. Get used to it!" On the Lord Mayor's doorstep with accordions, Melbourne, 2017. (Photographer, anonymous, Creative Commons, *Insurrection News*, 2017)

Business District. It's an echo of similarly unkind ordinances in similarly world-class cities elsewhere, like the one that inspired Food Not Bombs' early struggles in San Francisco circa 1989. (More on that in a moment.) Because the mayor's proposal would disrupt what little slumber Melbourne's rough sleepers get, the organizers have taken the fight to Doyle's own place of rest. One cardboard sign reads, "No More Good Night's Sleep for the Idle Rich." I was invited to a "party" via a mysterious text message that told me to bring an instrument (hence the accordion). Only when I arrived at the rendezvous and saw the others—mostly punks and anarchists from earlier protests—did the penny drop. It's a more impromptu sort of direct action than my FNB days, but I stay on.

Tomorrow, as a counterpoint to the narrative that will emerge in the commercial news media, a celebratory account of tonight's events will appear on insurrectionnewsworldwide.com, along with several photographs and pixelated faces. In addition, my own after-the-fact contribution to the affair will be an offer to draft a communiqué to Doyle's neighbors, as some of my anarchist friends from Seattle have done after public disruptions, to cultivate latent sympathies among bystanders (or mitigate their antipathy). The rest agree, and a collaborator offers to deliver copies to the neighborhood's letterboxes tomorrow evening. (Some collaborators will later tell me that my letter was too polite—always my problem, I suppose.)

In the morning, Melbourne's *Herald Sun* newspaper will describe us as "homeless" and a "rabble" (e.g., Bolt 2017). And though it's true that many of the people here have experienced homelessness, the word *rabble* does no justice to their shared anarchist ideals and tactics. I'm not sure that enough of us are present to constitute a rabble, anyway. Still, the word *does* connote a spontaneous, decentralized, uncivil sort of political action, heedless of the norms of liberal protest. The sort of anarchic sovereignty that Hakim Bey (1985) might have called a temporary autonomous zone. So, in that sense, perhaps some of those here might take it as a compliment.

I'm reminded that in the era before liberal capitalism, the dissent of feudal serfs often took the form not of a *march* or a *demonstration* (the chief action words of today's mass-mediated protests), but of a *hurly-burly*, an onomatopoeic event defined by the cacophony of voices raised in anger (Woodbridge 2001). The word *rabble* has similar roots: it referred to a stream of undecipherable syllables. In this way, the rabble assembled tonight are echoing a long history of raucous poor people's movements, from the hurly-burlies of Tudor England to the *caceroladas* of Argentina's last financial crisis. (Indeed, I make this very point in my letter to Doyle's neighbors.) And although I suspect nobody here knows it, we are reinterpreting a scene from 1995 in which the volunteers of San Francisco Food Not Bombs assembled in front of Mayor Frank Jordan's house to do much the same thing for similar reasons (Parson 2010, 133).

Although all these events emerged from their own particular historical moments, the resonances between them are clear. The spontaneous, defiant logic of the relatively powerless, galvanized by economic precarity and moved to action by the state's provocation, represents a form of counterpower that, although illegible to liberal institutions, nonetheless has often shaped the course of capitalism. As Saskia Sassen (2012) puts it, the powerless can and do still *make history* even without acquiring power in any traditional sense. "Powerlessness is not simply an absolute condition that can be flattened into the absence of power," she writes. "People becoming present and, crucially, becoming visible to one another can alter the character of their powerlessness" (1). In global cities in particular, she argues, conditions are ripe to bring them together and make them visible to one another. It is the shared social and spatial geography of these cities, woven as they are into a global fabric of cultural, economic, and material flows, that makes such history-making possible. Sassen (2011) describes these global sites of resistance collectively as the "Global Street." Simultaneously many places and no place in particular, the Global Street is a "space of flows" (Castells 1996), incipient wherever the city connects grassroots forms of resistance around the world, whether in word or deed. For tonight, in this otherwise quiet neighborhood, we could say that the Global Street is right here.

In part, the powerless make history by provoking the powerful. Homeless dissent has often been afforded a backhanded respect by elites, for example. In the 1500s, England's "sturdy beggars" were imagined to be dissimulating in order to conceal a dangerously vast, seditious conspiracy (Woodbridge 2001). So, too, the train-hopping hobos of the nineteenth-century American West (DePastino 2003). And in 2017, on talkback radio a few days after our visit, Melbourne's Lord Mayor will warn that "this may well be part of a new wave" of protest, implying that we might even have been paid for our dissent (3AW 693 News Talk 2017). "These weren't homeless people, they were well-organized, they were protesters," he said, apparently ignorant of the long history of well-organized homeless protests. Doyle even did me the honor of describing my letter as "very, very sophisticated" and quoting my favorite line—about the hurly-burlies and caceroladas. Largely mistaken, he insisted that the whole affair was "not anything that was spur of the moment." But he was not wholly wrong insofar as the conditions of the Global Street have been a long time in the making.

FIVE YEARS EARLIER AND AN OCEAN AWAY, another iteration of the Global Street found expression in Seattle. Although far removed in many respects, in this instance a rowdy milieu of anarchists again mobilized, provoked partly by the treatment of the city's homeless and public encampments—most especially the dispersal of Seattle's chapter of the Occupy Wall Street movement. And again, city authorities would overstate this group's organization and the threat they posed to urban order.

May Day in Seattle 2012 was hardly what criminologists Wilson and Kelling imagined when they first wrote about the dangers of broken windows, but a lot of broken glass was certainly left to be cleaned up afterward. Deliberately battered to shards by a handful of masked, black-clad anticapitalists during the annual May Day march—commemorating international workers' struggles—the ruined downtown display windows of Niketown and Wells Fargo, and the revolving glass doors of the Seattle courthouse, seem like a far cry from Wilson and Kelling's cracked and boarded-up panes. But they are not unrelated. At the center of both their broken windows theory of policing and the black bloc's May Day vandalism is a shared fundamental belief: symbolic disruptions to public order are a threat to the routine workings of market society.

Echoing the narratives that circulated among activists after Seattle's chaotic World Trade Organization protests in 1999—when a few corporate windows were also smashed—a small counterpublic of Seattle anarchists buzzed privately about what many (though by no means all) felt was a palpable strike against capitalism on behalf of the workers. One local anarchist newspaper wrote: "This is what terrifies those who profit from us. Their worst nightmare is the reality of hundreds of people actively applauding, encouraging, participating in, and growing ecstatic at the sight of capital being attacked. They want to obscure this reality however possible, to prevent the contagion from spreading even further" (Tides of Flame 2012).

Meanwhile, a different, larger public bemoaned the "violence" inflicted on the built environment. One Seattle Police spokesperson opined, "It's such a shame that such a small group of individuals were able to hijack the event and dilute the message to one of violence" (Valdes and Johnston 2012). More dramatically, the manager of one vandalized store said she felt "almost like someone broke into my house" (Valdes and Johnston 2012). Officials and constituents alike repeated the word *violence* bitterly in contexts where *vandalism* would have been more precise.[1] That this disruption of urban aesthetics and property relations (and the expense primarily for several wealthy companies to replace their windows) seemed to merit such inflated rhetoric from *both* the insurrectionary anticapitalists *and* their detractors points out just how high the stakes have become for the maintenance of a symbolic order conducive to urban consumption.

High enough, indeed, that the FBI and local police authorities conducted joint raids on anarchists' houses in Seattle, Olympia, and Portland—complete with battering rams and flash grenades—to collect evidence for a grand jury ostensibly called to investigate the May Day vandalism (Kiley 2012; Plante 2012).[2] Up to eighty officers were supposedly involved in the raids, and the mere possession of anarchist literature and flyers was cited as evidence (Potter 2012a). Activists with no demonstrable connection to the vandalism were detained for months by the grand jury solely on the basis of political pamphlets and flyers collected during these raids. This fact demonstrates a monumental misunderstanding of anarchist politics: resonating with Lord Mayor Robert Doyle's warnings about the "new wave" of highly organized, sophisticated protests, the FBI described "anarchist extremists" more like an organized crime syndicate than the motley counterpublic of dissenting radicals I've come to know.[3] Both Doyle and the FBI reflect a certain paranoia about the fragility of the social order of cities like Seattle or Melbourne, and the capacity of raucous, symbolic disruption to undermine it.

Here, as in front of Lord Mayor Doyle's home, we find a junction of the Global Street, where the relatively powerless make history by provoking the powerful. In contrast to the state's almost comically mismatched paramilitary response, the anonymous culprits themselves likely emerged from an informal milieu of young "insurrectionary" anarchists, energized over preceding months by the tumult of Seattle's branch of the Occupy Wall Street movement.[4] Food Not Bombs moves in some of the same spaces as these insurrectionaries, from DIY community centers and anarchist cafes to assemblies like Occupy Seattle. Although FNB represents a different kind of anarchist project, our networks overlap with theirs. And from my vantage point at Occupy Seattle—behind a pot of free FNB soup—it seemed that the anger circulating within that milieu had been amplified and focused through their experiences with police. Before it was evicted at the end of 2011, the heterogeneous encampment of Occupy Seattle had become a crucial site of foment for these self-styled insurrectionaries, who had already mobilized the previous year in several massive demonstrations against police brutality (most notably the unprovoked killing of a deaf, homeless Native American man, John T. Williams, for carrying a legal carving knife). In its handling of Occupy Seattle, the police department (already under scrutiny by the US Department of Justice for excessive use of force) reportedly provoked and escalated tensions with these insurrectionary types—most infamously by pepper-spraying a nonresistant priest, a pregnant woman, and an eighty-four-year-old woman (KOMO Staff 2011), but also in numerous other moments of intimidation or antagonism reported anecdotally by protesters through their own grassroots information networks.[5]

In the wake of this long dynamo of force and outrage, the vandalism on May Day represented a cathartic public performance. So edified were local anarchists by the event that the annual May Day Anticapitalist March became a routine (some local anarchists might even say "ritual") feature of Seattle's political landscape from 2012 on, marked by minor skirmishes and symbolic displays of power—by both the hundreds-strong black bloc and the riot gear–clad ranks of Seattle Police—and, of course, the odd broken corporate window.

The spectacle of order, captured by a passing tourist. Seattle Police march in anticipation of the annual Anticapitalist March, May Day 2015.

NEARLY A QUARTER CENTURY BEFORE THAT, and approximately ten degrees due south, yet another bloc(k) of the Global Street played host to another motley, anarchic gathering—this time one of the early watersheds in Food Not Bombs' history. On June 28, 1989, homeless San Franciscans and their allies gathered in Civic Center Plaza and struck camp in front of City Hall. Their tent city—christened "Tenement Square" in solidarity with that year's Tiananmen Square protests in China—decried the city's treatment of shelterless residents (Parson 2010). The occupation went on for three weeks, and Food Not Bombs, at the invitation of some of the homeless protesters, moved its meals there from Golden Gate Park, running what became a twenty-four-hour soup kitchen for the duration of the occupation. Afterward, the Plaza would become one of San Francisco FNB's principal locations, and the group would face near daily arrests by the city police for months.

As FNB founder Keith McHenry relates the story, in the days leading up to the protest, shelterless San Franciscans told FNB of escalating police pressure to move on: the fire department had deliberately soaked their camps, and the police had confiscated their sleeping bags (McHenry 2012, 105). Exactly as Melbourne's Robert Doyle would attempt thirty years later, Art Agnos, the ostensibly progressive mayor of San Francisco, prohibited homeless campers from leaving tents or "[p]ersonal property in excess of what can be carried" in the parks (quoted in Parson 2010, 79). After delivering a letter to that effect to park inhabitants, police began ticketing homeless people and disposing of their belongings (79).

The ensuing protest proved a massive spectacle. The homeless and their allies turned out in force. As McHenry related to me, members of the press branded it "Camp Agnos." (To make the moniker stick, according to McHenry, one mercenary journalist went so far as to print it on T-shirts and distribute them among the campers). The organizers held daily concerts and other events, while Food Not Bombs volunteers maintained a 'round-the-clock presence. Bolstered by growing visibility and volunteers (several of whom described this moment to me), the group ran an impressive operation, with its own delivery van, on-site cooking equipment, and a rotating cast of characters, from Fred the cheesecake man (who worked at a bakery and always brought surplus cheesecake) to a Hungarian volunteer committed to dental hygiene (they distributed free floss). To echo the Chinese Goddess of Democracy statue in Tiananmen Square, they built a Goddess of Free Food. And finally, weeks into the protest, after negotiations broke down between homeless organizers and the mayor, members of FNB crossed the street and occupied the Mayor's Office itself for a day.

San Francisco Food Not Bombs occupies City Hall across from Tenement Square, 1989. (Photo courtesy of the foodnotbombs.net archives)

Having only months before arrived at a détente with the city after numerous arrests in Golden Gate Park for sharing food, Food Not Bombs' participation in Tenement Square didn't score them any points with local government. As in the other vignettes above, City Hall responded with a decisive, heavy hand—in this case filing a lawsuit and winning an injunction against FNB, which made its actions a misdemeanor offense, the basis of many of the hundreds of arrests members of the San Francisco chapter would ultimately experience. Indeed, according to Sean Parson (2010), this period of protest galvanized the Agnos administration into taking an even harder line against San Francisco's homeless. Yet it also raised the profile of the issue, making it impossible to avoid. And it drew significant attention and notoriety to FNB itself, which would prove the clarion to a period of expansion that carried on into the early 1990s.

ALTHOUGH THEY TAKE PLACE in disparate times and places, and are interpreted by diverse actors in different historical moments, the parallels between these three scenes are telling. They help us to tease out the relations between governance, rebellion, and the realpolitik of homelessness, encampment, and public order in aspiring world-class cities. In each case, conflicts over access to public space, particularly for each city's most vulnerable, precipitated anarchic, insurrectionary responses (whether directly or indirectly). And again, in each case, this response allowed otherwise relatively powerless people to shape the course of events without seizing power. Despite their differences, if we connect the dots between each, we might imagine the terrain so outlined—one avenue of what Saskia Sassen calls the "Global Street"—as a stage for the rehearsal of the kind of mass conspiracies we have been pursuing throughout this book. It is to these conspiracies we turn in more detail in this last section of the work.

5

A Recipe for Mass Conspiracy

"If the Police Had a Brain in Their Head They Would Have Just Ignored Us . . ."

"Freeeeeeeeeee fooooooooood," calls Carmen, loud enough for anyone within two blocks of the park to hear her. It's one of her favorite parts of the meal. Her voice echoes down the red-brick paving on these quiet winter nights in Occidental Park. Many people already know to expect us each Sunday, but if anyone wasn't aware—well, now they are. She rattles off the menu and translates it fluently into Spanish for the benefit of some of the diners who have come all the way from Mexico, Guatemala, and farther south for the privilege of joining Seattle's casual labor pool and eating in a downtown park of a Sunday. If a mass conspiracy requires a call, a clarion to activate it, Carmen might as well be it. Her weekly cry convenes an ephemeral constellation of diners and volunteers who might otherwise have little to do with each other. In a way, it's a microcosm of the multitudinous, heterogeneous assembly of conspirators convened worldwide under the slogan "Food Not Bombs."

Things *extra* and *other* (details and excesses coming from elsewhere) insert themselves into the accepted framework, the imposed order. . . . The surface of this order is everywhere punched and torn open by ellipses, drifts, and leaks of meaning: it is a sieve-order.
—Michel de Certeau

Although mass conspiracies as such are largely a paranoid figment, the term nonetheless suggests certain paradoxes that aptly describe Food Not Bombs. First, such a communion is simultaneously esoteric and public: anyone might be part of it, yet only conspirators themselves understand the conspiracy. The temporary, unlikely community that is FNB represents just such an eclectic constituency. Unbounded, convened by shared attention ("freeeee foooood"), yet hidden at the city's margins, largely illegible to the uninitiated—this is its counterpublic aspect, as we have already seen in this book. Second, the mass conspiracy of popular imagination is paradoxically organized and formless. It connotes a decentralized structure that operates in concert without any central cabal or coordinator, like a swarm or a murmuration. In part III of this book, we map out this formless, decentralized structure.

Just so, the FNB chapters I have known are both disorganized and reliable. With no formal division of labor and a diffuse, constantly revolving membership, they may transform drastically from one week to the next. Nevertheless, they persist and collectively grow over time. One Melbourne volunteer, for example, estimated the number of sometime-participants at one hundred citywide, and yet the core kitchen crew on any given day might be counted on one hand. In the same way, for every time sharing food in Seattle felt like a convivial, open-air party, there were others when only two or three of us showed up to do the work of ten and it felt like an impossible chore. Yet in my six years of regular volunteering we failed to serve perhaps only half a dozen weekly meals. With the same irrepressible spirit, upon delivering lunch to the park, one crusty Melbourne punk rocker, dazed by the effort of cooking and transporting it with too few hands in too little time, told me wryly, "It always feels like a miracle when we get down here." In spite of this (and notwithstanding occasional hiatuses as volunteer crews turn over), chapters in each city I visited have endured since the 1990s or earlier. Not only that, the number of chapters worldwide has grown throughout the past four decades in spite of—and, I argue, in response to—economic restructuring and exclusionary urban policing. How should we account for this? What is the recipe for such a mass conspiracy?

> What was happening was a transformation. The city was depopulating. They were moving out poorer people, wholesale. Moving in rich people. And they were picking and choosing who they wanted to have live there. And homeless people weren't a part of that. And there were thousands of them. And they were sleeping on the streets. They were, you know—thousands of people were living in Golden Gate Park—I lived in Golden Gate Park, I slept in a camp out there—and hundreds of camps out there. Huge masses of disaffected people just, just moving around from place to place. And it was freaking out the local administration. They didn't know what to do with these people. They tried all kinds of different methods. Trying to induce them to move out to other places. Taking away social services. Increasing crackdowns, and police repression and clearing out camps and things like that, and they made *no difference whatsoever*.
>
> —Peter, San Francisco FNB, on the background to the group's growth in the late 1980s

As we have seen in this book, the surpluses of the global city—people, places, and things—are some of FNB's most crucial ingredients. In this chapter, I argue that the affective provocations and spatial incursions of city governance (such as the forbidden gifts of the last chapter) galvanize and organize those surpluses into resistant formations. Indeed, the movement's growth coincides with the past forty years of widening inequality, gentrification, and the "revanchist" project to discipline urban underclasses and exclude them from public space (Smith 1996, 2002).

This argument is woven from claims I have made already in this book. First, I have argued that the rhythms of commodity exchange routinely devalorize and obsolesce places and things—former commodities that have use value but that are nonetheless rendered abject capital, withdrawn from market circulation, and enclaved in exilic spaces at the bottom of dumpsters, under freeways, or behind the no trespassing signs of vacant properties. These former commodities are Food Not Bombs' bottom line—the hundreds of pounds of wasted food recovered weekly in each city, for example, or the squatted kitchens and low-rent community spaces where that food is prepared. The stakes and the scale of this waste are heightened in the global city. Second, I have argued that, in the process, not only places and things but populations and economic practices are marginalized or devalorized, constituting both market-publics and harlequin, counterpublic fringes dislocated by the transformations of life and labor in the global city. Those fringes find one novel expression in Food Not Bombs. With the proliferation of networks of global cities, an emergent political terrain that Sassen (2011) calls the "Global Street" makes possible the circulation of people and political discourse, enabling the spread of Food Not Bombs chapters and their affiliated counterpublics across a transnational constellation of cities. And third, I have argued that many municipal governments, particularly in the high-stakes, symbolic economies of global cities, have taken decisive actions to valorize and enable such market-publics, adopting revanchist biopolitical regimes like zero-tolerance policing and urban banishment that marginalize non-market-friendly forms of life. It is within this political context that the agency of a political constellation like Food Not Bombs is made meaningful and consequential.

What this chapter adds is a description of the organizing logic animating these ingredients. What are the properties of a worldwide conspiracy to feed people? According to what principles does it grow? Like the proverbial blind men describing an elephant from different angles, political theorists have given many names to such unruly social formations. Some highlight their geometry (e.g., *assemblage, network, cell, fractal scape, dis-organization*).[1] Others invoke ecological metaphors (e.g., *swarm, rhizome*).[2] Yet others emphasize illiberal forms of sovereignty and political agency (e.g., *multitude, insurgent citizenship, temporary auton-*

omous zone).[3] All these descriptions capture something of the complex system that is expressed under the sign of Food Not Bombs. Yet here I am most inspired by the third theoretical tradition, particularly those who develop Deleuze and Guattari's (1987) influential description of the crab-grass-like form of power they call the "war machine." Building on their concept, Zibechi's (2010) model of urban insurrectionary movements as "dispersal machines" enables a description of the dynamic entanglements of state power and FNB's anarchic counterpower. Cultivated over decades, this nonviolent, decentralized escalation is what I call a *slow insurrection*. (For these reasons, it has even attracted the attention of the FBI, although they also misunderstand it completely, with at least one branch obscurely including FNB on its "terrorist watch list.")[4]

With this in mind, what I argue below is that the elements of Food Not Bombs are often organized, provoked, and amplified by the efforts of city governments to suppress them. Their slow insurrection is an affective dynamo, which in turn reconfigures the possibilities for an urban politics across two distinct arenas, both directly confronting state power in the public realm and remaking everyday life in other, counterpublic spaces. As Peter, a onetime dreadlocked itinerant involved during the early years of FNB's rapid growth and clashes with the police in San Francisco, put it, "If the police had a brain in their head they would have just ignored us. Right? And we would have just become another weird part of the landscape. And they just could've waited us out. And we would have, you know, eventually become bored and moved on, and done something else." Instead, they didn't, and the movement grew by leaps and bounds.

A Confederacy of Nomadisms

People answer the call of Food Not Bombs for many reasons. Francisco, for example, who we met at the beginning of the book, seems to come to eat and talk politics. He's part of the local milieu of activists for whom FNB is a well-known feature of the political landscape. He joins us at the park occasionally, and even more occasionally he lends a hand in the kitchen. Like many intermittent volunteers, he talks keenly about FNB, but it's only one thread of his politics. He is a veteran of an array of radical projects. More recently he has thrown his energy behind the local Wobblies (the Industrial Workers of the World, an international anarchist union of sorts). At the same time, Francisco's relationship to FNB is not formed by ideological conviction alone. It also affords him a measure of food security. Like many radicals, he leads a somewhat peripatetic existence. He's not always securely housed or employed. For some radicals, this is a principled refusal of wage labor and consumption. For others, it reflects the precarity of a life under late capitalism. It's often hard to disentangle these two factors. When we met him before, Francisco was couch surfing with a mutual friend and FNB collaborator. The last time I saw him, he was selling *Real Change*, Seattle's street newspaper, for extra income.

In many ways, he embodies the intersections of political ardor and personal dis-location that characterize the social worlds of Food Not Bombs. There's also Jules, the single mother we met in the introduction who let us crowd into her subsidized apartment to cook some Sundays. And Bela, the rock-and-roll journalist who hitchhiked around the world, wrote three books about his travels, and routinely slept on a piece of cardboard under an overpass after washing up FNB's dishes each week. There's Lupyta, who left Mexico to work as a nanny, teach Spanish, and improve her English, and who borrowed a car from her employers each week to come to FNB. Koa, the half-indigenous, half-haole crust-punk from Hawai'i. Suzie, the Jewish bike punk and musician who came to Seattle to start a new life and looked immediately for FNB. Ani, from Bangladesh, who was living at the nearby rescue mission, and found in FNB a more welcoming community, with better food. Corrina, the ecologist who moved to Seattle for graduate school. Vijay, the Sri Lankan refugee who took a vow of poverty. Kwame, the hacker who couch-surfs and squats around the world and earns almost no income in a given year. Mary, the punk rocker who runs her own DIY cleaning business. Matt, the freegan university student who often shows up with surprise dumpstered ingredients. Jason, the slightly cynical transgendered playwright. Anna, the neuroscience postdoc. Jon, who lived in his van. And dozens and dozens of others who became, for months or years, regular faces in the Seattle kitchen during my six years of weekly volunteering.

At first glance, FNB appears quintessentially heterogeneous. The specific congerie I've just described includes collaborators and friends who are middle class, working class, and penniless; white, black, South Asian, mestiza, and mixed race; US-born and recent migrants; university educated and high-school dropouts; and so on. Although some critics of FNB rightly point out that members hail most often from the privileged set of disaffected, majority white, English-speaking, university-educated types who gravitate toward radical politics, that narrow description does not capture the movement's makeup. As Carmen (herself a child of Latinx migrants from different countries) put it, "We definitely had a diverse group, from all walks . . . So I think we should talk about how within [FNB] chapters themselves, there's a kind of a representation of the demographic of those cities." Indeed, in my time, Seattle FNB kitchens brought together a broader spectrum of racial, ethnic, national, linguistic, classed, and abled backgrounds than I have seen represented in many other radical or progressive political projects. Across these differences, if a common thread emerges, it is uprootedness. For example, Peter, the punk rocker from San Francisco (himself homeless when he joined FNB) summed up the urban milieu from which FNB emerged in the late 1980s: "There was a lot of disaffected sort of people hanging around San Francisco at that time that didn't have a job. It wasn't—there was a recession going on . . . so people would just come up to the Food Not Bombs table to get something to eat, because they didn't have a job or anything else, and were sort of marginally living and we were helping them out. And they would sort of hang around and get to know us, and then eventually get involved." Peter describes here a variegated collective that assembled in San Francisco, like in the other chapters I have worked with. Unemployed graduate students. Underemployed dishwashers. Full-time activists. Squatters. And so on. In spite of this multiplicity, their labors were reliably pooled, made common in the endeavor of sharing food.

Across all these differences, the thread that has drawn many of us together is an estrangement with respect to the norms of urban market-publics. Ironically, although these market-publics often privilege "sedentarist" norms (McVeigh 1997) rooted in the territorial claims of businesses and property owners, the economic restructuring that corresponds to the growth of global cities has fostered myriad forms of cultural and economic *deterritorialization*: patterns of spatial and/or social displacement, from the vagrant's downward mobility to the migrant diaspora's global transit or the exodus of women's labor from its former place in the traditional patriarchal home (see Ong 1991; Appadurai 1996; Hardt and Negri 2004). These patterns of deterritorialization are compounded in global cities. (All roads lead to New York, or Tokyo, or London, or . . .) Indeed, some of them, like the migrant and feminized labor of many low-wage service sectors (think of Lupyta and Mary, whom I mentioned above), are crucial to the reproduction of the global city—yet they are often rendered spatially or discursively peripheral (Sassen 1996). So dis-located, James Holston (2009) terms their collective constituents "global urban peripheries."

Many of these deterritorialized lives and practices find a home in the ranks of FNB: cultural dislocations, from downward economic mobility to queered gender identity; geographic displacements, from itin-

There is this kind of Food Not Bombs that is like a traveler's Food Not Bombs. And at a certain point I kinda realized that—I would say this is maybe ten years ago [ca. 1998]—that there was probably thousands of people in the world that never really live any one place, and just go from Food Not Bombs to Food Not Bombs . . . I've been to kitchens in Cancun and you would meet people who were doing—who had done Food Not Bombs in Seattle, and they'd gone down the coast, were in San Francisco for a while—in fact there was a whole crew of kids from Australia that rented the house in Cancun to make the kitchen. And they had sold all their belongings in Australia, a car and all this stuff to raise money to get over here. And then they just traveled around. I just ran into a guy in Oaxaca who—one guy's from Poland and one guy was from Utrecht, Holland, and they were doing the same thing. They rode their bikes from Seattle . . . A lot of them, I guess, when I talked to them, left home when they were really young teenagers, cause their parents were brutal, or something like that. And then they just went on the road and they never stopped going on the road. And Food Not Bombs ended up being a perfect venue for connecting with people and never staying put. And then there's the people like the people from Utrecht who just decided they would go see the world, because they were tired of being in their town and they thought, "Well I'll go share what I've learned about Food Not Bombs from my town with people in their other towns, and then find out what people were doing in those towns and bring it back to my town."

—Keith McHenry, cofounder, Cambridge FNB (ca. 1981), San Francisco FNB (ca. 1988)

erancy to labor migrancy; economic marginalia, from dumpstered gift economies to off-lease, informal housing arrangements. Of the homeless volunteers, train-hopping anarchists, underemployed locals, uprooted university students, broke musicians and artists, ephemerally housed punks and hippies, domestic and international labor migrants (low-waged and well-paid alike), and activists visiting from abroad who often compose Food Not Bombs, it may be said that we comprise a confederacy of nomadisms.

Slow Insurrection

One effect of these dislocations is FNB's ephemeral, "cellular" organization, an antithesis to the sedimented "vertebrate" hierarchies of state power (Appadurai 2006). In some sense, Food Not Bombs is a postmodern, global heir to the "acephalous," stateless societies that were the chief concern of early political anthropology. But unlike them, it is organized by contingency rather than kinship. Indeed, there exists no better example than FNB of what Deleuze and Guattari (1987) called a "rhizomatic" structure. Where states, and indeed most modernist institutions, are organized in "arborescent," treelike fashion—hierarchical and tied to a fascicle root—rhizomes are chimerical and crabgrass-like, governed not by chains of command but rather connected by "lines of flight," contingencies that bring together and disperse heterogeneous elements. For perhaps obvious reasons, some anarchists and radicals have embraced the metaphor. One share-house in Austin, for example, called itself "The Rhizome." Another collective, a Seattle-based DIY social media network, called itself "Crabgrass."

But whereas many phenomena could be called rhizomatic, from the tumult of children on a playground to the ordered anarchy of the global capitalist economy (Hardt and Negri 2000), certain sorts of rhizomes are insurrectionary. Deleuze and Guattari (1987) name them "war machines," a poetic metaphor for those juggernauts of dispersed, self-sovereign forces that exist in relationships of intimate exteriority with the state's apparatus, enacting some measure of political autonomy. The term describes familiar antagonists such as Genghis Khan's Mongol "hordes," but also those ungovernable formations that erupt from within the state's own territory, like a bread riot. Building on this metaphor, Zibechi (2010) develops a model of spontaneous, insurrectionary, urban political movements, such as the Bolivian Aymara uprising of 2000, characterized by a rhizomatic "logic of dispersal," a form of counterpower that confounds the state's optics and undermines the development of statelike institutional hierarchies within the movement itself. In Zibechi's account, they are best understood not under the enduring, identitarian forms implied by a proper noun or definite article (as in "Occupy Wall Street" or "the women's movement"), but rather as *movement* itself. In other words, he emphasizes the dynamic motion of their components. This movement is constituted by everyday social and economic vectors that deterritorialize and reterritorialize people, fluidly bringing them into and out of formation with one another as their circumstances change. "In these movements," Zibechi argues, "the organization is not separate from everyday life; daily life is deployed as an arena for insurrectionary action" (2010, 46). Their fluid, disparate structure is therefore not purely deliberate. Necessity, too, is the mother of their invention. As we have already seen, structural and spatial forms of exclusion, or differential incorporation, compel collaborators to organize "at the edges of capitalism" (Grubačić and O'Hearn 2016). For Zibechi, these everyday forms of organization tend toward insurrection.

Food Not Bombs has followed just such a pattern of growth across forty years and countless cities, exclusively through nonviolent mutual aid and direct action. In this sense, it is a slow, global, pacifist sort of insurrection. Following Zibechi's model, FNB's insurrection is not distinct from its participants' everyday lives. Rather, its growth reflects not only acute moments of conflict and mobilization, but also a slow, partly submerged aggregation of people and things—dislodged surpluses held temporarily in each other's orbit sometimes out of necessity, sometimes in opposition to state actions, and sometimes for the sheer joy of it.

Francisco, for example, will move on to other projects before too long. Our cantankerous mutual friend, Koa, often grumbles about this sort of

Police visit Food Not Bombs at Tompkins Square Park, New York City, late 1990s. (Photo by Victoria Law)

"activist résumé-building," implying that such short-lived participation merely serves to accumulate symbolic capital among fellow activists. (I've heard FNB collaborators call this "anarcho street cred" or "punk points.") And to be sure, such a performance of affinity is one face of the "cultural politics of networking" that drives many radical political communities (Juris 2008). But this politics of identity reflects the deeper cultural logic of contingent, networked relationships that allows dispersed and dispersing movements like Food Not Bombs to convene, reconfigure, and disband fluidly as political circumstances change on the ground (Juris 2008; see also Day 2005; Escobar 2008).

In the immediate aftermath of disasters like Hurricanes Katrina and Sandy in New Orleans and in New York City, for example, while formal organizations took days or weeks to mobilize, Food Not Bombs was one of the first groups with boots on the ground, distributing food. The Red Cross even gave out FNB's phone number to those stranded in New Orleans in the days after the storm (McHenry 2012, 112). Similarly, as I type this, friends with FNB in Seattle, Santa Cruz, and elsewhere have adapted in order to continue sharing food in the midst of the 2020 coronavirus pandemic. FNB's flexibility was also one component of the logic of dispersal behind Occupy Wall Street's sudden global mobilization in 2011. Although to the casual bystander its tent cities seemed to emerge out of thin air, their growth in fact activated and extended long-standing networks of radical activists with shared practices and political notions. Some of them were transnational, convened through the counterpublic circulation of radical art and literature; others were rooted in space, place, and practice, from anarchist cafes and independent media centers to Food Not Bombs

Food Not Bombs with surplus shopping trolley at Tompkins Square Park, New York City, late 1990s. (Photo by Victoria Law)

> During the Loma Prieta earthquake in '89, we set up our operation in Civic Center. And started feeding people that were in the Tenderloin who didn't want to live in their apartments anymore because the earthquake had shook the plaster off the walls and they were sure it was going to fall down. And there was no electricity. There was no power. And we knew how to pirate the water out of the water mains in Civic Center, 'cause we'd done it before. And we set up a mobile operation there, and became recipients of the Red Cross—like brought us food and supplies and propane, and we became a whole part of that network. And I felt like, "Yeah!" like I was—like you had your hand on the ass of history.
>
> —Peter, San Francisco FNB, late 1980s

chapters (see Juris 2012; Dickinson 2013; Barnard 2016). As Keith McHenry pointed out to me, for example, FNB's expertise in the deployment of impromptu field kitchens was central to the smooth functioning of Occupy Wall Street in New York, and I could say the same thing of FNB's seven-day-a-week contribution to Occupy Seattle.

This flexibility and contingency makes movements like Occupy Wall Street or Food Not Bombs decidedly "antifragile" (Taleb 2012). In other words, they grow larger and more robust under pressure, even as specific individuals and instantiations are neutralized (for example, by being arrested, as we will see in the next section). Their logic of dispersal therefore lends them elasticity and resilience in response to the state. Working in conjunction with this dispersal is also a "logic of aggregation" (Juris 2012) that allows for manifold newcomers to join the fray at will through manifestations in (counter)public spaces like the encampments of Occupy Wall Street or the free meals of Food Not Bombs. (Think of Carmen's clarion call.)

The geometry of such insurrection is an emergent property, evolving from multiscalar, more-than-the-sum-of-their-parts relationships between individuals and the whole—like fractal patterns emerging from seemingly random events (see Escobar 2008). Like any emergent system, it evolves not only from the characteristics and capacities of these constituent parts, but also from their limits, incapacities, or exclusions. Even the most dispersed, rhizomatic network rests on shared patterns or protocols that exclude certain forms of relationality (Galloway and Thacker 2007). And in insurrectionary movements, these limits and exclusions militate against all but the most fleeting, informal hierarchies. Indeed, when asked by police who is in charge, FNB collaborators often respond: "We all are." Or, as Lisa told me of the earliest Seattle FNB feeds, "They'd show up and they'd say, 'Who's in charge?' and we'd say, 'You are!' Which they didn't really think was very funny, although we did." In such anarchic fashion, FNB doesn't take direction well. Nor does the confluence of differently deterritorialized people and things make for straightforward, linear planning.

Instead, like Clastres's (1977) "societies against the state," the group is organized partly by stumbling blocks to consolidated authority or control. In that vein, Corrina described a typical story of a police visit to Seattle FNB around 2006:

> The cop drives his car into the middle of the square—and, you know you don't really see vehicles in there very often—and he pulls out this big megaphone, and was like, [cop voice] "One of you, come over here." And we all look at each other, and we're like "No." And so eventually he keeps getting more and more upset ... And so we said "No, we're not—we don't have a leader or anything." So we all went up and talked to him as a group ... I think he was scared.

As Clastres put it, when faced with the prospect of singular or centralized control, "savages want the multiplication of the multiple" (2010, 274).

Consider also FNB's typical decision-making process. Embraced by many radical activists simply under the name *consensus*, this method is a formalized, anarchist answer to Robert's rules of order, an attempt to codify a nonhierarchical distribution of power. Although partly intended to emulate Indigenous political systems such as the Zapatistas and Iroquois, it has sometimes been critiqued for privileging Eurocentric, middle-class forms of subjectivity, argumentation, and deliberation (e.g., Kauffman 2015). And yet consensus-based organization may productively disrupt even these hierarchies (Polletta 2002). In practice, for example, less bourgeois participants routinely upset these norms and appropriate or reinvent the consensus process. Allan, another regular San Francisco volunteer in the early 1990s, wryly reflected on the difficulty of reaching consensus at the group's collective meetings when participants didn't share the same social background or even neurological profile: "You had to participate in that process, and we definitely had people who made that really challenging. Well, some of

> At that point we owned two trucks-slash-vans, and we had a rented storage space, and we were serving seven nights a week at City Hall, a couple lunches. One at City Hall, one in the Haight, serving once a week at Sixth Street and Mission, where the welfare hotels are. We had a food service in the Mission, at Sixteenth and Mission during that period. It was huge. It was unbelievable. And during the first Gulf War, which was during that time period, we were set up in Civic Center Plaza for weeks, 24-7. There was just a never-ending presence there, because the protests were happening day and night and that became like a little touch point for a lot of folks. Constantly trying to shuttle more food down there. I was volunteering at the food bank ... and at the end of my shift, they were kind of flexible about taking bulk food. So I'd put as much dried beans and dried rice as I could fit in a backpack and ride my bike down to the tent. I was doing that two or three times a week. We were getting produce and bagels, I was trying to get beans and rice and that kind of thing. I remember Rainbow Grocery was giving us like fifty pounds of beans and fifty pounds of brown rice a month, but we blew through that so quickly.
>
> —Allan, on the scale of San Francisco FNB in the early 1990s

them just because they didn't really care, so they would sort of not do the process. But also ... some of these people were crazy. And crazy people, you know, they don't really stick to process."

In similar fashion, FNB's surplus raw materials constitute another built-in limitation to the consolidation or calcification of institutional structures. Chapters experience a regular turnover not only of members, but of resources and infrastructure as food surpluses are cut off or underused kitchen spaces are reallocated. In my six years of full-time volunteering, for instance, we cooked in no less than a dozen kitchens. After one of Seattle FNB's few long-term hiatuses—when a kitchen space had become unavailable and core volunteers chose not to seek another one—Ingrate reflected that maybe the hiatus had been a good thing. Anticipating Zibechi's argument in a way, he said, "I don't like the idea of organizations existing into perpetuity... organizations tend to take on a life of their own. Which is fine, but I think that when you get into things that live forever, and that don't at some point die, or don't stop when they're no longer able to function healthily, you start looking at the same sort of thing as corporations ... I just think that it's good for it to die at some point, or it's good for it to stop and then for new things to start."

Obeying this logic, for forty years FNB has proven insurrectionary, demonstrating the capacity to upset hegemonic patterns of capitalist social reproduction in two crucial respects. First, it has mobilized forms of "insurgent citizenship" (Holston 2009) that challenge the politico-spatial order of the city and test the practical limits of state sovereignty. Second, it has established new, counterpublic "spaces of encounter" (Lawson and Elwood 2013) where very different constituents of the global urban periphery become visible to each other—gateways that make it possible to build new relationships across difference in ways that refuse the typical logics of class, consumption, and labor. I describe each of these below.

Like Water on a Grease Fire

So far, I have described the properties of a peaceful insurrection, along with its active ingredients, but not yet the recipe. To paraphrase Fanon, we need to ask: What sets these deterritorialized surpluses into motion? "What blows the lid?" (2004, 33). The myriad people and things drawn into Food Not Bombs are not inevitable cognates. The conjunction that links them—the grammar of this particular multitude—is partly authored by the state itself.

Police arrest Keith McHenry, San Francisco FNB, at Golden Gate Park, 1989. (Photo courtesy of Keith McHenry)

In other words, the very efforts of local governments to exclude Food Not Bombs and its constituents from the public sphere have often been the catalyst for its expansion, from forbidden gifts to aggressive antiprotest tactics. As Peter described FNB's San Francisco salad days, for example, "the government, the police, the social interactions [between participants and government] were really what was driving what was going on." When the San Francisco mayor's office targeted FNB, arresting more than a thousand volunteers between 1988 and 1992 for publicly dishing out vegan food from buckets, the result was to intensify grassroots organizing, media attention, and volunteer recruitment (Parson 2010). By August 1988, within two months of San Francisco FNB's first meal, the group was shut down by police in riot gear and nine volunteers were arrested (McHenry 2012, 103). The *San Francisco Chronicle* (which had apparently been tipped off by police) published photographs of the arrests, and the next week two hundred outraged protesters marched through the Haight Ashbury District—banging pots and pans—to the serving location. Twenty-nine of them were arrested. A series of such confrontations ensued, garnering national and international news coverage, and by Labor Day roughly a thousand protesters had arrived at Golden Gate Park, fifty-four of whom were jailed (McHenry 2012, 103). The local administration relented and issued a permit—a détente that lasted until the following year, when FNB renewed the city's ire by joining Camp Agnos at City Hall (see scene 5).

From 1988 to 1992, through numerous waves of escalation and détente, across multiple mayoral administrations, FNB played a crucial role in San Francisco politics, keeping antihomeless measures in the spotlight, generating countless hours of bad publicity for the city, and even prompting the *San Francisco Chronicle* to ask mayoral candidates how they would deal with Food Not Bombs (Parson 2010). Although such protracted conflict was unique to San Francisco (perhaps other cities learned San Francisco's lessons), FNB collaborators from Seattle, New York, Orlando, and Melbourne all told me of parallel instances of arrest or antagonism between FNB and local police or councils. These moments simultaneously organized government agencies' efforts and further mobilized FNB's ranks. In this way, from its earliest days, Food Not Bombs has emerged from the fringes or minorities of urban market-publics in response to efforts by municipal agencies to remake public space. Like water on a grease fire, such state apparatuses can remake, but cannot dictate, the political landscape of the city.

For reasons just such as these, Deleuze and Guattari described the relationship between insurrectionary war machines and state apparatuses as generative and dynamic. Defying Isaac Newton, their actions often prompt opposite but unequal responses. By turns, they corral or intensify one another, and the force relations between them are multiplied. Deleuze and Guattari define state apparatuses as "organs of power" (1987, 357) that exercise sovereignty over specific territories and social orders in such a way that "makes possible the undertaking of large-scale projects, the constitution of *surpluses*, and the organization of the corresponding *public* functions" (359; my emphasis). In precisely this way, sharing prohibitions and the municipal state apparatuses that enforce them play a key role in directing the circulation of food surpluses to certain marginal urban spaces, thus constituting the terrain of urban market-publics.

Ostensibly, the state apparatus brooks no challenge. Its sovereignty is, however, inherently limited. "The State itself," Deleuze and Guattari argue, "has always been in a relationship with an outside and is inconceivable independent of that relationship. The law of the State is not the law of All or Nothing . . . but that of interior and exterior. The State is sovereignty, but sovereignty only reigns over what it is capable of internalizing, of appropriating locally" (1987, 360). Where it encounters resistance, therefore, the state operates as an "apparatus of capture," not only prohibiting but also appropriating and reorganizing the forces initially aligned against it. When outdoor meal providers in Seattle resisted the city's sharing prohibitions, for example, the municipal state apparatus effectively co-opted their efforts by forming institutions like the Outdoor Meal Site and the Outdoor Meals Partnership Coalition, as we saw in the last chapter.

Nonetheless, this capture is never total. Its sovereignty is what de Certeau might call a "sieve-order" (1984, 107). The stuff of life leaks through. The term *war machine*, then, notionally represents those forms of life that exceed or evade its order. "It seems to be irreducible to the State apparatus," Deleuze and Guattari write, "to be outside its sovereignty and prior to its law: it comes from elsewhere" (1987, 352). This "elsewhere" might just as easily refer to the cultural no-man's-land of the dumpster or the squat as it does the geographic territory beyond the state's reach. A range of exilic, counterpublic forms of life like the ones I describe in this book are therefore breeding grounds for such productive externality. As Deleuze and Guattari put it, "collective bodies always have fringes or minorities that reconstitute equivalents of the war machine—in sometimes quite unforeseen ways" (366).

Deleuze and Guattari's mutually entangled, co-constitutive model of power therefore calls our attention to the complex, sometimes submerged ways in which a phenomenon like FNB simultaneously evades, antagonizes, remakes, and is remade by state agencies. Like the war machine, which exists apart from and is irreducible to the state apparatus, FNB operates largely "under the radar." It uses food that won't be missed and works in spaces that are overlooked or freely, publicly accessible, usually explicitly eschewing state permission. Also like the war machine, however, FNB periodically encounters and inspires state resistance and cultivates recurrent moments of mutual antagonism.

Testing the Limits

"Every Sunday cops were showing up and telling us to get the fuck out of there, but never ever arresting us," Kris told me, describing Seattle FNB's clashes with the police in Occidental Park during in the late 1990s. "Constantly threatening us with [arrest] . . . but they never really had any sort of legal action to take against us," he said. "It was obvious that they were just trying to bully us out of there."

Food Not Bombs' regular presence in the park represented a pragmatic limit to the power exercised by police to enforce city policy. Although the state had a range of legal recourses, such as the right to issue extrajudicial "parks exclusion" orders (introduced by Mark Sidran as part of Seattle's "Civility Codes"), Seattle FNB was able to avoid any such consequences and successfully defend their weekly claim on the territory of Occidental Park, creating a regular "temporary autonomous zone" (Bey 1985). In part, Kris attributed this to the group's assorted constituency. Many of them were "within-the-system educated": "Like people that knew exactly what to say to these people, and to show them that, you know what, we're not stupid. We're not just being bleeding heart liberals. We know what we're doing, and we know why we can do it." In other words, they knew how to challenge the police legally, morally, and pragmatically through avoidance and obstruction. "I had cops in my face every single week," he said. "And we all kept our cool, and they never arrested us."

In this way, Seattle FNB has been calling the city's bluff for nearly thirty years. One volunteer from the 1990s, a graduate student at the time, explained: "I started [volunteering with] Food Not Bombs about the fall of '94, and it seemed like that [police presence] all was just there from the very beginning . . . The police did come down occasionally and would say, 'You need to close down' . . . and then they'd leave and a lot of times we'd finish serving, and then clean up and leave. Sometimes they would show up and say, 'You have to close down now,' and would just stay there." In spite of at least four such periods of intensified pressure from police to pack up and leave, and shorter, more sporadic moments of tension, the group has held its ground in Pioneer Square neighborhood, usually in Occidental Park, every week for most of the intervening period since it formed in 1992 without facing arrest or exclusion.[5]

Through such resistance, a war machine reorganizes the state apparatus and vice versa. Just as state actions have incensed Food Not Bombs into action, so have FNB's actions sometimes bounded, sometimes provoked or intensified the state's efforts to control food distribution. In this sense, FNB bears out the assertion of political philosophers Hardt and Negri that "resistance is primary with respect to power" (2004, 64).

This dance of mutual delimitation is reflected juridically in the degree to which state apparatuses can effectively prosecute their restrictions. In Orlando, for example, group members were arrested for sharing food and subsequently appealed these prohibitions in court. Their initial appeals were successful, in fact, and according to one Orlando collaborator, the city, embarrassed, offered to negotiate a compromise. Rather than negotiate, however, the complainants pursued the appeal to a higher court; the policy was ultimately upheld by the Eleventh Circuit Court of Appeals, setting a troubling precedent for feeding prohibitions across the country.[6] Food Not Bombs also shapes the state's mobilization in less formal, more semiotic ways. Seattle FNB has, for example, become familiar by name among some city officials and social service agencies. Its antiauthoritarian politics and corresponding decentralization and informal organization elicit, as we saw in chapter 4, a certain degree of distrust and explicit frustration from some of them, which inevitably informs their reaction to unsupervised meal programs in general.

Maybe more importantly, Food Not Bombs and municipal state apparatuses demonstrably test the spatial and material limits of each other's sovereignty. In Seattle, for example, conflicts between FNB and the police have established certain territories as more and less defensible. As Lisa described to me, at its inception in the early 1990s Seattle FNB underwent a period of testing and negotiation, conflict and détente, during which they discovered where they could and could not effectively serve:

> At the beginning we would be mostly be fighting with the police. Because we tried to feed people in Pioneer Square—in the actual square—and the cops would get called on us every single time, because the merchants there didn't want the homeless hanging out. Even though they were already hanging out, they didn't want it encouraged and they didn't want us there. So every single feed we tried to do, the cops would be there, and they'd be harassing us, and threatening to arrest us, and taking down the license number on our van, and etcetera. . . . They'd say, "Well we have complaints, la di da di da." It was just the same routine every time. And so we'd end up having to leave or get arrested—which we weren't really interested in getting arrested, so eventually, I'm not sure how it came about, but we talked to somebody and . . . finally negotiated a place where we could feed where they

> I remember one of the other people who was really heavily involved at the time that they [the police] were, you know, threatening further repression if we came back to Occidental Park in early 2000, spoke with James Pugel, who at the time was a captain and is now a, assistant chief I believe, or whatever they call those. Deputy dawg? I don't know, something higher up. But he was from the West Precinct, and looks very dashing when he's coming at you, waving a club on a horse, apparently—another anecdotal thing. But he expressed to a member of Food Not Bombs that he was concerned because he'd heard that Food Not Bombs was an anarchist group. To which the individual from Food Not Bombs cheerfully said, "We are!" [laughing] Which probably didn't help matters. But, yeah, it was shits and giggles.
>
> —Ingrate, Seattle FNB, ca. 1998–2002

> weren't gonna harass us. And that was what used to be a triangle park... And that's where we used to feed. And once we started feeding there we never got harassed. I guess there was some agreement made with the cops or the city or someone that we could feed there, and that spot was okay because it was like a public park.

In this way, FNB convenes and claims space for a nonviolently illiberal political order that attenuates or thwarts outright the reach of state apparatuses. As the anarchist collective CrimethInc. puts it: "*It's not against the law if you don't get caught*, as every schoolchild and corporate CEO knows" (2004, 22; emphasis in original). In other words, insofar as a slow insurrection like Food Not Bombs can maintain a civilly disobedient practice as more than a merely symbolic gesture, it serves as a boundary marker, whereby the extent and enactment of the state apparatus is measured in practice against its claims over a territory.

To the extent that FNB's flexibility and humanitarian interventions are highly publicized, they also lay bare the limits of the neoliberal social compact. They reveal the lengths to which the neoliberal state cannot or will not go in order to meet the standards for welfare and human rights ostensibly guaranteed by citizenship. Ingrate (who has also worked in different parts of Seattle's homeless services sector) reflected on the long-term impact of FNB's civilly disobedient stance:

> For a long time, Food Not Bombs was the only outdoor meal program on Sundays. Because the city, well at this point, they don't want *anyone* serving outdoors. At all. And they really tried very hard to regulate that at the time. And most of the faith groups and whatnot that had done it... when they were told, "Oh, you can't do this," most of them were slightly less confrontational than Food Not Bombs and said "Oh, okay." And would just not do it, because the police had told them not to. And I like to think that Food Not Bombs had a bit of an effect on that, in that people were like, "Well, *those* guys do it."

Extending its discursive reach, the movement is also featured prominently in reporting on sharing prohibitions and the criminalization of homelessness by journalists and advocacy groups such as the National Coalition for the Homeless.

Resistance being primary with respect to power, the labors of organizations like Food Not Bombs represent a constitutive part of the city's political order. They redefine, through antagonism or evasion, what is politically and practically possible. Where municipal state agencies work to reproduce a market-public through forbidden public sharing, FNB represents one of the exceptional forms of life always already conjured into being, ontologically and substantially, in the process.

Gut Politics

Insurrections, slow or fast, are passionate affairs. The relation between power and resistance is not Euclidean or mechanical, but rather nonlinear and visceral. Its laws of motion are often felt rather than reasoned. Political movement and conflict excite not only politically coded sentiments, from "outrage" to "solidarity," but also an assemblage of more inchoate, embodied feelings and dispositions, from hunger to empathy to incandescent rage. (As I type this, I can still hear Koa, whose apt tirades on capitalism and the cops were often dotted, sometimes eclipsed completely, by a series of apoplectic, quasi-involuntary "fucks." His constant political consternation rendered the word somehow verb, noun, and adjective alike.) It is partly this gut politics that knits together a mass conspiracy. So it is with FNB, animated by hunger, empathy, mischief, and antiauthoritarian zeal alike.

As opposed to emotions or sentiments that are always already caught in culturally constructed "structures of feeling" (Williams 1977), Deleuze and Guattari use the term *affect* to describe those immanent dispositions, deeply rooted in the body, that are ontologically a priori with respect to culture. Affect has the capacity to challenge or destabilize the order of the state apparatus; as such, they attribute to it a certain "deterritorialization velocity" (Deleuze and Guattari 1987, 356). It has the power to dislodge people and things from their former place—such as the dis-placed surpluses I described above—and to reconfigure them in new assemblages. Their "war machine" therefore avails itself of such affects and hitches them to new political configurations and commitments, be they ad hoc or enduring. From the carnivalesque irreverence of costumed street protest to the blind panic and the kindness of strangers provoked by clouds of police tear gas (see Juris 2008; Graeber 2009), such common, visceral experience reterritorializes constituents within the social space of a movement and makes possible its growth.

This accounts largely for San Francisco FNB's virtually arithmetic growth during its intensive early conflicts with the city. Through the successive administrations of Mayors Art Agnos and Frank Jordan, the city's punitive approach to FNB both inspired and activated a range of political dispositions, from compassion for the homeless to antiauthoritarian outrage. As volunteers from that period explained to me, such gut responses quickly drew hearts and bodies into the fold, and the group metastasized. Police would arrest volunteers and confiscate their buckets of soup from Golden Gate Park, Civic Center, and other frontiers in the struggle for public space. Additional volunteers would emerge, revealing yet more soup (cleverly hidden from the first round of arrests). They, too, were arrested. Not only was the group's resolve hardened by the experience, but new recruits, moved to action by shock or outrage at the arrests, would join the fray. Before long, the group had a calendar to coordinate people who volunteered to risk arrest once a month. According to Keith McHenry, who co-originated FNB and brought it to San Francisco, as the number of arrests grew, grassroots and commercial media coverage increased too. First locally. Then statewide. Then nationally. And with the media coverage, volunteers and community support multiplied.

Cycles of conflict and détente between the city and FNB had telling impacts on the group's affective constitution. Sean Parson (2010) (like me, a Food Not Bombs collaborator-cum-researcher) notes an affect of mutual antagonism that upset their fragile peace at numerous stages, for example. Either public officials would resume the arrests and harassment, or FNB members would adopt new, equally civilly disobedient locations and tactics, lending a certain bilateral traction to the relationship. Indeed, this sustained antagonism lent FNB great staying power and political effect where many other charities were easily absorbed into the local homeless services industry (Parson 2010). As Peter described it, each phase attracted a different constellation of sentiments and dispositions. The conflict attracted more antiauthoritarian volunteers inspired by "fighting the cops," as he put it. And times of truce yielded more volunteers keen on the caring labor of "helping the homeless." In the absence of formal institutional structures or enduring membership, this affective spectrum accounts in large part for Food Not Bombs' growth and geometry.

This pattern is not limited to San Francisco or the late 1980s, of course. In the same way, in Seattle, New York, and elsewhere such periods of state pressure have become the impetus both for local media coverage and calls for community support, circulated via diverse counterpublic channels (punk shows, radical bookstores, self-published underground zines, flyers, and now social media and email), all traditionally accompanied by images of police arresting Food Not Bombs' members or ordering them to pack up and go home. Of course, these images provoke strong feelings—both for and against the group—and bolster their numbers.

Such feelings and dispositions do not simply float about, however, detached as a Cartesian cogito in search of an object. Rather, as Elizabeth Wilson points out in *Gut Feminism*, political affect resides deep in the body. "The gut," she writes, "is an organ of mind: it ruminates, deliberates, comprehends" (E. Wilson 2015, 5). One early San Francisco FNB volunteer brought this point home to me when he described why he eventually distanced himself from the group, explaining that the outrage and anxiety of those clashes with the police lived on in his limbic system, close to the surface and easily triggered, even years later. "It's really easy for me to feel those feelings again," he told me simply. Similarly, Keith McHenry has traced his experience of long-term chronic nerve pain to the stress of his arrests and prosecution by the State of California for FNB-related activities under the state's Three Strikes law (which would have mandated a life sentence had he been convicted). In such ways, embodied experiences of anger, abjection, empathy, and so on inhabit different bodies differently and are mobilized accordingly (a point to which we will return in the next chapter).

This partly accounts for the movement's motley makeup. The various axes of motivation Peter described articulate with different, viscerally felt affects and embodied histories. Carmen explained, for example, why sharing food resonated with her own precarious background: "You know we had lived in shelters, and then I'd been in foster care. And, like, volunteering in something that has to do with foster care will *never* make me feel safe. Ever. I think it's worthwhile, but I don't think I'll ever feel safe doing it. Whereas cooking a meal for

> There would be periods of crisis where the police would crack down and throw us all in jail and come, you know, confiscate our equipment. And . . . then we'd get a whole group of people that were interested in that sort of activity, that civil disobedience. It really wasn't civil disobedience because we were—the police weren't really arresting us. They were just roughing us up. Throwing us in jail, and then kicking us back out again. . . . I was just picked up, thrown in jail, and then released without charges. And as each time happened they just got worse and worse. You know they would just, take my glasses and stomp on 'em you know, and tear my shirt off and throw me in the tank, you know, and tell the other inmates that I was gay. Things like that. Strip searches. Body cavity—yeah, good times. So as that, you know, kind of went on, the collective changed a little bit. It became more and more groups of people that were interested in fighting the cops. And then we would reach a détente sort of with the authorities. . . . I think City Council members intervened 'cause it was so embarrassing. And we would reach an agreement and we would have a period of relative peace and calm. And the collective would shift again to a new group of people that were interested in helping homeless people and, you know, doing more social interactions and making food and trying to, you know, do something useful other than fight with the cops. And so the group would change back and forth in that sense.
>
> —Peter, San Francisco FNB, late 1980s

somebody is one of the—it's like a love language, right? So it's one of the few things that I feel like we can do. I keep going back to the word *tangible*. You see immediate results. You cook something, you feed someone!"

Perhaps, too, this gut politics explains why so many FNB activists intent on "fighting the cops" are young and white—with the privilege that comes of not having learned, as many people of color do, to avoid contact with the police for fear of institutionalized racism and police brutality. Indeed, white FNB volunteers are often conscious of their relative privilege and understand their actions as a deployment of it in defense of the unhoused and other vulnerable members of the community.

> We were in Pioneer Square and we watched a bunch of bike cops descend on this guy. And they knocked him—he was just walking down the street. I don't know what he did. But they pounced on him, and knocked him to the ground, and knocked his skull on the paving stones. And you could hear it crack, and it was, like—we were on the opposite end of the square. And I went over and I figured it would be safest for me to cause a fuss because I was dressed like a yuppie. Ha. Well not really, but I didn't have dreads or anything that would automatically make them not like me. And I, in the serious tone that I could, told the guy that I was embarrassed for my city that they could do that, and it made the police department look really bad . . . And he was very upset and he in retaliation—he probably said something too—but he got on his mountain bike and he like charged us and ran over our little plastic cup. And we just cracked up.
>
> —Corrina, Seattle FNB, on confronting the police while sharing food, ca. 2006

Political affects, however, are contingent, malleable states. As Deleuze and Guattari argue, affect is often incipient or virtual, a spectrum of capacities waiting to be made actual. The provocations of state apparatuses do exactly this, enervating, instantiating, and rearticulating the feelings and dispositions of would-be peaceful insurrectionaries. Kris, for example, a young, white punk rocker who moved to Seattle at seventeen—riding the crest of his enthusiasm for antiauthoritarian politics and punk rock—described his angry response to Seattle's feeding restrictions and its value in forming his activist identity: "At that time, in downtown, there was a lot of police presence, it was—which for me, at the time was *awesome*. Like it was—you know, I was an angry young man—but in a good way, like I wanted to *do* some stuff, and they [Food Not Bombs] took me in with open arms." Although he had developed an abstract sense of antiauthoritarianism from political readings and punk rock, he told me, the experience of police repression made his politics more experiential, more affective:

> They [the police] were just dicks. And it was really . . . for me it was definitely an identity-building experience. Because it was me, ques-

> tioning without really knowing why I was questioning. But it definitely fostered a question of authority, that I—you know, I was taught to hate cops, just through the scene that I was involved with, but never really had a real experience to hate—and just not cops but just authority—and question why. You know somebody says, "You can't feed people here," and I immediately was like, "Why can't I do that? Why can't I just feed my friends? In this public environment? We're not trying to promote anything other than the reality that people are hungry."

Like the cyclical San Francisco volunteers inspired by conflict or détente, Kris's involvement with the group was impelled by both compassionate and antiauthoritarian imperatives—to feed people and question authority, respectively. Both of these elements were articulated and amplified within these moments of police repression.

Such compassion and antiauthoritarianism represent different classes of affect, affirmative and negative. As we have seen, they both are generative. Indeed, negativity and antisociality are inescapable components of protest (see E. Wilson 2015). Hardt and Negri argue that transnational political resistance in the era of capitalist globalization has been driven partly by a shared, generalized negative affect that they simply call "the will to be against"—a virtual, incipient disposition common to a heterogeneous multitude insofar as they all have something to gain from the overthrow of global capital (2000, 35). This will is reflected, for example, in the shared informal slogan of the movements against neoliberal globalization in the late 1990s: "One No, Many Yeses." Of course, as Kris points out, affirmation and negation are not mere opposites. They are mutually entangled. The obverse of "the will to be against," Hardt and Negri argue, is the role of love in forging active transnational connections. It is not the intimate, exclusive love of romance, kin, or identity politics, but something akin to the Platonic *agape*. A sort of post-Enlightenment humanism—or even posthumanism for the vegetarians and ecologists: a love of one's fellow beings. Hardt and Negri's vision is too speculative, perhaps even too utopian, to tell us much of ethnographic value about any specific movement. But if we bracket their teleological aspirations, their vocabulary nonetheless suggests meaningful vectors of comparison to parse the ways in which global political movements may be structured in the twenty-first century. And sure enough, the multitude of Food Not Bombs volunteers with whom I have worked in three nations and half a dozen cities are often moved by both a "will to be against" and

"As with lots of things in the punk world, inspired by a record. It was the MDC Capitalist Casualties split seven inch which basically had information about Food Not Bombs and a picture of Keith McHenry being arrested on the front cover. And MDC did a song, 'Bombs, Not Food.' . . . I'm sure some people had heard of Food Not Bombs prior to that, but that was—for the people involved in the start, or the very beginning seeds—that was where people went 'Oh, what's this?'" —Jade, on the origins of Melbourne FNB in the early 1990s (Note, the picture is miscaptioned: that's not Keith, although these could be the same cops as in the last photo.)

a platonic love for the strangers with whom they break bread.

In these ways, the recipe for a global mass conspiracy to feed people seems to entail roughly equal parts "love thy neighbor" and "fuck the cops." This affective constellation has the "deterritorialization velocity" to circulate beyond its original context, linking people at a global scale. Food Not Bombs' global proliferation across the past forty years bears this out. By the time San Francisco's early pangs of antagonism and armistice had run their course, for example, FNB as an organization had grown by leaps and bounds both locally and abroad. Not only had the local San Francisco chapter dug in and metastasized but new chapters had begun to form as a result of the frenetic publicity both around the country and around the globe. These moments of affective encounter–cum–discursive circulation served as a kind of lightning rod for the generation of larger resistant counterpublics and helped to crystallize a discursive space and identity for such a phenomenon as Food Not Bombs. By 1992, there were enough chapters to organize a national meet-up, timed to coincide with San Francisco's celebration of the five-hundred-year anniversary of Columbus's "discovery" of the Americas

(McHenry 2012, 106). A decade later, dozens, perhaps hundreds, of chapters dotted the globe. And today, they remain impossible to number with any certainty.

Gateway Activism and Dog-Whistle Anarchists

Shared feeling easily begets political sentiment and identity. Common embodied experiences accumulate as solidarity. Collaboration fosters mutual aid. All of these are affective transformations that forge political communities. It was not lost on me, for example, how much more readily my FNB collaborators often came to each other's aid when one of us needed material assistance than did, say, many of my friends from graduate school. My colleagues were always good for a beer and a chat about Gramsci. But if I needed a place to couch-surf (because a tiny research stipend doesn't go far in the Seattle housing market) or store hundreds of dumpstered doughnuts, FNB was often a more tangible sort of community. Years later, I am grateful to know that affinity and goodwill persist. (Indeed, some of my old collaborators proofread drafts of this book. Thanks, folks.) Food Not Bombs transforms us, for better and sometimes for worse, and those transformations are reflected in the emergent form of the movement.

Food Not Bombs therefore articulates new configurations of affect, affinity, and identity for its constituents. It embeds them in the social worlds of radical politics and organizing—often for life. In this sense, Isaiah, a collaborator from New York City, called it a kind of "gateway activism." Isaiah had been a *bottom-liner*, a shared term in some North American anarchist circles for a "first among equals," one who has no special authority but takes responsibility for making sure things get done (dishes washed, kitchens cleaned, doors locked at the end of the night, and so on). The very term reflects an anarchist inversion of hegemonic assumptions about leadership and authority, which is among the affective transformations that come with long-term involvement in FNB. These experiences directly informed his subsequent political and personal choices to pursue work in grassroots organizations.

Similarly, Vikki, another New York City bottom-liner, explained the practical, affirming dimensions of FNB's "gateway" function: "I think in New York City, people come, and for some people—I don't want to say all, because it's not true for all—but . . . I think Food Not Bombs is a good entry point for a certain subset of people—like in their mid-teens to early twenties, of 'I want to get involved in something concrete, and I want to get involved in doing stuff, here's a really good, hands-on way to get

Unlike a lot of other types of activism, you know that the time and effort and the sort of spirit that is being put into the work is directly for good. It's directly benefiting other people, and it's directly addressing issues of hunger, issues of waste and consumption. It's directly—there's so many ways to be active, I always felt like, I never questioned why was I doing it, because I also felt good about doing it. I was taking something that was going to be thrown away, making it into something reasonably tasty—you know, the soup is sometimes a little bland—and feeding myself, feeding my community, and feeding people who are hungry. . . . You can be an activist on a lot of other issues and people say, "What's the point of protesting? What's the point of that?" But you really can't question the point of Food Not Bombs. Because you're feeding people and that's something that everybody needs. And you're doing it primarily with food that would otherwise be tossed. . . . And you can really easily see how somebody who's never really been an activist who gets involved could be really politicized through Food Not Bombs. Really brought into a totally different mindset. Because it really does run so counter to the American value system around food and around consumption. It really is very radical.

—Erin, San Francisco FNB, ca. 1990

involved in doing stuff' . . . and then people sometimes tend to move on to other activist stuff." Vikki herself found FNB to be a gateway into the world of anarchist politics and punk rock, a far cry from her Chinese American community in Queens. "I think for me," she said, "Food Not Bombs was definitely like the entry into Lower East Side politics and squatting and doing that kind of work that I might not have gotten involved with otherwise." She went on to become a long-term organizer in several local DIY community programs and a freelance political journalist with a prolific body of research and writing (as we saw in chapter 2).

Even as it opens certain doors, however, Food Not Bombs closes others. Its transformations of affect and affinity both enable and exclude different forms of sociality. Although collaborators' shared feelings, attitudes, and dispositions are far from homogenous, they can actively alienate people who don't share them. Like almost any activist project, they exclude people who don't fit. Writing of similarly decentralized, unstructured feminist conscious-raising groups in the 1970s (perhaps also a kind of slow insurrection), essayist Jo Freeman observed that in the absence of formal structures and hierarchies, *informal* structures and elites often emerge, excluding or marginalizing some participants along the lines of class, race, and social capital. She called this "the tyranny of structurelessness" (Freeman 1972). In the same way, we might speak of a certain tyranny of affect that excludes or marginalizes would-be participants whose embodied modes of being-in-the-world do not readily articulate with FNB. New volunteers, for instance, have sometimes complained of a distinctly cold shoulder upon their first visit to the Seattle FNB kitchen (a point to which I'll return in the next chapter). And unsurprisingly, although shared dispositions draw FNB collaborators to align with groups with like political sensibilities—to cook for antiwar protests, to circulate radical zines, to organize punk rock shows to raise money, and so on—they often eschew potentially productive relationships with others. In Seattle, for example, Food Not Bombs has only rarely developed relationships with the other less radical meal providers in the city (as we saw in chapter 4).

At worst, these affective affinities manifest as an antagonism toward political difference. Peter put this into perspective for me when I ran into him by chance in the mêlée of Occupy Seattle. Amid the multitudinous crowd of protesters and tents—punctuated by fractious disagreements between libertarians, unionists, communists, liberal homeowners, homeless advocates, and others—he wryly singled out one animated group of black-clad twenty-somethings arguing zealously against complying with the cops. He called them "dog-whistle" anarchists—borrowing a term often applied to the Far Right—whose strategic word choices covertly signal shared virtues, ideological frameworks, and mythologies to those who know to listen for them. As Peter put it, many dog-whistle anarchists had a hard time reconciling themselves to duality and didn't feel comfortable in the company of strangers until they heard certain political catchphrases, communicating shared affinities and antagonisms.

Many seasoned radicals recognize the type. Anarchist essayists Carla Bergman and Nick Montgomery (2017) identify such dogmatic rejections of difference as part of a broad, sometimes toxic phenomenon they call "rigid radicalism." Similarly, Kris recalled (with the gentle sarcasm born of solidarity) the skepticism with which he was greeted by certain "holier-squatter-than-thou" Food Not Bombs volunteers when he visited the Portland chapter:

> Literally, I would be in the van, going to the feeding, and having people be, like, doing their conspiracy theories and like pointing at me like "Who are you? Like, I don't even know you ... he could be a Fed ... And you know what, I was thinking, you know, "Even if I was a Fed, what am I going to do to you?" Like, they [the Feds] *do* do these things [infiltrate grassroots groups] but you're not *that* radical. [laughing] You're just feeding homeless people. You're not Ted Kaczynski, you know? And I know that's what the Feds want to find out, but they're going to, you know, get in a van with you and be like, "Alright, this guy is just kind of a twat."

It's worth noting that Kris is describing a simpler time before September 11, 2001. During the 2000s, the FBI's intensified surveillance efforts became more onerous even for peaceful insurrectionaries (as I described in scene v), a situation that threatens to repeat itself under contemporary nationalist governments. Nonetheless, as the anthropologist and activist David Graeber argued, such a hostile "security culture" can undermine the growth and diversity of theoretically open, public-facing movements like FNB (2009, 10–11), fostering an unwelcoming, rigid radicalism. In like fashion, I witnessed at least one Seattle volunteer be asked not to return to the kitchen because she was suspected of being a Fed. (Perhaps she was, but it was equally plausible that her politics—including her military service, about which she claimed to have mixed feelings—just made people uncomfortable.) This hostility toward difference can also be expressed subtly through a simple negative affect, as Kris described on subsequent visits to the Lower East Side FNB: "It was the same way in New York City. At ABC No Rio . . . which is a famous old squat that turned into a publicly owned community center . . . they would even have flyers up, you know: 'Come and Help Food Not Bombs.' And I'd go, show up every week, and [simulating his own enthusiastic attitude], 'You guys need any help?' [And then, simulating their unimpressed, cold response,] 'Mmm, who are you?'" With some irony, he described this antagonism toward difference as "the closed-minded scene of the 'open-minded' people."

As I write this, however, I think of an invaluable conversation I had with Avery, a Seattle FNB collaborator, squatter, and punk rocker from the early 1990s who has a healthy skepticism about the heady politics of his past. I admitted how much I, too, had been embarrassed by my own youthful zeal and sanctimony. Although he sympathized, he offered this perspective: as narrowly idealistic as he now found such personalities, he admired them, he told me. Even missed them. Because, for all their narrowness and visceral antagonisms, their spirited convictions cultivated a commitment to change and possibility. The energy contained therein (following Deleuze and Guattari, we could say "velocity"), he said, was what made movements possible.

And here, perhaps, is where we might find one of the key intersections between antiauthoritarian antagonism and caring labor. For although I have written here about the tyranny of affect, the difference between Food Not Bombs and some other radical, counterpublic endeavors is that FNB is fundamentally embedded in a practice of helping others. As such, whatever affective conflicts it fosters are just as readily redirected and translated into an empathetic connection across difference. Perhaps it is for this reason that, eclipsing the frustrating moments of political or cultural antagonism, I have so treasured the informants, collaborators, and friendships I have made through Food Not Bombs.

Conclusion

Despite the powerful wake it leaves in the lives and landscapes it transects, Food Not Bombs' legacy is hazy to the casual observer. Until recently, its existence was recorded mostly in the annals of anarchist ephemera. Hand-painted banners. Photocopied zines. Inconsistently updated websites. Flyers taped to café walls. Beyond the audiences for these media, FNB leaves a deceptively small textual footprint. For most of its existence, researchers seem to have ignored it. News cycles quickly forget it. Service providers and public officials alike often regard it as deviant or incongruous.

Like most rhizomes, therefore, FNB's most important implications often fall below a threshold of public visibility. In this chapter, I have argued that its unseen entanglements amount to a sort of slow insurrection, albeit one that operates at temporal and spatial scales that render it illegible to many observers. Not only do its periodic, nonviolent clashes with city authorities shape the terrain of urban space and enforcement; in its local and global growth it amounts to a "many-headed hydra," a heterogeneous multitude of deterritorialized people, places, and things that forges new possibilities for political affinity and upheaval (see Linebaugh and Reddiker 2000).

Like the ancient, unsung barbarians of James Scott's *Against the Grain* (2017), who lived beyond the reach of the ancient state and whose antagonisms and exchanges with it left a definitive impression upon its form, the tools, techniques, and human resources of FNB's particular hydra are no less significant than the state apparatus, but they *are* more easily lost to the mists of time and political discourse. In the absence of such traces, we are left with a mistaken impression of city politics as governed primarily by municipal state apparatuses and their attendant market-publics.

Yet, as I have argued in this chapter, slow insurrections like FNB represent a nonviolent war machine with which these publics and apparatuses share an ontology. Food Not Bombs has played a crucial role in setting territorial limits to the sovereignty of municipal state apparatuses and in building networks and capacities that erupt onto the urban political stage in more legible ways. Not only does FNB represent one of the training grounds where people practice and refine radical forms of political action and organization, such as the public agglomerations and consensus-based protocols that defined the viral spread of Occupy Wall Street. It also

The way people do politics is changing. The way people are organizing and involving themselves in activities is altered forever. And I think Food Not Bombs was a beginning part of that. . . . It's a mosaic. It's a bringing together of all kinds of disparate factions and pieces, and they're all sort of working together, but not through any, you know, giant control. And so I think that's what really inspired me to work with Food Not Bombs at that time, you know, it's just a different way of thinking. And since I left Food Not Bombs and went on my own way, I've just noticed that, it just, it just went viral. . . . There's not going to be marches in the street anymore. There's not going to be takeovers of government. It's going to be small, autonomous, disparate groups, sort of working to solve their own problems in their own city, in their own way. And it's going to be different. And it's going to be chaotic. And it's going to get messy. But it's all people doing their thing and trying to take a certain amount of control over their life. And Food Not Bombs was trying to do that around homelessness and poverty, housing, hunger sort of issues. And they served a need or a function that wasn't being fulfilled by the society that they were—the group of, you know—the community they were living [in], and they filled that niche. And if that need changes, then they'll just sort of adapt to it, because that's what people do. They adapt. They change. And they, you know, they're not—people aren't like bureaucracies. They're not monolithic. They're not. You know, they're complicated.

—Peter, on the political legacy of San Francisco FNB and everything after

builds concrete logistical capacities, from assembling ad hoc field kitchens to facilitating consensus-based meetings.

What I hope emerges from this chapter is a complex picture of the ways in which the work of power and resistance actively make thinkable the possibilities for ordering social life in the city. Whereas participants in both Food Not Bombs and governmental agencies may sometimes see their role in urban politics as independent of or reactive to larger urban economic and cultural trends, I have tried to point to certain key moments in which they actively shape the urban landscape, especially the geography of eating and surviving in the city. The forbidden gifts of the previous chapter therefore become occasions for a mass conspiracy like FNB with the capacity to challenge some of the territorial claims and investments of the market-public. It does this both materially, by rearticulating public parks, wasted food, and dis-located people with one another, and discursively, by convening supportive urban counterpublics and by making concrete and visible the impact of feeding prohibitions and other urban policies.

In these ways, Food Not Bombs has represented an important trend in resistant social forms, one that emerges from fundamental changes in urban cultural economy and state apparatuses during an era of neoliberal globalization. As I have written, Food Not Bombs is attendant to the growing disparities and bourgeois symbolic orders of globalized cities, and to their increasingly market-centric, often heavy-handed approaches to governance. Not only this; we cannot help but notice now (following Hardt, Negri, and the latter's Operaista compatriots) the ways in which FNB resembles, in its decentralization and spontaneity, the flexible, globalized, post-Fordist kinds of economic organization that have driven these urban changes. Thus anarchic, war machine–like structures like Food Not Bombs, Occupy Wall Street, and other conspiracies have grown in prominence compared with party-based activist groups that looked more like state apparatuses and dominated an earlier era of the Left (see Graeber 2004). Our examination of Food Not Bombs' proliferation therefore identifies a microcosm of larger changes in government and resistance.

SCENE VI

WHEN I FIRST GOT TO THE KITCHEN

When I first got to the kitchen, I was early. There was nobody around. But the front door was wide open. So I walked in and made myself at home on one of the beaten-up secondhand couches upstairs.

In part, that was how I knew I was in the right place.

Food Not Bombs kitchens are often radically open affairs. There are no background checks. No managers (the odd bossy cook notwithstanding). They're accustomed to strangers showing up and making themselves at home in the kitchen. In fact, they often depend on it: volunteers are entirely at-will, and the turnover is rapid.

But without anyone to welcome me in, an open door alone wasn't enough to go on. I had asked the taxi driver to wait while I popped in to make sure I wasn't in the wrong place. Someone formerly affiliated with Melbourne FNB had given me the address for this place—a shared Do-It-Yourself arts warehouse with a kitchen. But it is in the nature of FNB to be ephemeral, so the address could easily have been out of date. I couldn't be sure from outside.

The locale was a clue. The faded Brunswick warehouse was at the end of an industrial cul-de-sac, literally and figuratively: the warehouses on this dead-end street had seen busier, brighter days as part of the suburb's textile industry. But by this point, in 2006, most of those jobs were gone, and the buildings shared space in the neighborhood with Melbourne's punks, artists, broke twenty-somethings, and adventurous young, urban professionals who all appreciated the cheap rent (Melbourne's property boom hadn't quite hit yet) and proximity to the city's Central Business District. The warehouse's original company sign lingered on the terra-cotta brick façade in tall, midcentury lettering, but the wide-open garage doors and the secondhand bicycle parts peeking out from inside were evidence that artists had taken up residence. The van out front was stenciled with spray paint: "brand new pre-loved." More evidence. A likely place for an anarchist soup kitchen.

What really gave the place away was the interior décor, if that's the right word. Not a concerted style like mid-century modern, but a distinct aesthetic nonetheless. One of lived-in-ness and enthusiastic making-do. Although this was my first visit to Melbourne's Food Not Bombs—and just the second FNB chapter I'd ever cooked with—I had only to pop in for a moment to affirm that I was in the right place before sending the taxi driver on his way. I was twenty-six, and after only a year or so of having worked with Food Not Bombs in Seattle, sharing space in the kinds of communes, co-ops, punk houses, squats, independent art spaces, and other locations where the group cooked and put on benefits, I would have known the place blindfolded. Literally. I wrote in my field notes: "The warehouse already felt familiar. It smelled like a co-op. I don't know exactly what that smell is, but it contains no artificial colors, preservatives or sweeteners. There are stencils and flyers on every wall. And every wall was a different color. No pastels. I was early. But there were couches." The explicit semiotics of the walls alone would have been a giveaway—announcements for punk shows, radical political slogans, cheeky subversive art, and other countercultural writings on the wall that bespeak the circles within which FNB moves in cities around the world. But what's even more interesting is that I already recognized the smell. Political slogans, musical genres, and art styles all enjoy a certain international circulation. Can the same be said of scents? I've heard punk rockers in different cities (themselves infamously pungent) joke that patchouli and sage "smell like hippy." Do some things "smell like Food Not Bombs"? What does it mean that this kitchen in Melbourne smelled so much like the kitchens in which I'd cooked in Seattle, or some of the FNB kitchens I would visit thereafter?

To say they smelled alike, on the face of it, is not to say all that much. But it hints at other, more important comparisons between the unspoken sensory landscapes cultivated and inhabited by people working in different corners of the world, ostensibly in the name of a common project. Smell is simultaneously visceral and habituated. It's the embodied sensory evidence of a particular kind of everyday life, embedded in memory and accumulated in a single place over time in ways that language can't always capture (and that social science often overlooks).

If the kitchens smelled alike to me, it was not simply because cooks in each place had a shared love of parsley or basil. There were more layers. A base note of compost and gray water, recovered from the sink for flushing the toilets. Middle tones of slightly overripe produce and slightly overripe traveling punks with limited access to shower facilities. Hints of nutritional yeast. (A favorite seasoning for some Food Not Bombers, sometimes called "hippy flakes" or "punk powder," depending on one's affinities.)

These layers cannot, of course, be divorced from the evidence of the other senses. The sense memories both cultivated and awakened in the kitchen turn cooking into a kind of cultural apprenticeship in the approaches to consumption, hygiene, and domesticity that inhere in a community (Sutton 2001). In my field notes I jotted down some of the various other traces left behind in the Brunswick warehouse, and the practices and sensibilities that seemed to underwrite them:

> The toilets at the warehouse are more or less communal, covered in wonderful graffiti, both the scribbles and the murals, the stencils and the sketches in spray paint. They could use a good scrub. There's a note on the wall outside the stalls, where the toilet paper and the sinks and the mirror reside, reminding anyone concerned that the warehouse is a communal space and if anyone has a spare minute, they might think about tidying the toilets. . . . The tables and the walls and the pipes and the sinks all have a bruised skin, like they've been saved from the tip and put together without worry about the shiny and the right-angled, without worry about the showroom floor which so many middle-class kitchens are working to re-create. Under the table in the middle, pots and pans and cutting boards and Tupperware and colanders and big stainless-steel bowls all mingle like a drunken high-school social. There's a locked cupboard with "FNB" stenciled on it and some of the more indispensable things are kept in there, like the giant soup pots and mixing bowls and the really sharp knives . . . next to the big waxed boxes of recently collected produce. Some of their stuff looks a lot mankier than the stuff we get in Seattle, but it's still serviceable. Adjacent to this back wall is a long wall with two fridges (one stenciled "FNB"), a gas range, a wall full of chalk messages to the "bombers," a sink and some drying racks. No one has cleaned between the sink and the fridge in years. The sink isn't really part of the cupboard-bench it's attached to, but it's pretty stable. There's a bloody hot tap above it, and under it two buckets, to collect grey water. Besides which there's no plumbing for it to drain away. And outside the sink, the cherry blossoms have just started to come out. Warehouse residents come in and out without much ado, although they're friendly and know the basic drill, and sometimes help cook or eat.

"Yo! Don't get Food Not Bombs veggies moldy don't unplug the fridge!!!" Traces and instructions for an ephemeral contingent in the ABC No Rio Kitchen, New York City (Photo by Victoria Law)

In the absence of an interlocutor, therefore, the space itself told me a great many things. To my senses, it communicated the kind of radical hospitality I had met in other FNB spaces—walls as egalitarian communication medium, strangers invited to stop in and eat or to take up chores. The smell of slightly overripe produce and the condition of the couches and kitchen fixtures told stories about regular practices of salvaging and scavenging would-be garbage. The bucket under the sink suggested a self-conscious ethic of conservation. The condition of the floor eschewed showroom aesthetics and a bourgeois paranoia about disease. A range of recurring modes of everyday living with which I had some familiarity and yet in which I was at that moment also being schooled. Practices and sensibilities that, I was learning, tend to deposit these same sensory traces wherever Food Not Bombs goes. The smells, the cluttered walls, the second-handedness of the couches all play a role in cultivating the practices and sensibilities of the people who live amid them. They matter quite a lot, in fact, in building scenes and social movements.

6 Embodying Otherwise

Toward a New Politics of Surplus

"Whichever Food Not Bombs You Visit, It's Always the Same Food"

Waste almost inevitably has a whiff of anarchy about it. Ejected from within any given social world according to its peculiar norms, waste (or contact with it) carries within it the possibility of subverting those norms. Our "mass conspiracy" is assembled from the experiments and improvisations of a heterogeneous constellation of people making do with the detritus at hand. The resulting transnational assemblage of goods, spaces, and bodies reimagines the pathways of value that make the city. In its overlooked corners, neglected warehouses, and underused kitchens, make-do becomes know-how and innovation scales up to constitute new forms of embodied political and practical common sense that confound the organizing principles of liberal markets and publics. Food Not Bombs and projects like it hold out the political possibility of embodying otherwise.

Consider a quotidian example: the recipe for "Glory Soup," invented one hectic Sunday afternoon in the Seattle FNB kitchen. Before any vegetable has even seen a chopping board, the dish's first definitive element is the kitchen complement. Perhaps a dozen of us—mostly punks and broke train-hoppers, some university students, one software engineer, locals and international visitors alike, straight folk and self-identified queers—piled into an impossibly small, aging studio apartment, one of the last affordable places in Se-

This is a doorway, this beautiful ruined house with its facade of vines & mirrors, and the world behind it has a thousand faces . . . It's asking you, where can we go when we let go of what binds us?
—Hibickina

attle's rapidly gentrifying Belltown neighborhood. We had recently lost our previous kitchen space and struggled to find another one available on Sunday afternoons. At the last minute, one Food-Not-Bomber volunteered her place, barely fit for purpose. Most of the available surfaces became de facto chopping boards. There was room for two or three of us around the stove, atop which a singularly massive stock pot nicknamed Big Mama was the only thing that fit on the tiny appliance. The next step was to pick up ingredients. Somebody (without a license, I later learned) had borrowed my car to visit Pike Place Market but our usual donors turned up relatively empty-handed, so we found ourselves with a single large box of assorted produce and whatever else was in the fridge. Given the space, the equipment, and the ingredients, the only thing to do was to make a single enormous pot of soup—and put literally everything we had into it, from tofu to pineapple to a jar of peanut butter. Equal parts stone soup and George's Marvelous Medicine, the hearty purple sludge turned out to be a hit at the park. Though the recipe beggared belief, diners came back for seconds. Upon much deliberation, we named it "Glory Soup" because, against the odds, it was delightful. Rather than the chaos sometimes misattributed to anarchists and their cookbooks,[1] the alchemy of such happy accidents is actually remarkably dependable. As Francisco put it after traveling across the US, "Whichever Food Not Bombs you visit, it's always the same food."

The kitchen practices, ethics, and aesthetics that emerge from these shared improvisations make a mockery of many received culinary wisdoms, and a few political ones too. Yet they become de rigueur for Food Not Bombs collaborators who develop new vernaculars and new forms of common sense that are experienced in deeply embodied

Glory Soup,
an Approximate Recipe

Ingredients: Pumpkin (1 large) • Squash (1 small) • Tofu (10 packets) • Garam masala (too much) • Cinnamon (a dash) • Ginger (3 inches) • Maple syrup (¼ cup) • Peanut butter (1 jar) • Cashews (1 handful) • Macadamia nuts (1 ½ cup) • Curry paste (4 inch log) • Pineapple (1, chopped) • Beets (3, grated) • Dill (a bunch or two, whole—stems and all) • Savory (1 packet) • Onions (1) • Potatoes (2) • Cauliflower (3 fleurettes—1 purple, 1 orange, 1 white) • Broccoli (stems only) • Lettuce (scraps) • Cabbage (scraps) • Arugula (scraps) • Kale (scraps) • Collard (scraps) • Grapes (1 bunch) • Dates (5 handfuls) • Bananas (3) • Soy milk, vanilla (1 carton) • Carrots (2) • Walnuts (½ cup) • Water (6 pitchers) • Salt and pepper (to taste)
Directions: Boil water • Add ingredients • Blend some [in a blender] • Burn bottom of pot
Serves: 30+

—From the author's notes, post facto, Seattle FNB, ca. 2006

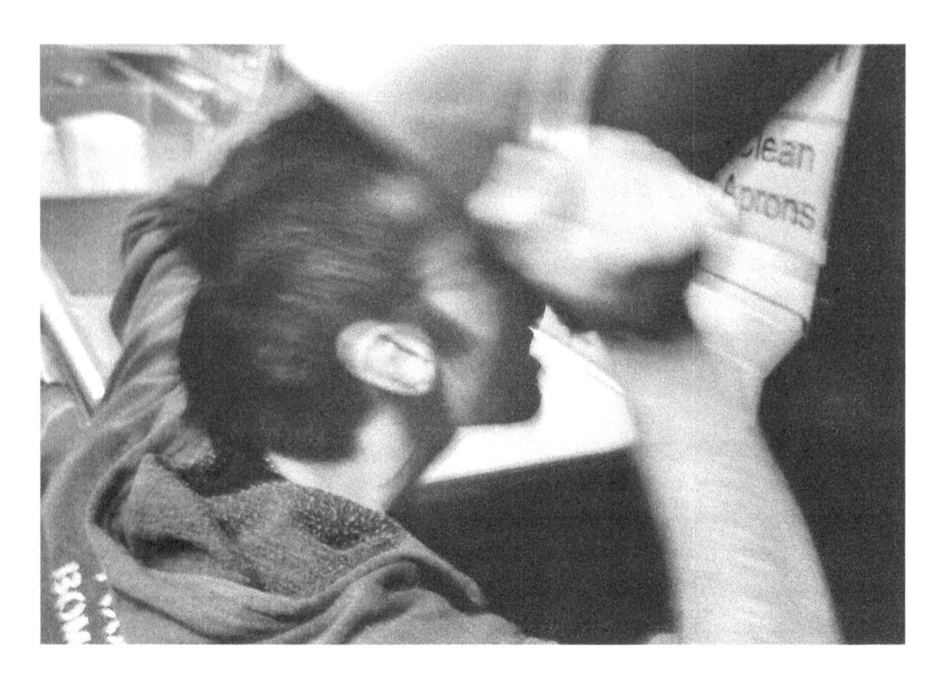

The author finishes the last of the Glory Soup, ca. 2006. (Photo by Wilson Shook)

ways. Tastes. Aesthetic norms. Modes of deliberating under pressure and collaborating across difference. If the embodied practices of "doing cooking" reproduce larger patterns of kinship, gender, class, and political organization (de Certeau and Giard 1997), then these emergent, embodied dispositions make thinkable new kinds of "gastro-politics" (Appadurai 1981), new landscapes—aesthetic, ethical, pragmatic, and political—that often remain illegible within the cherished political categories of Left and Right alike. This illegibility is part of what makes it a "conspiracy." Food Not Bombs and endeavors like it, I argue, create the conditions to queer hegemonic categories of embodiment, such as race, class, and sex, and interrogate their privileged incorporation by prevailing markets, publics, and institutions, cultivating emergent spaces of embodiment, contact, and collaboration across difference.

> One of the most fun things is that you have a pile of rutabagas and you have an hour to try to figure out how to make it taste good.
>
> —Corrina, on improvising with the scavenged materials at hand, Seattle FNB, ca. 2005

This chapter therefore explores the possibilities for what I'll call *illiberal embodiment*—both of the personal body and the body politic—incipient within the discarded surpluses of liberal markets and publics. Edible food discarded by supermarkets. Homes shuttered by real estate speculators. People displaced by gentrification or abandoned by neoliberal welfare "reforms." And so on. The ethnographic worlds of anarchist soup kitchens, DIY community centers, and other shared social spaces constituted by dumpster-divers, squatters, and other scavengers reconfigure people, places, and things devalorized by market and state in ways that tell us much about the material and discursive constitution of class, capital, and state power.

In particular, the high-stakes markets and publics of "world-class" cities incorporate and exclude bodies according to diverse kinds of enculturated affects and dispositions, from genteel germophobia to homelessness, all underwritten by class, race, nation, gender, sexuality, and ability. Those people who are rendered outsiders are diverse, ranging from underemployed students to radical queers, from undocumented migrants to homeless itinerants—all of whom come together through projects like FNB.

> As someone who was homeless and addicted, I found FNB randomly walking through a rainy Occidental Park one dark winter night. The following Sunday I latched onto the group like a lamprey. Its values, approach, and access were and still are unique. So it's very possible to find volunteers from those you serve.
>
> —Jon, Seattle FNB, late 2000s

These people are not outsiders a priori, however. As we have already seen in this book, their exclusion is biopolitical, constituted by practices and dispositions that reproduce bodies themselves. Picking up where chapter 4 left off, therefore, here I argue that it is not just surplus people, places, or things that are excluded from liberal markets and publics, but rather modes of embodiment, and especially embodied economic practices. These exclusions are conditioned by the contemporary configuration of market, public, and state that anthropologist Elizabeth Povinelli (2011) calls "late liberalism," a term I think with in this chapter. As such, I distinguish between those late liberal embodiments that structure market-publics, and those illiberal embodiments that organize a slow insurrection—and, indeed, reframe the very domain of the political, transcending mere exclusion. Projects like FNB, I argue, bring excluded goods and bodies together in novel, out-of-place formations, ephemeral but politically meaningful, that are not wholly legible according to the hegemonic terms of liberal markets and publics.

If the previous chapter concerned itself with parks and the spatial politics of municipal state apparatuses, this chapter concerns itself with kitchens and other spaces of counterpublic production. If the downtown parks where so many Food Not Bombs collaborators share their wares represent extremely public interventions in the politics of eating and surviving in the city, then the kitchens where they cook represent a reciprocal to these public actions—one not so much private as counterpublic, where their labors and experiences are shared across difference, one in which people come together and make something new out of the matter at hand.

Excursus: How to Recognize Difference

This chapter wrestles with a question posed in numerous guises to FNB and movements like it: "So what?" It's often a rhetorical question—dismissive of them for failing to play by familiar rules of engagement or make themselves legible within existing terrains of the political. It asks which differences make a difference, implicitly flattening the labors of FNB and movements like it into insignificance according to the terms of power and privilege that constitute liberal markets and publics. This book offers one account of how to constitute a politics *otherwise*.

Participants and critics alike often frame the social worlds of my co-conspirators within liberal imaginaries. Despite FNB's anarchism, for example, a popular slogan is that "Food Is a Right, Not a Privilege," invoking liberal traditions of "natural" rights or "human" rights. Meanwhile, detractors on the Left disparage practices like dumpster-diving and squatting as "drop-out culture" or "lifestyle activism," rebuking precisely such activists' disengagement from prevailing political and economic institutions. Both frames rely on liberal vernaculars that render illegible modes of living and organizing otherwise.

Indeed, late liberalism is organized by a discursive project of recognition that disciplines difference according to the norms of liberal markets and publics (Povinelli 2011). Therein, difference is either erased—reduced to homo economicus or the individuated neoliberal subject—or neutralized, as in that neoliberal co-optation of identity politics that evacuates embodied difference from identity. On the Right, for example, this erasure valorizes shallow corporate representations of "diversity," and on the Left it upholds essentialist conceptions of feminist or antiracist politics that ignore the dissent and differences among their constituents. Queer essayist Pat Mosley (2017) calls the latter "peak liberalism," a form of rigidly partisan identity politics that envisions different positionalities strictly as competitors on a one-dimensional, zero-sum terrain of privilege and therefore obscures the fluid intersections of struggle highlighted by the very feminists of color who originally popularized the term *identity politics* (e.g., Lorde 2007), along with unexpected vectors of solidarity that emerge from them.

In the same vein, even among progressives, FNB's politics are sometimes dismissed as merely white privilege in radicalism's clothing, its members characterized as disaffected youth for whom the protections of whiteness undermine their intended (or pretended) radicalism. To be sure, the privileges are real. In white-majority nations like the US and Australia, FNB and its affiliated movements are largely, though far from exclusively, white. The intersections of material, cultural, and social capital this affords them are indeed a topic of vigorous conversation for many participants. However, their detractors' narrow representation of these movements' political significance along a single vector of privileged identity *itself bears a resemblance to the liberal project of recognition*. In the process, it overlooks the everyday mutual aid of the confederacy of nomadisms described in the previous chapter. In this way, the liberal project of recognition that excludes many of them from political representation may also render the politics of their ephemeral collaborations illegible. In other words, those critics who write off FNB as simply a white, middle-class movement erase the contributions of countless participants who identify otherwise. As Carmen (our Latina co-conspirator with lungs of steel from chapter 5) put it, "I'm kind of annoyed that this is being framed as like a white people thing or a privilege thing, because it's absolutely not. It's a community effort . . . I mean, anything grassroots is the opposite of establishment, right?" In other words, whereas whiteness and privilege are inherently invested in and vested by the status quo, FNB represents one effort, however partial, to organize beyond those hierarchies.

So we have to ask ourselves, *What differences do we fail to recognize* when our work is reduced to a paradoxically disembodied liberal politics of identity? Part III of this book aims, in part, to make such differences visible.

To capture these unexpected intersections and avenues for both political agency and mutual aid, this chapter emphasizes embodiment over identity. It takes its cues from queer and feminist theorists who draw our attention to the untidy and intersectional *matter* (read: both "topic" and "materiality") of "enfleshment" where flesh-and-blood bodies, practices, and subjects intersect (e.g., Weheliye 2014; see also Butler 1993). Throughout this book, following Gibson-Graham's call to "queer economy" (2006, xxxvi)—in other words, to "read for difference rather than dominance" (xxxii) and valorize that which is illegible within hegemonic capitalist imaginaries—I have theorized the proliferation of economies and subjectivities with a queer or abject relationship to prevailing markets and publics, assembled from bodies and goods these markets and publics have discarded. Within such projects of reclamation is the raw material for postliberal political formations and unwritten futures.

Dirty Habits

The social worlds that foster Food Not Bombs are dirty. Not necessarily filthy, although on occasion they're that too. But more often the sensory landscapes of dumpster-divers, squatters, punks, FNB chapters, and other anarchist projects bear out the familiar dictum that "dirt" is merely matter-out-of-place. In *material* terms, they're harmless. (As we saw in chapter 1, FNB and dumpster-diving proved safer than eating at many commercial establishments.) But in *semiotic* terms, the sights and smells of anarchist soup kitchens and their ilk are beyond the pale of public decency. Like the larger counterpublics in which they are embedded, they are crowded with signifiers of obsolescence, valuelessness, disorder, and waste. They share a rough, unfinished aesthetic, from salvaged pots and battered appliances to dumpster-dived produce and a patent rejection of bourgeois body ritual. These elements are the phenomenological residue of shared practices of waste reclamation and other affiliated nonmarket, counterpublic modes of embodiment.

> It was donated by, I think, a couple of German boys. I'm not entirely sure. But, it was a smaller van than that [current] one and it was a fucking *nightmare*. The side door was broken. When I started, I'd have to get in—and it was summer—and I'd jump in one of the windows or one of the doors. I'd get in and I'd have to get inside and kick the back door to get it open. It was so hot and you'd be sweltering and punching it and kicking it to get it—and it totally looked dodgy every time I went to get in there—people, anyone who walked past would just be seeing me kicking it, you know, having a full go at this poor van. But eventually it got stolen. Fuck knows why.
>
> —Alicia, Melbourne FNB, ca. 2001–2005

Most of the FNB kitchens where I have cooked, for example, have shared a certain *je ne scent quoi*—that common sensory palette described in scene vi (overripe produce, unwashed punk rockers, and so on). Consider the punk house where I stayed while in Buffalo. Most shared punk houses have a catchy, irreverent name that is carried on by the generations of punks who live and hang out there years after the name's origin has been forgotten. This one was called "The Death Trap." It proudly displayed a repurposed sign on its front door (apparently from the sixties) that read "Hippies Enter by the Back." I wrote in my field notes: "The Death Trap was once the Food Not Bombs house. The 'FNB' remains inside one of the upstairs cupboards, along with a Brews Not

The “Scribble Squat” kitchen, Food Not Bombs, and donated veggies, Seattle, 2006. (Photo courtesy of Nancy Jean Chase)

Bombs Buffalo poster in the hallway. The house is covered in stencils and scrawled notes and sketches and posters and photographs and collages and the dishes are piling up in the sink. I don’t think I heard a toilet flush the whole time I was there. The landlord asks no questions.”

The Death Trap, too, smelled familiar. “I remember that smell,” replied my friend Chopper, a vegan punk, bassist, and FNB collaborator from Buffalo, when I told her what this chapter was about. “There’s a *reason* they called it the Death Trap,” she explained, only half joking. Its olfactory profile paralleled the visual and tactile traces that had built up over time from heavy traffic, earnest use, and perhaps too little scrubbing. Although FNB kitchens are far from homogenous, many of them—like the Death Trap, the FNB warehouse in Melbourne, the Abel Smith Street anarchist bookstore in Wellington, the Scribble Squat in Seattle’s Central District, ABC No Rio in New York City (as I’ll describe below), and any number of other spaces in North America and Australasia where I’ve helped cook or met

So we'd do these Street Feeds, and just kind of randomly, whenever we were having a protest. And then later on—I can't remember exactly when I heard of Food Not Bombs, more like in the early nineties—the housing and homeless activism got more alive and was kind of connected to the gentrification of Seattle. And at that point there was still a lot of low-income housing downtown and the city hadn't been gentrified that much yet. The convention center hadn't been built—and the convention center displaced four or five low-income housing buildings downtown. There was a lot of abandoned low-income housing areas in the downtown area, and so there was a lot of activism starting up about occupying those buildings. So then, that really was sort of around the same time as I started squatting. So there was these public occupations where we'd take over buildings, large buildings downtown. But at the same time smaller groups of us were squatting in houses, kind of more secretly, just places to live for free. And then we started doing the Street Feeds more regularly at all of our protests, and then we started hearing about Food Not Bombs in San Francisco. And I can't remember exactly how or where I heard of it, but we started hearing stories about Food Not Bombs and how it was kind of cool because all you had to do was just declare yourself a Food Not Bombs. It wasn't like "apply and be accepted" or anything. It was just totally anarchistic: just say you're Food Not Bombs. There's no rules, you just take the banner and go with it. So eventually, like after I'd lived in a couple different squats, probably in maybe '91 or '92 or so, I actually sort of got organized with a few people and started doing a regular thing that we actually started calling Food Not Bombs.

—Lisa, on the origins of Seattle FNB

Food Not Bombs collaborators—share some or all of these familiar sensory traces.

Such traces reflect a repertoire of embodied practices and dispositions that become second nature for many FNB collaborators—at odds with the embodied practices and dispositions that animate prevailing market-publics. Pierre Bourdieu (1977) might have called this repertoire a counterpublic "habitus" or "hexis." Habitus, as he described it, is a kind of socialized second nature: everything happens as if by design in a given social world because the social, economic, and political patterns within which individuals live are imprinted upon them as a set of seemingly commonsense predispositions, which tend to reproduce those same social, economic, and political patterns. *Hexis* refers to embodied habitus, from body language to culinary preferences. Anarchist organizers often acknowledge the importance of radical habitus by another name in their embrace of "prefigurative politics," a theory of change that calls for political actions that transmit by example shared practices and dispositions around which a new society could eventually coalesce. Food Not Bombs represents a quintessential form of prefigurative politics, bypassing existing power structures and momentarily enacting new relationships of mutual aid (see Parson 2010; Shannon 2011). After all, most people who find their way to Food Not Bombs do not start out dumpster-diving, squatting, or sweeping communal kitchens. Rather, these become common sense in response to the excesses and exclusions of the "mainstream" societies into which they have been born. The life-ways that accumulate as such counterpublic habitus are not easily summed up. They are not exclusive to Food Not Bombs.

They are not part of a distinct cuisine like "Tex-Mex" or a contiguous aesthetic formation like "modernism." It is tempting to name them after a specific movement—punk rock, for example, because many of these spaces are nurtured by punkers. But this misses the diversity of the people implicated therein.

Like a Dada collage, the embodied practices and life-ways shared among FNB participants and their counterpublic milieu are a kind of ad hoc *detournement*, a Situationist term for the politically subversive dislocation of objects from their everyday contexts. They have as much to do with alienation from prevailing, market-centric habitus as they have to do with any particular shared ethos or ethnos. Their kitchens reflect as much a rejection of the hypersanitary, perfumed and deodorized foodways of the supermarket and the *Better Homes and Gardens*–inspired kitchen as they do an embrace of any gastronomic or domestic aesthetic. (As Patricia told me, Seattle FNB's menu was "always nutritious, occasionally delicious.") This alienation is the germ, if you'll forgive the pun, that develops into shared counterpublic forms of habitus and embodiment.

A sidenote about risk: The casual observer, habituated to a market-centric, bourgeois habitus, might conflate this unorthodox common sense with bad hygiene and food safety. They would usually be wrong. Consider one Seattle Meals Partnership Coalition member I spoke with, for example, who questioned FNB's food safety practices because FNB at one point used ten-gallon plastic buckets to transport and serve the food. And although there's nothing unsafe about serving food from buckets (most vegan food need not be kept at a consistent temperature), to a certain bourgeois sensibility it looks out of place. Nonetheless, sharing food, space, or cutlery with FNB collaborators has never given me any serious misgivings about my health or safety. In my experience, FNB kitchens are usually peopled by cooks with carefully considered diets and dietary politics—part and parcel of their rejection of bourgeois culinary norms. And almost invariably, bottom-liners in each FNB kitchen are well-versed in food safety, taking extra responsibility for making sure the food is worth eating.

The Downward Mobility of Abject Economies

These dirty habits are deliberate symbolic rejections of the status quo, to be sure. More than that, however, they facilitate a dis-interpellation of goods, people, and embodied practices from the hierarchies of value that structure privilege and poverty in market-publics. Dominant foodways, in contrast, may serve, in Althusser's terms, as a kind of "ideological state apparatus," "interpellating" individuals as subjects—which is to say calling them to identify with and misrecognize themselves within hegemonic conceptions of nation, state, market, public, and so on (Allison 1991; Althusser [1971] 2014). Practices like dumpster-diving and squatting disrupt this. As we have seen throughout this book, such cultural dis-locations with respect to prevailing publics—especially market-publics—allow a motley constellation of outsiders and surpluses to come together in new counterpublic configurations.

As Dylan Clark (2004) argues in his ethnography of dumpster-diving punk rockers in Seattle, those markers of newness, tidiness, cleanliness, and safety that confer capitalist exchange value are not only constitutive of the commodity—and in their absence, of valuelessness and waste—but at a larger scale, they are some of the signifiers that constitute bourgeois identity and whiteness. By his logic these are tertiary but constitutive components of what Audre Lorde called the "mythical norm," that set of embodied signifiers (she lists "white, thin, male, young, heterosexual, Christian, and financially secure" but we can surely add more) within which, she says, "the trappings of power reside" (2007, 116). In this sense, as you will remember from chapter 1, "*the downward descent into a dumpster is literally an act of downward mobility*" (Clark 2004, 11; emphasis in the original).

This mobility is complicated, of course, by the privileges and struggles different participants bring to it. For example, although many a young white radical has keenly disavowed their whiteness and (over)identified with experiences of racial oppression, the cultural and social capital of whiteness or bourgeois heritage nonetheless inflect many of their countercultural spaces. To some degree, such privileges mitigate the symbolic pollutions of detritus and waste reclamation—whereas people of color and people living in poverty are often read as polluted without so much as touching a bin. Moreover, notwithstanding that dumpster-diving isn't illegal in the United States and is rarely prosecuted in Australia, potential contact with the police may be riskier for the people of color, the economically precarious, the disabled, and the nonpassing queers and transgender folks I met through FNB and dumpster-diving than for the white, middle-class, able-bodied, or straight dumpster-divers and squatters.

Across this constellation of embodied differences, however, such scavenging remains transgressive and never entirely risk-free. (Indeed, the only dumpster-diver I knew who reported police contact was a young, straight, working-class, cis-gendered white man dumpstering with a few other white punks behind a Buffalo supermarket. He was assaulted by an officer, then driven across town and released, without charge, far from home in the middle of the night.) To varying extents, therefore, participants share these embodied risks and transgressions with one another.

To describe these transgressive dis-interpellations, here we might borrow the terms *counteridentification* and *disidentification* from queer theorist José Esteban Muñoz (1999). In contrast to direct interpellation within hegemonic symbolic systems, for Muñoz "counteridentification" reflects a performative turning-against that nonetheless "validates the dominant ideology by reinforcing its dominance through . . . controlled symmetry" (11). In a sense, counteridentificatory subjects remain trapped in prevailing structures of meaning. Muñoz offers the contrasting examples of the assimilationism of Black liberals like Booker T. Washington, who called for Black interpellation within liberal social contracts, and the separatism of Black nationalists like W. E. B. Du Bois, whose stance left intact the logic of exclusion it rebuked (18). For Muñoz, such assimilation and separatism, identification and counteridentification, are of a piece. Similarly, for many dumpster-divers, a righteous but fragile anticapitalism represents a pattern of counteridentification—adhering almost religiously to symbolic languages that embrace the dirty or deviant classifications that bourgeois society imposes on them. For example, a litany of anarcho-punk band names popular with FNB collaborators illustrates the point—"Filth," "Nausea," "Capitalist Casualties," "Shoplifting," and others.

It is all too easy to end our story here (and many do), either romanticizing or dismissing these symbolic rejections as mere gestures (heroic or hubristic, respectively). But transgressive practices like dumpster-diving do more than merely breed reactionary anticapitalist identities. In contrast to such counteridentifications, therefore, Muñoz invokes the term *disidentification* to describe a signifying practice that sidesteps the dichotomy: "Disidentification is the third mode of dealing with dominant ideologies, one that neither opts to assimilate within such a structure nor strictly opposes it. . . . Instead of buckling under the pressures of dominant ideology (identification, assimilation) or attempting to break free of its inescapable sphere (counteridentification, utopianism), this 'working on and against' is a strategy that tries to transform a cultural logic from within, always laboring to enact permanent structural change, while at the same time valuing the importance of local or everyday struggles of resistance" (11–12). Muñoz describes here the signifying practices of many queers of color, for whom no stable recourse to identity (resistant or hegemonic) is possible. Their queerness often estranges them from mainstream communities of color, while their race and rejection of bourgeois norms mark them as Other in the predominantly white spaces of mainstream gay culture. Disidentification, then, describes the renegotiation of unstable or compromised identities in ways that are not easily legible. In contrast to the political endgame of legibility that often demands public recognition or redress (in the formula, for example, of "Black Lives Matter" or "We Are the 99 Percent"), disidentification facilitates a politics often liberatory from within but opaque from without—queer counterpublics that refuse inclusion in heteronormative publics.

Brittle anticapitalism notwithstanding, FNB and the punk scene in which it is embedded also foster just such spaces of liberatory illegibility, as we saw in chapter 2. Indeed, Muñoz himself identifies punk counterpublics as spheres of disidentificatory discourse (see also Hebdige [1979] 2005; Greene 2012). Similarly, Chicana punk rocker Alice Bag described the liberatory potential of the early Los Angeles punk scene—a kind of "home" where she felt freer to find a powerful feminine voice than amid the misogyny and gendered violence she associated with her Chicano childhood. "It was an exciting and hopeful time," she writes tellingly, "when our *ethical and aesthetic values were being demolished and rebuilt*, where each one of us on the scene could challenge one another in an attempt to tear down the old icons and virtues" (Bag 2011, 297; my emphasis). In such ways, people come to punk rock, anarchism, and other radical counterpublics through diverse pathways of exclusion, counteridentification, and disidentification—be they personal trauma, gender nonconformity, neurodiversity, or other stigmatized identities. As my friend and FNB co-conspirator Koa suggested bluntly, "We're all broken." Not everyone would accept his superlative, negative framing, but the embodied differences Koa highlights are nonetheless important parts of the punk landscape, of anarchist politics, and of FNB.

In this context, the "downward mobility" of punks, dumpster-divers, and FNB volunteers amounts to a disidentificatory signifying practice. Beyond rejecting consumerism, it serves a creative function that echoes and transforms the marginalization many participants already experience. The FNB kitchen, too, functions as such a site of downward mobility and disidentification, a semiotically gregarious space marked by a paucity of economic and cultural capital, for the encounter between people and things who, in ways small or large, permanent or passing, precipitate from Lorde's mythical norm.

What is especially important about such disidentifications in FNB's case, however, is that they do more than perform an identity. They also establish new patterns of political and economic organization. Michael Warner (2002) reminds us that counterpublic performance has the power to affectively transform both audience and actor, and as we saw in the last chapter, the "deterritorialization velocity" of such shared affective transformations is the force that knits together new political and economic configurations like Food Not Bombs.

In this way, FNB's resignifications are more than merely discursive. They are necessarily embodied, material practices that, in Muñoz's sense, labor to enact structural change and capacitate everyday struggles. FNB participants scavenge. They cook. They eat. They do unpaid caring labor. They seek shelter (if only a couch for the night). In each city, I met a wide range of people for whom dumpster-diving, squatting, and other kinds of scavenging made possible new lives and new communities. And in aggregate—across hundreds of FNB chapters in dozens of countries and innumerable networks of dumpster-divers, squatters, and so on—these practices constitute an economy, however marginal, in the strictest sense of the term: a system for distributing goods and services.

This beyond-the-pale economy that disidentifies and reorganizes both excluded bodies and abject capital is therefore an abject economy—*abject* because it is not legible according to the norms of market exchange but also not separable from them (Giles 2018). It becomes possible where the meaning of market exchange breaks down. In contradistinction to prevailing liberal economies, it relies on a principle of surplus and on the capitalist economy for its raw materials (just as markets themselves rely on such aftermarket economies to make their surpluses disappear). The constellation of squatters, dumpster-divers, FNB chapters, and other scavengers I have described is one example of such an abject economy.

If such new configurations of nonmarket value underwrite novel forms of counterpower, as I argued in the previous chapter, a crucial dimension of this counterpower is articulated at the scale of the body. It is the disidentification of embodiments and embodied practices that renders the slow insurrection of phenomena like Food Not Bombs significant at precisely the same time that they are rendered illegible to markets and their publics. To make this case we must turn first to the relation between embodiment and "late liberal" configurations of power, before returning to the kitchen and identifying the significance of illiberal forms of embodiment.

Liberal Embodiments

"I have friends that wouldn't do Food Not Bombs with me, even though I'd invite them, because it made them uncomfortable to be around homeless people," Carmen told me. She clarified: "There were people that *avoided sharing food* because of how uncomfortable it made them being faced with their own privilege." She is highlighting the ways in which dominant configurations of privilege, prejudice, and abjection maintain an order that organizes bodies and practices—like eating—and keeps them apart from one another spatially and socially. These are the kinds of patterns of enfleshment and exclusion that scale up to produce the liberal markets and publics that dominate the world-class city. As we have seen throughout this book, no market is "free," nor is any public self-evident. They are the effects of constellations of institutions, affects, and everyday practices—all of which are fundamentally embodied.

We have already explored some of those embodiments, from the urbane, sheltered hexis of bourgeois park-goers envisioned in Seattle's Downtown Parks Initiative to their reciprocal, hungry bodies tucked under the freeway at Seattle's official Outdoor Meal Site. To make sense of them, we must now ask what larger liberal regimes of embodiment find expression through that market-public. Where its publicness is instrumentalized (e.g., through policy), what forms of embodiment are both reproduced and publicly recognized? Where the classical liberal public is a rights-bearing public, for example, which bodies achieve the "right to have rights" (Arendt [1951] 1968, 177)? And what becomes of those bodies that do not? Once we have explored such questions, we can begin to say what the illiberal embodiments of a slow insurrection might mean.

Here, we need to connect certain ontological dots across three scales of analysis: on-the-ground forms of habitus and hexis; collective formations of identity and enfleshment; and the broad biopolitical structures of late liberalism (Povinelli 2011). In naming the multiscalar assemblages so constituted, I suggest a framework to trace the distribution of late-liberal discipline across a spectrum of differences that crisscross the fleshy palimpsests that are our bodies, impoverishing or privileging them in different ways, but always already incorporating them into the biopolitical regimes of market and state. These assemblages are what I call *liberal embodiments.*

Late liberalism comprises not just paradigmatic liberal institutions like private property, free markets, or the rights-bearing individual, but rather the broader configuration of cultural, economic, and state power that maintains them in our current era. It therefore weaves together many threads—from the direct administration of racialized state violence to the selective deployment of compassion in the public sphere and the normative discursive power by which differences are disciplined and logics of economic calculation privileged. In this way, it represents the latest stage within an entangled genealogy of liberal democracies and laissez-faire capitalism dating back to the French and American Revolutions, and the doctrines that inspired them. Povinelli's framework captures congruencies between a wide range of contemporary liberal iterations, from the postcolonial condition of indigenous peoples who remain excluded from the liberal social contract, to the heteronormative discipline of reproduction and caring labor under contemporary welfare regimes. It is relevant to our inquiry here, therefore, as it anchors specific political-economic formations like the global city or the market-public to larger epistemes, ideologies, and regimes of value.

Two features define late liberalism: neoliberalism, which Povinelli envisions as a form of governmentality that measures the value of all social life according to the criteria of the market; and that project of recognition described earlier, with the paradoxical imperative to mark and manage the participation of a spectrum of social differences in a realm defined by the abstract individuation of its participants. We might therefore define *late liberalism* most succinctly as that set of contemporary biopolitical technologies and discourses by which difference is incorporated into the social contracts of market and state. It responds equally to challenges both from within and without, recuperating or co-opting resistance from indigenous movements, postcolonial studies, poor people, people of color, feminists, and myriad Others. The doctrine of multiculturalism, in which difference and culture are celebrated and made economically productive at the same time as they are politically annulled, is a classic project of late liberalism. Marriage equality is another.

Indeed, as I described earlier, even more radical, critical voices are partly absorbed within late liberal vernaculars—consider FNB's invocation of *rights*, or the conception of cultural *property* that underwrites criticisms of "cultural appropriation," or even the master term common across the political Left, social *justice*. (Of course, sound *illiberal* arguments also exist for sharing food, respecting others' cultural traditions, equitably distributing power and opportunity, and so on—some of which we have already covered in this book.)

In this incorporation and management of difference, late liberalism is intimately concerned with bodies. It works simultaneously at numerous scales: the scales of the shared ideologies and apparatuses that underwrite market and state, and the scale of habitus and hexis, the concrete embodied practices and dispositions through which those ideologies and institutions are materialized. Markets are simultaneously founded, for example, on everyday waste-making practices that produce abject capital and the larger institutions, prejudices, and valorizations that surround the waste once it's made. We therefore require a name to capture such multiscalar assemblages. I call them *liberal embodiments*. They marginalize bodies and modes of enfleshment to produce surfeit and scarcity, privilege and poverty.

At first blush, liberal embodiments might be seen in any of the myriad sorts of hexis by which liberal markets and publics are sustained and privileged over other forms of political and economic behavior. The visceral trust placed in over-the-counter medicines as opposed to home remedies, for example. Or the social anxieties and fears of contagion and deviance buried in our endocrine responses that prompt the individuated consumption of transport, security, and name brands.

But liberal embodiments also encompass a broader range of affects, identities, and hexeis than the things that keep us working and shopping. As we have seen, subjects are *differentially incorporated* into the basic structure of liberal capitalism precisely according to their form of embodiment. Eva Cherniavsky writes: "I am calling 'incorporation' or 'incorporated embodiment' a specific idea of the body as the proper (interior) place of the subject, and my claim is that incorporation emerges as the privileged form of embodiment for a modern social and economic order predicated on mobility: the geographic mobility of the labor force relative to centralized manufacturing zones, for example, or the abstract mobility of 'free' economic agents to enter into and terminate contractual relations" (2006, xv). In this way, Cherniavsky's framework draws our attention to a spectrum of embodiments that are constitutive of capitalist social relations. The bodies of the undocumented day laborers who frequented FNB's Sunday dinners are no less incorporated into late-liberal formations, for example, than the bodies of bourgeois tourists who visited Pioneer Square's bars and restaurants, with their distinct palates and preferences. In other words, where Marx and Engels predicted that all class struggle could be subsumed within the antagonism between bourgeoisie and proletariat, for Cherniavsky, class qua class is merely one of many social relations of production and consumption. These relations entail both everyday forms of habitus and hexis, and larger relations among collectively incorporated identities. All of these relations constitute capital, and all of them are embodied. The same can be said of their integration into the larger projects of late-liberal governmentality that enable these relations of production and consumption.

Thinking about liberal embodiment this way cuts against the grain of the more celebratory usages of *liberal* and the correspondingly pejorative, theoretically narrow use of *illiberal*. Indeed, in this vexed moment of political upheaval, in which centrists from Madeline Albright to the editors of the *Economist* publicly worry that liberalism faces an existential threat from right-wing populism, many commentators conflate *illiberal* with *authoritarian*, as if the only choice facing us is between liberal democracy and autocracy. Yet, as FNB's slow insurrection demonstrates, this dichotomy is a false one; beyond a liberal framework of law and rights, infinite political possibilities exist, some of which are peaceful, inclusive, and respectful of difference. If liberalism is truly in decline, we will need to expand our illiberal imaginaries beyond the terms on offer from the Far Right.

Moreover, we cannot accept the conceit that liberalism itself is a reliable guarantor of freedom or enfranchisement. Povinelli echoes a long line of critics who identify the state of exception as the very condition of possibility for the liberal social contract. Liberal regimes have always depended on processes of structured exclusion or partial incorporation. Whereas some readers might see the illicit figure of the undocumented migrant laborer, for example—economically incorporated but legally without sanction—as anathema to a nominally rights-driven liberal order, we might identify at least certain modes of "illegal" immigration as profoundly liberal embodiments insofar as they are materially and discursively produced, perpetuated, and made legible by late-liberal regimes. Indeed, the threatening figure of the illegal immigrant has been carefully, salaciously deployed to consolidate state power and reify white, propertied personhood along the border. In this book, we have explored similar exclusions with regard to the sharing prohibitions that exclude surplus goods, surplus bodies, and nonmarket economic practices from public spaces. We might similarly identify the criminalized, "uncivil" homeless body so rebuked by some Seattle politicians—and deployed as a polarizing wedge issue in phobic language that closely echoes prejudices against the illegal immigrant—as a form of liberal embodiment too. Not coincidentally, many of those homeless and hungry bodies we fed during my time with Seattle FNB were also undocumented day laborers from Mexico and Guatemala. Although they were doubly disenfranchised, they were thoroughly economically incorporated. Indeed, the incessant construction industries of the global city depend on them.

The biopolitical force of Povinelli's late liberalism, therefore, rests not on a sacred recognition of rights, but rather on the power to distribute entitlements and to organize lives and bodies according to them—to "make live" or "let die," in Foucault's (1986) famous formulation. And where bodies are differentially incorporated, it exercises the capacity *to make live differently*, capacitating myriad lives and embodiments in such ways as to enable the projects of market and state. In this fashion, we might imagine a spectrum of racialized, classed, gendered, sexualized, and differently abled embodiments, from the undocumented migrant or homeless panhandler—both herded into different kinds of encampments—to the bourgeois white consumer, from the victorious beneficiaries of marriage equality to the objects of legislation prohibiting transgendered subjects from using their preferred bathroom. These examples all amount to liberal embodiments insofar as they reflect a differential incorporation made specifically legible within regimes of production, consumption, and governance. They produce legible, embodied modes of vulnerability and exploitation too complex to simply call "poverty," although that is their starkest consequence. In this way, the overlapping politics of race, class, citizenship, sexuality, gender, and ability have classically been shaped by liberal projects of embodiment. This is true whether we are describing their ontological basis in technologies of governmentality and biopolitical incorporation—from Jim Crow to the War on Drugs, from the law of coverture to the erosion of *Roe v. Wade*—or in those liberatory and redemptive movements that have aimed to incorporate them differently, from the civil rights movement to marriage equality.

Each of these things are examples of liberal embodiment. They persist as historically specific formations largely to the extent that they are policed, figuratively and literally, by liberal institutions. Differential embodiments of race in the United States, for example, continue to be underwritten by the expansion of the carceral state and the militarization of the border. Differential embodiments of class are underwritten in part by the criminalization and regulation of the homeless. The latter example throws into particularly sharp relief the entanglements between the axis of collective embodiments and the axis of hexis. As we have already seen in this book, most vagrancy laws do not, after all, criminalize homelessness itself, nor poverty, black and brown skin, mental illness, or queerness—though poor people, people of color, neurodiverse people, queers, and

LGBT communities all are overrepresented among the homeless—but rather a range of non-market-friendly embodiments that are juridically and spatially excluded from the public sphere. In just such ways are personal embodiments key components of larger liberal assemblages of embodiment. It is partly the exclusion of these personal embodiments from public protection—and their corresponding production as discursively legible and disciplined objects—that constitutes larger liberal embodiments themselves.

Illiberal Embodiment: Bodies That Matter out of Place

At this point, the reader could be forgiven for feeling a familiar post-Foucauldian paralysis. Is there not the smallest gesture that escapes liberal discipline? No resistance that may not be reenrolled in the biopolitical projects of market and state? However, whereas Foucault famously said, "one can never be 'outside' power" (1980, 141), it *does* have interstices. As Povinelli puts it, late-liberal discourses live in an ongoing process of "aggregation" and "disavowal." In this book we have already explored some of these disavowals at length, from the abject capital abandoned by the global city to the nonmarket forms of economic life banished from its parks and sidewalks. Among those goods, bodies, and practices disavowed lies the possibility for reassembling what Povinelli, ever prosaic, calls "the otherwise"—those forms of subjectivity that dis-integrate or circumnavigate late-liberal norms. In the previous chapter, we saw the otherwise at work in the form of a long, slow insurrection. To emphasize only its insurrectionary capacity, however, is still to privilege a liberal imaginary, with respect to which our mass conspiracy appears as sheer, oppositional alterity. We need to think beyond these negative dialectics. What sort of an alternative politics might they enable? To capture this, I outline below how such disavowed embodiments might be constellated in enduring assemblages that I call illiberal embodiments.

But first, a caveat: Illiberal embodiments should not be confused with "resistance" or "agency," concepts that theorist Alexander Weheliye suggests "assume full, self-present, and coherent subjects working against someone or something" (2014, 2). Whether through "strenuous denial or exalted celebration" (2), the two notions obscure other sorts of freedoms. "Why are formations of the oppressed," Weheliye asks, "deemed liberatory only if they resist hegemony and/or exhibit the full agency of the oppressed?" (2). By contrast, he calls us toward the messy ontological grounds of everyday lives.

In the course of Food Not Bombs' work and the related endeavors of anarchists, punks, dumpster-divers, squatters, and other counterpublic praxes, illiberal embodiments emerge from just such everyday moments in which liberal assemblages of embodiment are temporarily suspended or disarmed. Moments as simple as the willingness to let a homeless stranger sleep on a spare couch or floor; as unpredictable as the collaboration of Seattle software workers, recovering junkies, and devout Muslim immigrants around the FNB kitchen; as fleeting as the joy of finding the perfect peach in the dumpster. (These examples are not hypothetical, of course.) They attenuate the liberal embodiments of propertied, sheltered citizenship; racialized and socioeconomic segregation; and market-centric consumption, respectively. We mustn't romanticize these moments as resistance, but they nonetheless add up to a distinctive social world, and they *matter*—both in the sense of being important to participants and making a material difference.

There's a lot of people involved in Food Not Bombs that didn't really grow up the way I did. I mean I really grew up blue-collar, you know? Working class, and like I grew up in a hood. And a lot of the people involved in Food Not Bombs aren't very street smart... And so, I always felt that Food Not Bombs is also a really good place for people getting involved that come from upper-middle-class, suburban backgrounds to work with people who are homeless and come from a lot of different backgrounds. And it teaches them how to communicate, and they have to put on some tougher skin.

—Koa, Seattle FNB, 1990s–2000s

Above all, they matter on the terrain of the body. Illustrating this, Weheliye uses the term *habeas viscus* ("you shall have the flesh") to "signal how violent political domination activates a *fleshly surplus* that simultaneously sustains and disfigures said brutality" (2014, 1–2; my emphasis). While he writes from within Black feminist studies, his framework equally helps us think about a broader range of disavowed surpluses. Sometimes framed negatively as "bare life" for their abandonment (e.g., Agamben 1998), both Weheliye and Povinelli instead emphasize the positive materiality of those bodies whose abjection is the ontological precondition of biopower. Weheliye writes, "the flesh, rather than displacing bare life or civil death, excavates the social (after)life of these categories: it represents racializing assemblages of subjection that can never annihilate the lines of flight, freedom dreams, practices of liberation, and possibilities of other worlds" (2014, 2). In this way, Weheliye gestures toward a positive politics of waste and surplus analogous to the one I have essayed in this book, an illiberal politics within which something other than the lack and exclusion usually denoted by terms like *waste*, *abjection*, or *poverty* becomes imaginable.

The meaningful assemblages comprising such lines of flight, such other worlds, are what I would like to make visible with the term *illiberal embodiment*—from the queer, disidentificatory performances of Alice Bag to the mutual aid economies of FNB and other scavengers. These practices of freedom must be made meaningful in and through the body. Let us define an illiberal embodiment, therefore, as that larger assemblage composed of enfleshments, affects, practices, or hexeis that confound liberal recognition and incorporation and yet meaningfully organize participants' social worlds. It may evade liberal governmentalities altogether—ideally hiding in plain sight—or it may become visible but illegible to liberal vernaculars, as we have seen in Food Not Bombs' decades-long "slow insurrection."

This insurrection is illiberal by definition, revalorizing surpluses abandoned by liberal publics. Moreover, it serves a disidentificatory function, cultivating new forms of habitus and hexis that are not so much exceptional (excluded but legible) as abject (confounding and illegible) with respect to late-liberal governmentality. That abject habitus may facilitate coalitions and collaborations that cut across hegemonic lines of enfleshment. Povinelli (2011) describes such aggregations of people, things, and counterdiscourse simply as "radical worlds." To be sure, these worlds do not exist in a romantic, undiscovered country where people and things go on to lead social afterlives free of the logic of capital. But nor do liberal economies or polities command all spaces and social worlds equally. The churn of late liberalism's aggregations and disavowals creates interstices for assembling the otherwise. The ready availability of surpluses, therefore, and the embodiments that avail themselves of this waste, are the ontological substrate of Povinelli's radical worlds, along with the forms of nonmarket labor and identification capacitated by them.

Indeed, FNB is only the most prolific of radical political movements to be built from such abject capital. Its genealogy dates back to the free breakfast programs of the Black Panthers or the feed-ins of the San Francisco Diggers, which both served up grocery surpluses. Further, like FNB, many of them eschew the mechanisms of recognition and neoliberal governmentality expressed in formal nonprofit status, permits, grants, and so on.

Such radical "social projects," according to Povinelli, "disaggregate aspects of the social worlds and aggregate individual projects into a more or less whole . . . they are not 'things' so much as aggregating practices" (2011, 7). They represent queer rearrangements of prevailing discursive norms, complex assemblages of matter and meaning, of practice, affect, and signification.

FNB's conspiratorial, insurrectionary structure represents just such an illiberal assemblage, cultivating a heterogeneous and often ephemeral community. In this way, for example, FNB brings together sheltered and unsheltered people, both at public food-sharings and also in the kitchen, in relationships that are not possible under the sharp distinctions between volunteer-providers and "clients" typical of formally recognized soup kitchens or food banks. The community spaces, squats, and low-rent communal houses where FNB often cooks cultivate a permissive atmosphere and, importantly, tend to disavow any reliance on the carceral state. This permissive atmosphere, the informal structure, and the plenitude of its resources therefore cultivate "spaces of encounter"—sites within which a range of people may collaborate, with some of the usual

> We got to know all of [the homeless] really well. Because we were becoming front-line service providers . . . and we did crazy stuff. We would feed people that had been thrown out of shelters—so, violent, mentally deranged, alcoholic, chronic alcoholic—you know, people that were just not able to cooperate with any other social service network.
>
> —Peter, San Francisco FNB, late 1980s

Exterior of the Food Not Bombs kitchen, Lower East Side, New York City, 2016.

classed and racialized differences attenuated, if never entirely suspended (Lawson and Elwood 2013).

In this fashion, FNB and other anarchist projects become spaces of encounter for new arrivals in a city—including a transnational spectrum of itinerant, train-hopping punks and squatters, university students, precariously employed migrants from the Global South, tech employees, and others for whom FNB represented a welcoming space to touch down. To the extent that they create more egalitarian spaces of translocal encounter

Doing dishes at the ABC No Rio kitchen, New York City. (Photo by Victoria Law)

not premised on market or state recognition (and even hostile to these things), they queer national, classed, and racial imaginaries.

The privileges and oppressions of late liberalism do not, of course, simply disappear at the doorstep. As one Black punk rocker put it in James Spooner's brilliant documentary *Afropunk* (2003), his fellow white punks can often just "put on a suit" and blend back into mainstream society, a privilege not available to punks and anarchists of color. Indeed, participants often bring into the FNB kitchen the habitus of their privileges in the wider world. As Koa observed, for example, "There [were] some kids in the past who showed up [to volunteer] and who really acted like they were doing their charity work. And they had an attitude. And you know, homeless people already get a lot of attitude. And they're not gonna take some shit from some, you know, nineteen-year-old college kid." Yet whereas incorporated charities and homeless services often reinforce those hierarchies (Passaro 1996; Willse 2015), the grassroots, antiauthoritarian structure of FNB militates against them. As Koa told me, "There's been a couple of occasions that . . . we actually had to remove some people off the line and tell 'em 'Hey man, these people don't choose to be out here,' you know, and, 'You really don't need to be treating them with this kind of attitude.'" It is also telling that FNB meetings are still often dominated by heterosexual, cis-gendered men—sometimes dubbed "manarchists" by queer and feminist participants—who bring with them the baggage of masculine entitlement and ego. It is again, however, indicative of FNB's illiberal organization that it militates against such hierarchies, and feminist collaborators have often successfully used FNB's consensus process to censure aggressive manarchists. (And at least twice, in my experience, eject them from the chapter after problematic behavior.) My favorite example of feminist intervention, however, comes from the Seattle chapter during the early 2000s: the group established an all-male feminist dishwashing

> I handed over bottom-lining to this kid Peter, who lived in the Bronx. His parents owned a Chinese restaurant—he didn't know how to cook, for someone whose parents owned a Chinese restaurant. Food Not Bombs was his first foray into cooking. And he was very quiet, but he was very nice, and he was also very reliable. So I was like, "I can't do this anymore. Here are the keys. Can you bottom line?" And he was like, "Okay, sure," and he was fine for the first week, the first two weeks. And then—I think college must have started again—we had this influx of new people. It was, like, all these people who were white, late teens, early twenties, punk rock, sort of all spoke the same sub-cultural language. And Peter—who was this Chinese immigrant high-school or just-out-of-high-school kid from the Bronx—he was like, "I don't know how to talk to these people, I'm not comfortable with them," so he gave me the keys back and said, "You know, there are enough people here," and he left.
>
> —Vikki, on cultural clashes and exclusion in counterpublic "spaces of encounter"

contingent upon noticing that the typical gendered habitus of the wider society were playing out in the kitchen, and men had often been letting the women do all the washing up. As I've suggested above, therefore, late-liberal privileges do not command all spaces equally. Such spaces of encounter as these also often work to disrupt such privileges and to queer subjects' interpellation within liberal embodiments.

At the transnational scale, too, Food Not Bombs' remarkable global proliferation represents an illiberal assemblage of embodiments, simultaneously political and economic, that cuts across the vernaculars of nation, language, ethnos, and other vectors of readily legible transnational connection. Through my time with Seattle FNB, for example, I and other participants met visiting FNB activists, anarchists, and punks from Argentina, Australia, Canada, Colombia, France, Germany, Mexico, New Zealand, and Russia, not to mention dozens of US cities. Like many decentralized global social movements, they work with one another in what Day (2005) calls "groundless solidarity." Further, they produce social networks (online and offline) that circulate information even more widely, so that, for example, when I traveled to New York and met a volunteer from the Moscow chapter (Russia, not Idaho), I already knew to ask about their recent conflicts with local white supremacists (which had gotten one of her collaborators killed).

These networks represent more than mere acquaintance. They are the foundation for economic and political practices that are distributed transnationally. Volunteers from FNB in Texas, for example, arrive at FNB in Melbourne already adept at dumpster-diving and jump right in as regular volunteers. Punks from Arizona show up to eat at FNB in Seattle, realistically optimistic that they'll meet somebody from a shared punk house or a squat on whose floor to sleep that night. And they do. Anarchists from Russia show up in New York City and move seamlessly and immediately into the role of bottom-liner. Volunteers in Seattle move without a qualm from cooking in a well-lit, well-stocked, vacant industrial kitchen to cooking at a local squat by candlelight when it becomes the only space available. And when police approach the group in Seattle, San Francisco, or New York City, asking who is in charge, volunteers from each city reply instinctively with some version of either "no one is" or "we all are." The emergent political organization constituted by all these collaborations is all too often lost on outsiders or (mis)read within more familiar liberal vernaculars, as I described at the outset. Yet, to the extent that they are at all prefigurative, perhaps there will come a day when they are as politically intelligible as *nation*, *state*, *market*, *public*, and so on.

Conclusion

My first visit to New York City's famous former squat, ABC No Rio, in 2007—only my third new Food Not Bombs chapter—felt resoundingly familiar. Just as I had in Melbourne six months earlier and thousands of miles away (see scene vi), I was following street signs, looking for FNB at an independent gallery and community space in the city's Lower East Side, where lower property values (although it was rapidly gentrifying) prompted a wide range of people to call it home. Again, I knew the place only by reputation, although No Rio was somewhat more storied in punk and DIY circles than the Melbourne warehouse. And again, I had absolutely no trouble picking the place out.

"There was no mistaking it," I wrote in my field notes, "even without the stylized, hand-painted 'ABC No Rio' above the door in two-foot letters." The door was unlocked again, and unattended—maybe more unusual in the Lower East Side than it might have been in the run-down Brunswick cul-de-sac. This time, the building wasn't empty, but still, nobody stopped me to ask me what I was doing there. I had to introduce myself to one of them, newly arrived from Eastern Europe. But her embodied semiotics—dreadlocks, political patches, a sartorial palette of entirely black and olive drab, and a "Food Not Bombs, Lithuania" button (with a tree on it rather than the more familiar carrot-in-fist logo)—were already legible to me as "crusty punk" and wholly at home in the space, which felt as if it shared the radical openness and the patched-togetherness of FNB spaces I had already known. A patched-togetherness that echoed the patched-togetherness of the communities that pass through it.

Actually, the first thing I noticed when I walked in was a bulletin board near the front stairs advertising an upcoming punk show for a Melbourne band, on tour in the US, whose drummer I'd met at FNB's Brunswick warehouse. He helped *start* Melbourne Food Not Bombs. If this was a coincidence, by now it was hardly surprising. The networks that connect FNB make it feel like a small world after all. I missed the show in New York, but I saw the same band play in Seattle a few months later. (My FNB collaborator Koa was already a fan and copied their record for me.)

In spite of such remarkable transnational alignments, Food Not Bombs has no head office. No formal membership or secret handshakes. Although it applies some formal principles, agreed upon at a national gathering decades ago in San Francisco and published on a national website,[2] most volunteers have never read them. In lieu of a top-down mandate,

Food Not Bombs logo, Seattle.

FNB's efforts often feel just as much structured by happenstance, an emergent property of the assortment of individuals who've shown up, and the food they were able to rescue from the dumpster that day.

And yet Food Not Bombs chapters in hundreds of cities around the world persist in groundless solidarity as if coordinated by the same invisible hand. Perhaps, in a way, they are. Their labors are everywhere guided by the surpluses and scarcities of the market. The contiguity of their efforts globally, their paradoxical heterogeneity and regularity, their unstructured structure, become possible because participants acquire and reproduce the kinds of shared (or at least contiguous) embodied practices, sensibilities, and "commonsense" dispositions I have here called "illiberal embodiments." The ethic of improvisation, openness, utopianism, and fatalism so cultivated is a modus operandi familiar to almost anyone who has spent much time working with FNB. In aggregate, these improvisations and bricolage, assembled from leftover foods, cast-off furniture, low-rent kitchen spaces in borderline neighborhoods, and the people for whom they are home, amount to a kind of abject economy.

San Francisco Food Not Bombs signage, sometimes displayed at meals.

To make visible the linkages between the scale of these everyday practices and embodied dispositions and the larger political formations that they compose, in this chapter I have identified two species of assemblage within which they are implicated. I call the first of them *liberal embodiments*. These embodiments serve both to administer difference and to incorporate it within relations of production and consumption. As such, they also offer a framework for thinking beyond both reductive conceptions of class and essentialist variants of identity politics, and for theorizing distributions of privilege and impoverishment with respect to market and state. They also contribute to the disavowal, abandonment, and exclusion of surpluses from within liberal markets and publics.

In contradistinction to these liberal embodiments, to account for the shared radical worlds of Food Not Bombs, I have also tried to capture the possibilities for a novel, inclusively illiberal politics at the level of embodied practices and subjectivities—what Weheliye calls "different genres of the human." The range of embodiments excluded by liberal discourse and discipline represent the raw material for alternative lifeworlds. Echoing my earlier formulation, I describe those enduring constellations of everyday practice, shared vernaculars, and political horizons that constitute these worlds as *illiberal embodiments*. I insist on the political significance of these radical worlds in all their illegibility to and endurance alongside liberal forms of life and difference. Anarchists sometimes put this prosaically, insisting "another world is possible, and exists in the shadows of this one."

By grounding my argument in the materiality of body and flesh, I have argued that, to a large extent, that world may be built of abandoned or undervalued material surpluses of people, of places, and of things, in precisely the fashion that the globally contiguous ethnographic worlds of FNB are constellated. In wasted or undervalued spaces, fueled by those wasted surpluses, excluded bodies and practices are freer to convene, and to constitute enduring worlds wherein they may imagine their relationships differently than under the prevailing liberal discourses. A more radical world is in this sense not only possible, but it endures in the detritus of the political present.

ENCORE

A NEW ZEITGEIST

It's been at least five years since I saw Augusto. I've been away from Seattle following job prospects, but I'm back visiting now. And here he is in Occidental Park, just like old times. Aside from a new Freddie Mercury moustache, he seems little changed since our first meeting. Same old baseball cap. Same easy smile. I wonder if I seem the same to him.

I've known Augusto for more than a decade. Originally from Mexico, he's a longtime Seattleite now, and frequent FNB diner. He was one of the first people I met over dinner with Food Not Bombs. Just like today, he strolled over unhurriedly to eat with us. Just like today, he stuck around to chat—and continued to do so off and on for as long as I was involved. His English is better than my Spanish, but we carry on in both languages. He often wants to talk about Jesus. I often want to talk about capitalism. He usually has a more fatalistic, Hobbesian view of this life—nasty, brutish, and incorrigible. I'm usually more doggedly hopeful about the prospects of social change and a more egalitarian future. He's more jovially resigned, I more grimly preoccupied. We get along famously. It's almost like twelve years haven't passed.

But it's 2017, not 2005. Augusto is not optimistic about Seattle. He predicts unspecified global catastrophes. The financial crisis of 2008 is largely behind us, but as the economy continues to be reorganized, the "recovery" doesn't seem to have reached us here. Many people in the city feel more insecure than ever. More people sleep on the street every year. And Augusto knows intuitively that our housing crisis is not confined to this city or this moment. It is structural and global. From our vantage point on either side of FNB's growing soup-lines, he and I have both looked long and hard into the face of the new urban zeitgeist, precarity. Indeed, a president with barely veiled fascist sympathies is about to be inaugurated who has exploited that precarity with empty promises of prosperity. In the coming years, his administration will even intimate that the urban homeless could be rounded up and sent to camps, *literally*. Everyone seems worried about the future. For his part, Augusto is indulging in apocalyptic speculations, as befits his Catholic eschatology. For my part, I try to remember that it is precisely in times of crisis that we organize and lay the groundwork for the reconstruction to come.

Which of us has the better guess? Who can say what the future holds for Seattle? Or for Food Not Bombs? After a dozen years, we've both watched the city, country, and world transform. Augusto reminds me that some things don't change, others do. Whichever of us is right, FNB's work seems more important than ever.

Conclusion

An **Open Letter to** Lost Homes (Political Implications)

What the Future Holds

Seattle breaks my heart. When I began this work over a decade ago, around four thousand Seattleites were homeless. Now there are more than twelve thousand, many of them pushed into shelterlessness by transformations in the fabric of the city that hike housing costs and polarize incomes, displacing my old friends, neighbors, and communities to its outskirts. Meanwhile, Melbourne—my childhood home and the place where I now teach—has seen comparable rent increases, gentrification, and the stark growth of homelessness in its downtown core.[1] These changes have been the talk of both towns. Along with the other cities that feature in this book, they have been embedded in ongoing global mutations of urban place-making and economy, from the reorganization of postindustrial labor markets and transnational supply chains to the emergence of luxury real estate investment as a kind of global currency.[2] But as I argue throughout this book, what has made these places world-class boomtowns also makes them landscapes of great waste and want. Food is locked in their dumpsters while many are hungry. Properties sit empty in redeveloped neighborhoods while thousands sleep outdoors. This is the global city.

Augusto, from our encore, is surely right to see turbulent times ahead. Meanwhile, many of my Food Not Bombs collaborators imagine a different, more distant future. They redistribute the city's wasted surpluses in webs of generosity and frame their efforts as a kind of prefigurative politics, anticipating a time when capitalism and the state give way to something resembling their practice of mutual aid. It's a vision whose

> There are no cities to love.
>
> —Sleater-Kinney

spirit I share, even if I have argued in this book that FNB and the global city enjoy a messier, more symbiotic relationship than is usually acknowledged in such neat theories of change. Still, I envy both Augusto and my revolutionary collaborators their clarity. I am less certain what the future holds.

Nonetheless, opaque though it be, this book addresses itself to that future (as every book must, in some way). Behind its argument lie certain anxious questions. What will become of Seattle, Melbourne, and the other places described herein? Of Food Not Bombs? How will life change for their constituents, especially those who are most vulnerable? More ambitiously, what is to be done? Yet, for the most part, I have left prognostications and prescriptions aside. Anthropology refuses to offer up easy, definitive answers, instead insisting on the diversity and complexity of our social worlds. It rests on a certain faith that a rich portrait of those worlds holds value in itself, particularly for voices omitted from the blueprints and rationales of pundits and policymakers. Having attempted just such a portrait in the preceding pages, however, here I take the opportunity to venture some reflections on the political implications of this book. I've limited myself to four broad conclusions, each of which consolidates a thread of the book's argument.

These conclusions are not policy proposals or "solutions." I do not try to answer the questions strangers often pose to me when I talk about my work: How should we eliminate waste? How do we "solve" homelessness and hunger? What's my plan for a better world? They're good questions, but they are framed too broadly to give clear-cut answers—short of scrapping late capitalism and starting over. (An idea for which I have some sympathy, it's true.) Although I do make suggestions here, it is an impoverished understanding of research that measures its value in the number of plans and "action items" generated. As anthropologist David Graeber writes: "Normally, when you challenge the conventional wisdom—that the current economic and political system is the only possible one—the first reaction you are likely to get is a demand for a detailed architectural blueprint of how an alternative system would work. . . . Historically, this is ridiculous. When has social change ever happened according to someone's blueprint?" (2013). Notwithstanding the many ideological blueprints that have been deployed over the years, from Left and Right alike, although they are consequential, they rarely go to plan. As Angela Davis once put it when describing her activism in the 1960s, *the battles we won were not battles we even knew we were fighting.*[3] As Graeber points out, the legacy of the 1960s and earlier revolutionary moments was not to redesign society, but rather to invent and popularize forms of political and cultural *common sense* that had been previously unthinkable. New ideas and imaginaries are critical to social change, even if their effects are unforeseeable, myriad, and do not amount to line items or policy proposals.

New imaginaries are anthropology's specialty. As an exercise in cultural critique, it has a knack for challenging commonsense assumptions and revealing their unseen consequences. In this vein, what I have written here aims to unsettle popular myths about the efficiency of capitalism, to undermine prejudices about homelessness, and to rain on the parade of successful world-class cities' good fortune. Further, as a compendium of human potential, anthropology documents those spaces that incubate new ideas, alternative models, and "emergent forms of life" (Fischer 2003) with the potential to grow in scope and influence. The slow insurrections and scavenged counterpublics in this book represent just that. Movements like Food Not Bombs demonstrate that "another world is possible and exists now in the shadows of this one," as the common anarchist saying goes. Particularly in this historical moment in which liberal democracies face plausible existential threats from populism, demagoguery, and millenarian fatalism, such movements may inspire a renewed radical imagination—one that reclaims the terrain of illiberal politics from the Far Right and articulates a more inclusive, egalitarian vision of a future beyond liberalism.

Conclusion, the First

The market does not distribute resources efficiently; capitalism as we now practice it is built on great waste (which won't be solved with more capitalism).

This thought is no surprise to most Food Not Bombs collaborators. A reliable flow of edible waste and other surpluses is what makes the movement possible. It won't surprise some other observers either. Indeed, the issue of waste—particularly food waste—has lately captured the public imagination, giving rise to documentaries, government initiatives, and private enterprises (both charitable and for-profit) to reveal and reduce our food waste. And yet many of these efforts leave the logic of the market unquestioned. From legislation (like France's 2016 requirement that supermarkets donate unwanted produce) to food recovery charities that capture waste (like Australia's Second Bite or Washington's Northwest Harvest) or secondary markets that recapitalize it (like the growing discount supermarket chain Grocery Outlet, Boston's Daily Table restaurant, or California's Imperfect Foods delivery service), a plethora of efforts to

Believe me, the food is out there. Start by asking your local food co-op, if you have one, to save its wilted and spotty vegetables and other expired goods for you. Go to bakeries at closing time and ask for the bread they are going to throw away (bakeries tend to bake much more than they can sell for some reason; in my town they often put the bags of leftover bread out by the back door rather than in their dumpster in hopes that someone can use it). A local steakhouse gives us their leftover baked potatoes at the end of the night, plus their prepped lettuce and tomatoes—talk to restaurants and caterers about what they might be willing to donate. If you still need more food, go dumpster-diving: we have a standing Wednesday night date to go through three grocery store dumpsters to see what we can find, which yields enough not only to serve thirty or forty people the next day, but to put extra groceries out for people to take home. If you dumpster food, however, make sure that you are not stripping dumpsters other people depend on—we do our dumpstering in a suburban neighborhood where we are not competing with anyone.

—Liz (CrimethInc. Ex-Workers' Collective 2002)

address food waste fail to challenge the linear commodity chain that underlies the problem. They ignore the obvious: *in a capitalist market premised on individual consumption, food and other goods that lack exchange value must be abandoned or enclaved.*

Meanwhile, the ideological assertion that capitalism is the most (or even only) efficient way to distribute resources continues to hold sway in some circles, despite its recent disastrous failures, from global food crises to financial collapses. At its most extreme, this philosophy manifests in the prevailing neoliberal economic policies of many governments and financial institutions, which continue to leave the distribution of some very important things—food and shelter among them—largely in the hands of "the market." As I write this, for example, cities across the US debate rent-control measures to tame rent gouging and homelessness. Their detractors argue that rent control would disrupt the market and raise rental costs. Yet the market, left to its own devices, does much the same, manufacturing housing scarcity in places like Melbourne or San Francisco—just like it manufactures food scarcity. Indeed, at the height of the foreclosure crisis in the United States, there were roughly half a dozen vacant homes for every shelterless person.[4] The thousands of vacant properties kept off the market, like the thousands of pounds of viable food I have recovered from grocery stands, produce sections, and dumpsters, prove the "efficient markets" hypothesis flatly wrong.

Indeed, although a market exists for such surpluses (as The Daily Table and Imperfect Foods have wagered), markets are never disinterested conduits from supply to demand. In the everyday dealings of commerce, it is often more profitable to abandon the surpluses. The bruised avocado, the day-old bread, the juice that's close to its "sell by" date are cleared from the shelves to make space for newer, picture-perfect goods with more value for people who can afford to pay for it. Similarly, the vacant house is warehoused, off the market, until it can be rented to wealthier, gentrifying tenants. Free markets are free to pick and choose their clientele. Meanwhile, although it is true that a steadily growing number of food recovery charities redirect a portion of this waste from the landfill to people who experience food insecurity, they remain dependent on the economic logics of retailers and producers. In addition, such charities are often enrolled in enclaving, disciplining, and "regulating the poor" (Piven and Cloward 1971), a point I return to below.

To forgo such waste demands deliberately anticapitalist steps. Measures that unpick the commodity chain and supersede its "commonsense" logic of scarcity. These measures might be small or large. Consider the surplus food wasted by retailers because letting minimum-wage employees take it home without paying for it would be anathema to their business model. Why not start there, incentivizing employees' well-being over scarcity? Or expanding squatters' rights in cities with overwhelming vacancy rates? Such abundance-thinking scales up. In the middle of the twentieth century, for example, the philosopher Georges Bataille feared that the accumulating surpluses and productive power of Euro-American industry—which needed to be spent somehow in order to ensure constant growth—would be channeled into military production and a third massive "world" war. (Looking at the rest of the century, he wasn't far wrong.) His solution was a sudden emergency *wealth dump*. A one-off, no-strings-attached gift of massive proportions from countries with gargantuan surplus industrial output to those without. In some sense, this message is also behind the slogan "Food Not Bombs," which explicitly identifies the structural violence of hunger and food waste with the militarized violence of the state. To give away all the wealth dumped in the trash is also to value it under a different paradigm than the scarcity that animates empire.

Bataille was influenced by the Northwest American Indian potlatch, in which individuals' accumulated wealth was periodically given away in a massive communal celebration. In a modest homage to the potlatch, one can imagine a hybrid economy in which grocery stores set out their surpluses, free for the picking, say, every other Thursday, rather than throw them away. This might sound naïve. But it would surely represent a different sort of political-economic common sense. And for all we know, it might work. One can readily imagine the practical objections free-market ideologues and struggling retailers alike would raise. But as Nelson Mandela reminded us, many things seem impossible until they are done. Meanwhile, the current state of affairs leaves millions of households food insecure each year, so by that criterion, it, too, is not practical.

Less radical stop-gap measures might express the same logic. The expanding food recovery sector certainly has its place. Or selling the would-be waste for a pittance (rather than passing it onto secondary markets like those described above) might be a market-based approximation of my utopian Free Thursdays. Indeed, in small ways many small-scale commercial establishments already do this. Day-old bagels sell for half-off at my favorite cafes. One vendor at the Pike Place Market has a dollar table for produce that needs to be eaten quickly. These are valuable strategies and could be multiplied. However, they remain subordinate to the logic of the market. Without a community-driven or government-mandated incentive, they are moot if they cut into the retailer's profit margins (which are often thin to begin with). As long as the balance between the cost of raw materials and the spending power and choosy commodity aesthetics of certain sectors of the polity makes it more profitable for retailers to evacuate the shelves to make space for new, more expensive things, the waste is likely to go on.

That waste is amplified by a particular brand of late capitalism that privileges image-conscious, spectacular, wasteful kinds of "world-class" consumption—and to which Seattle and a growing number of cities have pinned their success. A shopping trip to Dubai might be a taste of the future for many of them. This world-class consumption will continue to create a world-class kind of waste too. In this era of mounting inequality and spiraling ecological crises, the stakes of that waste continue to rise.

Conclusion, the Second

Prejudices against things—particularly waste—are the basis for prejudices against people who consume things differently, particularly the unhoused.

Not long ago, an angry crowd of homeowners drowned out a panel of Seattle City Council members assembled to discuss homelessness. One local journalist described it as an unprecedented "cacophony of grievances" (Raftery 2018). Another called it a "Two Hours Hate" (Barnett 2018). Attendees jeered and taunted speakers about the tax dollars the city had spent "attracting" more unsheltered people to social services, rehearsing a pervasive, centuries-old myth that the unhoused are drawn from beyond the city, vermin-like, and can be driven away with austerity and punishment. But in fact most of them were Seattle residents before losing their homes (All Home 2018; see also Greenstone 2018); although they remain, they have become foreigners in their own city. What so excludes them? Like the immigrant, the dissident, and so many others, the homeless are imagined as one more of the "strangers at our door" (Bauman 2016). Under such pressures, visceral prejudices find their way into policy. With each new qualitative leap in its visibility, the crisis of homelessness awakens an ugly side of the putatively progressive, cosmopolitan citizens of the global city. And yet, as a demographic, the homeless are no categorical threat. They cannot be characterized by ethnicity, nationality, (dis) ability, or any other vector of difference (although virtually every kind of marginalization is overrepresented in their ranks). So wherefore the bitter estrangement?

Some part of the answer is that they consume differently. They might sleep in marginal spaces rather than pay rent. Eat what food recovery charities give them. Consume the castoffs of their sheltered neighbors. Antihomeless bigotry (for there can be no better word for it) therefore bears out anthropologist Mary Douglas's classic observation that a society's assumptions about what is dirty or clean, dangerous or safe, tell us more about their ordering practices than about the material reality of the things they're afraid of. The homeless consume "matter out of place" (Douglas 1984).

Indeed, to varying degrees, such prejudices are readily projected upon anyone who consumes differently—whether they violate taboos on squatting, eating out of the garbage, drinking milk that has outlived its expiry date, or simply shopping for secondhand goods. Those prejudices are expressed, for example, in news coverage of dumpster-diving, which often leads with the specters of disease or disgust and raises questions about identity theft and other kinds of criminality associated with scavenging. Class-inflected fears of things discarded by the market are thereby closely related to the stigmas attached to those who don't adhere to the norms of commercial life. In a sense, one reason that so many are so afraid of homeless people, poverty, and other kinds of perceived deviance is simply that they (apparently) don't participate in capitalism. Precisely such stigma is brought to bear politically against people who are homeless or whose forms of consumption are anathema to market-centric civility.

It has become part of my research methodology to invite those projections upon myself when I speak with journalists, students, friends, and colleagues about my work. I find myself interrogating their incredulity, fascination, and nervous laughter at the thought that an academic researcher with a comfortable abode would go so far as to eat what he finds in the dumpster. Fortunately for me, I have access to certain kinds of cultural capital that mitigate my scavenging. Racialized stereotypes of criminality, crassness, or dirt aren't superimposed on me from the moment I walk into a classroom. The letters after my name lend me (some) credibility. So I am rarely stigmatized in any lasting way by my association with waste. Nonetheless, I wear a blazer, in case it helps my audience take me seriously. And when I lecture publicly, I often take along a scavenged snack to share—often cookies made from dumpstered flour and chocolate, sealed smoothies, discarded on or near their "best by" date, or banana bread with dumpstered bananas. Although I always sample it ahead of time, to illustrate its safety, inevitably some people in the audience are too "grossed out" to try it.

I don't blame them. I once might have had the same reaction. Yet such socialized gut responses underwrite the economy as we know it. Without those prejudices, more people might scavenge for food and other goods. Perhaps more dumpsters would be locked or guarded. Fewer people might rely on the extremely conservative sell-by dates indicated by the manufacturer. Such wariness of unwanted goods extends to where they shop. Consider the Grocery Outlet, for example, where friends and students sometimes admitted that they felt uncomfortable shopping because the food isn't new or at its freshest. Even more telling is their nickname for it: "The Gross-Out." These prejudices manufacture scarcity and police the boundaries of the market.

Such stigma is more than simple classism. It is wrapped up in *abjection*, Julia Kristeva's (1982) word for our visceral sense of dread or disgust at certain hard-to-process experiences. The term perfectly captures the repulsion associated with waste and garbage, expressed in fears of disease or criminality and a diffuse, hard-to-name "gross-out" factor. Historically, this repulsion, and the accusations of poor hygiene and disease it inspires, have long formed part of the toolkit of oppression.

Consider, for example, the attitude of one Seattle bus driver I encountered toward the end of my research. A developmentally disabled man I had gotten to know, who was homeless and panhandled in my neighborhood, tried to enter the bus I was riding. He was prepared to pay his fare. Yet the driver wouldn't let him on. It was clear they had met before. With a forbiddingly outstretched palm, he said smugly, "You have a bad body odor, you may not ride with me." In my opinion, my friend had never actually smelled *that* bad, but regardless, access to housing and hygiene facilities is no criterion for entry to public property. All of this happened in a few seconds, and the bus pulled away before I could react. Before I got off, I tried to plead my acquaintance's case with the bus driver, who assured me that there were enough free shower facilities in the city that he didn't need to get on the bus smelling like that. I assured the driver (for all the good it did) that I'd spent a long time researching Seattle's network of homeless services and that he was flat fucking wrong. The city had (at that point) only *one* dedicated hygiene center and an inadequate handful of shelters with showers or laundry facilities.

In retrospect, I should have complained to King County Metro. Access to public buses is, after all, one of the quintessential civil rights struggles. It's also likely relevant that the driver was white, and my acquaintance was black; thus may racism, classism, ableism, and antihomeless prejudice intersect. And there is an additional, brutal irony in the fact that without public transport, my acquaintance (who walks with a limp) *couldn't get to the hygiene center to take a goddamn shower*. Which brings me to my next point: Such prejudices not only *reflect* differences and inequities in consumption practices, they also *enforce* them.

Conclusion, the Third

When prejudices based on the way people (fail to) consume are writ official, they regulate not only public space and public life but also access to resources, for example, making prohibitions against outdoor meal programs into de facto food policy.

In a way, this conclusion is an extension of the previous two. It is set apart here simply for emphasis. In this book I have described city policies that, in the name of health and safety, exclude people from public life and public space on the basis of subsistence practices anathema to a housed, market-centric public (sharing food in the park, sleeping rough, and so on). These policies have a direct impact on the ways in which those so excluded must access food, shelter, and other resources.

The economy as we know it is made possible by consumers' visceral taboos on those things it discards; those taboos in effect police a particular distribution of resources—they make sure the waste stays wasted. And if those taboos against wasted resources become the basis for social prejudices against people who consume them (by dumpster-diving, food-sharing, squatting, even shopping at the Gross-Out), then those social prejudices, too, police a certain distribution of resources. All the more so when they are written into law.

In this book, for example, I have described some of the ways in which city authorities invoke "health and safety" to defend ordinances that disproportionately target people who are homeless. Outdoor food-sharing prohibitions are the examples I have spent the most time on. They amount to a strategy to keep homeless people from congregating in public spaces in large numbers. City officials don't frame their reasons in this way, but it is disingenuous to suggest otherwise when the realpolitik of complaints from local businesses and NIMBY citizen groups has determined where outdoor meals are permitted with little or no input from the unhoused themselves. And although the courts have recently ruled that these forbidden gifts violate the free speech of meal providers (Eleventh Circuit Court of Appeals 2018)—a promising start—this ruling has so far had no definitive effect on indirect restrictions, which rest on more intricate regimes of public amenity and health statutes. Similarly, a federal court has ruled against any explicit criminalization of homelessness or encampments where adequate alternative shelter is not available (Ninth Circuit Court of Appeals 2018); however, this has not in itself slowed Seattle's policy of "sweeping" homeless encampments.

What becomes legible as public health and safety in these situations is distorted by the abjection and matter-out-of-place that many identify with homelessness. Fears of violence associated with outdoor meals are greatly exaggerated, for example. Although a certain amount of unruly behavior is inevitable, in my experience, on the infrequent occasions it escalates into physical conflict, it is practically never conflict between perfect strangers, and even less often does it involve both homeless and nonhomeless people. We did follow some basic precautions at FNB (we didn't hand out metal knives, for example), but we never felt particularly at risk of injury. In my six years with the group, I witnessed maybe two fights between people who already knew each other. That's it. And of course, if these outdoor meals were more numerous and better resourced rather than prohibited, the risks might be further diminished.

One could even argue that the health and safety risks to a general public—one that includes unhoused people—are in the long-term *exacerbated* by these sorts of antihomeless policies, which make life harder, more precarious, and therefore more violent for people who experience shelterlessness—and thus for everybody who shares the space of the city. One of the implications here is that feeding prohibitions—along with a whole range of antihomeless measures, "civility" ordinances, "quality of life" laws, and so on—do more harm than good for a city, especially for its most vulnerable citizens, and ought to be scrapped.

The real value of sharing prohibitions for public health and safety, then, is at best ambiguous, though it is clear that they answer to *perceptions* of health and safety on the part of businesses, residents, and the city officials who are obliged to respond to them. Their official response is, in effect, to keep matter in its place and dispel the appearance of danger or disorder. It is not a stretch to call these policies prejudice writ official. In a sense, this is understandable, as prejudices, rational or not, *can* impact economic order. Indeed, if prejudice is a legitimate worry for cities, municipal governments might work to address it and build stronger relationships between estranged communities like the shelterless and the housed. (Picture, if you will, reeducation camps to help middle-class people overcome a fear of their homeless neighbors. I am only half-joking. After all, in Seattle's increasingly polarized economy, acts of harassment and assault against the unhoused have escalated in recent years.)

All of this gives one the sense that certain kinds of people are not considered part of "the public." Antihomeless prejudices, for example, often have the effect of excluding people from public space, public visibility, and public protection. I therefore use the term *market-public* to describe the imagined boundaries drawn around a majority of citizens who adhere to the norms of the market and whose distorted sense of stability, safety, and decorum seems to be threatened by the conduct of those people who do not consume as they do. This distinction is rarely stated openly. But it is often implicit in antihomeless policies, and it has broad consequences politically and materially.

This conclusion builds on the ideas of Michael Warner (2002), who points out that no single such thing as "the" public can possibly exist. We are too diverse, speak far too many different languages (literally and metaphorically), and have far too many sources of information and frames of reference to ever really be described as having a unified, homogenous "public" interest. And yet modern politics relies on our belief in such a public. Governments decide what they think is best for it. Journalists report what they think it wants to hear. And so on. Warner suggests that we think in terms of *many* publics. Perhaps infinitely many. A conservative public and a progressive public. A punk public, a hippy public, and an academic public. A Spanish-speaking public and an English-speaking public. And many others. (And of course these often overlap.) A public is not like an ethnicity or a subculture, a nation or a party. It does not necessarily share cultural values, opinions, or even prejudices. It simply shares a set of norms for how and about what to communicate. But some publics pass for "the" public, Warner argues, and their shared norms and interests become the focus of concern for public officials. In this way, I am suggesting that market-publics are often mistaken for *the* public, particularly when cities are determining what sorts of policies to make about public spaces.

In excluding people from that public, feeding prohibitions like Seattle's effectively police the ways in which food can change hands in the public spaces of the city. In other words, in this case, a policy about public space and image *is also a kind of de facto food policy*. One of the more serious implications here is that when regulating public space, cities like Seattle must deliberately consider their impact on food security and on the accessibility of other vital resources. Not only are sharing prohibitions a de facto food policy, they are a market-centric one. They limit the means by which food can circulate in public space primarily to a field of commercial exchange. They stifle alternative sorts of food distribution by which people might avail themselves of the enormous food surpluses of the commercial waste stream—which become the raw materials of Food Not Bombs and other meal programs. So in a way, antihomeless prejudices come full circle: if a visceral prejudice against the reclamation or recirculation of waste serves as the basis for social prejudices against people who might access that waste, those latter social prejudices, levied against homeless people and other transgressive consumers, have the indirect effect of impeding the recirculation of wasted goods.

And, of course, more is at stake than what happens to the food. By way of a reminder (to myself as much as to you, my reader), as I type this, a friend of mine has just sat down adjacent to me at a Seattle cafe. He's homeless, shuffling between friends' couches and the street. He tells me he has just spent four days—and his twenty-eighth birthday—in jail for "trespassing." In this case, apparently that means getting caught sleeping in a warm garage adjoining the public library. Although a vacant garage is not surplus in the same way that commercial food waste or abandoned real estate is, in a less direct way the fact that it goes to waste is also a result of market-centric prejudices at work in policy. It certainly doesn't sit empty because there aren't people who would rather be sleeping somewhere dry and warm.

Conclusion, the Fourth

Out of these exclusions, new forms of resistance emerge; they, too, remake the city (although, to paraphrase Angela Davis, we don't always make the difference we think we're making at the time).

Food Not Bombs, in its scrappy, ambitious way, renegotiates the terms of urban life. In hundreds of cities around the world it recovers some edible sliver of the commercial waste stream and gifts it to that hungry remainder who've been left out of those cities' world-class aspirations.

In the process—along with other mutual aid networks and no-strings-attached gifts, such as Homes Not Jails, Really Really Free Markets, and Food Forests—Food Not Bombs makes publicly thinkable and practically viable, on a very local scale, an alternative economy. This is what Francisco meant, all those years ago, when he called it a "mass conspiracy." FNB's particular brand of sedition recasts the systematic exclusion of people and things from the market and makes of it an alchemic manifesto—a shared program and training ground for a slow, peaceful insurrection that turns waste back into food and abjection into political organization, in ways that add up over decades and make a material difference to city governments, political radicals, and hungry people. It might even make long-term social change possible. In other words, my fourth conclusion is simply *to keep it up*.

I write this with my FNB co-conspirators in mind. Maybe there's even something confessional about this conclusion. There were certainly times when I needed to hear it. I remember already feeling burned out after my first two years in FNB. Any given Sunday entailed eleven hectic hours of picking up donations, driving, cooking, sharing, washing the dishes, and dropping off our leftovers (yes, even we had leftovers) at one of several shelters or tent cities at the end of the night. Those hours fell unevenly on a few shoulders. We usually had enough people to cook. Regulars and occasional volunteers. Traveling radicals, passing through. Local punks, anarchists, artists, and students who made a social event of it. Cooking is the fun part—all arms and ebullience, conversation and controlled chaos. Many of them also joined us in the park to serve or eat. Serving can be fun, too, although it's often colder and wetter than the kitchen. But even when it's not fun, it's affirming. FNB represents a vital DIY supplement to the patchy safety net of formal nonprofit food pantries and emergency meal programs. And in the process of sharing food, we learned a lot about ourselves, homelessness, and the city we lived in. Sometimes we were obliged to "fight the cops" (as one FNB friend put it) who periodically came to evict us from the park. That, in turn, often drew new volunteers who were moved to join in an act of nonviolent civil disobedience.

In contrast to these shared labors, however, picking up the food and washing the dishes were often lonely tasks. There were rarely more than two of us at the beginning or the end of the day. My vision was blurred by the time it came to mopping the floor of whichever share-house, church, community center, or squat was kind enough to loan us their kitchen that day. Finding transport could be a struggle, though we always managed. We were often late to the park. But in six years, I can think of only two occasions that we didn't make it. With no permanent kitchen, just enough money from the occasional benefit concert to buy rice and oil, and an ephemeral crew of volunteers for whom FNB was often just one of too many commitments, such consistency was a remarkable accomplishment. But that was easily forgotten amid the frustrations it entailed. I'm not proud to admit that the phrase "pushing shit uphill" occurred to me often that year.

Fuck, Where Is Everyone Soup (a Recipe)

INGREDIENTS: onions, garlic, black pepper, corn, celery, potatoes, rice, tomatoes, dried oregano, vegetable oil, dried basil, any other vegetables that aren't being used (since almost no one showed up)
[DIRECTIONS:] Start heating water for the soup, and a separate pot for the rice. Cut the onions & celery, and sauté them in vegetable oil until the onions are slightly browned. Dump them in the soup pot. Let it cook for a while. Cut up potatoes & tomatoes into reasonably sized chunks and add them to the soup. Mince the garlic, sauté and add liberally to the soup. Cut the corn off the cobs, and add both the kernels and cobs. Add rice and all other vegetables. Season with pepper, oregano & basil. Let it simmer until the potatoes are cooked. Remove the corncobs & serve. Cuss the no-shows throughout.

—"Pokey '92" (2007)

It was also easy to be dismayed at the scale of waste and want in the city, and at local government's sometimes mercenary treatment of its most vulnerable citizens. After volunteering with FNB for even a short time, it became easy for me to see the imprint of antihomeless prejudice in Seattle's public life and policy. It could be harder to see our own impact. The paradox of the grassroots organizer is that they often feel equally frantic about the urgency of their work and helpless to make a difference. I remember at the time describing what would become this book as the story of how "I fought the law and the law won."

I'm glad to say I was wrong. But I wasn't alone. Other FNB collaborators from Seattle, San Francisco, Melbourne, New York City, and elsewhere shared the same burnout. One twenty-something woman from New York described to me times during the mid-2000s when she had to pick up donations from a local grocery store on her own, carrying the produce to the kitchen in buckets, on foot, *via the subway*. Enough food, mind you, to make a meal for dozens of people who would be waiting in Tompkins Square Park for FNB each week. One day, in tears, she finally decided that her own well-being was important too and quit. Frank, a middle-aged punker who helped organize the Melbourne chapter in the early 2000s, summed it up pithily: "There's always a core of reliable people. Then you've got your unreliable people. . . . It doesn't matter what chapter, there's usually someone who's doing too much."

What I lacked when I was twenty-seven was the critical distance of Angela Davis's reflections on her youthful activism: she might have told us that we had won battles I didn't even know we were fighting. Indeed, the research for this book helped me find some measure of that perspective, for which I am deeply grateful. It was cathartic and clarifying to interview former longtime FNB "bottom-liners," firsts among equals who took additional responsibility for getting things done, who shared with me the benefit of their years of hindsight and reflection. They taught me two lessons.

First, they reminded me that the movement's persistence and its impact for the people involved—from casual diners to bottom-liners—are an end in themselves. I had lost sight in all the hustle. As Vikki from New York City put it, "This is something hands-on that I can do. It's not some weird theoretical thing that may or may not happen—like 'Come the revolution, we will eradicate hunger.' It's like, 'Oh! No, I can chop vegetables and wash dishes.' Great. Wonderful. And I saw concrete results by the end of the day." In other words, the caring labor of Food Not Bombs is its own "victory." Not heeding this point, in a very early draft of this work I wrote that I had felt somehow exploited after putting in so much time. I wrote that, in FNB, "the division of labor in grassroots organizations is not necessarily more equitable than in the for-profit economy," to which Meg, one of my Seattle contemporaries and a former bottom-liner, replied that the problem is precisely the opposite. She wrote to me:

> I think that frustration, which I certainly felt at times too, comes from being accustomed to a hierarchical and individualistic society . . . feeling compelled—by yourself—to do something yourself, in order that it gets done, is not the same as inequity. It's entirely equitable actually, that those who want to see it done, whether it's finding a new kitchen or mopping the floor instead of just leaving, or doing the pick-up by bike instead of by car, if that's how they think it *should* be done, do it, instead of telling someone else to. If anything the difficulty is that it's way more equitable than we're generally used to.

I take her point. As she suggests sanguinely, these movements congeal a critical mass of uncoerced—perhaps at times unrequited—caring labor. And although the work of washing the dishes or mopping the floor is not as storied as Food Not Bombs' high-visibility campaigns of civil disobedience, the movement would be impossible without it.

And second, my fellow bottom-liners helped me to recognize such caring labor as the raw material of new political forms. It represents a distinct kind of political common sense that organizes the movement—something quite apart from the adversarial contests that dominate our political spectrum (although FNB is not immune) and more like the Quaker practice of "radical hospitality" that FNB arguably inherits indirectly, along with their principles of formal consensus. Through this caring labor, and the relationships of mutual aid it enables, communities and economies are built that are qualitatively different from those of the market-public. They swap Hobbesian scarcity for debt-free generosity. Consider the friendships built on the shared joys and frustrations of an all-consuming project like Food Not Bombs. The bonds forged after falling asleep on your feet washing dishes together at the end of the day. Hitting the mother lode at the Juice Dumpster. And so on. As Mary, from Seattle FNB, put it, "The collaboration makes such a difference." Notwithstanding the exhaustion and political despair so common to activism, she went on: "I can get as discouraged as the next person, but it makes all the difference in the world . . . that there's also this action that I'm taking in the world, that's not just about doing symbolic action, but that's also creating a greater sense of a community for myself." Such tangible solidarity often inflects the way we share food, shelter, information, and company long after we've moved on from a given FNB chapter—whether that means looking out for one another at a protest or couchsurfing with one another during periods of housing insecurity. (I've done both.) Thus do FNB and similar DIY projects weave diverse strangers into relationships of solidarity and subsistence.

> Seattle FNB has been the germinal [*sic*] for numerous projects, including the Alternative Healthcare Access Campaign (AHAC), which provides free acupuncture, naturopathic medicine, homeopathy, and massage to homeless and poor folks, and Mutual Aid Legal Fund Collective (which raised money for anarchists facing legal battles). Members and ex members have been involved in numerous direct actions, protests and campaigns throughout the world including the Infernal Noise Brigade (RIP), opening squats in Europe (and everywhere), Anarchist Peoples of Color Seattle (APOC), forest defense throughout Cascadia, Left Bank Books, Not In Our Names Seattle, Critical Mass, etc. Our membership has included punk kids and hippies, anarchists and green party types and community council members. As long as people can agree to the basic FNB principles: nonviolence, vegetarianism, and consensus decision-making, they are free to participate. We are building community one bowl of soup at a time. The Revolution Will Be Catered!
>
> —"Pokey '92" (2007)

In some way, the content of FNB's mass conspiracy amounts to a thin but enduring web of material solidarity, even across great distances, made possible precisely by the initial exclusion of people and things from prevailing public spheres. In turn, this solidarity enables larger, shared tendrils of radical community among veterans of FNB—enduring networks linked by FNB-adjacent concerns, from homeless advocates to organic farmers. For this reason, more than one FNB collaborator described it to me as a kind of "gateway activism." Such long-term connections and caring reciprocities lend a dense texture of mutuality and interdependence to life in the countercultural scenes of which FNB is a part.

Solidarity, caring labor, and shared economies are the backbone not only of specific movements but also of a larger radical milieu where new forms of common sense are incubated. In this way, for example, FNB and affiliated movements like Indymedia establish the conditions of possibility for even more visible movements like the World Trade Organization protests of the 1990s and 2000s, or Occupy Wall Street in 2011. FNB is one of the enclaves where illiberal forms of organization and embodied practices—from dumpster-diving to consensus-based decision-making—are shared and kept alive in ways that flout hegemonic, market- and state-centric kinds of common sense. Not only do these erupt in epochal moments like Occupy, they potentially bear fruit over a much longer term. If a postliberal future (however near or far off that may be) is organized along more consensual, participatory, democratic principles, it will be in part because social movements like FNB cultivated them and passed them down across generations, as prefigurative movements always have.

One notion that has helped me to think about these larger social spheres is the *counterpublic*. Like any other "public" in most respects, a counterpublic is distinctive in that it cannot take its publicness for granted the way some others can. It can never mistake itself for the "mainstream" public. So, we could talk about a punk counterpublic, a queer counterpublic, a Mormon counterpublic, and so on. Food Not Bombs and the caring relationships that it comprises therefore contribute to a nonmarket kind of counterpublic—one that makes it possible to renegotiate a life in less market-centric terms.

All of which is far from the Sisyphus-like task I identified with when I was twenty-seven. At that age, I was still thinking of politics in agonistic terms. In other words, I envisioned social change as a matter of competition and conflict between opposing sides. I was under the spell of political rhetoric about immediately "overthrowing" or "abolishing" capitalism. My thinking was framed by the metaphor of political work as a "battle," the militarized, partisan ontology of absolutes and either-or thinking all too common in antiauthoritarian circles. (The irony is that we inherit these ideas from the state itself.) Although conflict with the state may be sometimes inescapable, FNB taught me that it is embedded in larger, dynamic systems, and different, more ecological metaphors are necessary to see them.

As J. K. Gibson-Graham (1996) point out, one of the most daunting aspects of capitalism is the belief in its absoluteness—a crisis of vision suffered by both procapitalist ideologues and anticapitalist activists (like twenty-seven-year-old me). Through such black-and-white lenses, we cannot recognize the complexity, hybridity, and already existing diversity of our political and economic systems. To the extent that we accept the metaphors of battle, overthrow, and abolition as the measure of our successes against such a monolith, the kinds of successes FNB makes possible remain invisible. Deprived of this sense of immediate efficacy or forward motion, radical activists often turn instead to cultivating a vanguardist identity characterized by the politics of "purity" (Shotwell 2016) or "rigid radicalism" (Bergman and Montgomery 2017). In this vein, Vikki described her disillusionment with the paralysis of such abstract, agonistic politics after bottom-lining for New York City FNB: "I think I became a lot less tolerant of the 'isms'—that you, like, sit around and have meetings and nothing concrete comes of it. Or we sell newspapers. Or sort of all those 'isms' that don't seem to actually *do* anything that you can see, or is tangible. So I think that's both for anarch-ism and anarch-ists that sit in meetings and don't tend to do anything, and other 'ists' that tend to do that. So I think [my involvement in FNB] sort of really reduced my tolerance for that."

In response to these "isms" we might paraphrase David Graeber to ask: When has social change ever happened by replacing wholesale one thing we don't like with another thing we do like? Rather, as Gibson-Graham suggests, "post-capitalist" economies don't depend on an ideological purity. They are happening now, *in tandem* with capitalist economies. They are messy. They are heterogeneous. And they are growing.

Food Not Bombs' own messy, heterogeneous growth over the past four decades bears out Gibson-Graham's argument. It enacts a marginal, non-market economy that requires few doctrinal agreements except that the food be free, that it be vegetarian, and that each chapter be organized by consensus. Aside from that, anybody can chop carrots. Indeed, what is remarkable about FNB is the diversity of the identities and backgrounds of people who come together around the kitchen. As Kris described his teenage introduction to Seattle FNB's radical hospitality, "It was just a complete mix of students, activists, anarchists, punks . . . even a couple of old ladies who gave a fuck . . . there was no sort of weirdness if you showed up in a cardigan and a pair of jeans, or a pair of zippered-up pants and rags. It just didn't matter." Although FNB most often attracts people from punk and anarchist subcultures, during my time in Seattle I also cooked with Microsoft employees, Indigenous activists, shelterless people, domestic workers from the Global South, hippies, graduate students, transgender playwrights, refugees, ecologists, junkies, marine biologists, radical queers, Quakers, Muslims, Sikhs, single mothers receiving welfare, apolitical stoners, military recruits, and others. (Notwithstanding that in its openness, FNB also inevitably draws a cohort of politically exclusive and self-righteous collaborators whom Kris described as "the closed-minded scene of the 'open-minded' people.") Perhaps Food Not Bombs' greatest strength, therefore, is its potential to become a *contact zone*—a kind of mutable space where people from different classes and social worlds come together and develop shared political projects and shared mutual understandings in spite of their divergent perspectives (Lawson and Elwood 2013). Such contact zones make possible a politics not dictated by ideology, identity, or class interest.

Messy, heterogeneous movements like FNB resonate with another common anarchist metaphor, the notion of "growing the new society in the shell of the old." The prefigurative image of politics-as-ecosystem captures the tangled, paradoxical, chaotic process of social change in which FNB plays its role. Like invasive species, movements like FNB work simultaneously *with*, *within*, and *against* the systems of which they become part. This makes them both insurrectionary and slow. Such entanglements don't make for easy slogans or policy proposals, but they are consequential nonetheless. As we heard in chapter 5 from Peter, a core volunteer from FNB's early days in San Francisco, "If the police had a brain in their head they would have just ignored us. Right? And we would have just become another weird part of the landscape. And they just could've waited us out. And we would have, you know, eventually become bored and moved on, and done something else." Instead, they provoked a long, slow insurrection that continues to this day.

More and More to Do

The city is an endless onion. Without a singular, essential core, it hangs together, layer upon layer—some submerged, some at its surface, each a world unto itself yet intimately adjoining the others. Peel back its postcard-perfect rows of fruit and vegetables, find its dumpsters. Peel back the dumpsters, find a world of scavengers. And behind their ad hoc kitchens and squats, assembled in neglected corners of the housing market, hides the invisible hand of gentrification. And behind that, the world-class suits and shoppers who browse those postcard-perfect rows of produce on any given Sunday. The social infrastructure of the metropolis is at once disparate and recursive. This book has attempted to capture some of its seams and entanglements.

An upset or shift in one stratum cascades unevenly across the whole onion. Throughout the book, I have also tried to capture some of the compound mutations of the city as it relays crises of various scales through its fabric and reorganizes. Indeed, this manuscript may be born into an entirely new urban world, as I make my final edits in the midst of an unprecedented pandemic, one that has hollowed out the gathering spaces of cities around the world and exposed their existing socioeconomic fault lines—those who can afford it hide indoors from the disease while those who cannot are forced to work in low-waged services that remain essential, or else they have no home in which to take shelter. In this way, the sudden, acute crisis of a brand new virus amplifies the longer, slower effects of what Richard Florida (2017) called the "new urban crisis" of social and spatial polarization that now affects cities large and small in most corners of the world. At the same time, the "global city" has come to mean something new, as the world economy continues to be reorganized in the wake of the previous global financial crisis and old-guard megalopolises like New York and Tokyo lose traction to upstarts like Seattle and Bangalore—many of which begin to echo one another in uncanny ways, from the bivouacs of shelterless pavement dwellers to the gated enclaves of IT workers.

As the city transforms in all these ways, slow and fast, the excesses and exclusions I have described throughout this book may set the terms of public life in the city in brand new ways in the years to come. But so, too, do slow insurrections like Food Not Bombs. They cobble together new kinds of survival circuits, and in the process they make thinkable alternate forms of labor, consumption, organization, and cross-class solidarity. Indeed, as I write this, in the midst of the pandemic, FNB co-conspirators who appear in these very pages have been instrumental in organizing some of the thousands of new, city-based mutual aid networks that have sprung up around the world to render assistance directly to those people who are most vulnerable to the effects of the novel coronavirus and its larger social catastrophes. Their years of caring labor, reciprocity, and insurrectionary generosity with FNB have trained them and steadied their hands in anticipation of the current crisis. Although we cannot know what the coming years portend for the twenty-first-century city, we can be certain it will be globally refashioned by their efforts, as it is by the ongoing global reorganization of capital. The co-conspirators quoted throughout this book have, in Ani DiFranco's (2003) immortal words, "less and less to prove," and "more and more to do." In all of these ways, we might say that Food Not Bombs and the global city represent twin faces of our urban future.

notes

Introduction: Of Waste, Cities, and Conspiracies

Epigraph: Walter Benjamin, *The Arcades Project*, translated by Howard Eiland and Kevin McLaughlin (Cambridge, MA: Belknap Press of Harvard University Press, 1999), 13.

1. For a partial list, see "2020 Food Not Bombs Locations," https://foodnotbombs.net/info/locations/.

2. To qualify for low-income housing with the Seattle Housing Authority, a family of three must make less than 80 percent of the area median income, which at the time of her comment was $72,250 per year.

3. This described the number of "affordable" units mandated in 2019 to be part of these current developments under the city's Housing Affordability and Livability policy.

4. Roughly following Sassen's model of global city development, Seattle, New York City, San Francisco, and Melbourne each had experienced a decline in manufacturing jobs by the opening of the twenty-first century; growth in information technology, producer services, and other white-collar work; and a coinciding growth in casual or low-waged service work (see, respectively, Gibson 2004; Sassen 2001; Pratt 2002; Pamuk 2004; Beer and Forster 2002; Randolph and Holloway 2005).

5. Each city except Seattle ranked in the top three tiers of the global urban hierarchy described by Derruder et al. (2003), according to their connectivity within networks of corporate service firms; Seattle ranked fourth, "rarely if ever mentioned as world cities" (883). Only three—New York, San Francisco, and Melbourne—made it into the top fifty cities in terms of their share of headquartered corporate offices and subsidiaries (Godfrey and Zhou 1999). And while Seattle trails behind according to those criteria, the greater Seattle metropolitan region outshines the relatively provincial Melbourne according to the individual financial worth of some of its "pro-

ducer services," including the corporate headquarters of Fortune 500 companies such as Nordstrom, Starbucks, Weyerhaeuser, Nintendo, and information technology giants Microsoft and Amazon, as well as many of their smaller competitors and contractors. In terms of the city's concentration of economic decision-making power and its hefty share of international financial transactions, Sparke (2011) and Gibson (2004) both reckoned Seattle a "global" city; the latter explicitly compared the city's labor market and geography to Sassen's archetype.

6. *Many headed hydra* is a term Peter Linebaugh and Marcus Rediker (2000) use to describe the socially and geographically diverse, transnational proletariat unified in its relationship to landowners and power brokers under the conditions of European colonialism, slavery, and agrarian capitalism during the seventeenth century.

Chapter 1 : The Anatomy of a Dumpster

An earlier draft of this chapter appeared in *Social Text* 118 32(1) (spring 2014). Epigraph: Steinbeck (1939), 348–49.

1. This figure comes from Kantor et al.'s 1997 survey of US food waste. The US Department of Agriculture tracks both "food loss," the total amount of food thrown away, and "food waste," foods thrown away that may have been recoverable. Much more recent estimates for food loss are available (e.g., Buzby et al. 2014); however, estimates for "food waste" across the entire food system, such as Kantor et al.'s, are much harder to come by.

2. For example, vacant housing stock in the US rose steadily from 13.677 million vacancies, or 12 percent of the total housing stock, in 2001 to 18.574 million vacancies, or 14 percent of the total housing stock, in 2011. This increase was consistent over the intervening years, piqued only slightly by the recession in 2009 (Callis and Kresin 2011).

3. During 2010, for example, according to the World Bank global food prices rose to near the levels of the 2008 food crisis, pushing an estimated 44 million people into poverty (Poverty Reduction and Equity Group 2011, 6).

4. The United Nations Environment Programme, for example, has cited inefficiencies in the global food system that result in massive food waste, directly contributing to food crises like the 2008 price hikes (Nellemann et al. 2009).

5. Between August 2008, at the outset of the crisis, and the end of the following year, December 2009, food stamp participation increased nationally from 29 million people to a record 39 million—or one in eight Americans (Food Resource and Action Center 2009). In Seattle and across King County, according to the Department of Public Health: "In 2008, the number of people visiting King County food banks increased by over 72,000 people, a 30% increase compared to 2007; the number of people visiting food banks continued to increase through 2009 and 2010" (Public Health Seattle & King County 2020).

6. In 1996, food represented 22.2 percent of all commercial waste sampled in Seattle (Cascadia Consulting Group et al. 1997); in 2000, it represented 25.0 percent (Cascadia Consulting Group with Seattle Public Utilities Staff 2002); in 2004, 29.9 percent (Cascadia Consulting Group, Sky Valley Associations, with Seattle Public Utilities Staff 2005); in 2008, 31.6 percent (Cascadia Consulting Group with Seattle Public Utilities Staff 2008); and in 2012, 29.8 percent (Cascadia Consulting Group with Seattle Public Utilities Staff 2013).

7. As part of President Roosevelt's New Deal, for example, the federal government subsidized the slaughter of food animals, the dumping of milk, and the burning of food crops in order to diminish the supply and stabilize declining prices.

8. Rathje and Murphy (1992, 9) note that the distinction between *trash*, *garbage*, *refuse*, and *rubbish* emerged at a time when cities separated their garbage into wet and dry: *Trash* referred to discards that were "at least theoretically dry," such as newspaper, boxes, and cans. *Garbage* referred to the wet discards such as food remains, yard waste, and offal, which were slopped to feed pigs in some US cities until the 1950s. *Refuse* referred to both of these categories collectively. *Rubbish* was even more inclusive, referring to both refuse and construction and demolition debris.

9. Rathje and Murphy (1992) noted that scrap metal accounted for up to three quarters of all ocean-borne bulk cargo that leaves the Port of New York and New Jersey—1.6 million long tons every year.

10. Georges Bataille, for instance, imagined that waste itself was sovereign, situated in the ambiguous realm between profane and sacred wherein it was above the law. Bataille's "accursed share," in the work of the same name, represents waste or excess, a quantum of energy that must be squandered by a given social order. He called it, and the lives within which it was spent, "sovereign" to the extent that they are abandoned by this order, set free of their social moorings. As such, he wrote, "Life *beyond utility* is the domain of sovereignty" ([1976] 1991, 198; my emphasis; see also Bataille [1949] 1991, 33, 57–58, 129–30). Agamben's point, however, is that nothing is ever actually set entirely free of its social moorings.

11. Michel Foucault coined the term *biopower* to refer to recent historical configurations of power that, in contrast to the authoritarian power of earlier sovereign rulers who could mete out death by decree—to "take life and let live," he said—now worked structurally, through institutions that make live and let die (1986, 136). Agamben's insight is that this regulation of life is, in principle, limited neither to the modern age nor to state-centric institutions.

12. Certainly the state is implicated in defining capitalist property relationships—decreeing in some places, for example, that dumpster-diving amounts to theft from the proprietor or waste disposal company (see O'Brien 2013 and Edwards and Mercer 2007, respectively). The norms of market exchange, however, do not always require state intervention to enforce their exclusions. Indeed, in the United States, the right to pick through

other people's trash has been upheld by the Supreme Court (*California vs Greenwood* 1988), which held that law enforcement does not require a warrant to search a suspect's trash. Yet dumpster-diving remains rare.

13. News media use these terms to describe the stockpiling in warehouses of dairy products by the European Union to subsidize its dairy exports. Although this practice was suspended in 2007, it was temporarily reinstated in 2009 (Waterfield 2009).

14. One article from Orange County, for example, associates dumpster-diving explicitly with "collecting printed information that could be used to steal someone's identity" or (inexplicably) "scavengers [who] have been caught swiping bikes and other stuff from garages" without describing any other sort of dumpster-diving at all (Big 105.9 FM 2011). And in recent coverage of my own work by local media, the question of the legality of dumpster-diving received as many column inches of text as the question of food insecurity, and more than the scale of the waste—which I attempt to foreground in my interview (see McNerthney 2011).

15. In Kafka's short story *Before the Law* (from *The Trial*), a man from the country petitions a gatekeeper for entry to "the law." The gatekeeper responds ambiguously that he "cannot grant him entry at the moment," although it may be possible in the future. The gate to the law stands permanently open, but the gatekeeper says, "If it tempts you so much, try going inside in spite of my prohibition. But take note. I am powerful. And I am only the most lowly gatekeeper." The man from the country waits for a lifetime, and then on his deathbed asks why no one else has tried to gain entry. The gatekeeper replies, "Here no one else can gain entry, since this entrance was assigned only to you. I'm going now to close it" (Kafka 1971).

16. Following Claude Levi-Strauss's "culinary triangle" ([1966] 1997), which poses a structural opposition between the categories of "cooked" (equated with sociality), "raw," and "rotten" (both antisocial categories), Clark suggests that in (super)market societies, the category of "cooked" has become identified with commodification. For people who, like the punks in Clark's work, reject such market-based logic, these structuralist categories may retain their meaning, and yet their revulsion is displaced from "rotten" waste to the "cooked" economic system responsible for it. Thus does trash maintain a structural relationship to nontrash.

17. The Joint Center for Housing Studies of Harvard University (2011) noted that despite declining incomes, because of a demand for rentals in the wake of the foreclosure crisis and a general trend toward inflation in the rental market, 48.7 percent of US households were paying more than 30 percent of their income on rent, and 26.1 percent were paying more than half of their income on rent. These values represent increases from 41.2 percent and 20.7 percent, respectively, in 2001, with a full two percentage points of the increase occurring between 2007 and 2009 alone. In Seattle, for example, despite the crisis in housing prices, rental costs have increased steadily every year for more than the past two decades, with a particularly steep in-

crease of roughly 10 percent between 2007 and 2008 alone and a subsequent increase of roughly 5 percent between 2008 and 2009 (US Department of Housing and Urban Development n.d.).

18. These lines are from T. S. Eliot's "Little Gidding" (1942).

19. The anarchist Mikhail Bakunin was famous for writing, "The passion for destruction is also a creative passion" (1842). He would likely not have appreciated the resonances with the economic theories of Joseph Schumpeter ([1950] 2008), whose notion of "creative destruction" would be influential on future neoliberal, free-market ideologues.

Scene ii : Reckoning Value at the Market

At first glance, armed with Marx's labor theory of value, it is hard to explain why a thing should be thrown away, if it can only gain value through productive labor. On the basis of such simplifications, some cultural economists have largely dispensed with the labor theory of value altogether, deeming it cumbersome or deterministic. Marx's theory, however, ultimately describes a particular, culturally specific regime of value (determined by the availability of exploitable, socially productive labor)—incidentally, not wholly incompatible with the liberal theory of prices (determined by supply and demand). The theory's strength is its emphasis on the relationship between exchange, production, and social-cultural reproduction. This theoretical apparatus is invaluable to ethnographers and cultural critics because it keeps in focus the real activities of human beings—in fields, in factories, in offices, or at points of sale—that might otherwise be obscured in the abstraction of the Market.

Chapter 2 : Market-Publics and Scavenged Counterpublics

Epigraphs: Bataille (1949) 1991, 21; Hawkins 2005, 47.

1. In the United States, the system owes its historical origin to the US Department of Agriculture's surplus commodity programs, which originally absorbed agricultural surpluses to prop up food prices during the Great Depression. Some of these surpluses were destroyed outright. Others were channeled into school lunches and other early federal welfare programs, and they continue to be channeled into the national network of food banks and soup kitchens (Poppendieck 2010; Dickinson 2014).

2. Warner (2002) lists seven organizing principles that define a public. Each helps draw the ethnographer's attention to social processes and structures through which economic value is reckoned and public-ized. Publics are self-organized; "a relation among strangers" (76); addressed to a subject that is "both personal and impersonal" (81); constituted "through mere attention" (87); "the social space created by the reflexive circulation of discourse" (90); able to "act historically according to the temporality of their circulation" (96); and a kind of "poetic world-making."

3. Consider, for example, the prolific writings of Chris Rufo, an anti-homeless activist, former Seattle City Council candidate, and member of the conservative thinktank the Discovery Institute who has taken to *City Journal*, the *New York Post*, and Fox News, among other avenues, with the claim that homelessness primarily results not from poverty but rather from individual addiction and mental illness, that "city-sanctioned encampments in Seattle have become magnets for crime and violence," and "homeless individuals are 38 times more likely to commit crimes than the average citizen" (Rufo 2019). This grossly (and perhaps willfully) misrepresents the statistics from the linked source he provides, headlined "In Seattle, 1 in 5 People Booked into Jail Are Homeless: The Arrests by Police Are Mostly for Nonviolent Crime" (Kroman 2019).

4. Bernard Harcourt (2001), for example, has taken the theory to task both for its methodological flaws in data gathering and, more importantly, for its epistemological validity. Although some criminologists have found statistical correlations between broken windows theory–based policies to maintain order and declining crime rates, the *epistemological* foundations of these correlations are fundamentally flawed. Writing in defense of the theory, Corman and Moran (2005) inadvertently make this case for me by quoting New York Mayor Rudolph Giuliani, an influential proponent of the theory: "There's a continuum of disorder. Obviously murder and graffiti are two vastly different crimes. But they are part of the same continuum. And a climate that tolerates one is more likely to tolerate the other" (237). Giuliani's epistemological slippage is precisely the problem with the theory: it takes a perceived "continuum" and a qualitative "climate" as quantifiable facts, rather than as relativistic and mutable prejudices and social relationships. An unrepentant Kelling (2009) similarly defended the theory on the basis that it "worked" statistically; he did not problematize the social, cultural, and epistemological bases of the principles by which it was supposed to have functioned—citing on one hand statistical correlations between aggressive prosecution of misdemeanors and declining crime rates, and on the other hand experimental studies of theft under controlled clinical conditions. Though useful epistemological comparisons and relationships may be drawn, Kelling, and the broken windows theory in general, seems instead to ignore them. In essence, Kelling's argument seems to treat cultural frameworks and social relationships as a "black box" that can be reliably compared and quantified, an argument anathema to anthropology. (For further analysis, see Harcourt 2001; Braga, Welsh, and Schell 2015.)

5. This has been demonstrated in numerous ways. Lurie, Schuster, and Rankin (2015) have demonstrated that because marginalized groups—including racial minorities; women; individuals who identify as lesbian, gay, transgender, queer, or questioning (LGBTQ); individuals with a mental disability; incarcerated individuals; and veterans—are overrepresented among the homeless, they are therefore disproportionately affected by laws that

criminalize homelessness. And Beckett and Herbert (2010) demonstrate that urban exclusion orders that banish individuals from specific regions of downtown Seattle disproportionately affect poor people and people of color, for example. Before it was ruled unconstitutional, New York City's "stop and frisk" program authorized police to detain and search anyone they deemed to look suspicious; they then disproportionately stopped ethnic minorities and poor people (New York Civil Liberties Union 2012). And with a nearly 90 percent failure rate (i.e., nine of ten people who were stopped and frisked weren't doing anything that merited further action; New York Civil Liberties Union 2012), the stop and frisk program illustrates the importance for policy makers and their sympathetic market-publics not so much of cost-effective crime prevention as of the visible demonstration, for the benefit of market-publics and/or marginal counterpublics, of governmental commitment to maintaining a particular kind of public order.

6. The initials "MDC" have stood for a range of things over the years, from "millions of dead cops" to "multi-death corporation," although they have always referred to the same band.

7. A Really Really Free Market is a recurrent event organized in a public space in which a variety of goods and services are given away, rather than sold or bartered. Like Food Not Bombs, Critical Mass, and other anarchic projects, Really Really Free Markets are entirely voluntary, nonhierarchical endeavors with no formal membership.

8. Warner writes that "speaking, writing, and thinking" for the benefit of strangers "involve us—actively and immediately—in a public, and thus in the being of the sovereign" (2002, 69). His usage seems compatible with that of Agamben, for whom "sovereignty" is the license exercised by individuals and institutions to define relations of exception. Yet Warner also suggests that public and counterpublic sovereignties can exist simultaneously. The latter is perhaps parallel to Bataille's "accursed share": that "surplus taken from the mass of useful wealth," which was "sovereign" in its radical externality ([1949] 1991, 59). Agamben (1998, 112) criticized Bataille for mistaking the object of sovereignty for sovereignty itself. Yet one might read in Warner's description of the ambiguous, subaltern relationship between public and counterpublic a resolution of their differences.

9. From the song "Immigrant Punk" (Gogol Bordello 2005).

Scene iii : If You Build It, They Will Come

1. Short-term bocce facilities were actually first introduced in 2004, upon the recommendation of the design firm, before the more expensive changes were made in 2006 (Murakami 2004).

Chapter 3 : Place-making and Waste-making in the Global City

Epigraph: See Fanon (1963) 2004, 4.

1. New York was one of Sassen's chief examples and exhibits the same pattern today. In 2014, the top 1 percent of income earners in the city accounted for a whopping 40.5 percent of its income (New York City Independent Budget Office 2017). Their share peaked at 45.9 percent in 2007 (New York City Independent Budget Office 2017). Meanwhile, in the other cities where I have worked, income inequality is catching up quickly. In Seattle, for example, the rising tide of its tech industry's incredible growth has floated only some boats. In 2013, the top 20 percent of income earners brought in a per capita average of $248,000 per annum—$15,000 more than the previous year—overshadowing the mere $13,000 earned by the bottom 20 percent, a figure that hadn't budged since 2012 (Balk 2014). The pattern continued in 2016, as the top quintile earned $318,000 per annum—a whopping $40,000 increase over the previous year, comprising 53 percent of all income earned in the city and a 3 percent increase over 2015 (Balk 2017). The bottom 20 percent, meanwhile, again showed no change (Balk 2017). This growth made Seattle's top 20 percent the richest quintile of any US city except for Washington, DC, or San Francisco, its California competitor for software and high-tech industries (Balk 2017). Indeed, at that point, Seattle's income inequality had for the first time risen to match that of San Francisco, where top and bottom quintiles are similarly estranged (Balk 2017). Meanwhile, in the Southern hemisphere, Australian cities don't yet reflect such stark inequalities; however, the city of Melbourne exhibits comparable dynamics, clocking in with the nation's greatest inequality between top and bottom quintiles: a ratio of 8.3:1 (Biddle and Markham 2017). This social polarization is echoed by spatial polarization, with the ratio between home values in the richest and poorest neighborhoods growing from 3.5:1 a decade ago to nearly 5.0:1 today (Morton and Butt 2017).

2. Paralleling Sassen's (2001) description of New York City, Pamuk (2004) has directly associated rises in housing costs in San Francisco with the growing proportion of high-income workers employed in dynamic sectors of the global economy—particularly information technology (see also Pratt 2002). Similarly, Morrill (2008) has associated Seattle's growing housing costs (home values outpaced the national average growth by a third) with both the growing mean income and tertiary education of Seattle residents, both of which Gibson (2004) has directly associated with Seattle's successful competition within the hierarchy of global cities—particularly in the sectors of information technology, research and development, and other producer services. In Melbourne the dynamics of the labor market echo Sassen's conceptual blueprints less closely. Winter and Stone (1998), however, have attributed the marginalization of low-income workers at the bottom end of a hierarchy of housing tenure statuses (e.g., public housing, tenancy, homeownership) to a polarization of the Australian labor mar-

ket (and therefore the behavior of its upper strata in the housing market), which may echo Sassen's polarization thesis. Similarly, on the metropolitan scale, more directly paralleling Sassen's description of spatial polarization and segregation in global cities, Randolph and Holloway (2005) identified a growing spatial polarization and concentration of social disadvantage in low-income neighborhoods in both Melbourne and Sydney, which they identify in part with the polarization of the labor market resulting from Australia's liberalized economic restructuring and integration within the global economy.

3. The Pioneer Square Community Association unsuccessfully lobbied the Seattle City Council to step in to prevent the relocation of *Real Change* to the Pioneer Square neighborhood. They identified *Real Change* as a sort of homeless service and wrote a letter to the City Council, arguing that the neighborhood had its "fair share" of such institutions and requesting that the Council intervene (Krishnan 2010).

4. For contrast, compare these stalls to the grocery stores of Christchurch, New Zealand, whose dumpsters I have also explored with local scavengers, which routinely featured discount racks for ugly produce and goods nearing their "best before" date—a last stop before the dumpster for frugal, undiscerning customers. This cut-rate commodity status is less common in the high-end grocers of Seattle, San Francisco, Melbourne, or New York.

5. In the US, for example, up to 50 percent of Apple's new iPhones are purchased to replace an old iPhone taken out of circulation (adjusted for the number of secondhand phones recirculated and reactivated) (Dediu 2011).

6. Places, as Logan and Molotch (1987) describe them, represent a unique kind of commodity, largely immobile, with "special use values" (the things that can be done in or on them, including commercial enterprise) and "special exchange values" (both rental and sale); moreover, they are not manufactured in the same way as most notional commodities, and their value is therefore more contingent on speculation and government regulation.

7. In Manhattan alone, for example, Picture the Homeless (2007) counted at least 11,170 vacant housing units warehoused, along with 505 vacant lots and 584 commercial vacancies. They cited several other cities, including San Francisco and Seattle, where grassroots activists identify similar patterns of abject spatial capital (18–19). If the empty lots in New York City were developed and these properties opened up to people without shelter, they calculated that more than enough space would be available for the estimated 20,253 unsheltered households in the city and that the problem of homelessness would evaporate overnight. In a similar fashion, the greater Melbourne metropolitan region contained an estimated 82,724 vacant properties (Cashmore 2015). That's enough to house all 22,789 people homeless in the state of Victoria three times over (Homeless Australia). Picture the Homeless (2007) noted that vacancies were disproportionately concentrated in neighborhoods of low-income residents and communities of color, per-

haps anticipating neighborhood-wide gentrification and revalorization. The organization concluded that especially in these low-income locales, many landlords were leaving their properties vacant to renovate and upgrade them—to take them out of the auspices of the city's rent stabilization policies—or, alternatively, they were often speculating on the growth of their properties' value as higher-income tenants gentrified these neighborhoods. In a similar vein, New York City's Right to the City Coalition (2010) noted that luxury condominiums in three of the city's neighborhoods (South Bronx, West Village, and Chelsea) sat vacant by the thousands at exorbitant prices (on average $943,514; $336,035; and $4.7 million per condo in each neighborhood, respectively), out of reach in comparison with the neighborhoods' annual median household incomes ($19,111; $35,000; and $92,000, respectively). The net effect on the market is to constrain the available housing supply and inflate housing prices.

8. Indeed, many of the development firms responsible for building new "landscapes of wealth" in globalizing cities, from software company campuses to luxury condominiums, are themselves transnational firms working equally in Seattle, Mumbai, or Shenzhen, for example (O'Mara and Seto 2012; see also N. Smith 2002). Such transnational flows of capital, whether via development firms, transnational investment consortiums, or individual speculators, can remake the very parameters of urban real estate markets. In this vein, Gibson (2004) describes the vicissitudes of Seattle's market for downtown office space, which dramatically elevated both the city's skyline and its median rent per square foot during the 1990s, directly fueled by the waxing and waning of Japanese finance capital. And in Melbourne, for example, the remarkable growth of home prices and the corresponding housing insecurity of low-income Melburnians has been directly related to the influx of international investment in real estate (van Hulten 2010). And in Seattle and San Francisco, soaring property markets have been shaped by intensive investment of Chinese finance capital (Moon and Mudede 2016).

Scene iv : Like a Picnic, Only Bigger, and with Strangers

1. The Project for Public Spaces, contracted to reconceptualize the park, suggested "relocating at least a couple of the totems to allow for activities [such as performances and games] to occur in the space" (2004, 17). Note also that the totems do, indeed, feature carved wooden teeth.

Chapter 4 : Eating in Public

Epigraph: Mauss [1954] 2002, 13.

1. In January 2018, the city of El Cajon arrested Food Not Bombs volunteers and other meal providers after banning the sharing of food in public parks, ostensibly in connection with a hepatitis A crisis (Winkley 2018). The ban was later rescinded.

2. In late 2017, the city of Atlanta began enforcing a long-disused ordinance requiring groups that distribute food to obtain a permit (Jilani 2017).

3. These cities include Seattle, Washington; San Francisco, California; New York City, New York; Worcester, Massachusetts; Buffalo, New York; and Orlando, Florida.

4. In a survey of North American cities in 2010, the National Coalition for the Homeless and the National Law Center on Homelessness and Poverty highlighted twenty-three case studies of cities with recent food-sharing restrictions, varying from explicit legal limitations on park use permits to selective health code enforcement to extrajudicial police pressure (National Law Center on Homelessness and Poverty and the National Coalition for the Homeless 2010).

5. In 2011, the City Council of Westminster proposed a bylaw forbidding any person to "distribute any free refreshment" in certain regions of the city (Bullivant 2011). And in 2006, eleven Food Not Bombs volunteers were arrested in Buguias, Benguet, in the Philippines (Food Not Bombs n.d.).

6. In 2016, Melbourne was Australia's fastest-growing capital city, with 1,760 new residents moving there each week (Australian Bureau of Statistics 2016).

7. The annual Melbourne Street Count found 247 people sleeping rough in the central city, a 74 percent increase over the previous count (City of Melbourne 2016).

8. For one journalist's summary of the *Herald Sun*'s coverage, see Martinkus 2017. Headlines included "Mob Rule as Leaders Go Missing in Action" and "Grand Slum: Homeless Street Camp Blights City Gateway."

9. In early 2017, the Melbourne City Council opened the matter for public commentary and received an overwhelming 2,556 responses, 84 percent of which opposed the bans (Dow 2017b).

10. Where most economic anthropologists have followed Mauss ([1954] 2002) in emphasizing the inalienable reciprocal obligations entailed in a gift (see Gregory [1982] 2016), Graeber reminds us that no society is without certain sorts of debt-free giving. Like other gift economies, such communal sharing affirms a bond between benefactor and recipient, but at the broadest scale possible, the bond of sheer humanity.

11. See www.linkedin.com/in/nicholaswells (accessed May 22, 2020).

12. See Parson 2010 for a more detailed account of the distinct periods and situations during which these arrests occurred.

13. One of Nickels's spokespersons explained, "The mayor's goal was safety first. If people are getting beat up they can't eat" (Young 2004). The explanation was less than credible, because it was experienced regular meal providers such as the interviewee quoted in this chapter who organized a campaign of civil disobedience in protest of the mayor's decision, continuing to serve meals outdoors.

14. The Outdoor Meal Site was hosted by a church for a year or so before moving to its current location.

15. Gibson (2004) describes at length the competing claims backed by asymmetrical configurations of political and economic power at stake in the relocation of a proposed homeless hygiene center in downtown Seattle in 1999. The hygiene center was initially planned to have been built at Third Avenue and University Street, but its location faced the future address of Benaroya Hall, now home to the Seattle Symphony. After developers learned about the hygiene center, bitter negotiations ensued between them, the city, and the hygiene center. The Mayor's Office, which had initially supported the hygiene center, reportedly did an about-face in response to threats by the Benaroya family, who underwrote the project, and other members of the downtown business community (224). Advocates for the center were ultimately forced to abandon their standing agreements with the city and prospective landlord and relocate their facility some distance from the downtown core.

16. In 2010, for example, in case studies of twenty-three North American cities with feeding prohibitions, the National Coalition for the Homeless found that fully half of these prohibitions had focused on restricting the use of public parks for sharing food. (Although, interestingly, in other cases, even free meal projects on private property were targeted through local zoning laws [National Law Center on Homelessness and Poverty and the National Coalition for the Homeless 2010].)

17. During my fieldwork, many outdoor meals were served at different times in Occidental Park and Pioneer Square. I cannot say whether many of these were permitted, but I suspect not. They were usually short-lived, appearing for weeks or months. One notable exception was a meal provider who for several years served hotdogs and potato chips, among other things, at nearby City Hall Park, at the same time as Food Not Bombs. (The line for his food was often longer than ours, and I used to walk over to let people in the line know we were sharing food in Occidental Park, in case they didn't want to wait in his queue.) Local homeless diners referred to the primary organizer as "the cowboy." Some said he had won the lottery. I spoke with him infrequently, but I understood that he had also been pressured to relocate to the official Outdoor Meal Site and refused. In recent years, as the number of unhoused Seattleites has grown, so, too, have informal outdoor meal projects proliferated—in the downtown region, however, they have been largely compliant with the OMS.

18. This estimate is provided by Operation Sack Lunch itself (www.oslserves.org, accessed January 27, 2017).

19. The Homeless Management Information System (HMIS) was mandated nationwide in 2006 for any service providers receiving federal funds, and individuals were required to show an HMIS-specific ID card whenever they slept at a shelter, ate at a soup kitchen, washed their clothes at a hygiene center, and so on. This has troubling implications for homeless individuals who would prefer not to be recorded as such. Several Seattle service providers have told me that the system is not only a time-consuming form

of red tape but also largely ineffective, because HMIS IDs are constantly lost and reissued under whatever name a person gives, lest a lack of ID constitute an obstacle to survival itself.

20. The *New York Times* described Las Vegas Mayor Oscar B. Goodman's defense of his city's feeding prohibition as follows: "'Some people say I'm the mean mayor,' Mr. Goodman acknowledged, but he defended the ordinance as part of the effort to steer the homeless to social service groups" (Archibold 2006). Even nationally recognized experts like Barbara Poppe, former director of President Obama's official policy on homelessness, has invoked this myth implicitly: she chastised Seattle and other cities for allowing new homeless encampments, calling it a "distraction" that allows people to continue living outdoors in an "unconscionable" manner, implying that this choice is one they would not otherwise make, despite the glaring gap between Seattle's emergency shelter beds and the Seattleites therefore forced to sleep outdoors (Beekman 2016).

21. It's worth acknowledging that a wide range of legitimate reasons exists for why homeless and hungry people might find their agency and their efforts at self-care, decorum, and hygiene compromised, from the extreme to the mundane, from the personal to the systematic. Their marginalization in public space and policy is certainly one. And these challenges are, of course, not inconsequential for a larger urban public. Public drunkenness, untreated mental illness, and communicable disease, for example, are real worries for homeless and nonhomeless people alike. But the blanket prejudices and exclusions I have described above inevitably *distort* rather than clarify the challenges—and solutions, for that matter—of homelessness.

22. As Samira Kawash (1998) points out, a certain disproportionate distrust underwrites the common municipal approach of relying almost exclusively on bureaucratic emergency shelter systems, in contrast to homeless-managed projects like tent cities, which often yield better recoveries, result in a comparable number or fewer calls to the police (by residents and neighbors of these encampments alike [see Ervin and Mayo 2004]), and of course cost far less.

Scene v: "Rabble" on the Global Street

1. It is worth noting that at least one person was injured in the wake of the black bloc's actions, a press photographer struck in the temple while trying to photograph them. It is all the more telling, then, that this interpersonal violence was not, by and large, distinguished rhetorically from the vandalism (Kiley 2012).

2. In a statement published on their website, the Seattle chapter of the National Lawyers Guild suggested that they discovered through Freedom of Information Act (FOIA) requests that these grand juries may have been, in fact, called *before* the May Day vandalism, in which case the ostensible argument given for the grand juries is incomplete. This statement seems to be

no longer available on their website, although a press release is still posted there, condemning the grand juries and raids for focusing on political affiliations and therefore potential infringement of citizens' First Amendment rights (National Lawyers Guild 2012). In her public statement (made before she was imprisoned for refusing to testify before the grand jury), however, Leah-Lynn Plante (2012) describes this FOIA request as well. Therefore, other antipathies between state agencies and anarchists are likely at work as well. Nonetheless, the vandalism has been given explicitly as the reason for these investigations and raids, which in itself is significant.

3. Declassified FBI training materials underline this absolute misunderstanding: a slideshow the FBI used to brief agents on "Anarchist Extremists" sums them up as "criminals seeking an ideology to justify their activities" (Potter 2012b). In fact, however, anarchists are an incredibly diverse group. Most anarchists I have spoken with during the course of this project, including some whose friends' houses were raided and whose acquaintances were arrested in the wake of May Day, have no ties to this particular sort of property destruction and hold mixed opinions about its tactical value. The only anarchist I've spoken with whom I personally suspect of being involved in that day's vandalism was a traveler who never gave me their real name; they are long gone from Seattle.

4. The public encampments of these decentralized, diverse "occupations" were themselves largely made up of people and forms of living alienated from the predominant market-public and its institutions (from overleveraged, underpaid students to dumpster-divers, from squatting radicals to foreclosed families to homeless youth—none of these categories is mutually exclusive, and several of them have included this book's humble narrator at one time or another). Indeed, during the course of my own participation and observation at Occupy (or "Decolonize") Seattle, one of the criticisms I heard from middle-class-affiliated participants was that the movement had been "co-opted" by radicals and homeless people. (Consider the unselfconscious comment of one apparently white, middle-class protester, made public at the Seattle General Assembly: "This demonstration shouldn't be about homelessness—it should be about *politics*" . . . as if homelessness weren't political.) Of course, I heard radicals and homeless people from Occupy Seattle adopting the same language of "co-optation." They complained about middle-class "dumpies," recently hurt by the recession, co-opting *their* movement. Both comments seem to miss the point of the movement's diversity and decentralization. But they do highlight the importance, if contested, of abject labor, bodies, and modes of living, in defining the movement.

5. Several occupiers I spoke with informally reported uses of excessive force on numerous occasions. Although I witnessed some degree of verbal abuse toward police, I neither saw nor have heard any evidence to suggest that occupiers showed any corresponding physical aggression. Note, though, that police pepper spray and batons seem to have done consider-

ably more bodily harm at protests this year than the insurrectionists, whose net insurrection amounted, by all appearances, to the kind of vandalism, rhetoric, and bruised forehead described above.

Chapter 5 : A Recipe for Mass Conspiracy

Epigraph: de Certeau 1984, 107.

1. See, respectively, Deleuze and Guattari 1987; Castells 1996, Keck and Sikkink 1998, Juris 2007, 2008, and Escobar 2008; Appadurai 2006; Appadurai 1996; Clark 2004.

2. See, respectively, Hard and Negri 2004; Deleuze and Guattari 1987.

3. See, respectively, Hardt and Negri 2004 and Virno 2004; Holston 2009; Bey 1985.

4. Although the FBI does not publicly release the details of its terrorist "watch lists," its direct surveillance has been documented in several ways, including the detention of one of my interviewees by airport security, who questioned them about their involvement with FNB, and the detention of another by the FBI itself after a protest. Anecdotes aside, their surveillance is sometimes evidenced in other ways; for example, according to Austin Indymedia, "In a guest lecture at the University of Texas School of Law on Wednesday, FBI Supervisory Senior Resident Agent G. Charles Rasner listed Indymedia, Food Not Bombs, and the Communist Party of Texas as 'Terrorist Watch' cause groups in Austin. . . . Rasner then placed the FBI's Central Texas 'Terrorist Watch List' on the screen. On a list of approximately ten groups, Food Not Bombs was listed seventh. Indymedia was listed tenth, with a reference specifically to IndyConference 2005. The Communist Party of Texas also made the list. Rasner explained that these groups could have links to terrorist activity. He noted that peaceful-sounding group names could cover more violent extremist tactics" (Food Not Bombs 2006).

5. On one occasion, however, at a Reclaim the Streets protest, several members were issued parks exclusion orders from Victor Steinbrueck Park, where the protest was happening, and their pots, pans, and soup were confiscated. The order, however, did not disrupt the group's regular Sunday dinners.

6. See the decision in *First Vagabonds Church of God, Brian Nichols, Orlando Food Not Bombs, Bryan Hutchinson, Benjamin B. Markeson, Eric Montanez, Adam Ulrich v. City of Orlando Florida*, filed by the US Court of Appeals for the Eleventh Circuit, April 12, 2011.

Chapter 6 : Embodying Otherwise

Elements of this chapter appeared in an earlier form in David Boarder Giles, 2018, "Abject Economies, Illiberal Embodiment, and the Politics of Waste," in *Relational Poverty Politics: Forms, Struggles, and Possibilities*, edited by Vicky Lawson and Sarah Elwood, 1–24 (Athens: University of Georgia Press).

Epigraph: CrimethInc. 2003, 18.

1. The original *Anarchist Cookbook* was, many anarchists feel, misnamed, because its instructions had little if anything to do with egalitarian politics.

2. "1. The food is vegan and free to all. 2. We have no leaders and use the process of consensus to make decisions. 3. That Food Not Bombs is dedicated to nonviolent direct action towards creating a world free from domination, coercion and violence [*sic*]" (http://www.foodnotbombs.net).

Conclusion : An Open Letter to Lost Homes

Epigraph: These lyrics come from the Sleater-Kinney song, "No Cities to Love," on the album of the same name (2015).

1. Rough sleeping in Melbourne's Central Business District grew by 74 percent between 2014 and 2016, for example (City of Melbourne 2016).

2. See Madden and Marcuse 2016.

3. This remark was made as part of a public lecture given by Dr. Davis at the University of Washington on June 16, 2007. I regret that I did not write down her words verbatim at the time (for which reason they are not placed in quotation marks). Colleagues of mine, however, have heard her make substantively the same comment at subsequent lectures, and I am therefore satisfied that I am not misrepresenting her comments. Regrettably, I am not able to find a published version of them.

4. This figure is based on estimates before the recession that indicated 2.5 to 3.5 million Americans experienced homelessness (National Law Center on Homelessness and Poverty n.d.) and 18.6 million properties stood vacant (Callis and Kresin 2011). These numbers must, of course, be qualified in numerous ways. The vacant properties may include lots and structures unsuitable for occupancy. Nonetheless, as a broad snapshot of land tenure in the United States, it strikes an important note.

bibliography

3AW 693 News Talk. 2017. "RUMOUR CONFIRMED: Homelessness protesters take fight to Lord Mayor's private home," broadcast February 26. Accessed December 28, 2020. https://www.3aw.com.au/rumour-confirmed-homelessness-protesters-take-fight-to-lord-mayor-s-private-home-20170226-gulu2e/.

Adolph, Carolyn. 2018. "Seattle-Area Housing Prices Are Rising $5 an Hour, Every Hour, Every Day." 94.9 FM, KUOW, July 15. http://archive.kuow.org/post/seattle-area-housing-prices-are-rising-5-hour-every-hour-every-day.

Agamben, Giorgio. 1998. *Homo Sacer: Sovereign Power and Bare Life*. Stanford, CA: Stanford University Press.

Agger, Ben. 2004. *Speeding Up Fast Capitalism: Cultures, Jobs, Families, Schools, Bodies*. Boulder, CO: Paradigm.

Ahmed, Sara. 2004. "Affective Economies." *Social Text 79* 22(2): 117–39.

All Home. 2018. *Count Us In: Seattle/King County Point-in-Time Count of Persons Experiencing Homelessness, 2018*. Report compiled by Applied Survey Research. Accessed November 15, 2018. http://allhomekc.org/wp-content/uploads/2018/05/FINALDRAFT-COUNTUSIN2018REPORT-5.25.18.pdf.

Allison, Anne. 1991. "Japanese Mothers and Obentōs: The Lunch-Box as Ideological State Apparatus." *Anthropological Quarterly* 64(4): 195–208.

Althusser, Louis. [1971] 2014. *Lenin and Philosophy and Other Essays*. Translated by Ben Brewster. London: New Left Books.

American Civil Liberties Union. 2008. "Federal Judge Strikes Down Homeless Feeding Ban." September 26. Accessed December 30, 2020. http://www.aclu.org/racial-justice_prisoners-rights_drug-law-reform_immigrants-rights/federal-judge-strikes-down-orlando.

Anderson, Benedict. 1983. *Imagined Communities: Reflections on the Origin and Spread of Nationalism*. New York: Verso.

Appadurai, Arjun. 1981. "Gastro-Politics in Hindu South Asia." *American Ethnologist* 8(3): 494–511.

Appadurai, Arjun. 1986. "Introduction: Commodities and the Politics of Value." In *The Social Life of Things: Commodities in Cultural Perspective*, edited by Arjun Appadurai, 3–63. New York: Cambridge University Press.

Appadurai, Arjun. 1996. *Modernity at Large: Cultural Dimensions of Globalization*. Minneapolis: University of Minnesota Press.

Appadurai, Arjun. 2000. "Spectral Housing and Urban Cleansing: Notes on Millennial Mumbai." *Public Culture* 12(3): 627–51.

Appadurai, Arjun. 2006. *Fear of Small Numbers: An Essay on the Geography of Anger*. Durham, NC: Duke University Press.

Appadurai, Arjun. 2012. "The Spirit of Calculation." *Cambridge Journal of Anthropology* 30(1): 3–17.

Appel, Hannah. 2018. "Race Makes Markets: Subcontracting in the Transnational Oil Industry." Social Science Research Council, "Race and Capitalism" series, December 18. Accessed November 14, 2019. https://items.ssrc.org/race-capitalism/race-makes-markets-subcontracting-in-the-transnational-oil-industry/.

Archibold, Randal C. 2006. "Las Vegas Makes It Illegal to Feed Homeless in Parks." *New York Times*, July 28.

Arendt, Hannah. [1951] 1968. *The Origins of Totalitarianism*. New York: Harcourt, Brace and Jovanovich.

Australian Bureau of Statistics. 2016. "Melbourne Our Fastest-Growing Capital." Media release, March 30. Updated March 29, 2017. Accessed February 2, 2018. http://www.abs.gov.au/ausstats/abs@.nsf/lookup/3218.0Media%20Release12014-15.

Bag, Alice. 2011. *Violence Girl: A Chicana Punk Story*. Port Townshend, WA: Feral House.

Badiou, Alain. [1988] 2013. *Being and Event*. Translated by Oliver Feltham. London: Bloomsbury.

Bakunin, Mikhail. 1842. *The Reaction in Germany: A Fragment of a Frenchman*. Archived at theanarchistlibrary.org. Accessed December 30, 2020. https://theanarchistlibrary.org/library/mikhail-bakunin-the-reaction-in-germany.

Balk, Gene. 2014. "As Seattle Incomes Soar, Gap Grows between Rich and Poor." *Seattle Times*, October 6.

Balk, Gene. 2017. "Seattle Hits Record High for Income Inequality, Now Rivals San Francisco." *Seattle Times*, November 17.

Baran, Paul A., and Paul M. Sweezy. 1966. *Monopoly Capital: An Essay on the American Economic and Social Order*. New York: Monthly Review Press.

Barnard, Alex V. 2016. *Freegans: Diving into the Wealth of Food Waste in America*. Minneapolis: University of Minnesota Press.

Barnett, Erica C. 2018. "Tonight in Ballard: Two Hours Hate." *The C is for*

Crank: News, Politics, Urbanism, May 3. Accessed November 15, 2018. https://thecisforcrank.com/2018/05/03/tonight-in-ballard-two-hours-hate/.
Bartelt, David. 1997. "Urban Housing in an Era of Global Capital." *Annals of the American Academy of Political and Social Science* 551: 121–36.
Bataille, Georges. [1949] 1991. *The Accursed Share: An Essay on General Economy*, volume I. New York: Zone Books.
Bataille, Georges. [1976] 1991. *The Accursed Share: An Essay on General Economy*, volume III. New York: Zone Books.
Bauman, Zygmunt. 2004. *Wasted Lives: Modernity and Its Outcasts*. Cambridge: Polity Press.
Bauman, Zygmunt. 2016. *Strangers at Our Door*. Cambridge: Polity.
Beckett, Katherine, and Steve Herbert. 2010. *Banished: The New Social Control in Urban America*. Oxford: Oxford University Press.
Beekman, Daniel. 2016. "Stop Opening Tent Cities, Homelessness Expert Tells Seattle Leaders." *Seattle Times*, February 26.
Beekman, Daniel, and Jim Bruner. 2019. "Amazon Drops Additional $1 Million-Plus into Seattle City Council Races, with Ballots out This Week." *Seattle Times*, October 15.
Beer, Andrew, and Clive Forster. 2002. "Global Restructuring, the Welfare State and Urban Programmes: Federal Policies and Inequality within Australian Cities." *European Planning Studies* 10(1): 7–25.
Benjamin, Walter. 1999. *The Arcades Project*. Translated by Howard Eiland and Kevin McLaughlin. Cambridge, MA: Belknap Press of Harvard University Press.
Bergman, Carla, and Nick Montgomery. 2017. *Joyful Militancy: Building Thriving Resistance in Toxic Times*. Oakland, CA: AK Press.
Berlant, Lauren. 2010. "Risky Bigness: On Obesity, Eating, and the Ambiguity of 'Health.'" In *Against Health: How Health Became the New Morality*, edited by Jonathan M. Metzl and Anna Kirkland, 26–39. New York: New York University Press.
Best, Joel. 1993. *Threatened Children: Rhetoric and Concern about Child-victims*. Chicago: University of Chicago Press.
Bey, Hakim. 1985. *The Temporary Autonomous Zone: Ontological Anarchy, Poetic Terrorism*. Brooklyn, NY: Autonomedia.
Biddle, Nicholas, and Francis Markham. 2017. "What Income Inequality Looks Like across Australia." *The Conversation* (Australian edition), July 6.
Bolt, Andrew. 2017. "Violent Left Stalks Lord Mayor." *Herald Sun* (blog), February 28. Accessed December 30, 2020. https://www.heraldsun.com.au/blogs/andrew-bolt/violent-left-stalks-lord-mayor/news-story/63b868420039e47e44fe0bc660cc033e.
Bourdieu, Pierre. 1977. *Outline of a Theory of Practice*. Translated by Richard Nice. Cambridge: Cambridge University Press.
Bourgois, Philipe. 2010. "Useless Suffering: The War on Homeless Drug

Addicts." In *The Insecure American: How We Got Here and What We Should Do About It*, edited by Hugh Gusterson and Catherine Besteman, 239–54. Berkeley: University of California Press.

Braga, Anthony A., Brandon C. Welsh, and Cory Schnell. 2015. "Can Policing Disorder Reduce Crime? A Systematic Review and Meta-analysis." *Journal of Research in Crime and Delinquency* 52(4): 567–88.

Brinegar, Sarah J. 2003. "The Social Construction of Homeless Shelters in the Phoenix Area." *Urban Geography* 24(1): 61–74.

Bullivant, Stephen. 2011. "Sweeping the Homeless—and Charity—from Westminster's Streets." *Guardian*, March 4.

Burkhalter, Aaron. 2012. "Under the Table." *Real Change News*, August 29.

Bush, James. 1999. "Street Fight Brewing over Civility Laws." *Seattle Weekly*, October 20.

Butler, Judith. 1993. *Bodies That Matter: On the Discursive Limits of "Sex."* New York: Routledge.

Butler, Judith. 2009. *Frames of War: When Is Life Grievable?* New York: Verso.

Buzby, Jean C., Hodan Farah Wells, and Jeffrey Hyman. 2014. *The Estimated Amount, Value, and Calories of Postharvest Food Losses at the Retail and Consumer Levels in the United States*. Economic Information Bulletin no. 121, February. Washington, DC: Economic Research Service, US Department of Agriculture.

Byrne, Thomas, Ellen A. Munley, Jamison D. Fargo, Ann E. Montgomery, and Dennis P. Culhane. 2012. "New Perspectives on Community-Level Determinants of Homelessness." *Journal of Urban Affairs* 35(5): 607–25.

Callis, Robert R., and Melissa Kresin. 2011. "Residential Vacancies and Homeownership in the Second Quarter 2011." Press release, July 29. Washington, DC: US Census Bureau News.

Cascadia Consulting Group, Inc., in cooperation with Seattle Public Utilities Staff. 2002. *2000 Commercial & Self-Haul Waste Streams, Composition Study, Final Report*. October. Seattle: Seattle Public Utilities.

Cascadia Consulting Group, Inc., in cooperation with Seattle Public Utilities Staff. 2008. *2008 Commercial and Self-Haul Waste Streams, Composition Study, Final Report*. July. Seattle: Seattle Public Utilities.

Cascadia Consulting Group, Inc., in cooperation with Seattle Public Utilities Staff. 2013. *2012 Commercial and Self-Haul Waste Streams, Composition Study, Final Report*. Seattle: Seattle Public Utilities.

Cascadia Consulting Group, Inc. and Sky Valley Associates, in cooperation with Seattle Public Utilities Staff. 2005. *2004 Commercial & Self-Haul Waste Streams, Composition Study, Final Report*. September 2005. Seattle: Seattle Public Utilities.

Cascadia Consulting Group, Inc., Sky Valley Associates, E. Ashley Steel, and Hopkins Environmental, in cooperation with Seattle Public Utilities Staff. 1997. *1996 Commercial and Self-Haul Waste Streams, Composition Study, Final Report*. September. Seattle: Seattle Public Utilities.

Cashmore, Catherine. 2015. *Speculative Vacancies 8: The Empty Properties Ignored by Statistics*. Prosper Australia. Accessed March 11, 2017. https://www.prosper.org.au/wp-content/uploads/2015/12/11Final_Speculative-Vacancies-2015-1.pdf.2015.

Castells, Manuel. 1996. *The Rise of the Network Society*. Oxford, UK: Blackwell.

Cherniavsky, Eva. 2006. *Incorporations: Race, Nation, and the Body Politics of Capital*. Minneapolis: University of Minnesota Press.

City of Melbourne. 2016. "StreetCount 2016: Final Report." September. Accessed March 9, 2019. https://www.melbourne.vic.gov.au/SiteCollectionDocuments/streetcount-2016-final-report.pdf.

City of Seattle and Applied Survey Research. 2017. "2016 Homeless Needs Assessment." Accessed January 8, 2018. http://coshumaninterests.wpengine.netdna-cdn.com/wp-content/uploads/2017/04/City-of-Seattle-Report-FINAL-with-4.11.17-additions.pdf.

Clark, Dylan. 2004. "The Raw and the Rotten: Punk Cuisine." *Ethnology* 43(1): 19–31.

Clastres, Pierre. 1977. *Society against the State*. Translated by Robert Hurley. New York: Urizen Books.

Clastres, Pierre. 2010. *Archaeology of Violence*. Translated by Jeanine Herman. Cambridge: Semiotext(e).

Cloke, Jon. 2013. "Empires of Waste and the Food Security Meme." *Geography Compass* 7(9): 622–36.

Coleman-Jensen, Alisha, Matthew P. Rabbitt, Christian A. Gregory, and Anita Singh. 2018. "Household Food Security in the United States in 2017." ERR-256. Washington, DC: Economic Research Service, US Department of Agriculture.

Cooper, Melinda. 2008. *Life as Surplus: Biotechnology and Capitalism in the Neoliberal Era*. Seattle: University of Washington Press.

Corman, Hope, and Naci Moran. 2005. "Carrots, Sticks, and Broken Windows." *Journal of Law and Economics* 48 (April): 235–66.

Coyote, Peter. 2008. Book reading at Book Passage, Corte Madera, CA, December 10. ForaTV. Originally archived at http://fora.tv/2008/12/10/Peter_Coyote_Emmett_Grogan_and_the_Diggers. Accessed December 22, 2020. https://youtu.be/iki6oDgPf48.

CrimethInc. Ex-Workers' Collective. 2002. *D.I.Y. Guide*. Salem, OR: CrimethInc. Ex-Workers' Collective.

CrimethInc. Ex-Workers' Collective. 2003. *Off the Map*. Salem, OR: CrimethInc. Ex-Workers' Collective.

CrimethInc. Ex-Workers' Collective. 2004. *Recipes for Disaster: An Anarchist Cookbook*. Salem, OR: CrimethInc. Ex-Workers' Collective.

CrimethInc. Ex-Workers' Collective. n.d. "How to Start a Food Not Bombs, By Liz." *D.I.Y Guide II* zine.

Curran, David. 2013. "Why Not a Giant Ferris Wheel in S.F.?" *SFGate* (blog), July 27. Accessed January 10, 2018. http://blog.sfgate.com/stew/2013/07/27/why-not-a-giant-ferris-wheel-in-s-f/.

Day, Richard. 2005. *Gramsci Is Dead: Anarchist Currents in the Newest Social Movements*. Ann Arbor, MI: Pluto Press.
de Certeau, Michel. 1984. *The Practice of Everyday Life*. Berkeley: University of California Press.
de Certeau, Michel, and Luce Giard. 1997. "The Nourishing Arts." In *Food and Culture: A Reader*, 2nd ed., edited by Carole Counihan and Penny Van Esterike. New York: Routledge.
Dediu, Horace. 2011. "How Many iPhones Are Being Discarded in the US?" Asymco, November 8. Accessed May 6, 2013. http://www.asymco.com/2011/11/08/how-many-iphones-are-being-discarded-in-the-us/.
Delaney, Samuel R. 1999. *Times Square Red, Times Square Blue*. New York: New York University Press.
Deleuze, Gilles, and Guattari, Felix. 1987. *A Thousand Plateaus: Capitalism and Schizophrenia*. Translated by Brian Massumi. Minneapolis: University of Minnesota Press.
DePastino, Todd. 2003. *Citizen Hobo: How a Century of Homelessness Shaped America*. Chicago: University of Chicago Press.
Derruder, B., with P. J. Taylor, F. Witlox, and G. Catalano. 2003. "Hierarchical Tendencies and Regional Patterns in the World City Network: A Global Urban Analysis of 234 Cities." *Regional Studies* 37(9): 875–86.
DeSilvey, Caitlin. 2006. "Observed Decay: Telling Stories with Mutable Things." *Journal of Material Culture* 11(3): 318–38.
Dickinson, Maggie. 2013. "Cooking Up a Revolution: Food as a Democratic Tactic at Occupy Wall Street." *Food, Culture, and Society* 16(3): 359–65.
Dickinson, Maggie. 2014. "Consuming Poverty: The Unexpected Politics of Food Aid in an Era of Austerity." PhD diss., Department of Anthropology, City University of New York.
DiFranco, Ani. 2003. "Evolve." Track 6, *Evolve* (compact disc). Buffalo, NY: Righteous Babe Records.
Douglas, Mary. [1966] 1984. *Purity and Danger: An Analysis of the Concepts of Pollution and Taboo*. London: Ark.
Dow, Aisha. 2017a. "Melbourne CBD Rough Sleepers Are Pretending to be Homeless: Victoria's Top Cop Graham Ashton." *The Age*, January 19.
Dow, Aisha. 2017b. "Proposed Homeless Camping Ban in Melbourne CBD Faces Strong Resistance." *The Age*, March 30.
Duneier, Mitchell. 2000. *Sidewalk*. New York: Farrar, Straus and Giroux.
Dwyer, Jim. 2010. "A Clothing Clearance Where More Than Just the Prices Have Been Slashed." *New York Times*, January 5.
Editorial. 2011. "Activists Should Feed the Hungry without Flouting Orlando's Ordinance." *Orlando Sentinel*, June 10.
Edwards, Ferne, and David Mercer. 2007. "Gleaning from Gluttony: An Australian Youth Subculture Confronts the Ethics of Waste." *Australian Geographer* 38(3): 279–96.
Elliott, James R. 1999. "Putting 'Global Cities' in Their Place: Urban Hierar-

chy and Low-Income Employment During the Post-War Era." *Urban Geography* 20(2): 95–115.
Ervin, Keith, and Justin Mayo. 2004. "Tent City Doesn't Seem to Affect Crime Rates." *Seattle Times*, May 21.
Escobar, Arturo. 2008. *Territories of Difference: Place, Movements, Life, Redes*. Durham, NC: Duke University Press.
Fahmi, Wael, and Keith Sutton. 2013. "Cairo's Contested Waste: The Zabaleen's Local Practices and Privatisation Policies." In *Organising Waste in the City: International Perspectives on Narratives and Practices*, edited by Maria Jose Zapata and Michael Hall, 159–80. Bristol, UK: Policy Press.
Fainstein, Susan S., Ian Gordon, and Michael Harloe. 2011. "Ups and Downs in the Global City: London and New York in the Twenty-First Century." In *The New Blackwell Companion to the City*, edited by Gary Bridge and Sophie Watson, 38–47. West Sussex, UK: Wiley-Blackwell.
Fanon, Frantz. [1963] 2004. *The Wretched of the Earth*. New York: Grove Press.
Ferguson, James. 1999. *Expectations of Modernity: Myths and Meanings of Urban Life on the Zambian Copperbelt*. Berkeley: University of California Press.
Ferrell, Jeff. 2017. *Drift: Illicit Mobility and Uncertain Knowledge*. Berkeley: University of California Press.
Fischer, Michael M. J. 2003. *Emergent Forms of Life and the Anthropological Voice*. Durham, NC: Duke University Press.
Florida, Richard. 2003. *The Rise of the Creative Class: And How It's Transforming Work, Leisure, Community, and Everyday Life*. North Melbourne: Pluto Press.
Florida, Richard. 2017. *The New Urban Crisis: How Our Cities Are Increasing Inequality, Deepening Segregation, and Failing the Middle Class—and What We Can Do About It*. New York: Basic Books.
Florida, Richard, and Benjamin Schneider. 2018. "The Global Housing Crisis." *CityLab*, April 11, accessed November 15, 2018. https://www.citylab.com/equity/2018/04/the-global-housing-crisis/557639/.
Food Not Bombs. n.d. "FREE THE SAGADA 11: Cainta, Philippines Food Not Bombs Volunteers in Jail since February International Day of Protest February 14, 2007." foodnotbombs.net. Accessed February 2, 2018. https://www.foodnotbombs.net/philippine_arrests.html.
Food Not Bombs. 2006. "FBI Officer Speaks at Law School, lists Food Not Bombs and Indymedia on 'Terrorist Watch List.'" Published to foodnotbombs.net. Retrieved from http://foodnotbombs.net/FBI_officer_lists_FNB_austin.pdf, June 22, 2018.
Foucault, Michel. 1980. "Two Lectures." In *Power/Knowledge: Selected Interviews and Other Writings 1972–1977*, edited by Colin Gordon, 78–108. New York: Pantheon.
Foucault, Michel. [1978] 1986. *The History of Sexuality, Volume I: An Introduction*. Translated by Robert Hurley. New York: Random House.

Fraser, Nancy. 1990. "Rethinking the Public Sphere: A Contribution to the Critique of Actually Existing Democracy." *Social Text* (25–26): 56–80.
Fredericks, Rosalind. 2018. *Garbage Citizenship: Vital Infrastructures of Labor in Dakar, Senegal*. Durham, NC: Duke University Press.
Freeman, Jo. 1972. "The Tyranny of Structurelessness." *Berkeley Journal of Sociology* 17: 151–65.
Friedmann, John. 1986. "The World City Hypothesis." *Development and Change* 17: 69–83.
Galloway, Alexander R., and Eugene Thacker. 2007. *The Exploit: A Theory of Networks (Electronic Mediations)*. Minneapolis: University of Minnesota Press.
Geddes, Patrick, Sir. 1915. *Cities in Evolution: An Introduction to the Town Planning Movement and to the Study of Civics*. London: Williams and Norgate.
Gibson, Timothy. 2004. *Securing the Spectacular City: The Politics of Revitalization and Homelessness in Downtown Seattle*. New York: Lexington Books.
Gibson-Graham, J. K. 1996. *The End of Capitalism (As We Knew It)*. Oxford: Blackwell.
Gibson-Graham, J. K. 2006. *A Postcapitalist Politics*. Minneapolis: University of Minnesota Press.
Gidwani, Vinay. 2015. "The Work of Waste: Inside India's Infra-economy." *Transactions of the British Institute of Geographers* 40(5): 575–95.
Gidwani, Vinay, and Rajyashree N. Reddy. 2011. "The Afterlives of 'Waste': Notes from India for a Minor History of Capitalist Surplus." In "Bio(necro)polis: Marx, Surplus Populations, and the Spatial Dialectics of Reproduction and 'Race.'" Special issue, *Antipode* 43(5): 1625–58.
Giles, David Boarder. 2015. "The Work of Waste-Making: Biopolitical Labour and the Myth of the Global City." In *Environmental Change and the World's Futures: Ecologies, Ontologies and Mythologies*, edited by Jonathan Paul Marshall and Linda H. Connor, 81–95. London: Routledge.
Giles, David Boarder. 2016. "Distributions of Wealth, Distributions of Waste: Abject Capital and Accumulation by Disposal." In *Anthropologies of Value*, edited by Luis Fernando Angosto-Ferrández and Geir Henning Presterudstuen, 198–218. London: Pluto Press.
Giles, David Boarder. 2018. "Sketches for a Theory of Abject Economies." *Arena Journal* 51/52 (July).
Gille, Zsuzsa. 2010. "Actor Networks, Modes of Production, and Waste Regimes: Reassembling the Macro-Social." *Environment and Planning A: Economy and Space* 42(5): 1049–64.
Glynn, Chris, and Emily B. Fox. 2017. "Dynamics of Homelessness in Urban America." Zillow Research, arXiv:1707.09380. Submitted July 28. Accessed November 15, 2018. https://arxiv.org/abs/1707.09380.

Godfrey, Brian, and Yu Zhou. 1999. "Ranking World Cities: Multinational Corporations and the Global Urban Hierarchy." *Urban Geography* 20(3): 268–81.

Gogol Bordello. 2005. "Immigrant Punk." Track 4, *Gypsy Punks: Underdog World Strike* (compact disc). Los Angeles: SideOneDummy Records.

Gordillo, Gastón R. 2014. *Rubble: The Afterlife of Destruction*. Durham, NC: Duke University Press.

Gordinier, Jeff. 2011. "Want to Get Fat on Wall Street? Try Protesting." *New York Times*, October 11.

Graeber, David. 2001. *Toward an Anthropological Theory of Value: The False Coin of Our Own Dreams*. New York: Palgrave.

Graeber, David. 2004. *Fragments of an Anarchist Anthropology*. Chicago: Prickly Paradigm Press.

Graeber, David. 2009. *Direct Action: An Ethnography*. Oakland, CA: AK Press.

Graeber, David. 2011. *Debt: The First 5000 Years*. Brooklyn, NY: Melville House.

Graeber, David. 2013. "A Practical Utopian's Guide to the Coming Collapse." *Baffler* 22 (April). Accessed May 2, 2013. https://thebaffler.com/salvos/a-practical-utopians-guide-to-the-coming-collapse.

Greene, L. Shane. 2012. "The Problem of Peru's Punk Underground: A New Approach to Under-Fuck the System." *Journal of Popular Music Studies* 24(4): 578–89.

Greenstone, Scott. 2018. "How Many Homeless People in Seattle Are from Here?" *Seattle Times*, October 26. Updated January 28, 2019. Accessed November 15, 2018. https://www.seattletimes.com/seattle-news/homeless/do-homeless-people-come-to-seattle-for-help/.

Gregory, C. A. [1982] 2016. *Gifts and Commodities*. London: HAU Books.

Grubačić, Andrej, and Denis O'Hearn. 2016. *Living at the Edges of Capitalism: Adventures in Exile and Mutual Aid*. Berkeley: University of California Press.

Guano, Emanuela. 2002. "Spectacles of Modernity: Transnational Imagination and Local Hegemonies in Neoliberal Buenos Aires." *Cultural Anthropology* 17(2): 181–220.

Gupta, Akhil. 2016. *The Future in Ruins: Thoughts on the Temporality of Infrastructure*. Public lecture, School of Social and Political Sciences, University of Melbourne, August 3.

Gupta, Akhil, and James Ferguson, editors. 1997. *Anthropological Locations: Boundaries and Grounds of a Field Science*. Berkeley: University of California Press.

Gustavsson, Jenny, Christel Cederberg, Ulf Sonesson, Robert van Otterdijk, and Alexandre Meybeck. 2011. *Global Food Losses and Food Waste: Extent, Causes, and Prevention*. Rome: Food and Agriculture Organization of the United Nations.

Guthman, Julie, and Melanie DuPuis. 2006. "Embodying Neoliberalism: Economy, Culture, and the Politics of Fat." *Environment and Planning D: Society and Space* 24: 427–48.

Habermas, Jurgen. 1991. *The Structural Transformation of the Public Sphere: An Inquiry into a Category of Bourgeois Society.* Cambridge, MA: MIT Press.

Hackworth, Jackson. 2007. *The Neoliberal City: Governance, Ideology, and Development in American Urbanism.* Ithaca, NY: Cornell University Press.

Hall, K. D., J. Guo, M. Dore, C. C. Chow. 2009. "The Progressive Increase of Food Waste in America and Its Environmental Impact." *PLoS One* 4(11): e7940. doi:10.1371/journal.pone.0007940.

Hall, Peter. 1966. *The World Cities.* New York: McGraw-Hill.

Halperin, David M. 1995. *Saint Foucault: Towards a Gay Hagiography.* Oxford: Oxford University Press.

Hamnett, Chris. 1994. "Social Polarisation in Global Cities: Theory and Evidence." *Urban Studies* 31(3): 401–24.

Hardt, Michael, and Antonio Negri. 2000. *Empire.* Cambridge, MA: Harvard University Press.

Hardt, Michael, and Antonio Negri. 2004. *Multitude: War and Democracy in the Age of Empire.* New York: Penguin.

Harcourt, Bernard E. 2001. *Illusion of Order: The False Promises of Broken Windows Policing.* Cambridge, MA: Harvard University Press.

Harvey, David. 1978. "The Urban Process under Capitalism: A Framework for Analysis." *International Journal of Urban Research and Regional Research* 2(1–3): 101–31.

Harvey, David. [1982] 2006. *The Limits to Capital.* Chicago: University of Chicago Press.

Harvey, David. 2007. "Neoliberalism as Creative Destruction." *Annals of the American Academy of Political and Social Science* 610: 22–44.

Haug, Wolfgang Fritz. 1986. *Critique of Commodity Aesthetics: Appearance, Sexuality, and Advertising in Capitalist Society.* Minneapolis: University of Minnesota Press.

Hawkins, Gay. 2005. *The Ethics of Waste: How We Relate to Rubbish.* Lanham, MD: Rowman and Littlefield.

Hebdige, Dick. [1979] 2005. *Subculture: The Meaning of Style.* London: Routledge.

Henderson, George L. 2011. "What Was Fight Club? Theses on the Value Worlds of Trash Capitalism." *Cultural Geographies* 18(2): 142–70.

Hetherington, Kevin. 2004. "Secondhandedness: Consumption, Disposal, and Absent Presence." *Society and Space* 22(1): 157–73.

Heynen, Nik. 2010. "Cooking up Non-violent Civil-disobedient Direct Action for the Hungry: 'Food Not Bombs' and the Resurgence of Radical Democracy in the US." In "Cities, Justice and Conflict." Special issue, *Urban Studies* 47(6): 1225–40.

Holston, James. 2009. *Insurgent Citizenship: Disjunctions of Democracy and Modernity in Brazil*. Princeton, NJ: Princeton University Press.
Holter, Scott. 2004. "Three Men and a Vision: A Trio of Real Estate Developers Says Seattle Has to Evolve to Remain Among the Country's Elite Cities. Here's How They Plan to Do It." *Washington* CEO 15(4): 51–56.
Homes Not Jails. n.d. About Us. Accessed November 8, 2011. http://www.homesnotjailssf.org/wb/pages/about-us.php.
Hopper, Kim. 1988. "More Than Passing Strange: Homelessness and Mental Illness in New York City." *American Ethnologist* 15(1): 155–67.
Howard, Joshua, David Tran, and Sarah Rankin. 2015. "At What Cost: The Minimum Cost of Criminalizing Homelessness in Seattle and Spokane." Homelessness Rights Advocacy Project, May 8. Accessed February 2, 2018. https://papers.ssrn.com/sol3/papers.cfm?abstract_id=2602530.
Insurrection News. 2017. "Melbourne, Australia: Anarchists and Homeless People Protest outside the Home of Lord Mayor Robert Doyle." February 27. Accessed July 12, 2018. https://insurrectionnewsworldwide.com/2017/02/27/melbourne-australia-anarchists-and-homeless-people-protest-outside-the-home-of-lord-mayor-robert-doyle/.
Iveson, Kurt. 2007. *Publics and the City*. Malden, MA: Blackwell.
Jilani, Zaid. 2017. "Atlanta Police Suddenly Enforce Old Law and Hand Out Tickets to People Feeding the Homeless." *The Intercept*, November 29.
Johansen, Bruce. 1982. *Forgotten Founders: How the American Indian Helped Shape Democracy*. Cambridge, MA: Harvard Common Press.
Johnson, Eric. 2019. "Seattle Is Dying." KOMO News Special and Commentary. Posted March 15. Accessed December 22, 2020. https://komonews.com/news/local/komo-news-special-seattle-is-dying.
Joint Center for Housing Studies of Harvard University. 2011. *Rental Market Stresses: Impacts of the Great Recession on Affordability and Multifamily Lending*. Cambridge, MA: Harvard University Press.
Jones, Timothy, Sarah Dahlen, Andrew Bockhorst, Kathy Cisco, and Brian McKee. 2002a. "Household Food Loss Comparing Tucson, Arizona and Wilmington, Delaware: Extrapolating the Tucson Household Data to the Nation." Report to the Economic Research Service, US Department of Agriculture. Tucson: Bureau of Applied Research in Anthropology, University of Arizona.
Jones, Timothy, Sarah Dahlen, Kathy Cisco, Andrew Bockhorst, Brian McKee. 2002b. "Commercial Refuse Food Loss." Report to the Economic Research Service, US Department of Agriculture. Tucson: Bureau of Applied Research in Anthropology, University of Arizona.
Juris, Jeffrey. 2007. "Practicing Militant Ethnography with the Movement for Global Resistance (MRG) in Barcelona." In *Constituent Imagination: Militant Investigation, Collective Theorization*, edited by Stevphen Shukaitis and David Graeber, 164–76. Oakland, CA: AK Press.

Juris, Jeffrey. 2008. *Networking Futures: The Movements against Corporate Globalization*. Durham, NC: Duke University Press.
Juris, Jeffrey. 2012. "Reflections on #Occupy Everywhere: Social Media, Public Space, and Emerging Logics of Aggregation." *American Ethnologist* 39(2): 259–79.
Kafka, Franz. 1971. "Before the Law." In *Kafka: The Complete Stories*. New York: Schocken Books.
Kantor, Linda Scott, Kathryn Lipton, Alden Manchester, and Victor Oliveira. 1997. "Estimating and Addressing America's Food Losses." *Food Review* 20(1): 2–13.
Kauffman, L.A. 2015. "The Theology of Consensus." *Berkeley Journal of Sociology* 59:6–11.
Kawash, Samira. 1998. "The Homeless Body." *Public Culture* 10(2): 319–39.
Keck, Margaret E., and Kathryn Sikkink. 1998. *Activists beyond Borders: Advocacy Networks in International Politics*. Ithaca, NY: Cornell University Press.
Kelling, George L. 2009. "How New York Became Safe: The Full Story." In "New York's Tomorrow." Special issue, *City Journal*.
Kiley, Brendan. 2012. "Political Convictions? Federal Prosecutors in Seattle Are Dragging Activists into Grand Juries, Citing Their Social Circles and Anarchist Reading Materials." *The Stranger*, August 8.
KOMO Staff. 2011. "Elderly Woman, Priest Pepper-Sprayed during Occupy Protest." *Seattle Post-Intelligencer*, November 15. Accessed November 15, 2018. https://www.seattlepi.com/local/komo/article/Elderly-woman-pepper-sprayed-during-Occupy-march-2271197.php.
Kopytoff, Igor. 1986. "The Cultural Biography of Things: Commoditization as Process." In *The Social Life of Things: Commodities in Cultural Perspective*, edited by Arjun Appadurai, 64–93. New York: Cambridge University Press.
Krishnan, Sonia. 2010. "Chilly Welcome for Real Change from Pioneer Square." *Seattle Times*, May 21.
Kristeva, Julia. 1982. *Powers of Horror: An Essay on Abjection*. New York: Columbia University Press.
Kroman, David. 2019. "In Seattle, 1 in 5 People Booked into Jail Are Homeless: The Arrests By Police Are Mostly for Nonviolent Crime." *Crosscut*, February 19. Accessed October 19, 2019. https://crosscut.com/2019/02/seattle-1-5-people-booked-jail-are-homeless.
Kropotkin, Peter. 1902. *Mutual Aid: A Factor of Evolution*. New York: McClure Phillips.
Laporte, Dominique. 2000. *History of Shit*. Translated by Rodolphe el-Khoury and Nadia Benabid. Cambridge, MA: MIT Press.
Lawson, Vicky, and Sarah Elwood. 2013. "Encountering Poverty: Space, Class, and Poverty Politics." *Antipode* 46(1): 209–28.
Lazzarato, Maurizio. 2006. "Immaterial Labor." In *Radical Thought in Italy:*

A Potential Politics (Theory out of Bounds), edited by Paolo Virno and Michael Hardt, 133–49. Minneapolis: University of Minnesota Press.

Lefebvre, Henri. 1968. *Le Droit à la Ville*. Paris: Anthopos.

Lepawsky, Josh, and Mostaem Billah. 2011. "Making Chains That (Un)make Things: Waste-Value Relations and the Bangladeshi Rubbish Electronics Industry." *Geografiska Annaler: Series B, Human Geography* 93(2): 121–39.

Levi-Strauss, Claude. [1966] 1997. "The Culinary Triangle." In *Food and Culture: A Reader*, edited by Carole M. Counihan and Penny Van Esterik, 28-35. New York: Routledge.

Linebaugh, Peter, and Marcus Rediker. 2000. *The Many-Headed Hydra: Sailors, Slaves, Commoners, and the Hidden History of the Revolutionary Atlantic*. Boston: Beacon Press.

Lipsitz, George. 1998. *The Possessive Investment in Whiteness: How White People Profit from Identity Politics*. Philadelphia: Temple University Press.

Logan, John, and Harvey Molotch. 1987. *Urban Fortunes: The Political Economy of Place*. Berkeley: University of California Press.

Long, Katherine. 2011. "Dumpster-diver's Thesis: Good Stuff Going to Waste." *Seattle Times*, November 3.

Lorde, Audre. 2007. *Sister Outsider: Essays and Speeches by Audre Lorde*. 2nd ed. Berkeley, CA: Crossing Press.

Lowe, Celia. 2006. *Wild Profusion: Biodiversity Conservation in an Indonesian Archipelago*. Princeton, NJ: Princeton University Press.

Lurie, Kaya, Breanne Schuster, and Sara Rankin. 2015. *Discrimination at the Margins: The Intersectionality of Homelessness and Other Marginalized Groups*. Seattle: Homeless Rights Advocacy Project, Seattle University; May 6. Accessed January 31, 2017. https://papers.ssrn.com/sol3/papers.cfm?abstract_id=2602532.

Luxemburg, Rosa. [1913] 1951. *The Accumulation of Capital*. Translated by Agnes Schwarzschild. London: Butler and Tanner.

Madden, David, and Peter Marcuse. 2016. *In Defense of Housing*. New York: Verso.

Malkki, Lisa H. 1997. "News and Culture: Transitory Fieldwork Phenomena and the Fieldwork Tradition." In *Anthropological Locations: Boundaries and Grounds of a Field Science*, edited by Akhil Gupta and James Ferguson, 86–101. Berkeley: University of California Press.

Marcus, George E. 1995. "Ethnography in/of the World System: The Emergence of Multi-Sited Ethnography." *Annual Review of Anthropology* 24: 95–117.

Marcuse, Peter, and Ronald van Kempen. 2000. "Introduction." In *Globalizing Cities: A New Spatial Order?*, edited by Peter Marcuse and Ronald van Kempen, 1–21. Malden, MA: Blackwell.

Martinkus, John. 2017. "How the Herald Sun Declared War on Melbourne's Homeless." *Crikey*, January 25.

Marx, Karl. [1865] 2000. *Capital*. In *Selected Writings*, edited by David MacLellan, 452–525. Oxford: Oxford University Press.
Marx, Karl. [1941] 2000. *Grundrisse*. In *Selected Writings*, edited by David MacLellan, 380–422. Oxford: Oxford University Press.
Mauss, Marcel. [1954] 2002. *The Gift: The Form and Reason for Exchange in Archaic Societies*. London: Routledge Classics.
Mayaram, Shail. 2009. *The Other Global City*. New York: Routledge.
McGregor, JoAnn. 2008. "Abject Spaces, Transnational Calculations: Zimbabweans in Britain Navigating Work, Class, and the Law." *Transactions of the Institute of British Geographers* 33: 466–82.
McHenry, Keith. 2012. *Hungry for Peace: How You Can Help to End Poverty and War with Food Not Bombs*. Tucson, AZ: See Sharp Press.
McNerthney, Casey. 2011. "UW Student Goes Dumpster-Diving—For School Credit." *Seattle Post-Intelligencer* (blog), September 2. Accessed September 3, 2011. http://blog.seattlepi.com/thebigblog/2011/09/02/uw-student-goes-Dumpster-diving-for-school-credit/.
McVeigh, Robbie. 1997. "Theorising Sedentarianism: The Roots of Anti-Nomadism." In *Gypsy Politics and Traveller Identity*, edited by Thomas Acton, 7–25. Hatfield, UK: University of Hertfordshire Press.
Meals Partnership Coalition. n.d. "Monthly General Meetings." Accessed February 2, 2017. http://www.mealspartnership.org/events/monthly-meetings/.
Miller, William Ian. 1997. *The Anatomy of Disgust*. Cambridge, MA: Harvard University Press.
Mitchell, Don. 1997. "Annihilation of Space by Law: The Roots and Implications of Anti-Homeless Laws in the United States." *Antipode* 29(3): 303–35.
Mitchell, Don. 2011. "Homelessness, American Style." *Urban Geography* 32(7): 933–56.
Moon, Cary, and Charles Mudede. 2016. "Hot Money and Seattle's Growing Housing Crisis: Part One." *Seattle Stranger*, August 10.
Morrill, Richard. 2008. "Gentrification, Class, and Growth Management in Seattle, 1990-2000." In *Global Perspectives on Urbanization*, edited by George M. Pomeroy and Gerald M. Webster, 43–92. Lanham, MD: University Press of America.
Morton, Adam, and Craig Butt. 2017. "Income Gap between Melbourne's Richest and Poorest Suburbs Is Widening." *The Age*, April 12.
Mosley, Pat. 2017. "Un-Identity: Climbing Down the Other Side of Peak Liberalism." Pat Mosley (blog), May 14. Accessed May 18, 2017. https://patmosley.blog/2017/05/14/un-identity-climbing-down-the-other-side-of-peak-liberalism/.
Muñoz, José Esteban. 1999. *Disidentifications: Queers of Color and the Performance of Politics*. Minneapolis: University of Minnesota Press.
Munro, Roland. 2013. "The Disposal of Place: Facing Modernity in the Kitchen-Diner." In *Waste Matters: New Perspectives on Food and So-*

ciety, edited by David Evans, Hugh Campbell, and Anne Murcott, 212–31. Malden, MA: Wiley-Blackwell.
Murakami, Kery. 2004. "Reclaiming Occidental Park." *Seattle Post-Intelligencer*, June 11.
Murakami, Kery. 2006a. "Occidental Park Foliage Falls to Groans and Glee." *Seattle Post-Intelligencer*, March 6.
Murakami, Kery. 2006b. "Occidental Park Reopening." *Seattle Post-Intelligencer*, September 6.
Nagle, Robin. 2013. *Picking Up: On the Streets and Behind the Trucks with the Sanitation Workers of New York City*. New York: Farrar, Straus and Giroux.
National Law Center on Homelessness and Poverty. n.d. "Homelessness in America: Overview of Data and Causes." Fact sheet. Accessed November 15, 2018. https://www.nlchp.org/documents/Homeless_Stats_Fact_Sheet.
National Law Center on Homelessness and Poverty and the National Coalition for the Homeless. 2009. "Homes Not Handcuffs: The Criminalization of Homelessness in U.S. Cities." July. Accessed June 10 2017. http://nationalhomeless.org/issues/civil-rights/.
National Law Center on Homelessness and Poverty and the National Coalition for the Homeless. 2010. "A Place at the Table: Prohibitions on Sharing Food with People Experiencing Homelessness." July 2010. Accessed January 29, 2018. https://www.nlchp.org/documents/A_Place_at_the_Table.
National Lawyers Guild. 2012. "Seattle Chapter of the National Lawyers Guild Urges FBI and US Attorney to Drop Grand Jury Subpoenas." Press release, August 1. Accessed May 2, 2013. http://nlgseattle.org/node/57.
Navaro-Yashin, Yael. 2003. "'Life Is Dead Here': Sensing the Political in 'No Man's Land.'" *Anthropological Theory* 3(1): 107–25.
Nellemann, Christian, Monika MacDevette, Ton Manders, Bas Eickhout, Birger Svihus, Anne Gerdien Prins, and Bjørn P. Kaltenborn, eds. 2009. *The Environmental Food Crisis: The Environment's Role in Averting Future Food Crises. A UNEP Rapid Response Assessment*. United Nations Environment Programme, GRID-Arendal, February 2009.
New York City Independent Budget Office. 2017. "How Has the Distribution of Income in New York City Changed since 2006?" April 19. Accessed January 10, 2018. http://ibo.nyc.ny.us/cgi-park2/2017/04/how-has-the-distribution-of-income-in-new-york-city-changed-since-2006/.
New York Civil Liberties Union. 2012. "Report: NYPD Stop and Frisk Activity in 2011," May 12. Accessed December 22, 2022. https://www.nyclu.org/en/publications/report-nypd-stop-and-frisk-activity-2011-2012.
O'Brien, Martin. 2013. "A 'Lasting Transformation' of Capitalist Surplus: From Food Stocks to Feedstocks." In *Waste Matters: New Perspectives on Food and Society*, edited by David Evans, Hugh Campbell, and Anne Murcott, 192–211. Malden, MA: Wiley-Blackwell.

Olsen, Hanna Brooks. 2017. "What Does a Sweep Cost, Anyway?" *Real Change News*, November 8.
O'Mara, Margaret, and Karen C. Seto. 2012. "The Influence of Foreign Direct Investment on Land Use Changes and Regional Planning in Developing-World Megacities: A Bangalore Case Study." In *Megacities: Action Models and Strategic Solutions*, edited by Frauke Kraas, Gunter Dill, Gunther Mertins, and Ulrich Nitschke, 81–97. New York: Routledge.
O'Neill, Bruce. 2017. *The Space of Boredom: Homelessness in the Slowing Global Order*. Durham, NC: Duke University Press.
Ong, Aiwha. 1991. "The Gender and Labor Politics of Postmodernity." *Annual Review of Anthropology* 20: 279–309.
Ong, Aiwha. 1999. *Flexible Citizenship: The Cultural Logics of Transnationality*. Durham, NC: Duke University Press.
Ong, Aiwha, and Ananya Roy, editors. 2011. *Worlding Cities: Asian Experiments and the Art of Being Global*. West Sussex, UK: Wiley-Blackwell.
Operation Sack Lunch. n.d. "Open Meal Service." Accessed December 22, 2020. https://www.oslserves.org/open-meal-service.
Packard, Vance. [1960] 2011. *The Waste Makers*. Brooklyn: Ig Publishing.
Pamuk, Ayse. 2004. "Geography of Immigrant Clusters in Global Cities: A Case Study of San Francisco, 2000." *International Journal of Urban and Regional Research* 28(2): 287–307.
Parson, Sean Michael. 2010. "An Ungovernable Force? Food Not Bombs, Homeless Activism and Politics in San Francisco, 1988–1995." PhD diss., Department of Political Science, University of Oregon.
Passaro, Joanne. 1996. *The Unequal Homeless: Men on the Streets, Women in Their Place*. New York: Routledge.
Passaro, Joanne. 1997. "'You Can't Take the Subway to the Field': 'Village' Epistemologies in the Global Village." In *Anthropological Locations: Boundaries and Grounds of a Field Science*, edited by Akhil Gupta and James Ferguson, 147–62. Berkeley: University of California Press.
Picture the Homeless. 2007. "Banking on Vacancy: Homelessness and Real Estate Speculation." Accessed December 22, 2020. https://www.picturethehomeless.org/project/banking-on-vacancy-homelessness-real-estate-speculation/.
Pike Place Market Preservation and Development Authority (PDA). 2009. *Executive Committee Meeting Minutes, Wednesday, August 19th, 2009 7:30 a.m. to 9:00 a.m.*
Piven, Frances Fox, and Richard A. Cloward. 1971. *Regulating the Poor: The Functions of Public Welfare*. New York: Pantheon.
Plante, Leah-Lynne. 2012. "Statement from a Resister." Burning Hearts Media. Vimeo video, 5:25. Accessed May 2, 2013. http://vimeo.com/burningheartsmedia/statement.
Pokey '92. 2007. *Food Not Bombs, Seattle: History! Recipes! & More!* Seattle zine.
Polanyi, Karl. [1944] 1957. *The Great Transformation*. Boston: Beacon Press.

Polletta, Francesca. 2002. *Freedom Is an Endless Meeting: Democracy in American Social Movements*. Chicago: University of Chicago Press.

Poppendieck, Janet. 1998a. *Sweet Charity: Emergency Food and the End of Entitlement*. New York: Penguin.

Poppendieck, Janet. 1998b. "Want amid Plenty: From Hunger to Insecurity." *Monthly Labor Review* 50(3): 125–36.

Poppendieck, Janet. 2010. *Free for All: Fixing School Food in America*. Berkeley: University of California Press.

Potter, Will. 2012a. "BREAKING: FBI and JTTF Raid Multiple Homes, Grand Jury Subpoenas in Portland, Olympia, Seattle." *Green Is the New Red* (blog), July 25. Accessed May 2, 2013. http://www.greenisthenewred.com/blog/home-raids-grand-jury-subpoenas-portland-olympia-seattle/6233/.

Potter, Will. 2012b. "Newly Released FBI 'Domestic Terrorism' Training on Anarchists, Environmentalists, Show COINTELPRO Tactics." *Green Is the New Red* (blog), May 29. Accessed May 2, 2013. http://www.greenisthenewred.com/blog/fbi-domestic-terrorism-training-anarchists-eco/6199/.

Poverty Reduction and Equity Group. 2011. *Food Price Watch (English)*. February 1. Washington, DC: World Bank Group.

Povinelli, Elizabeth A. 2011. *Economies of Abandonment: Social Belonging and Endurance in Late Liberalism*. Durham, NC: Duke University Press.

Pratt, Andy C. 2002. "Hot Jobs in Cool Places. The Material Culture of New Media Spaces: The Case of South of the Market, San Francisco." *Information, Communication, and Society* 5(1): 27–50.

Project for Public Spaces. n.d. "What Is Placemaking?" Accessed June 13, 2013. http://www.pps.org/reference/what_is_placemaking/.

Project for Public Spaces. 2004. "Creating a 'Square' in Pioneer Square: Draft, for Discussion." Report to the City of Seattle.

Public Health Seattle and King County. 2020. "Increases in Food Needs in King County, WA Spring-Summer 2020." Report date: August 2020. Accessed December 22, 2020. https://www.kingcounty.gov/depts/health/covid-19/data/impacts/~/media/depts/health/communicable-diseases/documents/C19/food-insecurity-brief-report-august-2020.ashx.

Rafter, Isolde. 2018. "The Day Seattle Nice Died." 94.9 FM, KUOW, May 3. Accessed November 15, 2018. https://kuow.org/stories/day-seattle-nice-died/.

Randolph, Bill, and Darren Holloway. 2005. "Social Disadvantage, Tenure and Location: An Analysis of Sydney and Melbourne." *Urban Policy and Research* 23(2): 173–201.

Rathje, William, and Cullen Murphy. 1992. *Rubbish: The Anthropology of Garbage*. New York: HarperCollins.

Reddy, Rajyashree N. 2015. "Producing Abjection: E-Waste Improvement

Schemes and Informal Recyclers of Bangalore." *Geoforum* 62: 166–74.

Regan, Gary, and Mardee Haidin Regan. 2006. "The Birth of the Cosmopolitan: A Tale of Two Bartenders." *Ardent Spirits* e-letter 7(6) (October). Accessed May 6, 2013. http://web.archive.org/web/20070707072947/http://www.ardentspirits.com/ardentspirits/Newsletter/vol7Issue06.html#cosmo.

Ren, Xuefei, and Roger Keil. 2018. "Editors' Introduction: From *Global to Globalizing Cities*." In *The Globalizing Cities Reader*, 2nd ed. Edited by Xuefei Ren and Roger Keil, xxiii–xxix. New York: Routledge.

Reno, Joshua. 2016. *Waste Away: Working and Living with a North American Landfill*. Berkeley: University of California Press.

Resnick, Elana. 2015. "Discarded Europe: Money, Trash and the Possibilities of a New Temporality." *Anthropological Journal of European Cultures* 24(1): 123–31.

Right to the City Coalition. 2010. "People without Homes and Homes without People: A Count of Vacant Condos in Select NYC Neighborhoods." Accessed December 30, 2020. http://cdp.urbanjustice.org/sites/default/files/People_Without_Homes_and_Homes_Without_People.pdf.

Robinson, Cedric. 1983. *Black Marxism*. London: Zed Press.

Rufo, Christopher F. 2019. "The Wrong Narrative: Seattle Elites Show Little Sympathy for a Woman Raped By a Homeless Man." *City Journal*, May 3. Accessed October 18, 2019. https://www.city-journal.org/seattle-elites-homeless-crime.

Sahlins, Marshall. 1972. *Stone Age Economics*. Hawthorne, NY: Gruyer.

Saint Mary's Food Bank Alliance. n.d. About Us. Accessed January 10, 2012. http://www.firstfoodbank.org/history.html.

Sassen, Saskia. 1990. "Economic Restructuring and the American City." *Annual Review of Sociology* 16: 465–90.

Sassen, Saskia. 1996. "Analytic Borderlands: Race, Gender and Representation in the New City." In *Re-Presenting the City: Ethnicity, Capital and Culture in the 21st-Century Metropolis*, edited by Anthony D. King, 183–202. New York: New York University Press.

Sassen, Saskia. 2001. *The Global City*. 2nd ed. Princeton, NJ: Princeton University Press.

Sassen, Saskia. 2011. "The Global Street: Making the Political." *Globalizations* 8(5) (October): 573–79.

Sassen, Saskia. 2012. "Occupying Is Not the Same as Demonstrating." SaskiaSassen.com. Accessed June 9, 2013. http://www.saskiasassen.com/publications.php#selected-articles.

Sassen, Saskia. 2015. "Who Owns Our Cities—And Why This Urban Takeover Should Concern Us All." *Guardian*, November 24. Accessed November 15, 2018. https://www.theguardian.com/cities/2015/nov/24/who-owns-our-cities-and-why-this-urban-takeover-should-concern-us-all.

Scandura, Jani. 2008. *Down in the Dumps: Place, Modernity, American Depression*. Durham, NC: Duke University Press.

Schmitt, Carl. [1985] 2005. *Political Theology: Four Chapters on the Concept of Sovereignty*. Translated by George Schwab. Chicago: University of Chicago Press.

Schumpeter, Joseph A. [1950] 2008. *Capitalism, Socialism and Democracy*. New York: HarperCollins.

Scott, James C. 2017. *Against the Grain: A Deep History of the Earliest States*. New Haven, CT: Yale University Press.

Seattle Downtown Parks & Public Spaces Task Force. 2005. Task Force Meeting #7 Summary, July 8, 2005. Accessed June 1, 2013. http://www.seattle.gov/parks/projects/downtown/minutes/07-08-05.pdf.

Seattle Downtown Parks & Public Spaces Task Force. 2006. Downtown Parks Renaissance: A Strategy to Revitalize Seattle's Public Spaces, Final Report March 16, 2006. Accessed June 1, 2013. www.seattle.gov/parks/projects/downtown/Report.pdf.

Semuels, Alana. 2018. "How Amazon Helped Kill a Seattle Tax on Business: A Levy on Big Companies to Fund Affordable Housing Awakened the Ire of Corporations." *The Atlantic*, June 13. Accessed November 15, 2018. https://www.theatlantic.com/technology/archive/2018/06/how-amazon-helped-kill-a-seattle-tax-on-business/562736/.

Shannon, Deric Michael. 2011. *Making Culture: Social Movements, Culture, and Food Not Bombs*. PhD diss., Department of Sociology, University of Connecticut.

Short, John Rennie. 2004. *Global Metropolitan: Globalizing Cities in a Capitalist World*. New York: Routledge.

Shotwell, Alexis. 2016. *Against Purity: Living Ethically in Compromised Times*. Minneapolis: University of Minnesota Press.

Sidran, Mark. 1993. "This Is the Best of Times to Keep This City Livable." *Seattle Times*, August 10.

Simmel, Georg. [1903] 2002. "The Metropolis and Mental Life." In *The Blackwell City Reader*, edited by Gary Bridge and Sophie Watson, 11–19. Oxford: Wiley-Blackwell.

Simone, AbdouMaliq. 2010. *City Life from Jakarta to Dakar: Movements at the Crossroads*. New York: Routledge.

Sleater-Kinney. 2015. "No Cities to Love." Track 4, *No Cities to Love* (digital download). Seattle: Sub Pop Records.

Smith, Neil. 1996. *The New Urban Frontier: Gentrification and the Revanchist City*. New York: Routledge.

Smith, Neil. 2002. "New Globalism, New Urbanism: Gentrification as Global Urban Strategy." *Antipode* 34(3): 434–57.

Smith, Patti. 1978. "25th Floor." Track 9, *Easter* (LP). New York: Arista Records.

Spangenthal-Lee, Jonah. 2008. "Bombs Away: City Cracks Down on Food Not Bombs' Meals for the Homeless." *The Stranger*, June 4.

Sparke, Matthew. 2011. "Global Geographies." In *Seattle Geographies*, edited by Michael Brown and Richard Morrill, 47–80. Seattle: University of Washington Press.

Spataro, David. 2016. "Against a De-politicized DIY Urbanism: Food Not Bombs and the Struggle over Public Space." *Journal of Urbanism* 9(2): 185–201.

Spooner, James, dir. 2003. *Afropunk* (DVD). Independently released.

Stallybrass, Peter, and Allon White. 1986. *The Politics and Poetics of Transgression*. Ithaca, NY: Cornell University Press.

Steinbeck, John. [1939] 2006. *The Grapes of Wrath*. New York: Penguin Books.

Stevens, Quentin, and Kim Dovey. 2004. "Appropriating the Spectacle: Play and Politics in a Leisure Landscape." *Journal of Urban Design* 9(3): 351–65.

Stoler, Ann Laura. 2013. "'The Rot Remains': From Ruins to Ruination." In *Imperial Debris: On Ruins and Ruination*, edited by Ann Laura Stoler, 1–37. Durham, NC: Duke University Press.

Straw, Will. 2010. "Spectacles of Waste." In *Circulation and the City*, edited by Alexandra Boutros and Will Straw, 193–213. Montreal: McGill Queen's University Press.

Stuart, Tristram. 2009. *Waste: Uncovering the Global Food Scandal*. London: Penguin.

Sutton, David E. 2001. *Remembrance of Repasts: An Anthropology of Food and Memory*. Oxford: Bloomsbury Academic.

Taleb, Nassim Nicholas. 2012. *Antifragile: Things That Gain from Disorder*. London: Penguin Books.

Tides of Flame. 2012. "May Day Statement from Tides of Flame." Press statement, May 2. Accessed May 2, 2013. http://tidesofflame.wordpress.com/2012/05/02/may-day-statement-from-tides-of-flame/.

Theodore, Nik, Jamie Peck, and Neil Brenner. 2011. "Neoliberal Urbanism: Cities and the Rule of Markets." In *The New Blackwell Companion to the City*, edited by Gary Bridge and Sophie Watson, 15–25. West Sussex, UK: Wiley-Blackwell.

Thompson, Michael. 1979. *Rubbish Theory: The Creation and Destruction of Value*. Oxford: Oxford University Press.

Trang X Ta. 2017. "A Space for Secondhand Goods: Trading the Remnants of Material Life in Hong Kong." *Economic Anthropology* 4(1): 120–31.

Tsing, Anna Lowenhaupt. 2004. *Friction: An Ethnography of Global Connection*. Princeton, NJ: Princeton University Press.

Tsing, Anna Lowenhaupt. 2015. *The Mushroom at the End of the World: On the Possibility of Life in Capitalist Ruins*. Princeton, NJ: Princeton University Press.

United States Court of Appeals, Eleventh Circuit. 2011. First Vagabonds Church of God, an unincorporated association, Brian Nichols, Orlando Food Not Bombs, an unincorporated association, Ryan Scott

Hutchinson, Benjamin B. Markeson, Eric Montanez, Adam Ulrich, Plaintiffs–Appellees–Cross Appellants, v. City of Orlando, Florida, Defendant–Appellant–Cross Appellee. No. 08–16788. Decided April 12, 2011.
United States Court of Appeals, Eleventh Circuit. 2018. Fort Lauderdale Food Not Bombs, Nathan Pim, Jillian Pim, Haylee Becker, William Toole, Plaintiffs–Appellants v. City of Fort Lauderdale, Defendant–Appellee. No. 16-16808. Filed August 22, 2018.
United States Court of Appeals, Ninth Circuit, District of Idaho. 2018. Robert Martin; Lawrence Lee Smith; Robert Anderson; Janet F. Bell; Pamela S. Hawkes; and Basil E. Humphrey, Plaintiffs–Appellants, v. City of Boise Defendant–Appellee. No. 15-35845. Filed September 4, 2018.
United States Department of Housing and Urban Development. n.d. Historical Fair Market Rents, Washington Metro Areas. Accessed December 22, 2020. https://www.hud.gov/states/shared/working/r10/emas/histwafmr.
Valdes, Manuel, and Gene Johnston. 2012. "Violence, Arrests at Seattle May Day Protests." *Seattle Times*, May 2.
van der Waal, Jeroen. 2015. *The Global City Debate Reconsidered: Economic Globalization in Contemporary Dutch Cities*. Amsterdam: Amsterdam University Press.
van Hulten, Andrew. 2010. *Global Flows, Gentrification and Displacement in Melbourne's Inner West*. Working Paper no. 49. Melbourne: Centre for Strategic Economic Studies, Victoria University.
Vaughn, Rachel A. 2011. *Talking Trash: Oral Histories of Food Insecurity from the Margins of a Dumpster*. PhD diss., Department of American Studies, University of Kansas.
Virno, Paolo. 2004. *A Grammar of the Multitude: For an Analysis of Contemporary Forms of Life*. Cambridge: Semiotext(e).
Vitale, Alex. 2009. *City of Disorder: How the Quality of Life Campaign Transformed New York Politics*. New York: New York University Press.
Waldron, Jeremy. 1991. "Homelessness and the Issue of Freedom." *UCLA Law Review* 39: 295–324.
Wallerstein, Immanuel. 1984. *The Politics of the World-Economy: The States, the Movements and the Civilizations*. Cambridge: Cambridge University Press.
Warner, Michael. 2002. *Publics and Counterpublics*. New York: Zone Books.
Waterfield, Bruno. 2009. "EU Butter Mountain to Return." *Telegraph*, January 22.
Weheliye, Alexander G. 2014. *Habeas Viscus: Racializing Assemblages, Biopolitics, and Black Feminist Theories of the Human*. Durham, NC: Duke University Press.
Wells, Hodan Farah, and Jean C. Buzby. 2005. "U.S. Food Consumption Up 16 Percent Since 1970." *Amber Waves*, November 1. https://www.ers

.usda.gov/amber-waves/2005/november/us-food-consumption-up-16-percent-since-1970/.

Wetzstein, Steffen. 2012. "Globalising Economic Governance, Political Projects, and Spatial Imaginaries: Insights from Four Australasian Cities." *Geographical Research* 51(1): 71–84.

Wilk, Richard. 2017. "How Can Economic Anthropology Contribute to a More Just World?" *Economic Anthropology* 4(1): 144–55.

Williams, Raymond. 1977. *Marxism and Literature*. Oxford: Oxford University Press.

Willse, Craig. 2015. *The Value of Homelessness: Managing Surplus Life in the United States*. Minneapolis: University of Minnesota Press.

Wilson, Elizabeth A. 2015. *Gut Feminism*. Durham, NC: Duke University Press.

Wilson, James Q., and George L. Kelling. 1982. "Broken Windows: The Police and Neighbourhood Safety." *Atlantic Monthly*, March.

Winkley, Lyndsay. 2018. "About a Dozen People Arrested for Feeding the Homeless in El Cajon Park." *San Diego Union Tribune*, January 14.

Winter, Ian, and Wendy Stone. 1998. *Social Polarization and Housing Careers: Exploring the Interrelationship of Labour and Housing Markets in Australia*. Australian Institute of Family Studies, Commonwealth of Australia, Working Paper no. 13, March.

Woodbridge, Linda. 2001. *Vagrancy, Homelessness, and English Renaissance Literature*. Chicago: University of Illinois Press.

Woolf, Virginia. [1927] 2016. *Street Haunting: A London Adventure*. Alcester, UK: Read Books.

Young, Bob. 2004. "Mayor Reverses Decision on Homeless Meal Program." *Seattle Times*, August 11.

Zibechi, Raul. 2010. *Dispersing Power: Social Movements as Anti-State Forces*. Translated by Ramor Ryan. Oakland, CA: AK Press.

Zukin, Sharon. 1998. "Urban Lifestyles: Diversity and Standardisation in Spaces of Consumption." *Urban Studies* 35(5–6): 825–39.

Zukin, Sharon. 2010. *Naked City: The Death and Life of Authentic Urban Places*. Oxford: Oxford University Press.

index